Providence and
the Invention of
American History

Providence *and the* Invention *of* American History

SARAH KOENIG

Yale UNIVERSITY PRESS/NEW HAVEN & LONDON

Published with assistance from the income of the Frederick
John Kingsbury Memorial Fund.

Published with assistance from the foundation established in
memory of Calvin Chapin of the Class of 1788, Yale College.

Yale University Press books may be purchased in quantity for
educational, business, or promotional use. For information,
please e-mail sales.press@yale.edu (U.S. office) or sales@yaleup.
co.uk (U.K. office).

Set in Minion type by IDS Infotech, Ltd., Chandigarh, India.
Printed in the United States of America.

Library of Congress Control Number: 2020948378
ISBN 978-0-300-25100-5 (hardcover : alk. paper)

A catalogue record for this book is available from the British
Library.

This paper meets the requirements of ANSI/NISO Z39.48-1992
(Permanence of Paper).

10 9 8 7 6 5 4 3 2 1

To my family

Contents

Acknowledgments

When I decided, in my first year of graduate school, that I wanted to write a book examining a forgotten legend and the origins of my newly chosen profession, I understandably met with some questions. How does one dissect the modes of thinking and research that have shaped one's own intellectual and personal formation? How does one write a story about a story, particularly if that story isn't true?

I am extraordinarily grateful for the support of mentors, friends, family, and dedicated professionals, without whom this book would not have been possible. I will name some of these people in the following pages, but my efforts will almost certainly be inadequate to the task.

The book originated in Jon Butler's research seminar. I am thankful for the many mentors who helped to guide this project from that inchoate stage into this finished book. Skip Stout took a chance on me when I was a master's student in liturgy hoping to switch to American religious history. His knack for storytelling and attention to big questions encouraged me to explore the larger stakes of the Marcus Whitman story. John Mack Faragher's commitment to rigorous research and deep historiographical understanding served as a model for both my research and writing. Tisa Wenger offered countless hours of sage wisdom in subjects ranging from secularism to gardening, and her ability to combine theoretical rigor and readable prose is an inspiration. Jay Gitlin has been an invaluable conversation partner, sharing his boundless love of all things western and introducing me to the joys of discovering local histories in old bookstores. Katie Lofton has been my most tireless mentor and advocate. As I transitioned from graduate school to a professorial life, she has been ever present with encouragement, advice, and, when necessary, gentle goading. I deeply appreciate her commitment to this book, particularly during the seasons when my own faith in it waned.

My path to academic life was somewhat circuitous, involving a music degree and divinity school. Several individuals helped to smooth that path. Lynn Szabo encouraged me to consider graduate school, and Thomas Hatina first recommended the Yale Institute of Sacred Music to me when attending an Ivy League graduate program seemed about as plausible as joining the circus. Gordon Lathrop's patient and cheerful mentoring enabled me to publish my first scholarly article. Serving as Bryan Spinks's research assistant gave me a first look at the research and publication process and a sense of the possibilities for uniting my interests in history, religion, and American culture.

Writing can be a lonely process, but I was fortunate to be connected to a tight-knit and collaborative group of colleagues. I am particularly grateful to Emily Johnson, whose house was my second home during my grad school years, and who taught me the joys of list making. Alison Greene and Sarah Hammond guided me as I navigated the transition to the religious studies program and inspired me to imagine the kinds of nuanced histories scholars could create. David Walker and Lucia Hulsether were crucial conversation partners in my theorizing this book, and Kati Curts, Alex Kaloyanides, Michelle Morgan, Tina Post, and Shari Rabin offered both incisive feedback and welcome moral support. I am grateful to the Lamar Center for Frontiers and Borders for providing weekly camaraderie, connection to the wider world of western history, and top-notch jam sessions. Sarah Bowman, Debbie Doroshow, Marie-Amelie George, Kate Irving, Erin Johnson-Williams, Ann Phelps, and Nate Widelitz also provided friendship and inspiration. Julie Middleton has supported me through thick and thin and has been a wonderful companion for thinking through life's big questions.

As I've begun the transitory life of an academic, I've appreciated the wisdom and support of my supervisors and colleagues, especially Reid Gomez, Christine Hahn, and Charlene Boyer Lewis at Kalamazoo College and Erick Castellanos, Susan Hangen, and Stacie Taranto at Ramapo College. I am continuously impressed by the curiosity and resilience of my students, whose questions have pushed me to rethink elements of my teaching and writing. I am also thankful for the friends and kindred spirits who have helped me create homes in these new places, especially Renee Lee-Miller, Sarah Friesen-Carper, Rachel Lonberg, Kristen Totten, and the inaugural members of the Kalamazoo ministers' cocktail club, also known as the Not Jeremys: Brian Lonberg, Barrett Lee, and Sarah Schmidt-Lee.

I am very grateful for the research assistance of the archivists, librarians, and other staff at the Beinecke Rare Book and Manuscript Library, Whitman College and Northwest Archives, the Oregon Historical Society Research Library, Washington State University Manuscripts and Archives, the University of Oregon Special Collections and University Archives, and the Oregon State Library. George Miles introduced me to the Elwood Evans papers, which were a gateway into the world of Pacific Northwest historians, and to the seemingly boundless resources of the Beinecke Library. Scott Daniels at the Oregon Historical Society conferred invaluable assistance and good-natured ribbing, greeting me during each of my research trips with the inquiry, "Are you president of Yale yet?" The staff of the Whitman College and Northwest Archives, the New York Public Library, and the Presbyterian Historical Society went out of their way to secure image scans despite the challenges caused by the COVID-19 pandemic.

The Beinecke Rare Book and Manuscript Library, the John F. Enders Research Grant, the Frederick Hilles Memorial Scholarship fund, the American Society of Church History, and the Ramapo College Faculty Development Fund afforded me generous support for research and presentations connected to this book.

My book is dedicated to my family. My grandparents, Frank and Charlotte Russell, did not live to see it reach fruition, but their influence is felt throughout. I have been profoundly shaped by my grandfather's love of learning, and my grandmother was my best sounding board for new ideas. My aunt Leona and uncle Denny have offered unconditional love and positivity (and much-needed reminders to get outside every once in a while). I'm grateful to my brother, Jon, and my sister-in-law, Stephanie Balascio-Koenig, for their inspiring commitment to excellent teaching and for some of the best adventures I've ever had in New York City. The Sabella and Bouvier families accepted me as one of their own, and their hospitality is unparalleled. My parents have been unfailingly supportive at every stage of my work on the book, and they have assisted in ways both large and small. When a research trip was derailed because of an unexpected archive closure, my mom reached out to the historical fiction author Jane Kirkpatrick, who shared her deep knowledge of repositories in the area. I have fond memories of my dad accompanying me on research trips to the Oregon Historical Society, helping to dig through mounds of correspondence and taking as much delight as I did in finding the stories buried within.

I started this book just after my husband, Jeremy, and I were married. In hindsight, beginning both a marriage and a graduate program within a two-week period seems extraordinarily foolish. Yet I can say, without hesitation, that it was the best decision I ever made. I am so grateful for our life together, for your humor and compassion, and for your resolute love.

Introduction

On July 3, 1923, President Warren G. Harding regaled the citizens of Meacham, Oregon, with a well-known patriotic tale: the daring 1842 ride of the Protestant missionary Marcus Whitman, the savior of Oregon. In stirring fashion Harding described how Whitman had raced from Oregon Territory to Washington, DC, arriving just in time to stop President John Tyler from signing a treaty granting possession of Oregon Territory to Great Britain. "Here was a man who, without a single companion, in the dead of Winter, struggled through pathless drifts and blinding storms, 4,000 miles, with his sole aim to serve his country and his God," Harding stated.[1] Whitman's "long ride and frozen limbs" convinced Tyler that Oregon should remain an American possession, and Whitman sealed the point by leading the first wagon train back to Oregon. "Never in the history of the world has there been a finer example of civilization following Christianity," proclaimed Harding. "The missionaries led under the banner of the cross and the settlers moved close behind under the star-spangled symbol of the Nation."[2]

The story of Marcus Whitman, as narrated by Harding, made an ideal subject for such a stump speech. It nodded to Oregon's regional history while placing that history within a broader framework of Protestant providentialism, Manifest Destiny, and American exceptionalism.

It was a story that many Americans had told over the decades since Whitman's death and that the citizens of Meacham would have known well. But it was not, strictly speaking, true. Though the story originated from an actual journey that Whitman made, its details had been so embellished by his fellow missionaries, local boosters, and Protestant authors that it little resembled Whitman's actual life. Harding was aware of these embellishments, and yet it was the Marcus Whitman of legend that he preferred. "I like the story of Whitman," he declared in defense of his use of the tall tale. "If it isn't true, it ought to be."[3]

The Marcus Whitman of legend was a rugged, intrepid pioneer who saw, before any other white American, the potential for the Pacific Northwest to become a part of the United States. He traveled to Oregon Territory in 1836 to become a missionary, but he intended to claim the region for the United States of America as well as for Jesus Christ. He crossed the Continental Divide on July 4, 1836, stopping to lead his party in prayer and plant an American flag on then foreign soil. He labored quietly among the Cayuse people until 1842, when, through a series of divinely orchestrated coincidences, he discovered that Great Britain and its secret allies, Jesuit priests, were planning to trick President Tyler into signing a treaty that traded possession of Oregon for a codfishery in Newfoundland. Ignoring the pleas of his wife and his fellow missionaries, Whitman jumped on his horse and rode away on his fateful trip, proclaiming, "Though I am a missionary, I am not expatriated."[4] He arrived just in time to prevent Tyler from ceding the vast Pacific Northwest to Great Britain and then, on the way back, blazed the Oregon Trail. The "Paul Revere of Oregon" was a faithful Christian, an even more faithful patriot, and for decades a national hero.[5]

The Marcus Whitman of history, by contrast, labored from 1836 to 1847 at an unsuccessful Protestant mission in the Pacific Northwest. The mission proved ineffective at winning the hearts and minds of the Cayuse people, prompting Whitman early on to switch his focus from converting Cayuse souls to encouraging white Christians to settle on Cayuse land. Relations between Whitman, his fellow missionaries, and the Native people they came to serve became so poor that Whitman's Boston-based supervisors ordered the mission closed in 1842. Whitman traveled to the eastern United States to protest the order and successfully kept his mission operating for five more years. But in 1847, after years of growing tension between Whitman and the Cayuse people, several Cayuse men attacked and murdered Whitman, his wife, Narcissa, and twelve other white Americans in a desperate attempt to rid their land of emigrants and the epidemic diseases they brought to Cayuse country. The Whitman Mission killings, also known today as the Whitman Incident, marked the end of the Cayuse missions and the beginning of years of violent encounters between encroaching Anglo-American settlers and the Cayuse and other neighboring groups. The tragic event made it both possible and necessary for survivors and contemporary observers to reimagine the legacy of Marcus Whitman and his mission: possible because Whitman was no longer able to testify to his own significance or lack thereof, and necessary because the disastrous end of Whitman's mission demanded that providentially minded Protestants find a way to redeem Whitman's apparent failure.

The story of Whitman's heroic ride to save Oregon first appeared in the months after Whitman's death, as his associates and other Anglo-American Protestants in the newly organized Oregon Territory struggled to make sense of his murder and the collapse of Protestant missionary efforts in the region. The so-called Whitman Saved Oregon Story eventually spread throughout the United States, inspiring poetry, pageants, statues, hagiographic biographies, sermons, and patriotic speeches like Harding's. By 1891 newspapers touted Whitman's 1842–43 journey as "the most famous ride in American history!," more thrilling even than the midnight ride of Paul Revere.[6] Then, at the January 1900 meeting of the American Historical Association (AHA), the Yale historian Edward Gaylord Bourne shocked the attendees and the nation by arguing that the Whitman story was a myth—a "complete legendary reconstruction of history" the like of which had not been seen since medieval times.[7] Through critical examination of source documents Bourne demonstrated that Whitman traversed the continent to meet with his missionary supervisors in Boston, not to converse with President Tyler in Washington, DC; that Whitman traveled with the 1843 wagon train but did not organize or pilot it; and that Oregon in 1842 was not in any danger of becoming a British possession.[8] The claim incited a ten-year controversy between Whitman's detractors, who argued that modern historical methods proved the Whitman story was false, and Whitman's defenders, who believed that the critics' logic was part of a larger pattern of skepticism bent on destroying traditional history and perhaps even Christianity itself.

The Whitman Saved Oregon Story was gradually stricken from history books, but the broader historical patterns it produced endured. The discipline of American history was recreated along the lines drawn by the battles over the Whitman story, dividing professional from amateur, Protestant from Catholic, providentialist from scientific historian. This book takes up the history of those conflicts, examining the historical formations that they both reflected and generated. It examines the ways in which religious communities and ideas shaped these forms of historical narration, including those that sought to remove religious language and theological interpretations from historical scholarship. And it explores how the divides still present in American historical consciousness—between the quest for a noble, usable past and the need to overturn false narratives, between religious practitioners and skeptics, and between academic history and popular history—grew out of nineteenth-century narratives and twentieth-century shifts in historical influence.

This book both intervenes in and provides a prehistory to the work of scholars interested in the professionalization and secularization of the American historical discipline. First among these is Peter Novick's *That Noble Dream,* which traces how the concept (or, rather, various concepts) of objectivity informed the American historical profession's development. A crucial aspect of Novick's analysis is the observation that the meaning of objectivity is and has always been contested: it is "not a single idea, but rather a sprawling collection of assumptions, attitudes, aspirations, and antipathies," born out of historical contingencies and misunderstandings.[9] In his introduction Novick discusses the possibility of viewing objectivity as a myth, drawing on religious studies theorists like Mircea Eliade, Bronislaw Malinowski, and Émile Durkheim. To Novick, the ideal of objectivity functions as an origin story, legitimating the new professional historical methods of the late nineteenth century; as a way to "safeguard and enforce" scholarly methods and rituals; and as a way to provide a sense of unity to a profession made up of diverse scholars.[10] But if objectivity is a myth, one that was necessary in order to legitimate and structure the emerging American historical profession, what ideology did it replace? What was, and is, objectivity's other, the spectral presence that continues to haunt debates about rationality in history? And how have objectivity and its other grown up together, mutually informing each other even as they repudiate one another? These are the questions that drive this book.

The creation, growth, and eventual disproving of the Whitman story illustrate how a single historical narrative could be circulated and transformed through changing historical networks and practices. Returning to the Whitman story provides a historical accounting for two major patterns in the writing of American history that continue to shape American discourse. On the one hand is providential history: a mode of historical labor marked by the conviction that God is an active agent in human history and that historical work can reveal patterns of divine will. Providential history was the dominant mode of history writing for much of the nineteenth century, and the Whitman story was a foundational piece of data for providential historians who sought to prove that the divine had a special plan for Protestant America. Providential history viewed the American story as one of progress, a triumphal narrative of the increasing prosperity of the American nation-state propelled by the ever-growing primacy of Protestant religion. It viewed the fates of Protestantism and the United States as coextensive, casting Protestant leaders as heroes and non-Protestants, especially Catholics, as either beneficiaries of Protestant's tolerant largesse or as enemies of the state. And it celebrated the triumph of white Protestant Christianity over heathen superstition, represented in particular by indigenous peoples. Providential historians were thus primarily interested in history as a means of creating a usable past, one that opened a window into American destiny, a sense of national and religious pride, and a set of shared moral principles.

Historians, most notably Nicholas Guyatt, have discussed how providentialism influenced American identity and American writing in the nineteenth century, but they have not explored how providentialism functioned as a discrete historical methodology, one that shaped the contours of academic American history.[11] Providential historians formed some of the first historical societies, collected archival materials, and engaged in regular discussion and peer review of historical works. Both providential history's professionalizing impulses and its vision of US history as fundamentally progressive played a crucial role in shaping the structures and ideological framework of American academic history. Though the providentialist vision lost out to newer historical practices, it bequeathed over a century of historical writing and cast a long shadow over popular history, where providential interpretations of history continue to appear in monuments, sermons, pageants, and historical tourism.

On the other hand is objective history, also referred to in this book as secular or scientific history.[12] Objective history aims to eschew sectarian bias and prioritize dispassionate reason and hard evidence. This mode of history is what we scholars typically think of when we discuss academic history, because its assumptions and methodology have prevailed in the academy since the early twentieth century. However, objective history's ascendance as the predominant mode of historical inquiry did not happen without controversy nor did its arguments originate within the academy. Appeals to objectivity first appeared not within academic circles but in the pleas of Catholics and other religious and racial outsiders who resisted providentialists' pejorative depictions of non-Protestants and nonwhites. Objectivity, in other words, did not preclude commitment to a cause or appeals to religious concepts; rather, it was first defined as a conviction that Protestant sectarianism clouded historical judgment and undermined reasoned argument. Only later, at the beginning of the twentieth century, did objective history begin to be defined as a quasi-empirical science, one with the power and prestige that such a definition implied. The rise of objective history entailed the gradual marginalization of overtly providential histories, which now exist primarily outside the academy in subcultures like that of the Christian Right.

On the surface, then, this may appear to be a straightforward tale of academic professionalization and secularization, and indeed, these two themes do appear in my book. Yet it reveals a far more ambivalent story, one in which providentialism, along with its hero tales like the Whitman story, is never fully eradicated. Providentialism lives on not only in circles that are marginal to the academy but also in the racial and religious measures of progress that the early objective historians deployed. The battle scars of the American historical discipline's professionalization and secularization continue to shape American dialogue about history, as providentialists, now marginalized from the academy, publicly condemn the so-called revisionist histories of scholars and form alternate communities of historical engagement separate from the halls of academic power.

Histories and Other Stories

Early twentieth-century historians explored the Whitman Saved Oregon Story in depth, but their work was primarily that of debunking: identifying which aspects of the Whitman story were false.[13] They also ventured theories about how the Whitman story came to be, theories that have been essentially unquestioned in historical scholarship until now. These early twentieth-century historians, particularly William Isaac Marshall, were nothing if not thorough, and this text both draws on and concurs with many of their conclusions about the Whitman story's incompatibility with archival evidence. However, this book's fundamental subject is not the Whitman story's truth or falsity, questions that have been explored at length in other studies. Rather, it examines what the Whitman story's creation, dissemination, and discrediting reveal about the ways in which Americans have conceptualized and narrated history, especially the history of the Anglo-American conquest of the West. The work of early twentieth-century historians in dismantling the Whitman story thus becomes part of this book's broad arc.

In addition to the early twentieth-century sources there is a large body of biographical material on the Whitmans as well as a smaller body of literature that explores the Whitman story and related myths in the context of western patterns of mythmaking and writing. The Presbyterian historian Clifford Merrill Drury, active from the 1930s to the 1970s, was by far the most prolific writer and editor of materials regarding the Whitmans and their associates, publishing two biographies of Marcus Whitman, a biography of Whitman's associate Henry Harmon Spalding, and multiple anthologies of the Oregon missionaries' letters and diaries. Drury was less interested in the mythology surrounding Whitman, which appears only in a short epilogue in his most thorough Whitman biography, *Marcus and Narcissa Whitman, and the Opening of Old Oregon.*[14] Other, more recent biographers of the Whitmans, most notably Julie Roy Jeffrey, have also focused primarily on the Whitmans' lives rather than their legacy in American memory.[15] A few scholars have briefly discussed the Whitman story in works published in the last twenty years: as a remnant of unsettled "Old World religious scores" and as an example of early twentieth-century historians' exclusion of Native voices from their work.[16] However, the Whitman story's wide-ranging influence on popular memory and professional history remains largely unexamined.

By exploring how an unlikely tale about a missionary helped to shape popular and academic understandings of history, my book draws on and expands on scholars' interpretations of the cultural legacies of US Protestant missionary work. While earlier scholarly histories of missions treat interactions between missionaries and their subjects, historians of missions have more recently begun to examine interactions between missionaries and their home cultures.[17] A primary function of nineteenth-century missionary narratives was to depict American expansion as a Christian duty ordained by divine providence.[18] Historians since Arthur Schlesinger have argued that imperialist ideals shaped American missionary work, but less studied is the way missionary narratives reinforced imperialist ideals in US popular culture.[19] In her essay "The Influence of American Missionary Women on the World Back Home" the historian Dana Robert argues that religious leaders recast stories of martyred missionaries, native resistance, and failed missions into tales of heroism, sacrifice, and delayed success, so that the public narrative of mission work was often very different from the reality at the missions.[20] The Whitman story exemplifies how this reframing was enacted, as Whitman went from failed missionary to "the great martyr to the cause of . . . the advancement of national development and Christian civilization."[21] Examining the mythology surrounding Whitman demonstrates how missionary history formatted history in the West. Christian historical writings were not peripheral to the American historical enterprise in the nineteenth century; rather, the roles of missionary, pastor, and academic historian were often blurred, and the patterns that providential history followed continued to shape scientific historical narratives of the West. The Whitman story offers an explicit example of how Protestantism persisted within academic historiography as the default practice and teleology for American expansion.

I thus also draw here on scholarship that examines the origins of the American historical profession, notably the aforementioned *That Noble Dream*. Novick's work is a foundational text in the study of the academic historical profession's development, and one with which all subsequent works of the history of historiography must contend. Novick's recognition that objectivity was a contested, poorly defined term is instructive for this project. However, Novick does not examine one of the main reasons objectivity was contested: because it called into question the place of providential narratives in academic historical work. Objective historians argued that historical work written from an ostensibly Protestant perspective, one that viewed American history as dictated by a divine plan, was incompatible with the demands and goals of proper historical labor.

Other scholars, Henry Warner Bowden and Elizabeth Clark among them, have examined the conflict between providential and objective history more thoroughly. In *Church History in the Age of Science,* Bowden examines the changing relationship between church history and secular history by tracing the changing relationship between the American Society of Church History and the AHA.[22] Bowden writes that this changing relationship can be summed up in two conflicting ideas about history: whether church history should be fundamentally guided by theological convictions or by the latest scientific theories and methodologies.[23] Clark provides a prehistory to Bowden's account in *Founding the Fathers,* which explores how four leading Protestant seminaries served as centers of graduate work in the study of church history in the nineteenth century, before the establishment of history doctoral programs.[24] Clark holds that scholars at these institutions served as key transitional figures between the sectarian study of church history and the discipline of the study of religion.[25] Both Clark and Bowden demonstrate that questions about the appropriate place of theological narratives played a pivotal role in shaping the development of the American historical profession. Their portraits of individual scholars show that the language of objectivity and science was not exclusive to those who sought to eliminate providential narratives from academic history; to the contrary, church historians often appropriated the language of science in idiosyncratic ways that synthesized the theological and the scientific.[26]

For all their interest in church history, however, neither Clark nor Bowden examines the discipline of comparative religion's influence on scholarly ideas about history, particularly through comparative religion's theories of myth. Comparative religion, a discipline that developed alongside history in the late nineteenth-century American academy, helped to cast myths as holdovers from supposedly primitive societies in which science and reason had not yet prevailed.[27] Comparative religionists' teleologies of the progress of civilizations from myth and superstition to science and reason afforded scientific historians a moral logic for refuting cherished myths in US history. If myths were the proper purview of primitive (nonwhite and non-Protestant) societies, then it behooved historians to purge the annals of United States history of myths. Clark's and Bowden's studies also focus on the narration of what one might call traditional church history: the histories of creeds, liturgies, and denominations. Providential history extended beyond such churchly topics to encompass the whole of US and world history and it placed special emphasis on a region often represented as being devoid of religion: the American West.

Scholarly explorations of historiography in and about the American West focus on a different kind of mythology than the narratives of providence and progress that shaped providential and objective history. These studies of history writing in the West emphasize two features not seen in more nationally focused work. First, they demonstrate that popular and academic history intersected in the early years of white western settlement, where organizations like historical societies, veterans' groups, and pioneer associations blurred the lines between the popular and the scholarly. Second, they illuminate how narrations of the Anglo-American conquest of the West helped to set the terms of historical inquiry from the nineteenth century to the present. Amanda Laugeson's *The Making of Public Historical Culture in the West, 1880–1910* traces the growth of the State Historical Society of Wisconsin, the Kansas State Historical Society, and the Oregon Historical Society, maintaining that these societies utilized both the legends of the West's pioneer past and the tools of the emerging historical profession to build a public historical culture in the West.[28] Kerwin Klein's *Frontiers of Historical Imagination* argues that Anglo-European and Native encounters in the West cast a long shadow over American historical work, for it was in representations of these frontier encounters that the "historical and nonhistorical defied and defined each other."[29] Klein plots a genealogy of scholarly writing about the West that begins with Frederick Jackson Turner and progresses through the twentieth century. In Klein's narrative, tensions between history as a narrative art and history as an analytical science parallel the tensions between indigenous peoples and white settlers described in scholars' accounts of the West. The historical profession itself, then, can be seen as a kind of frontier whose inhabitants make sense of each other through binary designations of historical versus nonhistorical, art versus science, story versus analysis.

Both Laugesen and Klein take up the American West as myth, and in so doing they stand in a long line of scholars beginning with Henry Nash Smith.[30] But religion is curiously absent in their analyses of this western mythology. One would not know from reading Laugesen that most of the Oregon Historical Society's early proponents were connected to the region's Methodist missions and were deeply committed to representing the Pacific Northwest as a Protestant space. History writing in the Northwest served as a way not only of establishing a regional identity in a recently and incompletely conquered region but also of narrating Protestant supremacy into a place still inhabited by indigenous people, Catholics, and religious skeptics and freethinkers. Similarly, while Klein asserts that historians of the American West often built their history on grand moral and philosophical visions, his exploration of the roots of these visions remains strictly within the realms of philosophy and literature, not theology. This is striking because Klein places Turner in a lineage of figures whose work was profoundly shaped by Protestant sensibilities, including Hegel and Emerson.[31] I argue that providentialism was as significant as European intellectual currents in shaping historians' moral visions of the American West, for providentialism both predated American historians' study at European institutions and guided many proto-professional historical endeavors, including historical societies, the teaching of church history in seminary contexts, and amateur historical writing.

Discussion of the marginalization of providential narratives naturally brings to mind scholarly conversations about secularization, and indeed, this book also draws and expands on many of these works. In recent years a growing number of scholars of religion have recognized the crucial part that Protestantism has played in the evolution of American secularism. Tracy Fessenden, in *Culture and Redemption,* has held that the secular is not the absence of religion but an ideological space profoundly shaped by and dependent on Protestant ideological commitments. The secular, she proposes, grew out of a deliberately asserted nineteenth-century Protestant hegemony, and the secular both obscured and more deeply embedded this hegemony by denuding it of its outwardly religious qualities.[32] I make a parallel argument here about the secularization of the American historical profession: the removal of overtly providential narratives from academic history writing was propelled by Protestant concerns with removing avowedly primitive, medieval accretions and returning to original texts, even as historians repudiated their fellow Protestants for their sectarian biases. I also complicate Fessenden's thesis in two ways. First, I locate the beginnings of a secular history of the Pacific Northwest in the writings of Catholic priests. Their appeals for an objective, nonsectarian history arose from the margins of Protestant power and received little attention until they were taken up and revised by Protestants, but they nevertheless represent an alternate vision of secularization. Second, I argue that the early twentieth-century secularization of the American historical profession was an enterprise propelled by Protestants and directed by broadly Protestant convictions. It was thus an intra-Protestant struggle, one in which both pro- and anti-secularizationists believed they were on the right side of church progress. My book thus reveals multiple conflicting providentialisms and secularisms, formulated differently and mobilized toward different ends.

Excavating the Whitman Story

The Whitman story evolved out of the history of the establishment and subsequent collapse of Marcus Whitman's mission among the Cayuse people. Chapter 1 returns to this oft-told tale to excavate what became the threads of the Whitman story. It situates the Whitman Mission within antebellum Protestant understandings of missionary labor as ordained by God and destined for success. Within this providential framework, the failure of a mission to win converts or implement any material change in the lives of missionized peoples would be viewed as incompatible with the divine destiny of mission work. As the possibility of Cayuse conversion and acculturation to Anglo-American values became more and more remote, Whitman began to renarrate his own missionary purpose so that it could be seen as a success. He came to the conclusion that the Cayuse people were providentially doomed to extinction and that his true purpose was to facilitate the Christianization of Oregon Territory by means of Anglo-American colonization of Native lands. After his death in 1847, his surviving colleagues amplified this mission of colonization in order to frame Whitman as a providential and patriotic hero.

Chapter 2 follows Marcus Whitman's surviving missionary associate, Henry Harmon Spalding, as he sought to redeem his and Whitman's missions in public memory through a twenty-six-year historical crusade. From 1848 until his death in 1874 Spalding wrote newspaper articles, lectured regionally and nationally, and eventually testified before the United States Senate in order to argue that the Oregon missionaries, Whitman first among them, were heroes and that Catholics were ultimately responsible for Whitman's death. In so doing Spalding created a providential history of the settling of Oregon in which Whitman served as a God-ordained hero of both Christianity and American expansion. Spalding's campaign demonstrates how Protestant–Catholic disputes in the Oregon Territory produced two conflicting narratives of Whitman's mission—one lauding Whitman as a hero, the other lamenting him as a missionary failure. It also illuminates the networks by which providential history spread: through churches, religious periodicals, and state and local governments.

Chapter 3 brings to the fore another of Whitman's missionary associates, William Henry Gray, as he participated in the first efforts to commemorate the Pacific Northwest's Anglo-American pioneers, including the Whitmans (and, importantly, Gray himself). In the 1870s and 1880s Oregonians took up the mythology of Whitman in their earliest attempts to create a regional history and in the process helped to make

Spalding's providential history a part of broader struggles over regional identity. Gray and his allies founded the Pioneer and Historical Society of Oregon, a Protestant-leaning organization that fashioned Whitman into a key symbol of Oregon's white Christian pioneer heritage. Meanwhile, the first detractors of the Whitman story sought to demonstrate that the West was abandoning local legends in favor of modern historical methods. As both Whitman's supporters and detractors used the Whitman story as a means to engage anxieties about the Pacific Northwest's rapidly shifting political, religious, and intellectual landscape they also drove the region's first efforts toward historical professionalization. The results were two conflicting historical methodologies: pioneer providentialism and pioneer secularism. These proto-professional methodologies both constructed the pioneer as an archetype for western identity and a model for the West's uncertain future.

Chapter 4 examines the nationalization of the Whitman story in the 1890s through the efforts of three figures: Stephen Penrose, the president of the struggling Whitman College, founded in Whitman's memory; Daniel K. Pearsons, a Chicago philanthropist; and Oliver W. Nixon, the editor of the *Chicago Inter Ocean*. As Whitman College teetered on the edge of bankruptcy, Penrose enlisted the two Chicago men to help raise a permanent endowment for the school. The Whitman story became the cornerstone of their fundraising appeals. Pearsons's financial resources and Nixon's wide-ranging media influence brought the Whitman story to a wider audience than it had ever reached. More than that, however, Penrose, Pearsons, and Nixon refashioned the Whitman story to appeal to Gilded Age sensibilities. In their narratives Whitman became an exemplar of white masculinity as well as a harbinger of America's late nineteenth-century imperial expansion, the hero of an imperial providential history. Whitman could thus be placed within other late nineteenth-century histories of the United States that emphasized the nation's superior racial stock, advanced state of civilization, and providential destiny to carry that civilization to the darker-skinned peoples of the world.

By the beginning of the twentieth century the Whitman story had achieved national fame, appearing even in scholarly histories of the United States. Yet shifts in American historical thought were about to lead to its undoing. Chapter 5 explores the controversy that arose in 1900 when the Yale historian Edward Bourne presented evidence at the AHA's annual meeting that the Whitman story was false. It traces the debate exemplified by Bourne and the school principal William Isaac Marshall, on the one hand, and the providential historians Myron Eells and William Mowry on the other, situating this controversy within the professionalization of the historical discipline and its relationship to the discipline of comparative religion. While the Whitman story was eventually stricken from most scholarly histories, the assumptions underlying that removal retained the racialized logic of earlier modes of history. Bourne, Marshall, and other scholars who advocated the new, scientific history methods placed their work within a broad teleology of progress that positioned their opponents as primitive, medieval believers in outmoded myths like the Whitman story. History must be purged of its myths, they argued, in order to distinguish modern Anglo-Americans from racial and religious others. Meanwhile, the Whitman story began to function in a kind of mythical capacity for those who continued to believe in it, serving as a signifier for the rejection of scientific history and the preservation of earlier moral and religious values.

The tale of Whitman's ride was a legend, but it was a legend with real consequences. For decades it played a central role in constructions of regional and religious identities. It helped Anglo-Americans narrate their way into lands that they had conquered only recently and incompletely. It allowed Pacific Northwest Protestants to envision the West as a Christian region, despite ample evidence to the contrary. It powered historical organizations, fundraising efforts, and public displays of the unity of Protestant and state power. Its changing iterations both reflected and shaped academic and popular history in the nineteenth and twentieth centuries, as providential narratives ceded ground—but never disappeared entirely—from academic historical writing. Even today historians struggle to navigate a path between the believer and the skeptic, the storyteller and the debunker. This book, focusing its lens on an Oregon missionary and those who both made and unmade his legend, explores how these tensions came to be.

Providence and the Scandal of Missionary Failure

"It does not become me to speak by way of complaint of any one; but I may safely say we are greatly wanting in spirituality, faith, prayer, & expectation of success," wrote an exasperated Marcus Whitman in 1840.[1] Whitman, his wife, Narcissa, and three missionary associates had traveled across the North American continent in 1836 to establish the first Presbyterian and Congregationalist missions among the Native peoples west of the Rocky Mountains. Since then the missions had fractured, torn apart by interpersonal conflicts and grudges over issues both significant and trivial. Meanwhile, the missionaries' relationship with their Native neighbors, the Cayuse, Nimiipuu, and Spokane peoples, had deteriorated as those peoples realized that the missionaries' teachings demanded wholesale rejection of their lifeways and justified Anglo-American colonization of their lands. Now, some of the missionaries wanted to leave in order to save their missionary organization "the embarrassment into which it must be brought by what will be laid before them by some members of the Mission."[2]

The Marcus Whitman of this letter—discouraged, frustrated, and uncertain—was a far cry from the Whitman who would later be known to historians and laypeople alike as a Christian martyr and a national hero. Seven years later, in 1847, several members of the Cayuse nation attacked Whitman's mission, killing Marcus and Narcissa Whitman and eleven other white Americans in a last-ditch effort to save their people from epidemic disease and the relentless, missionary-supported flow of white settlement. The Cayuse homeland erupted into war, and the Protestant missions in the region collapsed. None of this suggested that Whitman would someday be honored as a national hero.

After his death Whitman would undergo a dramatic transformation in both academic history and popular culture. Haunted by their missions' failure and eager to find a redemptive vantage point from which to envision their place in the Pacific Northwest, Whitman's missionary associates reinvented Marcus Whitman as a visionary and a sure-footed patriotic hero, one whose quick thinking and providential leading saved Oregon Territory from becoming a British possession. Tracing that hero story from its first iteration in 1848 into the twentieth century illustrates how changing versions of the Whitman story illuminate broader creations and conflicts in the history of American historical writing and thought. Two historical imaginaries would grow up around the Whitman story: the providential and the objective. Both drew from older traditions of historical thought but became increasingly routinized and institutionalized in the decades preceding and immediately following the founding of the American historical profession. As these strains developed, Whitman became, first, a providential figure and then a subject of the myth busting energies of objective history.

There were multiple reasons the story of Marcus Whitman lent itself to this kind of providential reimagining. The first is rooted in his life. From the beginning of his missionary career Whitman saw his work as being providentially guided. As he argued with other missionaries, suffered great personal loss, and ultimately redirected his missionary labor from evangelizing the Cayuse people to encouraging white Protestants to settle in the Northwest, he attributed all to divine providence. Providentialism was the hermeneutic that shaped Whitman's understanding of his own work and thus provided a template for subsequent providential narrations of his life. These two factors—Whitman's failure as a missionary and the providentialism through which he and his associates viewed their work—set a template for future reimaginings of Whitman's significance as a Christian martyr and American hero.

The history of Marcus Whitman and his mission is an oft-told story, one that began circulating with the Whitmans' deaths in 1847 and still appears, as an obligatory vignette, in recent histories of the American West. Historians have examined the Whitman missions as a classic case of cultural misunderstanding, emphasizing the Whitmans' inability to fully learn the Nez Perce language and respect Cayuse customs, the different ways in which the Whitmans and the Cayuse people understood medicine, and conflicts over increasing Anglo-American settlement.[3] Scholars of Native America have situated the Whitman Mission's history within a broader context of disruptions to Pacific Northwest Indian life in the eighteenth and nineteenth centuries as well as an intensification of preexisting Native prophetic and millennial traditions.[4] Still other scholars have focused on Whitman Mission's place in the history of Anglo-American colonialism, examining the mission as a case study in manifest destiny.[5] The short history of Marcus Whitman was all of these things: a history marked and inflamed by cultural conflict, a history that took place within a broader context of continuity and change in Plateau Indian life, and a history that both was inflected by and helped to further American expansion and Native dispossession.

In this chapter I revisit some of those arguments in recounting Whitman's short life and violent death, but my primary interest in retelling the Whitman story is to account for how Whitman's missionary life and death sparked such enthusiastic, dramatic, and widespread renarration, renarration that transformed not only Whitman's legacy but also the practices of writing and telling history in America. There were two reasons Marcus Whitman's missionary career was primed for such legendary recreation. The first is that the mission itself was a spectacular failure, a failure that was incompatible with the ways in which nineteenth-century America viewed missions. Marcus Whitman and his companions began their missionary labors at the height of the evangelical revivals of the Second Great Awakening, when American evangelicals evinced tremendous optimism about the ability of Christians to reform and evangelize the world. "The cause is the noblest on earth—the work the greatest—the sure results most durable and glorious," wrote Samuel Worcester in the 1820 report of the American Board of Commissioners for Foreign Missions (ABCFM).[6] Undergirding this growth in missionary labor was the evangelical conviction that God's providence ordered all things, including especially missionary labor. "The world was created as a theatre for [missionary labor's] existence. The machinery of Providence, and the relations of men, have been constructed to favor its operations," wrote Absalom Peters for the American Home Missionary Society in 1831.[7] Marcus Whitman, his fellow missionaries, and their American supporters were shaped by this conviction that God ensured missionary success.

But the Whitman Mission never won a single convert. Its existence was marked by years of infighting and frustration. The Whitmans were killed by the very people they had spent eleven years evangelizing, and the Whitmans' deaths plunged the region into war, foreclosing all future opportunities for Protestant evangelism. The collapse of the Whitman Mission demanded that the proponents of missions find ways to relocate God's providential guidance in what appeared to be a tale of missionary failure.

The second reason for the Whitman story's transformation lies within Whitman himself. As the creeping failure of his evangelistic efforts became apparent, Whitman reevaluated his own missionary purpose and found new ways of understanding the providence that had placed him in the Pacific Northwest. Midway through his missionary tenure, he shifted his efforts from evangelizing the Cayuse people to encouraging white, Protestant, American settlers to populate the Pacific Northwest—including, eventually, the Cayuse homeland. By the time Whitman was killed in 1847, he viewed his labor for American emigrants as the most important contribution he had made as a missionary. But before he became the Paul Revere of the West he was a missionary who knew he was failing to reach the Cayuse people, who was wearied by the never-ending feuds among his missionary associates, but who nonetheless believed that his work was advancing the cause of Christianity in the world. When later interpreters argued that Whitman was a hero of American expansion, then, their narratives, however exaggerated, were grounded in Whitman's own words and deeds. Whitman was the first to see himself as an agent of Americanization and a hero of Oregon settlement. Though his legend grew in ways he could not have anticipated, he was the template.

The "White Man's Book of Heaven" and the Providential Origins of the Oregon Missions

Little in Marcus Whitman's early life portended his later fame. He was born to Alice and Beza Whitman in 1802 in rural Rushville, New York. When Marcus was eight years old his father died unexpectedly, and his mother sent him to live with his grandfather in Plainfield, Massachusetts.[8] There, Whitman studied under the Presbyterian minister and teacher Moses Hallock. In 1819 an evangelical revival swept Plainfield, and Whitman, then seventeen, was among the converted. "I was awakened to a sense of my sin and danger and brought by Divine grace to rely on the Lord Jesus for pardon and salvation," he later wrote.[9] Whitman began attending Sunday school regularly and set his mind on becoming a minister. However, when his family convinced him he could not afford the cost of college and seminary training, he trained to become a physician instead.[10] After completing his medical training, he again attempted to study for the ministry but was forced to abandon his studies when he found himself, as he later told the ABCFM, "impaired by a pain in the left side which I attrebuted [sic] to an inflamation [sic] of the spleen."[11] He returned to his career as a physician, working in Wheeler, New York, and hoping for an opportunity to become more than just a town doctor.

In 1834 the opportunity materialized. A Presbyterian minister, Samuel Parker, arrived in Wheeler to raise support for a new mission to the Native peoples living west of the Rocky Mountains. Parker's interest in the mission had been sparked by a remarkable incident reported the previous year. In 1833 the Methodist periodical the *Christian Advocate* ran an article by a pious New York merchant named Gabriel P. Disoway, who recounted how "[four] chiefs of the Flat-Head nation" had traveled from their homeland west of the Rocky Mountains to St. Louis, Missouri, in search of the Bible and Christian teaching. Disoway included a letter from William Walker, a Christian Wyandot Indian who claimed to have met the chiefs in St. Louis while they were visiting the famed explorer William Clark.[12] Alongside striking sketches of the Indians' flattened heads, Walker reported the story of the chiefs' visit:

Some white man had penetrated into their country, and happened to be a spectator at one of their religious ceremonies. ... He informed them that their mode of worshipping the supreme Being was radically wrong. ... [H]e also informed him that the white people *away* toward the rising of the sun had been put in possession of the true mode of worshipping the great Spirit. They had a book containing directions how to conduct themselves in order to enjoy his favor and hold converse with him; and with this guide, no one need go astray, but every one that would follow the directions laid down there, could enjoy, in this life, his favor, and after death would be received into the country where the great Spirit resides, and live for ever with him.

Upon receiving this information, they called a national council to take this subject into consideration. Some said, if this be true, it is certainly high time we were put into possession of this mode ... the sooner we know it the better. They accordingly deputed four of their chiefs to proceed to St. Louis to see their great father, Gen. Clarke, to inquire of him, having no doubt but he would tell them the whole truth about it.[13]

Walker stated that Clark then gave the chiefs a "succinct history of man" and of Jesus Christ and "explained to them all the moral precepts in the Bible."[14] But two of the Flathead men sickened and died before they could bring the knowledge back to their homeland, and the fate of the other two chiefs was unknown. Against this uncertain ending, Disoway added his own coda, contrasting the Indians' physical deformity (their flattened heads) with their moral potential and painting a pathetic picture of the "simple children of nature" living in the wilderness, with no white men to guide them except the "sordid, demoralizing hunter and fur trader." Disoway closed with a plea: "Let the Church awake from her slumbers, and go forth in her strength to the salvation of those wandering in our native forests."[15]

There is a certain irony in the *Advocate* being the starting point for Whitman's mission, for it, like later tales of Whitman's heroism, was too good to be true. As historians have subsequently shown, Disoway's article and Walker's letter were based on an actual encounter, but the visit's details and import were greatly exaggerated in the retelling.[16] Four Native men did indeed travel to St. Louis and seek out William Clark in 1831: Black Eagle (Tipyeléhne Cimúuxcimux), Speaking Eagle (Tipyeléhne Íleesenin) or Man-of-the-Morning (Ka'áwpoo), Rabbit-Skin-Leggings (Hey'úuxchtonin'), and No-Horns-On-His-Head (Téewis Sisímnim'). They were not Flathead, however, but Nimiipuu, and none of the men actually had the flattened heads that had rendered them so striking in Walker's drawings.[17] Nor did the men have a conversation with Clark in which he explained the tenets of Christianity. No one in St. Louis at the time spoke Nimiipuutímt, the Nez Perce language, so the men were able to communicate only through signs. Instead of requesting the "white man's book" and Protestant teaching, the men visited a Catholic church, whose priests presented them with crucifixes and baptized the sick men before their deaths.[18] It was, in short, an ambiguous and ambivalent visit, one that demonstrated a desire for contact with white Americans and an interest in elements of white religion but not the desire for Bibles and Protestant missionaries that Disoway's story depicted.

The *Advocate*'s readers could not have known the story's murky details, however, and so the remarkable news of the Indians who crossed the continent in search of the Bible sent a spark through the churches of the eastern United States.[19] It was not the first time that Anglo-American Protestants had envisioned Native people crying out, as the Macedonians had in the New Testament, "Come over ... and help us!"[20] The idea of an Indian Macedonian cry had generated and justified missionary efforts since the Massachusetts Bay Colony included a desperate Indian on its colony seal.[21] However, American conquest of Native lands, intensification of white–Native violence, and the perplexing realities of cross-cultural ministry had undermined missionary efforts again and again, most recently when the American government forcibly removed the Cherokee and Choctaw nations from their ancestral homelands over the vehement protests of members of the ABCFM.[22] Meanwhile, politicians, scholars, and religious leaders trumpeted the notion that the Indians were a doomed race destined to die out or be irrevocably corrupted by unscrupulous whites in the face of unstoppable white expansion.[23] By the time the *Christian Advocate* published the story of the Flathead Indians, growing discouragement with national Indian policy and pessimism about Indians' future had led mission organizations like the ABCFM to shift their focus toward missions outside the North American continent.[24]

Walker's letter and Disoway's article thus reached the Christian press at an opportune time. Disoway's imaginative sketches of the delegation's flattened heads rendered the "Flat-Head Indians" both grotesque and compellingly exotic, underscoring the promise of an alluringly savage people needful of Christian teaching. These Indians were "honest, brave, peaceable"; they were notably free of vice; the women made excellent wives and mothers; the men were faithful to their wives; and they already had some understanding of an afterlife.[25] By Disoway's account this was a people primed for Christian instruction—indeed, one already living by Christian precepts in many ways. Once freed of their idolatry, they would surely be model converts. There could hardly have been an account more calculated to persuade hopeful missionaries that here, finally, was an Indian field where missionaries could succeed.

And missionaries were indeed persuaded. Just four months after the article was published, the Methodist Missionary Society appointed Jason Lee missionary to the Flathead Indians. With his brother, Daniel, Jason Lee established the first Protestant mission in the Pacific Northwest in 1834, in French Prairie near present-day Salem, Oregon.[26] Parker sought to do the same under the auspices of the joint Presbyterian, Congregationalist, and Dutch Reformed organization, the ABCFM.[27] The endeavor fell under the category of foreign missions because of the ambiguous nature of Oregon's boundaries in the early nineteenth century. At that time the area encompassing present-day Oregon, Washington, Idaho, and parts of British Columbia and Montana was known as the Oregon Country. From 1818 to 1846 the United States and Great Britain jointly held fur-trading rights in the region, but neither country could claim ownership. The missionaries would be some of the first US citizens to settle in what was then foreign territory.[28]

Though the board initially rejected Parker because of his advanced age—he was fifty-four— Parker persisted. He moved to Ithaca, New York, where the fervent revivals of the Second Great Awakening were sweeping the land with such frequency that the region later earned the nickname the Burned-Over District. He began preaching at churches in the area about the Indians of Oregon, hoping to raise funds and volunteers.[29] One of his rapt listeners was Marcus Whitman. After Parker's visit, Whitman wrote to the ABCFM to offer his services as a missionary, eagerly declaring his willingness to work as a "P[h]ysician Teacher or Agriculteralist" [sic]—any job that the board required. "My mind has long been turned to the missionary subject," he stated. "For the last Six months I have been mor[e] inten[t] upon it than b[e]fore, I wish soon to have a definit[e] course." Like Parker, Whitman was rejected at first. The board was concerned about his record of poor health and his unwillingness to work in the hot, tropical climates where most of the Board's missions were located.[30] But by 1835 both men had convinced the board to commission them, and they set off in the spring of that year to travel with the American Fur Company on an exploring tour from St. Louis to the yearly trading rendezvous near Green River, Wyoming, and then on to the lands west of the Rocky Mountains.[31]

The trip did not go smoothly. Parker and Whitman disagreed about costs, supplies, and division of labor. The company did not take kindly to the missionaries' insistence on temperance and Sabbath observance. "Very evident tokens gave us to understand that our company was not agreeable such as the throwing of rotten eggs at me," Whitman wrote to the secretary of the board, David Greene.[32] But when Parker and Whitman reached the site of the yearly fur-trading rendezvous, where Native and white traders met to exchange goods and socialize, their interactions with the Native peoples assembled there rekindled their hopes. They met with members of the Nimiipuu and Flathead (Bitterroot Salish) nations, and Whitman noted in his journal that these men were "very much inclined to follow any advise [sic] given them by the whites and are ready to adop[t] any thing that is taught them as religion."[33] Speaking through translators, members of the two tribes gave orations in which they declared their desire for religious knowledge. Tai-quin-su-watish, also known as Tackensuatis, or Rotten Belly, proclaimed, "He had heard from white men a little about God, which had gone only into his ears; he wished to know enough to have it go down into his heart, to influence his life, and to teach his people."[34] "They all made as many promises as we could desire," Parker marveled.[35] The field

Fig. 1. Painting by Drury Haight based on
a sketch of Marcus Whitman by Paul Kane.
Marcus and Narcissa Whitman Collection,
Whitman College and Northwest Archives,
Walla Walla, Washington.

appeared so promising that Whitman turned around to return to the US
and immediately seek partners for a mission while Parker continued the
journey to Oregon alone.[36]

Whitman's first missionary associate was his new wife. Before em-
barking on the exploring tour Whitman had proposed to Narcissa Prentiss,
the eldest daughter of a well-to-do family in Prattsburgh, New York. Little
is known of their courtship, which took place over the course of a single
weekend, but the two evidently saw their common interest in missions as a
sign of God's providence.[37] Like Marcus, Narcissa had applied to be a missionary and had been rejected, not because of her health but because of her
unmarried status. In the 1830s the ABCFM did not commission single
women for missionary work, and they preferred that male missionaries

Fig. 2. Painting by Drury Haight based on
a sketch of Narcissa Prentiss Whitman by
Paul Kane. Marcus and Narcissa Whitman
Collection, Whitman College and Northwest
Archives, Walla Walla, Washington.

marry in order to properly demonstrate Christian domestic life to missionized peoples.[38] This constraint had not always been applied with Protestant
missions in America. In the seventeenth and eighteenth centuries many
missionaries were single men, who were presumed to have fewer family
ties to distract or deter them from engaging in lonely, dangerous labor. But
changes in American concepts of gender and virtue at the turn of the nineteenth century had led to a new emphasis on the family as the center of
Christian piety and of women as the custodians of that piety.[39] The rise of
this "cult of domesticity" placed significant focus on female piety in general
and female missionaries in particular. Biographies of women like Harriet
Newell, a short-lived missionary wife who served briefly in India, achieved
popularity much like the *Life of David Brainerd* had done a half-century

earlier.[40] By the 1830s, the ABCFM not only preferred to send married couples as missionaries, they also commissioned missionary wives as "assistant missionaries," demonstrating the vital responsibility that women like Narcissa were expected to uphold in teaching indigenous women Christian gender roles, child-rearing, and domestic pursuits.[41]

Marcus and Narcissa were married on February 18, 1836. The next day, after a tearful farewell service, they embarked on their cross-country journey to Oregon.[42] They intercepted the missionaries Henry and Eliza Spalding, whom Marcus convinced to join the expedition to Oregon instead of their original assignment to the Osages. As the two couples began their journey they received parting instructions from the ABCFM. "Live near to God," wrote Secretary Greene. "Labor for him. Rely on his grace and spirit, and may his promises all be made good to you, and y[ou]r mission be as life from the dead to the benighted tribes of the remote west."[43]

The missionaries believed they had every reason to be optimistic. Native people living west of the Rocky Mountains had received Whitman and Parker with enthusiasm at the 1835 Rendezvous. Nimiipuu leaders made promises of future friendship and even sent two of their own young men, Tackitonitis (whom Whitman called Richard) and Aits (whom Whitman called John), to return East with Whitman to cement the bonds between the two peoples.[44] The missionaries also trusted in the story of the Flathead chiefs' journey in search of the Bible. The missionaries had not sought out the Indians; rather, the Indians had sought out the missionaries. Surely these were a people who were ripe for the harvest.

What the Whitmans did not and could not know was that the Native people at the Rendezvous desired contact with white Americans for far more complicated reasons than the experiences of Whitman's and Parker's exploring tour suggested. Religious exchange was, for the Nimiipuu and their neighbors, a determining feature of material exchange. A comment that a Nimiipuu leader known only as Charlie made to Parker hints at this: "These white men know everything. They know what rocks are made of, they know how to make iron, and how to make watches, and how to make the needle always point to the north."[45] For the Native peoples of the Oregon Country white religion was inextricably intertwined with other forms of knowledge and power, including those manifested in trade goods. The Native peoples of Oregon had come into contact with such goods through trade networks even before meeting white people face to face. The Hudson's Bay Company had established posts in Nimiipuu territory in the 1820s, and those posts proved to be centers of education about white material cultures and customs. The Roman Catholic chief factor of Fort Walla Walla, for instance, held Sunday services for all affiliated with the trading post and encouraged his Native neighbors and employees to observe the Sabbath, reject polygamy, and avoid liquor.[46] From these traders Native people around Fort Walla Walla also learned about Christian sacred objects like crucifixes and incorporated them into their material practices.[47] Under this arrangement access to novel material goods was closely associated with religious teaching such that religious leaders and trading partners were one and the same.

Moreover, the Nimiipuu and neighboring Native communities viewed spiritual power as something that could be acquired and integrated into existing systems of belief and practice. They readily incorporated Catholic elements into their rituals and lifeways, but the traders did not demand, nor did Native people seek, wholesale cultural transformation. Rather, they adopted elements of Christianity to varying extents and for a multitude of reasons: attaining spiritual power, forming new trading alliances, gaining material and societal prosperity, finding avenues for cultural reform.[48] The Native people at the Rendezvous likely saw white religion as one tool for addressing the rapid upheavals brought by white contact, white diseases, and the international economy of the fur trade—a tool that could add to existing cultural structures without replacing them. The Nimiipuu were not as remote and untouched a people as Disoway's account depicted. They had already had extensive contact with white people, had some knowledge of Christianity, and already operated as part of an international trading economy. They desired contact with and knowledge about Americans, certainly, but what they were requesting and what they would receive were worlds apart.

Great Expectations, Disheartening Realities

In the spring of 1836 the missionaries had little reason to doubt the auspicious origins of their mission or the promise of its success. They traveled by carriage to Pittsburgh, then by steamboat to Liberty,

Missouri, where they met William Henry Gray, the fifth member of their party. Gray had hoped to be appointed to Oregon as a missionary, but because of his youth and lack of education the American board had appointed him to be the party's manual laborer—a post that caused discord in the future. The missionary party then traveled overland with fur company caravans to the yearly Rendezvous.

For the missionaries, who believed all events were guided by God's providential hand, the overland journey confirmed their optimism about their future calling. "Indeed when we recount the mercies we have received we are constrained to say goodness and mercy have followed us all the way," wrote Whitman.[49] Though the party often had nothing to eat but buffalo meat, they did not go hungry. And the large size of their caravan—seventy fur company members with their wagons and cattle—ensured safe travel.[50] "I wish I could discribe [sic] to you how we live so that you can realize it," wrote Narcissa to her brother Edward and sister Harriet Prentiss as the mission party traversed the Great Plains. "Our manner of living is far preferable to any in the States. I never was so contented and happy before. Neither have I enjoyed such health for years."[51] The missionary party met several Nimiipuu at the 1836 Rendezvous, who greeted them warmly. "They expressed great satisfaction at seeing us & that we had not disappointed them but spoken truth," wrote Marcus.[52] The missionaries also met several Cayuse people, neighbors and allies of the Nimiipuu. The Cayuses were as intent on having missionaries as the Nimiipuu; Narcissa later wrote that the two groups "nearly came to blows" over where the Whitmans and Spaldings would settle.[53] Struck and moved by this enthusiasm, the missionaries continued on with the fur company but reassured the Cayuses and Nimiipuu that they would return.

The missionaries evidently did not realize it at the time, but their journey would have great import for the Protestant history of the American West. Narcissa Whitman and Eliza Spalding were the first known white women to cross the Rocky Mountains. As Narcissa later noted in her diary, it was an "unheard of journey for females."[54] The two women came to symbolize the opening of the West to Anglo-American families and, with that, the extension of American patterns of gender and domestic life.

At the time, however, the missionaries were interested primarily in making it to the Oregon Country safely. On September 1, 1836, the party arrived at Hudson's Bay Company Fort Walla Walla, where they were warmly greeted by the head of the fort, Chief Factor Pierre Chrysologue Pambrun, and his métis wife, Catherine.[55] They then traveled with Pambrun by boat to Fort Vancouver, near the confluence of the Columbia and Willamette Rivers, where they received a similarly warm welcome from Chief Factor John McLoughlin and his métis wife, Marguerite. After the long journey the missionaries were struck by the genteel nature of the traders and their wives, their use of such niceties as porcelain china and feather beds, and their willingness to support Christian teaching. "The means of sustenance and comfort we find here, so much beyond our expectations when we left home, calls for the most sincere praise and gratitude," wrote Narcissa.[56] Both chief traders held Sunday services at their respective forts, and McLoughlin had secured an Anglican priest, Herbert Beaver, to minister at Fort Vancouver. To the missionaries, who had no doubt read accounts of fur traders portraying them as men who rejected civilization and impeded attempts to civilize the Indians, this must have come as a surprise. "We see now that it was not necessary to bring anything because we find all here," Narcissa wrote to her family.[57] Narcissa and Eliza remained at Vancouver for two months while Marcus, Henry, and William Gray returned to Nimiipuu and Cayuse country to choose mission sites and construct homes.

The three men traveled northeast up the Columbia River, through the Cascade Mountains, to the homelands of the Cayuse and Nimiipuu peoples in the Columbia Plateau, the large, semiarid region between the Cascade and Rocky Mountains. At that time Cayuse territory comprised the lands between the Blue Mountains to the east and the Deschutes River to the west, encompassing parts of present-day northeastern Oregon and southeastern Washington.[58] Though the Cayuse people had made their homes in the Columbia Plateau since time immemorial, Cayuse society had changed markedly in the century before Whitman's arrival. Records by early explorers and traders indicate that in the eighteenth century the Cayuse people had expanded their territorial and economic reach, enabled by their quick adoption and superior utilization of horses. The semiarid river valleys along the Columbia River offered little in the way of farmland but abundant grazing territory.[59] Whitman's colleague Asa Bowen Smith wrote in 1838 that some Cayuses were rumored to have "a thousand horses apiece."[60] Moreover, their proximity to the Grande Ronde River Valley, a major trading artery between the Rocky Mountains and Fort Vancouver, placed them at the center of Columbia River trading networks. Together, these advantages allowed the Cayuse people to occupy a privileged place in the region.[61]

The Nimiipuu homelands were just northeast of Cayuse country, between the Blue and Bitterroot Mountains, in present-day eastern Washington and western Idaho.[62] The two tribes interacted closely and frequently intermarried, and in fact by the 1830s most Cayuses spoke a dialect of Nimiipuutímt called Weyíiletpuu rather than their ancestral language of Cayuse.[63] Like the Cayuses, the Nimiipuu had adapted to the changes brought by white contact by becoming excellent horse herders. Also like the Cayuse, the Nimiipuu homelands were well situated along trading routes that placed them in direct and indirect contact with whites as well as native tribes from across North America.

The two tribes had other similarities as well. Their locations between mountain ranges meant they were relatively protected from their neighbors, the Blackfeet, Bannocks, and Shoshones, but were also close enough to the Great Plains to participate in buffalo hunting and interact with Plains tribes. Both tribes engaged in seasonal cycles of travel to accommodate their region's limited resources.[64] And along with other peoples of the Columbia Plateau the tribes had common religious traditions: a strong interest in prophecy; the belief that all beings possessed spiritual power that could be beneficial, malicious, or neutral in nature; and practices meant to harness, increase, and manage that power.[65] Both the Cayuses and Nimiipuu had become acquainted with the Hudson's Bay Company and, through the company's proselytizing efforts, had sent prominent young men of the tribe to the Anglican Red River Missionary School in present-day Manitoba to learn more about white religion.[66] The Nimiipuu and Cayuses were not as materially destitute, as ignorant of white religion, nor as isolated from white civilization as the missionaries had been led to expect. Each tribe was adept at negotiating their interests with whites—as their success at persuading the missionaries to settle with them attested.

After surveying the region Whitman decided that he and Narcissa would settle among the Cayuse people at Waiilatpu, also known as Place of Rye Grass, near Fort Walla Walla. The Spaldings settled among the Nimiipuu at Lapwai, 110 miles away, near present-day Lewiston, Idaho. Gray alternated between the two mission stations to assist in construction, farming, and other manual labor.[67] The decision was ostensibly made to accommodate both tribes' insistence on having missionaries. But it also hinted at personal differences emerging between the Whitmans and Spaldings that would create problems in the future. Henry Spalding had attended school with Narcissa Whitman in the 1820s. During that time he had proposed to her, and she had rejected him. When Spalding was first asked to go to Oregon with the Whitmans, he had declared, "I will not go into the same mission with Narcissa for I question her judgment."[68] Spalding eventually relented, but he and Marcus Whitman bickered throughout the entire journey west, and rifts between the two families continued to simmer for the duration of their respective missions.[69]

The Whitmans' decision to settle among the Cayuses was a fateful one. When the Nimiipuu heard that the Whitmans would not be settling with them, they warned Whitman that the Nimiipuu "do not have difficulties with the white man as the Cayous do and that [you] will see the difference."[70] The Cayuses had become used to exercising their sovereignty within their homelands, and while they welcomed missionaries and traders they expected to do so on their own terms. They did not anticipate that asking the Whitmans to settle among them would invite the spread of American cultural and, eventually, demographic and political power.

In the meantime, however, the arrangement seemed advantageous to everyone. By November 1836 the men had built crude but habitable shelters, and Narcissa and Eliza journeyed up the Columbia River by boat to their new homes.[71] There, they planned to commence their missionary work of learning Nimiipuutímt, the language spoken by the Nimiipuu and Cayuse people; teaching the Cayuse and Nimiipuu to speak, read, and write in English; holding prayer meetings and Sunday services; and teaching and modeling American-style agriculture, housekeeping, and domestic pursuits. The missionaries understood Christianity as a set not only of beliefs but also of practices that aligned with their

Protestant, New England ways of life. Conversion to Christianity was thus synonymous with the adoption of Anglo-American cultural habits, including adherence to Anglo-American domestic patterns, literacy, private landownership, and, especially, settled agriculture.[72] "Although we bring the gospel as the first object, we cannot gain an assurance unless [the Indians] are attracted and trained by the plow and the hoe," Whitman explained.[73] The missionaries hoped to model these patterns of Protestant life in ways that would be sufficiently alluring to Native peoples to draw them to Christianity, "by exhibiting to them," in Whitman's words, "the beauties of that religion, 'by a well ordered life, and godly conversation.'"[74]

The Whitmans, the Spaldings, and Gray soon found that nearly every aspect of their mission work was going to be more difficult than they had expected. The basic work of survival took up much of their time: building shelter, securing supplies, growing crops, and raising livestock. Cayuse and Nimiipuu seasonal migration patterns meant that there was a constantly shifting population of Native people around the missions, and occasionally there were no Native people in the area at all. Henry Spalding wrote, "Today [we] may have a congregation of a thousand, who for the next two or three weeks or months may be upon the constant move through the plains & over the mountains in search of food."[75] Even when Native people were living near the missions the work of evangelization was slow and frustrating. The Nimiipuu language contained elaborate compound words, which confounded the missionaries. The language was not suited to communicating the complicated, sometimes labyrinthine doctrines of nineteenth-century Calvinism. The missionaries struggled to find Nimiipuutímt analogues for concepts like sin, atonement, and predestination. "As to any word which means to forgive I find nothing as yet. I doubt whether the people have the idea, any farther than thou *forget*," one of the missionaries lamented in 1840.[76] Neither Marcus nor Narcissa ever learned enough Nimiipuutímt to become fluent. In the meantime they taught the Cayuses and the Nimiipuu hymns in English, which they sang willingly without understanding the words.[77]

Neither did the Whitmans convince the Cayuse people to give up their seasonal migrations in favor of settled farming and individual landownership. Whitman and Spalding spent their first four years in the Oregon Country trying to secure enough plows, hoes, and cattle to provide the Cayuses and Nimiipuu with western-style agricultural tools.[78] Members of both tribes eagerly accepted what farming implements the missionaries supplied, but rather than abandoning hunting they used agriculture to supplement their existing patterns of subsistence. The introduction of agriculture created confusion and discord among members of the Cayuse nation, as those who planted crops often found that their neighbors helped themselves at will to the fruit of the fields.[79]

Moreover, when Whitman and Spalding distributed farming tools to the two tribes, they found themselves embedded in systems of gifting and trade that they did not understand. The Nimiipuu and Cayuse peoples viewed gift giving as an expression of mutual reciprocity, one that demonstrated the giver's generosity and largesse and one that established a pattern of free giving and trading in the future. They believed they had initiated this gift-giving relationship when they allowed the Whitmans and Spaldings to settle on their homelands.[80] The missionaries, however, viewed Native people's acceptance of farming tools as a sign of their willingness to abandon traditional lifeways and to accept the missionaries' form of Protestant Christianity, with all of its entailing commitments to Anglo-American patterns of life and work.[81] They were perplexed, then, when the gifts of farming tools led to more and more requests for goods. As the Methodist missionary Henry Perkins complained, "If we give the natives seed to plant, lend them axes, & hoes, to work with, they somehow think us under some obligation to feed them."[82] When the missionaries denied these requests, believing that granting them would compromise the industriousness and self-sufficiency they were attempting to inculcate, the Cayuses and their neighbors were perplexed and insulted by the missionaries' refusal to share food reaped from Cayuse land.

Conflicting understandings of material obligation also shaped interactions inside missionaries' homes. Narcissa Whitman placed great emphasis on maintaining a genteel household, and by 1842 her home boasted a cookstove, glass windows, and English china.[83] Such wealth seemed excessive to both white observers, such as the Indian agent Joel Palmer, and the Whitmans' Cayuse hosts, who felt that the Whitmans were "rich and getting richer by the house [they] dwell in and the clothes [they] wear."[84] Though the express purpose of the Whitmans' home was to serve as a model house-hold for demonstrating Christian domesticity, Narcissa attempted to rele-gate her Native visitors to a single "Indian room" inside the larger house, believing they were too "filthy" to be allowed in the rest of her home.[85] Rath-er than being inspired by Narcissa's vision of domesticity, the Cayuse people were baffled by the Whitmans' lack of hospitality, especially since the Whit-mans were guests on Cayuse land.[86]

As the Whitmans, Spaldings, and Gray began to realize the extent of the difficulties in their missionary project they quarreled among themselves. Personal difficulties had arisen among the party long before the founding of the missions. William Gray felt insulted by the board's refusal to appoint him as a full-fledged missionary and chafed under Whitman's and Spalding's demands that he carry out manual labor. He came and went as he pleased and devoted much of his energy toward trying, unsuccessfully, to establish his own mission away from the oth-ers.[87] Henry Spalding, meanwhile, was a difficult personality even under pleasant circumstances: as Gray described him, he was "quite impulsive, and bitter in his denunciations of a real, or supposed enemy."[88] But his history with Narcissa made the relationship between the mission fami-lies intolerable. In 1840 Narcissa lamented that Spalding "never ought to have come. My dear Husband has suffered more from him in conse-quence of his wicked jealousy & his great pique toward me, than can be known in this world."[89]

In 1837 the personal conflicts had been further inflamed when Gray left for the United States, apparently without notifying Marcus Whitman, to procure additional helpers for the mission and make a profit selling Nimiipuu horses. Through dramatic exaggeration of the mission's pros-pects he convinced the American board to appoint additional missionar-ies to the Oregon Country: Cushing and Myra Eells, Elkanah and Mary Walker, Asa and Sarah Smith, Cornelius Rogers, and Gray's new wife, Mary Augusta Dix. Whitman and Spalding had hoped for a massive influx of missionaries and industrious laypeople to extend the reach of evange-lism and agriculture widely over the region.[90] Instead, they received only eight souls, who arrived at the Whitmans' home without adequate sup-plies and too late in the season to build their own shelters. The Whitmans and the newcomers were forced to winter together in the Whitmans' cramped three-room quarters, where differences in personality and piety festered, leading to long-standing grudges.[91]

The new missionaries were Congregationalists, not Presbyterians like the Whitmans and Spaldings, and though the two denominations cooperated in missions and other evangelistic pursuits, they differed in their daily habits and sensibilities. The newcomers smoked pipes and drank wine; the Whitmans and Spaldings were teetotalers. The newcomers frowned on women speaking in prayer meetings, while Narcissa and Eliza were accustomed to praying aloud in public. Each side viewed the other as hopelessly impious.[92] The new missionaries found Marcus Whitman to be stubborn, Spalding duplicitous and emotionally unstable, Gray hotheaded and imprudent, and Narcissa moody and judgmental. Meanwhile, the original party lamented their guests' inconsiderate behavior, above all that of Asa Bowen Smith, who was resolutely despairing and critical, "in a fret all the time."[93] "We have a strange company of missionaries," noted Mary Walker in her diary. "Scarcely one who is not intolerable on some account."[94] When the new missionaries left in 1839 to establish new stations among the Spokanes at Tshimakain and the Nimiipuu at Kamiah, the grudges remained. In 1840 Asa Smith lamented, "I suppose this mission is not alone in having difficulty, yet I hope there is no other as bad as this. What will be the result of this mission I know not. Every thing looks dark to me. Nothing but the arm of God can save this mission from being a failure."

As the missionaries struggled to adapt to their new situation, additional newcomers arrived in the Oregon Country. The Catholics Francis Norbert Blanchet and Modeste Demers came at the behest of the Hudson's Bay Company, as many of the company's traders were Catholic. Beginning in 1838 Catholic priests began visiting Nez Perce and Cayuse country at the behest of the company. In 1847 four Catholic priests established a mission only a few miles from that of the Whitmans, shortly before the Whitmans were killed. The priests aggressively tried to woo Cayuses and Nimiipuu away from the Protestants, distributing crucifixes and offering free food and good trading terms, which made the Protestants' refusal to engage in gift giving look even more parsimonious.[95]

The Catholics required a less intensive reformation of material practices than the Protestants did. Celibate Catholic priests had no families to support or large-scale agricultural operations to maintain, so they were able to travel with seminomadic Columbia Plateau peoples on their seasonal rounds. For this reason they did not need Native people to be settled in order to have a consistent mission field, as the Protestants did.[96] Moreover, they identified conversion differently. To the Catholic missionaries Christianity entailed participation in the sacraments—an adoption of a new, albeit somewhat familiar set of religious practices— yet it did not necessarily entail changes in patterns of work, recreation, dress, farming, and property ownership. Protestants required more. Though they insisted that the experience of an inner, spiritual conversion was what made someone a Christian, they also believed that such an inner change would be marked by a new set of habits centered on a new set of objects. Western-style clothing, spinning wheels, plows, and cattle all served as proofs of conversion.[97] In the absence of these objects, the Anglo-Protestant piety that the missionaries sought to inculcate in the Native peoples of the Oregon Country would be impossible.

The religious conflict undermined the authority of both groups, as each depicted the other as idolatrous and illegitimate. The viciousness of the competition can be seen in the visual aids that the priests and Protestant missionaries created for use in their ministries. Ladders, as they were called, depicted the history of Christianity pictorially, with images signifying key events in salvation history placed in a kind of timeline. Branching off from the central timeline were heretics and other enemies of Christianity. The first ladder, created by the Catholic missionary Francis Norbert Blanchet, depicted Protestantism as a deviant, withered branch of Christianity. Subsequent Catholic ladders apparently depicted the errors of Protestantism in increasingly graphic terms, portraying Martin Luther and other prominent Protestants falling into the flames of Hell.[98] In retaliation, the Spaldings created a six-foot-by-two-foot ladder of their own, depicting Protestantism as the true branch of Christianity and the pope as the one falling into hellfire.[99] Such rancor rendered white religion increasingly divisive among the Nimiipuu and Cayuses. As the famed Nimiipuu chief Joseph (Heinmot Tooyalakekt), who would lead the Nimiipuu on their unsuccessful flight from the US military in 1877, later observed, it seemed that Christian churches could only teach Native people "to quarrel about God, as the Protestants and Catholics do. . . . [W]e do not want to learn that."[100]

There was one connection between the Whitmans and the Cayuses that the Catholics could not approximate, however: the Whitman's daughter, Alice Clarissa, born at Waiilatpu on March 14, 1837. A bright, friendly child, Alice learned to speak Nimiipuutímt when she was only a toddler. The Cayuses, delighted by the white child born on their land and speaking their language, nicknamed Alice Clarissa "Cayuse-Te-mi," or "Cayuse girl."[101] The elderly chief Umtippe, or Cut Lip, told Narcissa that "he [did] not expect to live long & he [had] given all his land to her."[102] As scholars have noted, the Cayuses' claiming of Alice Clarissa as their own may have been as much a subtle reminder of their sovereignty—Alice was a Cayuse girl, after all, because she was born on Cayuse land—as it was a statement of attachment to the child.[103] In any case, this tie between the two peoples was severed on June 23, 1839, the day two-year-old Alice Clarissa wandered off to get water and drowned in the Walla Walla River.[104] Narcissa never bore another child. From the time of Alice's death to the destruction of the mission, the Whitmans recreated their family by taking in abandoned Native, white, and métis children, but there would never be another Cayuse-Te-mi. This as well, to the missionaries, was a sign of God's providence—but a painful, mysterious, and uncertain sign, a harbinger, perhaps, of greater trials to come.

For the next several years the Whitmans, Spaldings, and their associates continued to struggle with interpersonal differences, competition with the Catholics, and the increasingly discouraging nature of their evangelistic efforts. Several of the missionaries wrote to the ABCFM expressing their frustrations with the missions' progress and with each other.[105] William Gray criticized Whitman's and Spalding's focus on convincing Native people to farm. "If they are engaged in teaching the Indians the values of their souls, I am confident they would not think so much about ploughs and mill irons," Gray wrote to the American board.[106] Smith wrote seven letters to the board complaining about the difficulties, suggesting that "the Mission [at Lapwai] better be given up to the Methodists & *Mr. Spalding advised to return home*" and that "it would be better that [Gray] *should return home* rather than go to another field."[107] The group had managed to resolve most of their differences by 1842: the Smiths agreed to be transferred to the ABCFM mission in Hawaii, while the Grays abandoned missionary work to take up farming in the Willamette Valley, about 280 miles southwest of the missions. But the damage was done. In September 1842 Marcus Whitman received an order from the American board stating that in light of the missions' setbacks the board had decided to recall Smith and Spalding, close the Whitmans' mission among the Cayuses and the Spaldings' mission among the Nimiipuu, and consolidate the other missions.[108]

The missionaries hastily called a meeting and determined that to save the Cayuse and Nimiipuu missions Marcus Whitman would travel cross-country to the ABCFM headquarters in Boston to speak with board members in person. Whitman left on October 3, 1842—the most inhospitable time for overland travel, as it required him to cross the continent in winter. Since he was leaving on such short notice there was no fur caravan to accompany him and provide safety and supplies. His only companion was the emigrant Asa Lawrence Lovejoy, newly arrived in the Oregon Country, and the occasional white and Native guides who accompanied him for segments of the trip. Because of rumors of war between the Lakota and Pawnees along the usual cross-country route, the men had to travel along a less direct southern route that took them through Taos, New Mexico; Bent's Fort, in present-day Colorado; and then to St. Louis. The journey took six months. Whitman and Lovejoy got lost at least twice on the unfamiliar route, and snowstorms and subzero temperatures often stopped them in their tracks. Lost in a snowstorm at one point, the men were forced to kill their pack mules and then Whitman's dog for food. Finally, after a grueling, nearly lethal journey Whitman arrived in the eastern United States. He was half starved, filthy, and clothed in trappers' garb and almost certainly had no idea that his cross-country trip would become a cornerstone of the history of the American West.[109]

Yet Whitman did have grand notions of what the journey would accomplish. Upon arriving in the eastern United States, Whitman went first not to Boston, where the ABCFM was located, but to Washington, DC. There, he met with James Porter, secretary of war, and possibly also with President John Tyler in the hopes of convincing them to sponsor a bill to provide additional protections to settlers traveling to Oregon.[110] Only then did he travel to Boston, where he convinced the disgruntled board to rescind its order closing the missions and made another plea for reinforcements.[111] Finally, after visiting friends and relatives in New York, he joined the wagon train of one thousand emigrants heading to Oregon Territory in the spring of 1843. Traveling with the wagon train, which he aided as physician, he made his way back to Oregon. His goal, throughout each of these journeys, was nothing less than to support a massive influx of Protestant settlers to claim Oregon for Christ.

Whether Marcus Whitman traveled west to save the missions or to save Oregon, as would later be claimed, is one of the most frequently trod debates in both academic historiography and popular memory. But this debate sets up a false dichotomy. The missionaries' understanding of Christianity was inseparable from American Protestant assumptions and mores, and their understanding of American identity was inseparable from Protestantism. In their view, to be American was to be Protestant. Other religions were foreign by definition. This reasoning can be seen in the stark distinctions Whitman drew in his plea to Secretary Greene: "I feel that this country must either be American or else foreign & mostly Catholick papal."[112] If work was progressing slowly with the Indians, which it was, and if Catholics were pressing in, as they were, then Protestants would have to be procured from elsewhere. As Whitman further explained, "I think our greatest hope for having Oregon at least part Protestant now lies in encouraging a proper attention of good men to go while the country is open."[113] The possibility of civilizing the Indians might be bleak, but the missionaries could still Christianize the Oregon Country by encouraging the emigration of American Protestants. The spiritual future of Oregon depended on it.

Whitman's New Purpose and the Collapse of the Oregon Missions

In March 1843 a triumphant Whitman returned to Waiilatpu with one thousand American emigrants in tow on their way to the fertile Willamette Valley. And with that dramatic arrival Whitman's own accounting of his mission shifted. Whereas his prior goal had been to make the Indians into Americans, he now sought to make Indian *lands* American. His letters reflecting on his 1842–43 journey renarrated the trip's purpose accordingly. "As I hold the Settlement of this Country by Americans rather than by an English Colony most important," he wrote to Narcissa's father in 1844, "I am happy to have been the means of landing so large an Imigration [*sic*] onto the Shores of the Columbia with their Waggons [*sic*] Families & Stock, all in Safety."[114] The mission's great purpose, from 1843 onward, was "to aid the white settlement of this Country & help to found its religious institutions."[115] Such settlement was bound to drive out both Native people and the missions that had come to serve them, but Whitman was not troubled about this. "When a people refuse or neglect to fulfill the designs of Providence," he reasoned, "they ought not to complain at the results & so it is equally useless for Christians to be anxious on their account. The Indians have in no case obeyed the command to multiply and replenish the Earth & they cannot stand in the way of others in doing so."[116] The mission that had been founded to answer the call of the four Native chiefs would now leave a legacy of Native displacement. This too, for Whitman, was God's providence.

The Cayuses, who at that time numbered no more than three hundred or four hundred people, must have observed the 1843 migration with trepidation. The Whitman Mission, located as it was between the Blue Mountains and the Columbia River, had served as a vital stopping point for emigrants since 1840. But this new emigration dwarfed all those that came before.[117] The historian Elliot West describes the Cayuses' experience as akin to "twenty-eight thousand western Indians passing through [Boston] toward settling on Cape Cod, announcing that even more were sure to follow."[118] In 1844 fifteen hundred settlers arrived; 1845 brought twenty-five hundred more. Some in the Cayuse tribe began to suspect that the Whitmans intended to displace them with the white newcomers. "They fear the Americans are going to overrun the country," observed Whitman.[119]

As more and more settlers poured into the country tensions with the Cayuses and Nimiipuu increased. Since the early years of the mission Cayuses' resentment over the Whitmans' use of their land had simmered and occasionally boiled over. In 1841 the Cayuse leader Tiloukaikt had demanded payment for the Whitmans' occupation of Cayuse land. Whitman, believing that the Cayuses had given their land freely, refused to pay. In retaliation, Tiloukaikt had insulted him, slapped him, and pulled his ears and beard.[120] Meanwhile, at Lapwai several Nimiipuu individuals had thrown Spalding into a fire when he tried to stop them from burning his cedar fence, a symbol of the Spaldings' claiming of Nimiipuu land.[121] By 1844 Cayuse demands for payment had become a regular occurrence. The Cayuses had indeed invited the Whitmans to settle with them, but they had done so with certain expectations of what the mission would entail: spiritual and technological knowledge that would make their lives better, reciprocal friendship, and a rival trading influence to help them in their dealings with the Hudson's Bay Company. When these anticipated benefits did not materialize, the Cayuses felt cheated, murmuring that the missionaries "do not give goods for nothing and give large prices for all we get of them and break their land for nothing."[122]

White settler violence further inflamed Cayuse resentment. In 1845, a contingent of Cayuse, Walla Walla, and Spokane Indians traveled to Sutter's Fort, near Sacramento, to trade horses for cattle. At the fort, a white American settler named Grove Cook accused Elijah Hedding (Toayahnu), a student at the Methodist mission and the son of the Walla Walla chief PeoPeoMoxMox, of stealing a mule. A few days later, Cook caught Hedding unarmed and shot him in cold blood. The missionaries had nothing to do with the death—indeed, they lamented the loss of one who they thought would have made a promising convert—but the Cayuse people still felt that the death signaled Americans' untrustworthiness, especially since Cook faced no consequences for the murder. Tauitau, also known as Young Chief, had been a firm supporter of the Whitman Mission in its early years. Now, however, he pointed out that "Elijah was sent by them to be educated and was regarded by them as a proper person to introduce them to the whites but that he was killed by Americans."[123] The fact that Hedding had been killed while attempting to bring cattle back to the Northwest must have suggested an ominous future for Native people who accepted the missionaries' call to make peace with the whites and adopt American-style agriculture.

Whitman's medical practice also created distrust among the Cayuses. In Cayuse culture a medicine man, or *tewat,* held great spiritual power that could be used to heal or to destroy. If a patient under the care of a tewat died, the family of the deceased had the right to kill the tewat in retribution.[124] Hudson's Bay Company traders, however, reinforced fears about white medicine by describing their own medical practices as sorcery and using the threat of white medicine to control Native people through fear. In 1812 an unscrupulous trader in Astoria had told some Chinook and Clatsop Indians that he had a vial of smallpox. He had but to "draw the cork" and the pestilence would "sweep man, woman, and child, from the face of the earth!"[125] Hence when Cayuses died from diseases they looked to Whitman as the cause. When Chief Waptashtak-mahl died in 1845, his son told Whitman, "I [Whitman] had killed his Father—and that it would not be a difficult matter for me to be killed."[126]

All of these factors led the Cayuses to become disenchanted with the missionaries' teachings. In 1846 the Nimiipuu chief Ellis shared with Whitman some of their complaints. According to Ellis, "Their main position was that religion was too sacred a thing for failable [sic] beings to practice and in as much as they could not so keep its holy requirements as not to come short and sin it was better to have nothing to do with it. Another position was that those who proffessed [sic] to follow the practices of religion came so far short that it led them to think it was better for them not to have any thing to do with it or with the Bible but to take their own judgment in the matter."[127] The Cayuses had grown tired of the Whitmans' unattainable demands for Native conversion and their failure to live up to their own missionary teachings. In 1847 the Whitmans assembled members of the Cayuse tribe and offered to leave Waiilatpu. "We live at all times in a most precarious state," Whitman wrote, "not knowing whether to stay or go nor at what time nor how soon.[128] The Cayuses assured them that they wanted them to stay. Their decision to remain proved fatal.

For several years prominent Cayuse leaders had suspected that the Americans were planning to kill them in order to take their lands. In 1845 Tauitau had accused the Americans of seeking to obtain the Indians' "country + property" using "pioson [poison] and infection."[129] These charges were given some basis by the fact that several years before, some Cayuses had been sickened by eating melons that Gray had laced with an emetic in order to prevent their being stolen; others had nearly died when they mistakenly ate meat that Whitman's employee had laced with arsenic in order to bait and kill wolves.[130] In addition, there was no question that the flood of newcomers contributed to the spread of novel diseases to the Pacific Northwest. Since the beginning of white contact the indigenous peoples of the Northwest had been ravaged by plagues of measles, cholera, and dysentery. The Whitman Mission, a way station on the Oregon Trail, housed many emigrants who required medical care or were too ill to continue their journey, further spreading disease in the region.[131]

Like other Christian missions in the North American West, the Whitman Mission inadvertently served as a disease vector, a place where people carrying Old World diseases mixed with nonimmune populations in close quarters. Missionaries rarely realized their culpability in spreading disease: germ theory was in its infancy in the nineteenth century, and white Christians were more likely to attribute the high rates of disease and death to God's providence as a sign that the Indians were a doomed race.[132] As Narcissa Whitman wrote less than a year before her death, "There have been many deaths among [the Indians] and quite a few of the influential chiefs have been killed or died from sickness. The providence of the Lord seems to be turning and overturning among them in various ways—and may he continue to do it for good until 'he shall come whose right it is to reign.'"[133]

Native people, on the other hand, drew clear associations between missionaries, American settlers, and devastating disease. The Cayuses were aware of the staggering losses among the Native peoples living near Jason Lee's Methodist mission in the 1830s, where successive waves of smallpox, malaria, and other illnesses had all but obliterated the Kalapuyas and Anglo-Americans had moved onto their former lands.[134] They would have been greatly alarmed by any disease outbreak at the Whitman Mission.

In the fall of 1847 growing resentment against the missions and American settlement reached a tipping point. The caravan that had traveled to California with Elijah Hedding in 1845 returned carrying measles, which ravaged the Cayuse, Nez Perce, and Spokane peoples as well as the missions and the Hudson's Bay Company forts.[135] The disease was particularly virulent among Native people. Those who were not killed by measles often succumbed to the dysentery, or "Bloody Flux," that followed.[136] Spalding wrote, "It was most distressing to go into a lodge of some ten fires and count twenty or twenty-five, some in the midst of measles, others in the last stages of dysentery, in the midst of every kind of filth, of itself sufficient to cause sickness, with no suitable means to alleviate their inconceivable sufferings, with, perhaps, one well person to look after the wants of two sick ones. They were dying every day, one, two, three, and sometimes five, in a day, with the dysentery; which very generally followed the measles. Everywhere the sick and the dying were pointed to Jesus, and the well were urged to prepare for death."[137]

At Waiilatpu Whitman cared for both white and Native victims of the outbreak, but nearly half of Whitman's Native patients died, while only one white child succumbed to the epidemic. Whitman's treatments likely increased mortality among his patients. While his exact course of treatment for the 1847 measles epidemic is not recorded, he regularly utilized bleeding, blistering, emetics, mercury-based drugs like calomel, and other purgative treatments that would have further weakened already frail bodies.[138]

Meanwhile, a métis trader named Joe Lewis began spreading rumors that Whitman and Spalding had brought on the epidemic by using poison. Lewis, like many bicultural traders, enjoyed a position of influence because of his ability to act as a culture broker between whites and natives.[139] Lewis had lived in the eastern United States and also had knowledge of Americans' dealings with Native people there. He had previously warned the Cayuses of the fate of Native tribes in the East. In light of Lewis's claims, several Cayuses decided to test Lewis's poison theory by having Whitman treat two of their men: one sick with measles, the other healthy. Both died within days. The answer was clear.[140]

In the midst of the epidemic Henry Spalding traveled to the Whitman Mission bringing concerning news. While visiting the lodge of PeoPeoMoxMox, the father of the young man who had been murdered by Americans in 1845, a Nimiipuu man entered and asked, "Is Dr. Whitman killed?" Spalding observed that the man seemed to be expecting an affirmative answer.[141] At the same time, four Catholic missionaries were on their way to establish a mission near that of the Whitmans, a move that was sure to increase sectarian tension. Whitman and Spalding sought the counsel of Istachus, a Cayuse leader who had long been an ally of the missions. Istachus warned the men that Whitman was in danger.[142] But dozens of emigrants were wintering at Whitman's station, making a quick evacuation impossible. The Whitmans thus remained at the station, hoping the threat would subside.

On the morning of November 29, 1847, Marcus Whitman attended the burial of three Cayuse children who had died of measles. According to survivors' testimony, Whitman noted, ominously, that there were far fewer people at the burial than expected. Later that afternoon a group of Cayuse men, including chief Tiloukaikt and Tomahas, came to the Whitman Mission. Cayuse and settler accounts differ as to the reason for the visit. Cayuse oral tradition states that the men sought to confront Whitman about his suspected malfeasance in the measles deaths, whereas the surviving mission residents stated that the visitors requested medicine.[143] The visitors may have believed that the medicine would prove the poisoning allegations to be true. In any case, an argument ensued. Tomahas tomahawked Whitman in the head, fatally wounding him, before rushing back outdoors. As Whitman lay dying other attackers moved through the outbuildings of the mission, killing the adult men and teenaged boys who were teaching school and performing manual labor. Narcissa and the other inhabitants of the mission house locked the doors and hid, but not before Narcissa was shot in the shoulder through a window. Finally, one of the men persuaded the wounded Narcissa to come out from the attic where she had sought refuge with other mission residents. The men carried Narcissa outside, where they shot her and then trampled her body in the mud before shooting two teenaged boys who were still hiding with their sisters in the attic. By the end of the day the attackers had killed nine people.[144] The Whitmans, however, were the victims of most of the attackers' wrath. A half century later, archaeologists investigating the site discovered that someone had split open Marcus's and Narcissa's skulls with Whitman's own surgical saw.[145] Such violence testifies not only to the degree of bad feeling between the Cayuses and the missionaries, but also perhaps to the fear that even in death Whitman's spiritual power might pose a danger to the tribe.

Except for Narcissa, the attackers killed only adult and teenaged males. They took the fifty-four surviving men, women, and children as prisoners, hoping they could use the captives to negotiate a peace and prevent white retaliation. The situation quickly deteriorated. The tribe was still reeling from its own horrific losses, and Tiloukaikt was unable to maintain order among his band. Ten days after the initial attack the captors killed two more sick teenagers, Crockett Bewley and Amos Sales. Three other children died of measles during the captivity.[146] Finally, after a month, Hudson's Bay Company factor Peter Skene Ogden was able to negotiate the captives' release. The survivors were taken down the Columbia River to settle in the Willamette Valley.[147]

For months after the attacks Nimiipuu and Cayuse country was marked by uneasy quiet punctuated by the threat of chaos. The Hudson's Bay Company forts waited in constant readiness for all-out war. American settlers lobbied for guaranteed government protection. Under the guise of bringing the perpetrators to justice, the Americans in Oregon organized a militia to exact revenge on the Cayuses. The ensuing Cayuse War raged until 1850, when five Cayuse men surrendered to stand trial and end the violence.[148]

One by one the missionary stations folded as first the Spaldings and then the Walkers and Eellses were escorted to the Willamette Valley under armed guard. There, they attempted to rebuild their lives and to make sense of the missions' failure. Henry Spalding spent the rest of his life trying to prove that his religious enemies, the Catholic priests, masterminded the violence at Waiilatpu. William Gray became involved in the earliest efforts at commemorating Oregon history and thus, having control over the narrative, refashioned himself as more than an unappreciated manual laborer. Cushing Eells would build a school in Whitman's memory, not for the Cayuse people but for the white Protestants who now occupied the Cayuse homeland. Each, in his own way, rewrote the history of the Oregon missions and of the Oregon Country. In doing so, they made Whitman into a patriotic hero, a martyr of flag and cross.

The tale of Whitman saving Oregon, then, has its roots in a much more ambivalent history than Whitman's later fame would suggest. In the face of his failure to evangelize the Cayuse people whom he had come to serve, Whitman turned his efforts away from the Cayuses and toward American emigration. The result was the destruction not only of Whitman's life but also of his mission, the missions of his companions, and the Cayuse people's sovereignty over their lands. But it was precisely the murkiness of this history that demanded its refashioning into something clearer, nobler, and more in keeping with Protestant understandings of missions as being guaranteed "sure results most durable and glorious." Henry Spalding would be the first to find ways to realign the history of Marcus Whitman and his mission with a providential understanding of Christian triumph and American destiny.

Providential History

Early in 1866 Henry Spalding stood before the assembled crowds at the First Congregational Church in Walla Walla, Washington, to deliver the fourth installment of his lecture series on the history of Protestant missions in Oregon. Nearly two decades earlier this region had been marked by the failure of Marcus Whitman's mission and a decade of white–Native violence. Now there was a city of a thousand white settlers, with more on the way. The Cayuse people had been removed to a reservation on the homelands of their neighbors, the Umatillas.[1]

Just as the Cayuse homeland had been transformed in the course of twenty years so had the history of the missions. As Spalding looked out on the residents of the rapidly growing settlement, he proclaimed the history of God's providence in allowing humble missionaries to be the means of securing Oregon Territory for the United States. Spalding proclaimed, "Our Gracious God, when the auspicious moment came to develop his plans, took His own way, chose His own instruments, to open this overland route and secure a basis for the settling of the country, to accomplish which so many lives, so much treasure and so much wisdom had failed. . . . He did not select John Jacob Astor, as the right hand of the American Government, but He chose four Indians from the Rocky mountains, two white women and one white man, without wealth to aid them or a military power to protect them."[2]

The "four Indians" were the Nimiipuu delegation of 1831 who had journeyed to St. Louis in search of Christian teaching. The "two white women" were Narcissa Whitman and Spalding's wife, Eliza. And the "one white man," was Marcus Whitman, who, "[reached] Washington in March, 1843, through terrible sufferings and hazards ... not an hour too soon to save this country from becoming a British province."[3] Marcus Whitman was no longer a failed missionary. He was now, through Spalding's efforts, a patriotic hero.

Two decades after Whitman's untimely death and the Oregon missions' abandonment, Spalding had reinvented the missions' legacy. He had created a regional history, one that recast the missions as a success for nationalism if not for evangelism, relegated Indians to the margins and Catholics to the role of villains, and made Protestantism central to the founding and future of the Oregon Country. He was joined in this effort by other local religious and political leaders concerned about the influx of irreligious and Catholic settlers in the region, the social tumult and moral decline caused by the California Gold Rush, and the coming of a statehood that looked little like the one that the former missionaries and their Protestant allies had envisaged. Each of these groups would take up the early history of Oregon settlement, transforming it into a providential allegory.

Spalding's historical crusade is indicative of a broader story in the conjoined histories of religion and nation—conjoined here by the very historiography Spalding helped fashion. In the turbulent decades of the 1850s, 1860s, and 1870s Protestants turned to history to narrate a religiously and ideologically unified Pacific Northwest in the midst of perplexing disunity and conflict. Specifically, they turned to a particular mode of historical practice: providential history, which I define as the use of oral and documentary evidence to interpret past events in order to determine the work of God or of another unseen force in history. Providential historians did many kinds of work that would be recognizable to professional historians today—amassing oral and written evidence, examining the work of other historians, and offering interpretations of the causes, effects, and meaningfulness of various events. But they differed from later professional historians in notable ways. Most significantly, they believed that God acted in human history and thus that even if events had an immediate, earthly cause they also had a more fundamental divine cause.[4] The divine purpose behind earthly events might not always be immediately evident, but if one could determine the purpose, one could determine the larger arc of history. As the ABCFM missionary and providential historian Hollis Read wrote, "History, when rightly written, is but a record of providence; and he who would read history rightly, must read it with his eye constantly fixed on the hand of God. Every change, every revolution in human affairs is, in the mind of God, a movement to the consummation of the great work of redemption."[5] To providential historians like Read, appealing to divine will was not only an acceptable methodological move but also a theological imperative. Understanding the direction in which God was moving in history would not only help the providential historian understand history, it would give her insight into God's larger plan of human redemption and prosperity.

This redemption, which for providential historians like Spalding entailed the global dissemination of Christian teaching and principles, would be accomplished through the divinely chosen American nation. Specifically, this redemption would be realized by divinely chosen American Protestants, including ministers, politicians, and especially missionaries. Because missionaries often served, knowingly or unknowingly, as the vanguard of American settlement or political influence in a region or both, they were vital to the coextension of American power and Protestant religion that providential historians believed fulfilled God's ultimate purpose. Thus, in the eyes of Spalding and his associates, even if Protestants were a minority in Oregon they were at the center of Oregon's founding and its future. The large numbers of Catholics and lapsed Protestants who moved into the region might outnumber faithful Protestants, but they did not ultimately change the narrative. Churchly historians could make Oregon a Protestant society in writing if not in fact.

My argument here draws from and expands upon other recent work on the influence of providence in American history, principally the historian Nicholas Guyatt's *Providence and the Invention of the United States, 1607–1865*. Guyatt explores changing ideas about American providence from the colonial period through the Civil War and argues that providentialism "played a leading role in the invention of an American national identity before 1865."[6] To Guyatt, providentialism entails several epistemological and theological commitments, which may or may not coexist: the belief that God intervenes in the history of nations, the belief that America is specially ordained to play a critical part in world history, and the belief that biblical prophecy can explain contemporary events. Guyatt traces the influence of providentialism in helping Americans develop a separate national identity from Great Britain, justify or contest structures of racial hierarchy, and preserve a sense of national unity in the face of the Civil War.

Yet providentialism in the nineteenth century was not manifested only in intellectual and political discourses about racial or national difference. As Spalding's work shows, providentialism also served as a narrative ritual, a method by which stories—sermons, histories, novels, personal testimonies—were given a familiar structure, teleology, and interpretive framework. Readers of these stories knew that no matter how dire the challenges the subjects faced, all suffering ultimately served God's greater plan of world redemption.

Missionaries played a central role in contributing to and further disseminating providentialist stories, both through their own storytelling and by serving as central subjects of providential narratives. As the historian William Hutchison has shown, nineteenth-century American missions were "rooted both in a Christian, a-nationalistic zeal for expansion and active evangelization, and equally in a fervent belief, less obviously Christian but just as religious, that Americans were under special obligation to save and renovate the world."[7] Not only was missionary work rooted in these dual convictions, but missionary writing like Spalding's also dramatized these convictions and, through vivid descriptions of harrowing trials, miraculous victories, and exotic locales, helped to make them accessible and attractive to the broader public. In an era when many Protestants considered secular novels to be idle or even sinful reading, Protestant missionary periodicals and biographies afforded readers a spiritually sanctioned source of exciting narratives. Julie Roy Jeffrey, a biographer of Narcissa Whitman, observes that for women like Narcissa, whose pious families did not allow them to read novels, "the newspaper must have provided a picture of a wonderfully exciting and exotic life that contrasted sharply with the daily female routines of [small-town New York]."[8] Missionary stories also offered a counter to Catholic hagiographies, regaling Protestant readers with heroes whose

daring deeds entertained as well as gave spiritual uplift. Electa Van-
Valkenburg, a pious Presbyterian from Spalding's old church in Prattsburgh, New York, wrote of hearing the story of the ABCFM Oregon
missions "in our missionary meetings & monthly concert meetings,"
and, much as Catholics did with icons of saints, VanValkenburg kept
framed pictures of Spalding and his family on display so she could "point
those to [them] that have heard the story."[9]

By reading missionary stories, Protestant laypeople could participate vicariously in them, praying for their missionary heroes and imagining themselves in the stories they read. Eastern Protestants who would
never have the chance to visit another country or cross the Rocky Mountains could read missionary tales as a way to experience such foreign
places. Thus missionary tales became one way of linking eastern readers
to the American West. As Rev. Huntington Lyman wrote to Spalding in
1871, "How I long to see the great Oregon and California!! Your description of your sublime ride over the great mountains, fills me with new
longing to ride there too."[10]

Spalding's crusade aimed to develop a providential history of the
Oregon missions and to have this history ratified by churches, political
leaders, and, ultimately, the United States Senate. The controversy over the
Oregon missions' legacy helped forge two conflicting strains of history
that continued to reverberate into the twentieth century: one, exemplified
by Spalding, was overtly Protestant in its sympathies and providential in
its methodology; a second, exemplified by Spalding's rivals Jean-Baptiste
Brouillet and John Ross Browne, claimed objectivity while adhering to a
tacit providential framework. These histories were not simply academic
exercises; rather, they were embedded in regional and national conflicts
about race, religion, and expansion, and they influenced government
policy on missions, Native peoples, and religious rivalry. To nineteenth-
century Americans history making was a state enterprise as much as it
was an academic or religious one. The federal government itself solicited
histories of events, including two histories of the Oregon missions, and
histories also served as a means by which emerging states like Oregon and
Washington could link themselves to a national story.

The legend of Marcus Whitman was bound up with Pacific Northwest history from its beginning. Since historians first disproved the Whit-

man Saved Oregon Story at the turn of the twentieth century, scholars have argued that the story did not emerge until the late 1850s, when the ABCFM missionaries used the tale to bolster their claims to their former mission property.[11] But the language of Whitman saving Oregon appeared quickly after his death, indicating that it was more a reflection of Spalding's historical project of redeeming the missions and placing Protestants at the center of Oregon history than an invention to win back property.

This story has many potential beginnings, settings, and characters. Other Protestants allied with Spalding or fought his interpretations. There were Catholics who struggled to counter Spalding's accusations in an era of deep anti-Catholic sentiment. There were Cayuse and other Native peoples who resisted the imposition of Protestant explanations of the Whitman Mission's destruction and preserved their own version of events through oral histories, even in the face of war, population loss, and forced removal. Each of these groups make appearances in the book, but here I foreground Henry Spalding for two reasons. First, Spalding was the most prominent early disseminator (and likely the inventor) of the legend that Marcus Whitman saved Oregon from becoming a British possession. Consequently Spalding was one of the most effective early contributors to making Marcus Whitman into a hero and enshrining the myth studied here. Second, Spalding's work, more than other early histories of the Oregon missions, exemplified the methodology of Protestant history writing that shaped church history into the early twentieth century. The legend Spalding helped create and the methodology surrounding that legend thus provided both the data and the historical model against which scientific historians would later rail and, through their criticisms, produce a new understanding of history. Moreover, it was Spalding's single-mindedness that resulted in the hegemony of one particular view of Whitman's legacy, the version of events that Catholics, Native peoples, and even rival Protestants would have to struggle for decades to amend.

Spalding, Providence, and the West

In many ways Henry Harmon Spalding made for an unlikely public historian—certainly, an unlikely public historian to achieve such a wide and lasting audience. As a missionary he was intensely devoted to his cause, but he was also stubborn, tactless, paranoid, and harsh in his judgments of others. When these traits inevitably led to conflicts with colleagues and supervisors, Spalding viewed the incidents as persecution. When the *Missionary Herald* published a letter in 1841 in which a fellow missionary mildly criticized the Oregon missions, Spalding complained, "Really it seems that wicked men & devils, church & state, good men & missionaries, have united their influence to destroy Indian missions & so make the assumed annihilation of the whole race the more certain."[12] As early as 1840 Spalding's colleagues Marcus Whitman and Asa Bowen Smith had worried that "the man will become deranged should any heavy calamity befall him."[13] The attack on the Whitman Mission occurred seven years later, a "heavy calamity" by any measure. Spalding viewed the killings—and virtually every subsequent hardship he or his loved ones suffered—as part of a Catholic conspiracy to drive out and discredit the Protestant missionaries of Oregon, a conspiracy reaching into the highest echelons of the US government. Some observers, then and now, considered him to be an inveterate liar, hopelessly deranged, or both.[14]

Spalding's success attests in part to his tireless perseverance. Throughout his career he wrote hundreds of letters to politicians, newspaper editors, church leaders, and influential community members, seeking a sympathetic hearing and a public forum. When one outlet rejected him, he immediately sought another. As the editors of the *Albany States Rights Democrat* expressed in a rather dubious compliment, "He may be insane, but it is the same kind of insanity with which Columbus, and Fulton, and Morse, and Field, were afflicted when trying to impress their earnest convictions upon the public."[15]

But more than that, Spalding's success attests to the power of a specific Protestant vision of history in the mid-nineteenth century. Spalding was educated by some of the leading Protestant figures of his day, he was well connected with regional and national Protestant networks, and he was a missionary and a minister, vocations that automatically conferred respect among other Protestants. Moreover, the ways in which he reenvisioned the history of Oregon missions turned a story of missionary failure—a narrative which, according to the conventions of missionary history, would be a terrible scandal—into a story of missionary, Protestant, and American triumph. Such a narrative aligned with

Fig. 3. *Henry Harmon Spalding,* photograph by
Matthew Brady, 1871. Henry Harmon Spalding and
Eliza Hart Spalding Papers, Presbyterian Historical
Society, Philadelphia, PA.

Protestant assumptions about themselves and their world: that American Protestants were the heroes of the divine drama of world redemption and that those who opposed American expansion and Protestant
supremacy were enemies of God, doomed to be cast aside in the
ongoing progress of world history. And it did so in a Western way,
bringing together the northeastern-based literatures of missionary hagi-
ography and anti-Catholic exposés with the conventions of Indian captivity tales and stories of pioneer bravery. In the hands of Spalding,
Whitman simultaneously became a sainted martyr, a cautionary tale of
Catholic evildoing, a testament to Indian savagery, and a buckskin-clad
hero traversing the snows of the Rockies.

Spalding's background and training enabled him to create such a hybrid history and motivated him to use the force of his personality to spread his history as widely as possible. Unlike the missionary physician Marcus Whitman, Spalding was a minister by trade and possessed a seminary education. It was an education begun late in life, with great difficulty, and steeped in the evangelical reform sensibilities of the early nineteenth century. Spalding was born out of wedlock to Howard Spalding and an unknown mother in Bath, New York. His mother gave him up to another family, the Broats, when he was only fourteen months old.[16] Spalding's home life was, as one historian describes it, hellish, and when Spalding was seventeen his abusive foster father cast him out of the house.[17] From that point forward Spalding was determined to support himself and get an education, although he was extremely shy and barely literate. He boarded with various ministers and schoolteachers, and in those evangelical circles he was introduced to the ardent revivals of the Second Great Awakening and to the burgeoning evangelical missionary movement. While working as a schoolteacher he came across the ABCFM tract *The Conversion of the World*, which argued that a concentrated missionary effort could convert all of the world's estimated six hundred million heathens in only twenty-one years. Spalding was attracted to this grand scheme, and despite his poverty and lack of formal education he resolved to become a missionary.[18] In this way Spalding was a representative type in the growing American nation. To Spalding the West would become a site of opportunity as he moved from New York to Ohio and eventually Oregon territory. Westward migration offered Spalding a chance to create a new narrative for himself in the absence of familial and eastern authority figures.

With the help of scholarships for indigent students, Spalding was able to attend Western Reserve College and Lane Seminary, where he undertook a curriculum that would have included the general sciences, classical languages, theology, and church history.[19] During this time Spalding met and married Eliza Hart, a pious farmer's daughter who had a strong desire to be a missionary. Eliza was already suffering from the lung disease that eventually claimed her life, but she was a devoted partner in all of Spalding's pursuits. While Spalding studied at Lane, Eliza not only took in boarders to help pay expenses but also attended as many classes at Lane as she could. Later, as a missionary with the Nimiipuu, Eliza demonstrated an aptitude for native languages and innovative missionizing techniques, such as the use of simple watercolor images to communicate biblical concepts to Native audiences. Spalding found her "a companion who has ever proved a most worthy and beloved wife."[20]

Both Western Reserve and Lane were at the center of several antebellum evangelical movements that would shape Spalding's attitudes both as a missionary and a historian. First, both institutions were manual labor schools at which students spent a certain amount of time doing agricultural or industrial work each day in order to develop good health and industrious work habits.[21] Manual labor became central to Spalding's understanding of his ministry with the Nimiipuu. To Spalding, missionary success meant not only persuading the Nimiipuu and other Native peoples to convert to Christianity but also teaching them "to work cloth, raise cattle, establish schools & mills, laws, & friendship to our Government."[22] Judged by these measures, Spalding believed, the Protestant missions to the Oregon Indians had ultimately succeeded whereas the Catholic missions had ultimately failed.

Second, both schools were at the forefront of the drive to Christianize the American West by sending evangelical ministers and godly laypeople to settle there. Lyman Beecher delivered his famous "Plea for the West" while a professor at Lane. Beecher proclaimed that "the religious and political destiny of our nation is to be decided in the West" and that the West's future "must affect powerfully the cause of free institutions and the liberty of the world."[23] Spalding would later ascribe the same significance to the West in his lectures, claiming that the settling of the West was ordained by God to "speed the chariot wheel of human salvation" to the world and that the West was a crucial battleground in the struggle between Protestantism and papism.[24]

Third, both schools were rent by antebellum controversies over abolition and academic freedom. In 1833 a professor's protest in favor of racial equality disrupted Spalding's graduation ceremony at Western Reserve College, and it was during Spalding's tenure at Lane Seminary that the school fractured over the issue of abolition, the bulk of the student body leaving for newly founded and staunchly abolitionist Oberlin. Spalding, who was a more conservative colonizationist, stayed at Lane, but he would have been surrounded by the heated debates.[25]

Thus during Spalding's time at Lane he was exposed to the model of education he would use in his Indian ministry, to the notion that the American West figured prominently in world salvation history, and to the expectation that bitter controversy was an inescapable part of academic and religious life. All of these influences shaped Spalding's understanding of his missionary work and of the broader meaning of the Whitman Mission's destruction.

Spalding was exemplary in his resolute devotion to the cause of missionary history, but not in his interest in interpreting the recent past. After the violence at the Whitman Mission it seemed that all Oregonians became lay historians. As the killings turned into a war and the war gave way to a public trial, the accused, the survivors, and those who observed from a distance all attempted to construct a narrative of the missions and determine the causes of the violence that had torn the Cayuse homeland apart. Most observers pointed to the immediate cause of the measles epidemic of 1847 and the circulating rumors that the Whitmans and Spaldings were poisoning the Cayuses in order to take their land.[26] But beyond that, observers disagreed about whom to blame. Some white settlers claimed that the fault lay entirely with the Cayuse people and that the killings were simply a senseless manifestation of Indian viciousness. George Curry, the editor of the *Oregon Spectator,* insisted that "there are no mitigating circumstances. [The Cayuses] knew the enormity of their conduct. Their unpardonable insult was achieved with the coolest determination and the most unmistakable intention."[27] Critics of the mission, including Catholics, Hudson's Bay Company traders, and the Cayuses themselves, asserted that the missionaries had sown the seeds of violent conflict for many years before it actually occurred by refusing to pay for the mission land, encouraging white settlement, and disrespecting Cayuse customs.[28] Finally, Protestants like Spalding insisted that the Cayuses could not have acted alone, that someone, whether Hudson's Bay Company agents or Catholics, must have incited the Cayuses to commit a crime they would never have engaged in otherwise.

In debating these various causes Oregon settlers developed two conflicting strands of regional history. One, developed by Catholics and other critics of the Protestant missions, blamed the Protestant missionaries for inciting the violence through their incompetence or their greed or both. This critical historical school originated as a way to vindicate the Catholic missionaries in the face of the accusations of the Protestants. Later, it was taken up by emerging professional historians eager to demonstrate their differentiation from churchly historians like Henry Harmon Spalding and his successors. The second thread, providential history, mapped the Whitman Mission's fate onto existing Protestant tropes of Indian capriciousness, Catholic conspiracy, and a virtuous, expanding Protestantism inextricably tied to American national destiny. It was this second narrative that Spalding came to champion, thereby creating an account that would buttress existing nativism and justify colonial expansion.

The *Oregon American* and the Legacy of Protestant Anti-Catholicism

Ironically, Spalding escaped the violence at the Whitman Mission only because a Catholic missionary saved his life. The French-Canadian priest Jean-Baptiste Brouillet had arrived in the Walla Walla Valley only two days before the bloodshed at Waiilatpu. On December 1, 1847, two days after the killings, Spalding was traveling to Waiilatpu to visit his daughter Eliza, a student at the Whitman Mission's school. He had no idea that several Cayuse men had just attacked the mission, killed his associates the Whitmans, and taken Eliza captive with the other surviving women and children. A few miles from Waiilatpu, Spalding met two Cayuse men traveling with Brouillet.[29] The Cayuse travelers, believing Spalding had been conspiring with Whitman to cause the measles epidemic raging among them, planned to kill Spalding, but Brouillet warned him to leave before they could do so. Spalding immediately turned back toward his home at Lapwai, not knowing whether his family there was dead or alive. After a grueling five-day journey Spalding arrived at Lapwai, barefoot, starved, and so changed in appearance that the Nimiipuu men who met him did not recognize him.[30] He was relieved to find that his family was alive, if not altogether safe. The Nimiipuu were deeply divided over whether to ally with the Americans or the Cayuses, and they worried that the American militia would use the Whitman killings as an excuse to attack and displace them as well as their Cayuse neighbors. For several weeks they did not allow the Spald-ings to leave, considering them "hostages of peace."[31] Finally, in January, the Nimiipuu agreed to escort the Spaldings safely to Fort Vancouver, where they were reunited with their daughter Eliza and the other freed captives of the Whitman Mission.[32]

While he and his family had been held at Lapwai, Spalding had written to Bishop Augustine-Magloire Blanchet of the Catholic mission at Waiilatpu and to William McBean of the Hudson's Bay Company, in-sisting that "it is our wish to have peace.... [W]e do not wish the Amer-icans to come from below to avenge the wrong." He also begged Blanchet for assistance, stating, "We cannot leave the country without help."[33] But as soon as he, his family, and the captives were safe at Fort Vancouver, it became clear that Spalding wanted war. As word of the killings spread through the more thickly settled Willamette Valley, American settlers formed a hastily organized militia of five hundred souls to apprehend the perpetrators.[34] Spalding pledged five hundred dollars of ABCFM money to the war effort, casting himself, as he explained to his mission-ary supervisor David Greene, "upon the Patriotism of those churches who contribute to the funds of our Board" and who no doubt would understand that their donations must be rerouted from Indian evange-lism to Indian killing.[35]

Thus when the Oregon Country's only newspaper, the *Oregon Spec-tator*, published the earlier letter in which Spalding had requested peace with the Indians and aid from the Catholic bishop and the Hudson's Bay Company, Spalding was incensed. He had written the letter under duress and had never planned on making it public.[36] But more than that, the vio-lence at Waiilatpu had further inflamed Spalding's preexisting hatred of Catholics. Like all the Protestant missionaries in Oregon—and like nine-teenth-century American Protestants more generally—Spalding believed that Catholicism was a heretical, perhaps even satanic organization that drew innocent people into despair and degradation and undermined American democracy through obedience to the pope, a foreign prince.[37] Throughout his missionary tenure Spalding had anxiously filled his letters with fears about Catholicism worldwide. When the government of the Sandwich Islands chose to offer freedom of religion to Catholics as well as Protestants, Spalding saw the news as "most horible [sic]" and blamed the decree on the arrival of a French Man of War.[38] When Catholic soldiers volunteered for the US military during the Mexican War, Spalding saw their enlistments as nothing more than a ruse, writing, "Every catholic of the U S who has taken the oath of allegiance has done so merely to blind the eyes of our Government."[39] To Spalding, as for many nineteenth-century American Protestants, American democracy and Catholicism were fundamentally incompatible. Adherence to or even toleration of Catholicism could be achieved only through force and would result in the certain downfall of the United States.

Given these predilections, it is not entirely surprising that Spalding's first reaction to the news of his letter's exposure was to suspect that a nefarious Catholic plot was afoot to discredit Protestant power in the Oregon Country and establish Catholicism as supreme. When Oregon's American Protestant residents read Spalding's letter, Spalding wrote, "[they] felt greatly mortified to see me in the dust, at the Bishop's feet begging my life."[40] As Spalding saw it, this embarrassing incident could serve only one purpose: the priests were gloating, reveling in the power they had insidiously obtained through scheming and bloodshed in the Oregon country. Spalding imagined what the priests were thinking. "Behold ye inhabitants of Oregon, especially ye adherents of the Catholic church, how speedy and complete is my victory," Spalding wrote in the voice of his imagined enemies. "Arrived but yesterday, today you see a missionary of the heretics, who has been 11 years in the country, at my feet, begging his life and the life of his countrymen, held as slaves by the Indians. He feels my power and acknowledges it in this letter."[41] This insult, real or imagined, would lead Spalding to become an unusually influential early interpreter of Oregon history, a quest that consumed the rest of his life. "If God spares my life to go on with the work," he declared, "the world will be confounded at the doings of Romanism."[42]

Ever since receiving word of the Whitman killings, Spalding, along with many of the other Protestant survivors of the violence, had felt that the rival Catholic priests must somehow be to blame for the violence.[43] The Protestants and Catholics had, after all, engaged in vicious rivalry for converts subsequent to Catholic missionaries' arrival in the Pacific Northwest in 1838. Given this history and Protestant suspicions of Catholic behavior generally, the priests' actions during the attacks and their aftermath came under intense scrutiny. Three issues above all raised Spalding's ire. First, Brouillet, the priest who later saved Spalding's life, had traveled to the Whitman Mission the day after the killings to baptize the Cayuse children there who were dying of measles. Spalding viewed these baptisms as a sign that the Catholic Church sanctioned the recent violence.[44] Second, one of the main figures implicated in the attacks, the métis trader Joe Lewis, was Catholic.[45] Most damning, however, was the accusation that the priests had failed to protect a young female teacher at the mission, Esther Lorinda Bewley, from being sexually assaulted. One week after the attacks Five Crows, the chief of a neighboring Cayuse band twenty-five miles south of the mission, took Bewley as his wife. Since Five Crows was a prominent leader, a longtime ally of the Whitmans, and had not been involved in the attacks, he evidently believed that this union would protect Bewley and ease tensions between the Cayuses and white settlers. Bewley, however, was still recovering from measles and had just witnessed the murder of her brother; she consented to the union only under duress. When Bewley attempted to seek refuge at St. Anne's Catholic mission the priests offered to host her during the day but said she must spend her nights with Five Crows.[46] The priests argued that all of these actions were designed to appease the Cayuse attackers and help save the lives of the captives, but their defenses fell on deaf ears.[47] To the Protestants such actions mapped perfectly onto established tropes of Catholic conspiracy, anti-American activity, and sexual depravity.

Other Oregonians may have viewed the Walla Walla priests with suspicion, but Henry Spalding transformed this generalized distaste into a specific historical crusade. First, he attempted to have his version of the attack on the Whitman Mission published by the *Spectator*. But the *Spectator*, avoiding sectarian conflict in order to maintain the widest possible audience in Oregon, refused to publish Spalding's inflammatory account.[48] This only deepened Spalding's conviction that a Catholic conspiracy was afoot. He redoubled his efforts and managed to get a series of letters published in a new paper, the explicitly Protestant *Oregon American and Evangelical Unionist*, started by Spalding's friend and future brother-in-law, the Oregon minister John Smith Griffin, and printed on the same press that Spalding had once used to print Nimiipuu

Bibles at his mission in Lapwai.[49] In the nine issues of the paper's run during 1848 and 1849 Spalding set out his first history of the missions in a series of letters to the editor, his friend Griffin. The letters were published as a public debate between Spalding and the Oregon Territorial Legislature member and Catholic convert Peter Hardeman Burnett, but it was clear what side the paper took in the debate: the editors introduced Burnett as "an American lawyer turned Papist."[50] Unlike the *Oregon Spectator*, which attempted to assume a journalistic neutrality in its reporting, the *Oregon American* served as an expressly sectarian outlet in Oregon Territory.

In the *Oregon American* Spalding set out the history that he continued to refine for the next twenty-five years. Like a prosecutor, he obtained notarized testimonies from witnesses to and survivors of the violence at Waiilatpu, as he "did not wish to use in such horrible matters, any thing that would not bear the strictest examination."[51] In Spalding's telling, the attack on the Whitman Mission (which he recounted in grisly detail) was caused not by missionary failures or cultural misunderstandings but rather by the scheming of villainous Catholic priests. According to Spalding, "The priests had told the Indians everywhere . . . that the Protestant missionaries were causing them to die; that they were poisoning them; that it was the Americans who had brought the measles among them; and that God had sent that sickness to them to show his hatred against the heretics."[52] This accusation was the crux of Spalding's claim against the Catholics and the narrative that would persist in Protestant circles into the twentieth century. Spalding interpreted Brouillet's assistance as a ploy to direct attention away from his and his fellow priests' involvement in the killings. More significantly, Spalding transformed Whitman into a martyr in the holy war to determine whether Catholics or Protestants would rule the Oregon Country. According to Spalding's second letter in the *Oregon American*, Whitman had expected this martyrdom and accepted it fully, allegedly stating to Spalding, "Now if the Indians do not allow us to leave, my days are few, but if I am to fall by Catholic influence, I believe my death will do as much good for Oregon as my life can."[53] Spalding cast the Whitmans as victims who were killed because Catholic missionaries resented their work to model, plant, and uphold American institutions and values through their missionary work. "Let all Americans," Spalding proclaimed, "whether they sympathise [sic] with religion or not, remember that these Missionaries were Americans,—were their own fellow citizens,—were with themselves engaged in sustaining free and virtuous institutions, the glory of all true Americans."[54]

Already, at this early point, the germ of the Whitman Saved Oregon Story was present in Spalding's letters: in his highlighting of Whitman's bravery in facing death, his invocation of the missionaries' Americanism, and his depiction of Catholics as necessarily un-American and opposed to US interests. An additional document from 1848 supports this conclusion. Just a few months after Spalding began publishing in the *Oregon American,* the Protestant *Boston Recorder* published an obituary of Whitman, reprinted from the *Chicago Herald.* In its penultimate paragraph the obituary included the first reference to Whitman saving Oregon, asserting, "In the winter of 1842, Dr. Whitman made his last visit to the United States, clothed in skins. He then performed, almost alone, the perilous journey across the plains, traversing their snows and swimming their icy streams, that he might communicate important intelligence to the American Board in regard to their stations, and prevail upon his countrymen to commence at once an emigration, in order to save Oregon from the grasp of Great Britain, as well as to preserve it from the power of the Jesuits, with whose schemes he had become acquainted."[55] While the obituary was uncredited, it is almost certain that the account of Whitman's ride was derived from Spalding. A true preacher, Spalding reused key phrases and evocative details in all his lectures and writings, language that matches the account in the *Boston Recorder* obituary.[56] Moreover, Spalding knew the *Herald*'s editors from his college days. Both the *Herald*'s principal editor, James Barr Walker, and its assistant editor, James Shaw, were students at Western Reserve College during Spalding's time there.[57] Spalding also corresponded with another classmate and friend of Walker's, Dudley Allen, who regularly published Spalding's letters in the (Hudson) *Ohio Observer,* a paper for which Walker had previously served as editor.[58] At this early date, less than a year after Whitman's death, Spalding was the only surviving companion of Whitman's who had both the knowledge of Whitman's affairs and the connections in the Midwest to influence such an article.

Spalding's narrative radically reimagined the history of the Oregon missions, but it did so along lines that would have been familiar to Spalding's American Protestant readers. Accounts of saintly missionary martyrs and evil Catholic priests were popular reading for Protestants in the mid-nineteenth century. Hagiographic missionary biographies like *The Life of David Brainerd* and the *Memoirs of Harriet Newell* circulated widely among Protestants and helped shape their expectations of the contours of missionary character and missionary work.[59] These accounts recast missionary lives through the lens of divine providence, assuming that no missionary's life or work was wasted and that each missionary had been divinely ordained for some good purpose, whether or not that purpose was readily obvious. Harriet Newell, for instance, had died at nineteen and spent less than a month in her intended missionary field of India, but a sermon attached to her memoir as an epilogue encouraged readers to see that her early death was not in vain because "her character has, by Divine Providence, been exhibited upon the most extensive theatre, and excited the attention and love of Christian nations."[60] Such writings taught Protestants, including missionaries like Henry Spalding, how to interpret experiences as successes when they might have been seen as failures.

Popular literature also taught Protestants how to view Catholics. Salacious alleged exposés of convents, most notoriously the *Awful Disclosures of Maria Monk of the Hotel Dieu Nunnery of Montreal,* presented sinister depictions of Catholic religious life, in which lustful priests and sadistic nuns drew in unsuspecting women, then subjected them to rape, physical abuse, and other horrors.[61] The *Awful Disclosures of Maria Monk* was circulating in Oregon Country as early as 1838, likely brought there by Protestant missionaries.[62] Other texts, many of them purportedly written by ex-priests, described Catholic plots to undermine American democracy and place the nation under the authority of the pope.[63] To antebellum American Protestants, Catholics' allegiance to a foreign prince made them inherently antidemocratic and un-American, their rejection of Protestant patterns of domesticity made them inherently deviant, and their preference for what Protestants considered undue secrecy—keeping nuns cloistered, conducting services in a foreign language—made them dangerous.[64] Thus Spalding's insistence that Catholic priests were responsible for killing Protestant Americans through manipulation and intrigue fit neatly with other accounts that Protestants, including Protestants in Oregon, would have heard and read. His history confirmed what Protestants assumed about themselves and the world around them, namely, that their work was truly meaningful, that they lived in a world in which all things were ordered by God, and that their enemies were as diabolical as they suspected. Such a history was primed to succeed among devout evangelical Protestants in a frontier setting rife with religious struggle.

The articles had the desired effect among the *Oregon American*'s readers, sparking letters of indignation at Catholics' abhorrent treatment of Oregon's Protestant missionaries. A representative letter from "O.B.," demanding to know whether the Catholics had a permit to live and work in Oregon, stated, "Perhaps that petticoat gentry (Priests) may reply that they have a permit from the ten horned beast, (Pope of Rome,) that [sic] despoiler of the virginity of every Republic on which he lays his withering hand."[65] Much to Spalding's and Griffin's dismay, however, Oregon was not made up solely of devout evangelical Protestants. The *Oregon American*'s readership was so small that the paper lasted for only nine issues, with long interruptions in printing schedule, until 1849.[66] Though most of the estimated ten thousand white emigrants who settled in Oregon between 1840 and 1850 were probably Protestants by background, only about one-tenth of them joined churches when they arrived in Oregon. Early church records for the Oregon Country are strikingly low: the First Congregational Church of Portland was established in 1851 with ten members; the First Congregational Church in Oregon City, then the most prominent settlement in Oregon, had three members; and all the Baptist churches in the region had a combined total of ninety-five members.[67] This low involvement in formal religious institutions set an enduring pattern in the Pacific Northwest that would earn it the modern-day nickname of "the None Zone."[68]

Yet institutional religious adherence was not the only part of the story of Oregonian religiosity. Protestantism was not only a matter of formal religious affiliation but also a set of sensibilities and practices that served as identity markers in the Pacific Northwest and in the United States generally. In Oregon Territory, with its rapidly growing settler population, active and ongoing resistance from Native communities, and only inchoate American political structures, such identity markers grew more important, not less. Those who did not care enough about the cause of Protestantism to subscribe to Griffin's paper still worried about the presence of nonwhite non-Protestants, religious and racial others presumed to be unwilling or unable to contribute to American democracy. The years after the *Oregon American*'s failure proved this to be the case.

The Trial of the Cayuse Five and De Facto Oregon Protestantism

As Spalding was writing his anti-Catholic history, the Oregon Country was changing. The attack on the Whitman Mission proved to be the impetus needed for the American government to make Oregon a US territory, which it did on August 14, 1848.[69] With the advent of formal territorial status, the balance of power in Oregon shifted. From 1818 to 1846 the US and Britain had formally held joint possession of the Oregon Country, and white settlement was concentrated around a few locations in and around the Willamette Valley. Native communities outside of the Willamette Valley were able to maintain a degree of autonomy by their physical distance from white settlements and by playing the two empires against each other.[70] But with the rush of American settlers in the 1840s and the coming of territorial status in 1848, the balance of power shifted decidedly toward the Americans. Increasingly, these Americans came in large wagon trains that had experienced or heard rumors of Indian violence, and they were disposed to view Native people with fear and hatred.[71]

The Cayuse attack on the Whitman Mission further inflamed settler hatred. Shortly after the Oregon provisional government learned of the attacks, Oregon settlers organized a militia of five hundred men, and federal troops followed. Governor Joseph Lane vowed that "the whole tribe will be held responsible, until those, whoever they may be, concerned in that melancholy and horrible affair, are given up for punishment."[72] In April 1850, after two years of intermittent fighting between the Oregon territorial militia and the Cayuses, the US ally Tauitau surrendered five Cayuse men—Tiloukaikt, Kiamasumpkin, Tomahas, Isaiachalakis, and Klokamas—to be brought to Oregon City for trial.[73]

Oregon settlers hoped the trial would bring the Whitman affair to a satisfactory resolution. Instead, it further highlighted divisions around race and religion in the developing Oregon Territory. Despite a veneer of judicial impartiality, the trial amounted to what later historians and Cayuse tribal members have considered a "public lynching."[74] The federal marshal Joe Meek, whose daughter, Helen, died of measles while she was a captive at the Whitman Mission, served as bailiff and, later, executioner. Judge O. C. Pratt rejected all of the defense's motions, including calls to move the trial to a less hostile county outside the Willamette Valley, to dismiss the case on the grounds that the attacks had taken place on Cayuse territory outside of US jurisdiction, and to accept evidence that the Cayuse killing of Whitman was in accordance with Cayuse law, or *tewatat,* governing the punishment of malicious medicine men.[75] These rulings made it clear that the trial could have only one outcome.

The town of five hundred people had no courthouse, so the trial took place in a tavern, with hundreds of onlookers crowding in to see the theatrics.[76] Four white American Protestant survivors of the attack on the Whitman Mission—Eliza Hall, Elizabeth Sager, Lorinda Bewley (now Lorinda Chapman), and Josiah Osborne—testified for the prosecution. Henry Spalding, perhaps motivated by his conviction that the Catholics bore ultimate responsibility for the killings, testified for the defense. Alongside him were two other defense witnesses: John McLoughlin, the former chief factor of the Hudson's Bay Company Fort Vancouver, a practicing Catholic, and the husband of a métis woman, and Istachus, commonly called Stickus, a Cayuse leader. This division of witnesses made visible the shifting power dynamics of Oregon Territory, with an all-white roster of American Protestant settlers facing down representatives of the two communities that had preceded them in the Oregon Country: Native people and mixed-race fur-trading families.

On May 24, 1850, the jury, composed of twelve white male settlers, including at least one who had known Whitman personally, condemned the defendants, now known as the Cayuse Five, to death. The Cayuse Five's defense lawyer tried to petition for a last-minute pardon, but Governor Lane had already resigned his post and left for the California Gold Rush.[77] The men were hanged on June 3, 1850, and buried without ceremony in an unmarked grave somewhere on the north side of Oregon

City. The location of the grave was subsequently lost to history, making it impossible for the Cayuses to retrieve and repatriate the remains.[78] Despite the finality of the verdict and the executions, the trial raised more questions than it answered and highlighted the fragility of state structures in Oregon Territory. The Cayuse Five had always insisted that they were innocent and that the real perpetrators had already died during the Cayuse War. Tiloukaikt, when asked why he had surrendered if he was innocent, had proclaimed, "Did not your missionaries teach us that Christ died to save his people? So die we to save our people."[79] Some observers suspected it was not justice but hatred of Indians that had been served in the trial. The *New York Tribune* observed, "Much doubt was felt as to the policy of hanging them, but the *popularity* of doing so was undeniable."[80] The status of Indians and Catholics as anti-American others was further underscored when the five Cayuses refused to meet with Spalding before their deaths and instead requested an audience with the Catholic Archbishop Francis Norbert Blanchet. With another priest, Auguste Veyret, Blanchet recorded the Cayuses' statements of innocence and baptized them before their execution.[81] Thus in a very public way the Catholic priests allied with the Cayuse Five at a time when hatred of Indians was at a peak in the Willamette Valley.

Yet this alliance was as tenuous as the Catholics' position in Oregon Territory. American Protestants in Oregon had been suspicious of their Catholic neighbors ever since the beginning of white settlement. Most Catholics in early Oregon were retired French-Canadian traders who had come to the Oregon Country with the Hudson's Bay Company. They spoke French, married Native women, and created mixed-race enclaves at places like French Prairie, in the Willamette Valley.[82] Such characteristics reinforced Anglo-American Protestants' notions of Catholics as separate, foreign, and suspicious.

The Whitman killings brought these anti-Catholic sentiments to the fore. After the attack on the Whitman Mission, Spalding had briefly convinced Colonel Gilliam, the leader of the Oregon militia, that the priests were responsible for the violence. Gilliam resolved that he would "shoot or hang the first one of [the priests] they should meet," but Bishop of Walla Walla Augustine Blanchet was able to intercept Gilliam and explain that no priests had been involved in the killings.[83] When the Cayuse Five went on trial in 1850 the *Oregon Spectator* and papers in the eastern United States erroneously reported that two Jesuit priests stood trial as well.[84] Later in 1850 the citizens of Linn County, Oregon, where Spalding lived, passed a resolution asking the Territorial Legislature to appoint a special committee to determine "the influence of Jesuits and hierarchical agents among the Indian tribes." If such influence was found to be insurrectionary the legislature should ban all Catholic priests from having any interaction with Native peoples in Oregon Territory. The resolution assumed the danger of "papal intrigue," accusing Jesuits and Hudson's Bay Company traders of "trying to bribe our Senators in Washington" and "subvert the dearest interests of our Territory."[85] In fact, none of the Catholic missionaries in Oregon belonged to the Jesuit order. Instead, the term "Jesuit" served as a stand-in for any Catholic activity believed to be conspiratorial, anti-American, or dangerous.[86]

As the volatile environment of nativism among Oregon's white Protestant settlers intensified in the wake of Spalding's accusations and the Cayuse Five trial, Spalding's rescuer Jean-Baptiste Brouillet determined that he had to speak out on behalf of Oregon's Catholics. Brouillet could address Oregon Protestants' suspicions in several ways. First, he could defend his own actions and the actions of the Hudson's Bay Company, with whom the Catholic missionaries were closely associated. Second, he could provide a critical account of the Protestant missionaries and of Protestantism in Oregon more generally, drawing on his personal knowledge to refute Spalding's claims, highlight the failings of the Protestant missionaries, and criticize the overly close relationship between Protestant religious and American national expansion. If these approaches failed, he could focus attention on an even less sympathetic group: the Cayuse and other Native peoples of Oregon Territory. Brouillet used all three strategies, and his defense presaged the historical arguments of later critics of Whitman.

As early as 1848 Brouillet had drafted a rejoinder to Spalding, but it was not until after publication of Spalding's history in the *Oregon American,* the trial of the Cayuse Five, and the near-passing of the several anti-Catholic bills in the Territorial Legislature that Brouillet made his history public. Unable to find a sympathetic newspaper outlet in Oregon Territory, Brouillet first published a series of articles in a Catholic newspaper, the *New York Freeman's Journal*, in 1853. Later that year he published the collected letters as a pamphlet. Its full title left no doubt about Brouillet's interpretation of events and his reasons for writing: *Protestantism in Oregon: Account of the Murder of Dr. Whitman and the Ungrateful Calumnies of H. H. Spalding, Protestant Missionary.* Brouillet assembled testimonies and written evidence with the same zeal as Spalding, but he put these accounts in service of a very different narrative. Brouillet's was not a providential history but a debunking history: it moved through each of Spalding's claims and presented written and oral evidence to the contrary, often using Spalding's own words against him. In this way Brouillet prefigured the professional historians who later refuted the Whitman Saved Oregon Story in the late nineteenth and early twentieth centuries.

Whereas Spalding insisted that his religious claims were inseparable from his historical interpretations, Brouillet's use of the term "providence" was far more sparing. More often Brouillet invoked the concept of objectivity, arguing that "every unprejudiced reader" who "considers the following facts" would agree with his interpretations.[87] Brouillet highlighted the many failings of the Protestant missionaries and of US Indian policy in general. He argued that "there existed, among the Indians, long before the arrival of the Bishop of Walla Walla and his clergy, strong causes of dissatisfaction against the Protestant missionaries and the Americans in general" and that the attack on the mission was a sign of animosity "that had been fermenting for years."[88] Using primary source evidence, including materials from Spalding's own *Oregon American* letters, Brouillet demonstrated the ways in which the closely intertwined aims of religious and national expansion had caused the Protestants to lose Native people's trust. He also asserted that the priests' actions before, during, and after the killings were perfectly reasonable and not malicious given the perilous circumstances. Finally, he emphasized that the responsibility for the killings lay entirely with "the evil-disposed Indians among the Cayuse nation," who, as "poor untutored savages," acted out of confusion and superstition.[89]

This was the basic outline of the narrative that professional historians would continue to develop. Like those histories, Brouillet's narrative presumed the ongoing progress of enlightenment, in which objective truth ruled over even deep-seated sectarian disputes. The preface to the second edition of *Protestantism in Oregon* evinced dismay that "at this remote day" there were those whose prejudices would not "yield before the penetrating rays of truth."[90] Brouillet's evidence was so clear, he insisted, that "every candid mind" would acknowledge the rightness of his argument.[91] This was a deft rhetorical move in that it implied that any Protestant reader who disagreed with his account was blinded by sectarian hatred, while Brouillet himself was not embroiled in the same sectarian conflicts. The assumptions that Brouillet's results were replicable if readers followed the same path of evidence, that objective reading was possible and desirable, and that readers who were unable to evaluate sources objectively had allowed religious prejudices to blind their common sense prefigured the convictions of professional scientific historians like Edward Gaylord Bourne, Thompson Coit Elliott, and Joseph Schafer.[92]

Yet Brouillet's history differed in key ways from later invocations of scholarly objectivity. First, Brouillet's narrative grew out of a different setting. He was not a professionally trained historian nor was he writing for an academic audience. Instead, he composed his history as a member of an embattled community and as an eyewitness to the events he described. He was, then, intimately involved in the history he interpreted, and he liberally included his own experiences, reactions, and opinions in his narrative. Second, Brouillet's history was explicit in its political purpose. He sought to defend the Catholic missionaries and Oregon's Catholic population in general from accusations that endangered their existence in the Oregon Country. In other words, though he felt that any disinterested observer would agree with his conclusions, he was not a disinterested observer himself. Brouillet's sense of objective history did not preclude histories written by eyewitnesses with a personal interest in how the events would be interpreted. Instead, his definition of objectivity lay in the standard of evidence he utilized and in his differentiation from less enlightened peoples: the "poor untutored savages" of the Cayuse nation and the "religious fanaticism" of Protestants like Spalding.

Thus Spalding's "History of Protestant Missions in Oregon" and Brouillet's *Protestantism in Oregon* exemplified competing narratives of early Oregon history, including competing debates about the relative positions of Protestant and Catholic settlers in Oregon. More importantly, they represented early versions of the narrative forms that would continue to shape Pacific Northwest historiography, nationalism, and sectarian loyalty for future generations of history writers. Both narrative forms were ultimately progress tales. But while Spalding's and Brouillet's histories differed in their visions of progress, they were remarkably alike in their definitions of progress's opposite: heathen superstition and religious fanaticism, both of which were doomed to be overshadowed by the light of truth.

Spalding Goes to Washington

Both Spalding's and Brouillet's histories and the ideological battles that generated them might have remained in the Pacific Northwest if not for a chance clerical misunderstanding and the US Congress's practice of commissioning histories to explain thorny political and military situations. But in the late 1850s these factors converged to make the fights over Whitman's legacy national in scope, drawing the federal government and churches across the United States into the fray.

The killings of the Whitmans had set off a cycle of violence that lasted well beyond the trial of the Cayuse Five. Even before the trial and execution of the five men the Cayuses and their neighbors worried that Americans would use the attacks as an excuse to seize Native lands with abandon. The actions of the US regional and national governments had already proven that this fear was accurate. In 1848 H. A. G. Lee, Oregon Territory's superintendent of Indian affairs, had declared that in light of the Whitman killings "the territory of said Cayuse Indians [is] forfeited by them, and justly subject to be occupied and held by American citizens."[93] In September 1850 the United States Congress passed the Donation Land Act, which granted 320 acres of land to any adult white male who settled in the Oregon Country before December 1, 1850, and 640 acres to any married couple if they resided on the land for four years. Settlers arriving after December 1, 1850, but before December 1, 1853, could claim up to 320 acres, still a generous amount of land.[94] At the same time, the territorial government and the US Congress began making plans to relegate all the remaining Indian tribes in the Pacific Northwest, including the Cayuses, to reservations.[95]

These policy decisions soon began affecting the Cayuses and other Indians of the Oregon Country. In 1851 the US government established an Indian Agency in Umatilla, near the Cayuse homeland, underscoring its intent to claim authority over the region.[96] In 1855 a US delegation held a meeting with leaders of the Cayuse, Walla Walla, and Umatilla nations. Through veiled threats and ominous tales of Native tribes who unsuccessfully resisted reservation life, US agents convinced tribal leaders to sign a treaty that ceded most of their homelands to the US and established a joint reservation on the remaining territory.[97] Members of the Cayuse and other Plateau tribes who had not supported the treaty banded together with the Yakama people and other allies in a desperate attempt to protect their lands against white encroachment. Oregon and Washington volunteer armies pursued the Cayuses and their allies, unencumbered by the structures of the regular army. In December 1855 the First Oregon Mounted Volunteers murdered and mutilated the body of the Walla Walla chief PeoPeoMoxMox, who was a prisoner in their custody.[98] The following year the Second Regiment of Washington Volunteers killed at least fifty Cayuses, including women and children, in what became known as the Grand Ronde Massacre.[99] Meanwhile, settlers in southern Oregon and northern California engaged in similarly brutal conflicts, what the historian Boyd Cothran has called "a conflagration of state-sponsored Indian killing."[100]

Although US forces ultimately prevailed in dominating and displacing Native peoples in Oregon and Washington Territories, the territorial and national governments found the violence troubling because of its potential to place a chill on western settlement.[101] In response the US House of Representatives sent J. Ross Browne, an agent of the departments of Treasury and Indian Affairs, to gather information about the violence.[102] Browne compiled a history of settler–Native conflict in the Pacific Northwest, complete with his interpretations of the reasons for the unrest and the unstoppable force of Anglo-American expansion.

Neither the House's request nor Browne's response was unusual. In fact, the United States legislature and members of the presidential cabinet frequently assumed the responsibility of requisitioning authorized histories of events, sometimes in order to aid in policy making or allocation of military or monetary resources and sometimes simply for the public record. In 1833 the House had authorized Secretary of State Andrew Livingston to commission a documentary history of the American Revolution, which was approved and published in 1836.[103] In 1840 the Senate published twenty-five hundred copies of Robert Greenhow's *Memoir, Historical and Political, on the Northwest Coast of America.*[104] In 1846 the Senate Committee on Indian Affairs unsuccessfully attempted to commission a report on "the true history of the relations between the United States and the several Indian tribes or nations, from the revolutionary war down to the extinguishment of the Indian title eastward of the Mississippi."[105] Browne's history would ideally help the House to address questions about settler safety and to determine whether further military action would be needed.

Browne embarked on a two-month tour of the Oregon Country, during which he conversed with "all the leading citizens" and "nearly every federal officer in the country."[106] The American settlers, unsurprisingly, denied that they had committed any wrongdoing, and Browne concurred. He concluded that, like all Indian wars, "the primary cause" was "the progress of civilization, to which the inferior races, from their habits and instincts, are naturally opposed." Browne's view was that the Whitman killings and the subsequent wars could not have been prevented. Rather, they were the inescapable product of the advancement of white, American civilization over Native peoples, an advancement that was both necessary and inevitable. "It was a war of destiny," he insisted.[107]

Browne's report might have gone unnoticed in the Oregon Country were it not for a miscommunication that made it appear as if he was siding with Oregon's Catholics. While he was in Oregon, Browne became acquainted with both Spalding's accusations and Brouillet's response. Browne, a nominal Protestant, was deeply unimpressed with the "bitterness of feeling existing between the different sects" and concluded that "as little dependence can be placed upon the statements of one side as by the other."[108] Nevertheless, he sent Brouillet's *Protestantism in Oregon* back to the House along with his own report, perhaps in order to quell the rumors still circulating about the Catholics' responsibility for the Whitman killings. In 1858 the House of Representatives Committee on Military Affairs published Browne's report as Executive Document No. 38 and attached *Protestantism in Oregon* to it. Browne had never intended for Brouillet's account to become part of the public record.[109]

It is not clear exactly when Spalding discovered that Brouillet's narrative had been published by the US Congress as part of Browne's report. Congressional documents were printed, first and foremost, for the use of members of Congress, and there is no known report of the document in extant Oregon newspapers. But the report appeared amidst several other blows to Spalding from the federal and territorial governments. In 1850 Spalding was appointed Indian Agent among the Nimiipuu, allowing him to return to his former mission field at Lapwai. He was fired within the year for his irascible nature, however, and the resulting public quarrel between him and Superintendent of Indian Affairs George Dart convinced the American Home Missionary Society to temporarily dismiss Spalding as a missionary as well. Largely due to the testimony of Dart the federal government determined not to compensate Spalding or any of the other former Oregon missionaries for land and property lost when they were forced to flee their missions, under the rationale that the missionaries had voluntarily abandoned their claims after the Whitman killings.[110] Spalding interpreted this judgment as an insult to the missionaries, an accusation that they had "turned missionary apostate" by leaving their posts in the thick of the Whitman crisis.[111]

In the midst of Spalding's campaign against his mission board and the US government Spalding's beloved wife, Eliza, died of tuberculosis. He believed that Eliza's condition had been worsened by the stress of the Whitman Mission attack and the struggle to make ends meet in the years following. Although Spalding eventually remarried—to the sister of his anti-Catholic partner in publishing, J. S. Griffin—he idolized Eliza for the rest of his life, using the memory of his "angel wife" as the motivation for his crusades.[112] "God willing I shall defend her pure character," Spalding declared to the ABCFM in 1866, "though I shall have to face the Black Republicans and papists."[113]

After Eliza's death Spalding continued to try to return to Lapwai, finally succeeding in 1863. Again he ran afoul of government officials, who this time also stripped him of his salary. The furious Spalding considered this "highway robbery," and noted that "23 Jesuite [sic] missionaries remain unmolested in the same field."[114] Now Spalding began to believe (without evidence) that Jesuits had infiltrated the US government in a grand conspiracy against the Protestant missions in Oregon, a conspiracy that reached all the way to President Abraham Lincoln and his successor, Andrew Johnson.[115] "Has the Spanish Inquisition been resurrected to be incorpered [*sic*] into our once Free government," Spalding inquired rhetorically. "Alass [*sic*] it is no dream I write, Robbed of my home, and stripped of almost everything, and the spotless character of my angel wife slandered by two Presidents."[116] Thus when Spalding discovered the existence of Executive Document No. 38, sometime before March 1866, he interpreted it as a "libel on Oregon history," as yet another part of the plot to destroy Protestant missions in Oregon, besmirch the reputation of Spalding and his associates, and "gratify, manifestly, the great band of Jesuits in our land—who, number (the Oregonian says), with their friends, 4,000,000 in the States and 200,000,000 in the world."[117] The entire federal government, swayed by a great Catholic army, seemed to be working to erase his legacy, a legacy that Spalding still believed had been guided by divine providence.

Spalding embarked on a grand scheme to shape public memory. The insults, he believed, were national in scope. Thus his response would be national as well. No longer would he debate the cause of Whitman's death in a self-published local newspaper. Rather, he declared, "I am replying by giving a history of the first settling of this country."[118] Spalding's history would prove the importance of the Oregon missions, not just to the region or to Protestants but to the entire nation. It would demonstrate that "the arm of God was apparent in the settlement and development of this mountain-licked region" and that the missionaries were the instruments of that divine arm.[119] And Spalding took his case before the very body he believed had wronged him: the United States Congress.

Spalding began by publishing a series of articles in the San Francisco–based religious newspaper the *Pacific,* of which his missionary friend George Henry Atkinson was editor. He then adapted the articles into a series of nine lectures he delivered at the newly founded First Congregational Church of Walla Walla in 1866. The lectures were a format that suited Spalding's dramatic, sermonic method of storytelling, and his lectures, judging by the report of the *Walla Walla Statesman,* were well attended. "I am sent from every direction to deliver these Lectures," he reported. "The community are indignant at the conduct of the Catholics."[120] As he announced in the first installment, the series had four purposes: to "correct grave and widespread mistakes concerning the first settling of this coast by American settlements"; to "defend the unsullied character of [his] angel wife," whose character had been "cruelly and shamefully slandered"; to "answer the oft-repeated question, 'What good has missions done among Indians?'"; and "to lay before the citizens of this coast the Herculean and hazardous labors of Dr. Whitman and his lady associates in securing this country to his Government."[121] Whitman's heroism would be the lynchpin of the lecture series.

In these lectures Spalding set forth a more developed providential history than in his articles of 1848 and 1849. Now, with the hindsight of nearly twenty years, he could attribute greater significance to the Oregon missionaries' work. Since Spalding's first publications in the *Oregon American*, Americans had struck gold in California and fought a Civil War. To Spalding both of these events were part of God's providential plan for American-led world redemption. As he explained at length, "In the progressive development of human redemption, the great end of this created world ... the allwise God had determined that these vast gold and silver mines, in and west of the Rocky Mountains and throughout the Pacific slope ... should, in these last days, be developed and given to the commercial world, and by American hands ... in part to speed the chariot wheel of human salvation, and in part to meet the stupendous National Debt to be incurred by our terrible war waged in behalf of human rights and the last command of Jesus Chsist [*sic*], 'go teach all nations' and against the combined despots of earth who thought to lay both in the new made grave of our American Republic."[122] In Spalding's schema, divine providence had saved the wealth of the gold mines for the exact moment when it could be best used to aid the American nation in its struggle for union and international supremacy. This was an expressly American kind of providence, one in which the divine intervened in world history specifically to protect and ensure the prosperity of the American nation.

This expanded providential history included a new take on Marcus Whitman. In 1848 Whitman had been primarily a religious martyr, a figure of sectarian importance. Now, Spalding made Whitman into a national hero fit for the lectures' grander scope. In the years since Whitman's death Spalding and the other surviving Oregon missionaries had

magnified Whitman's memory among themselves, adding various details and flourishes to the deeds that Whitman himself had claimed: ensuring that Protestants would settle the Oregon Country and leading the
first large wagon train to Oregon.[123] These additions had coalesced into
a story that Spalding either imagined or invented, one whose particulars,
while extremely improbable, nearly perfectly dramatized the conventions of Spalding's providential, anti-Catholic convictions. This more
intricate, more exciting version of the Whitman Saved Oregon Story
would become the standard Protestant narrative of the Oregon missions
into the twentieth century.

According to this new narrative, Whitman had been dining at Fort
Walla Walla with several Hudson's Bay Company traders and the Catholic
priests Francis Norbert Blanchet and Modeste Demers when they received a letter stating that a large train of emigrants would be arriving
soon from Red River, Manitoba, Canada. Upon hearing that news, "a
young priest ... not thinking that there was an American at the table,
sprung [sic] to his feet, and swinging his hand exclaimed, 'Hurrah for Columbia, Oregon; America is too late; we have got the country.' In an instant, as by instinct, Dr. Whitman saw through the whole plan clear to
Washington, Fort Hall and all. He immediately rose from the table and
asked to be excused, sprang upon his horse, and in a very short time stood
with his noble 'cayuse' [horse], white with foam, before his door, and without stopping to dismount he replied to our anxious inquiries with great
decision and earnestness, 'I am going to cross the Rocky Mountains and
reach Washington this winter, God carrying me through, and bring out an
emigration over the mountains next season, or this country is lost.'" Whitman then undertook his perilous journey to Washington, DC, where he
discovered that Secretary of State Daniel Webster, who "lived too near
Cape Cod to see things in the same light with his fellow statesman who
had transferred his worldly interests to the Pacific Coast," insisted that the
Oregon Country was a wasteland "fit only for the beaver, the gray bear,
and the savage" and that he "had about traded it off with Gov. Simpson [of
Great Britain], to go into the Ashburton Treaty, for a cod fishery on Newfoundland." But Whitman would not be deterred: he demanded to meet
with President John Tyler. Tyler, seeing Whitman's "frozen limbs" and rec-
ognizing his "missionary character," promised him that "if the Doctor

could establish a wagon route through the mountains to the Columbia River ... he would use his influence to hold on to Oregon." Whitman then rounded up a group of one thousand emigrants and led them over the Rocky Mountains to Oregon, proving that Oregon could be settled by Americans and ensuring American possession of the country. The Hudson's Bay Company and their henchmen, the Jesuit priests, never forgot that Whitman had caused Oregon to slip from their grasp. Four years later they tricked members of the Cayuse tribe into killing Whitman. But they were too late. American settlers flooded Oregon, claiming it for the United States and for true Christianity.[124]

As historians from Hubert Howe Bancroft to Cameron Addis have demonstrated, most of the claims in Spalding's new narrative are false: there was no meeting of Whitman, the Hudson's Bay Company, and the Catholic priests; there was no plot to trade Oregon for a codfishery; and though Whitman traveled with and aided the emigration of 1843, he did not organize or lead it. Yet most of Spalding's Protestant readers did not doubt the narrative. They believed it, circulated it, and even signed petitions verifying it. Protestant readers were not inclined to doubt the claims of a missionary—or of a story that depicted a missionary as heroic, the Protestant missionary enterprise as patriotic, and the settling of the West as divinely ordained.

Moreover, Spalding had not conjured the narrative out of thin air; he had collected substantial evidence—of a sort. By his own report he had begun amassing materials related to the Whitman killings in 1848. In the 1860s he created questionnaires to send to early settlers of the Oregon Country, soliciting testimonies to support his version of events. These materials relied on the memories of events that occurred twenty years earlier, memories that were shaped by Spalding's leading questions.[125] Only one of the witnesses, Asa Lawrence Lovejoy, had direct knowledge of the events; he had accompanied Whitman on his journey east but did not go with him all the way to Washington. The others offered their memories of the attack on the Whitman Mission or simply stated their belief in Spalding's narrative.[126] Nevertheless, testimony constituted evidence for Spalding's readers, and many commented on the "authentic documents" that supported Spalding's "truthful history."[127]

Capitalizing on the success of the lectures, Spalding turned toward gaining a hearing in Congress. Beginning in 1866 he drafted and circulated a petition to local churches and political leaders calling on the House of Representatives to correct the mistakes they had made in Executive Document 38.[128] The petition, in its final form, stated that "a grievous wrong has been done [to] Dr. Whitman and his martyred associates, in the passage by the Thirty-Fifth Congress of Executive Document 38" and that the undersigned "in common with the patriotic citizens of the Pacific coast ... unite in asking Congress to rectify this wrong."[129] The petitioners asserted that the earlier House document contained "all slanders of the worst description." "It was only as the Jesuits were running Congress at the time," added Spalding's old friend J. S. Griffin, "that the [House] ever published such scandal."[130] After amassing the testimonies into a single narrative, Spalding proclaimed, "Oregon has made & written her history a glorious history, a history written not in blood, but in characters of light & hope, known & read of old men, to take its place along side the chapters that are making up the wonderful history of this wonderful Nation."[131]

Spalding bolstered this "glorious history" with signatures from members of Oregon's Protestant community. Among those signing on to Spalding's version of events were Methodist, Baptist, Presbyterian, Congregational, and Christian (Disciples of Christ) congregations; Joel Palmer, the superintendent of Indian affairs in Oregon; D. W. Ballard, the governor of Idaho; several members of the Washington Territorial government; and George Abernethy, the former provisional governor of Oregon. Such support attested to the ongoing presence of Protestant figures in the regional governments in the Pacific Northwest. Yet it also demonstrated the extent to which these Protestant leaders worried about their status in the region as they fought to enshrine fellow Protestants as the Oregon Country's true founders and to repudiate Brouillet's pro-Catholic history.

Before the document was even completed Spalding sought the aid of various Protestant luminaries to gain a hearing before Congress. He found allies in Henry Winslow Corbett, a US senator, businessman, and one of Oregon's leading Republican statesmen, and Joseph Showalter Smith, the Oregon representative-at-large. Corbett was a member of Portland's First Presbyterian Church, where the newly installed minister,

A. L. Lindsley, was an acquaintance of Spalding's and a supporter of the Oregon missions.[132] Smith was a schoolteacher, a lawyer, and a devout Methodist.[133] Spalding's story roused the politicians' sympathies, and they were impressed by the patriotic nature of his claimed deeds. As Smith stated, "We have many, many missionaries, from all parts of the earth, but, your services are for our own land, and for the poor Indians."[134] Smith agreed to take the document before the House Committee on Indian Affairs, and Corbett did the same with the Senate's committee.[135]

Having secured support in the US legislature Spalding undertook a cross-country journey, but a very different one from that Marcus Whitman had taken in 1843. The land that had once been linked by trading networks of Native peoples was now traversed by railroads. The speed of mail had increased exponentially, so that instead of surprising his visitors, as Whitman had done, Spalding was able to travel east as an expected and respected guest. He stopped in Chicago, Philadelphia, New York, Boston, and his old hometown of Prattsburgh. In each location he delivered parts of his lectures, gained more signatures for his petition, and was featured in local papers as the venerated "father of pioneer missions in Oregon."[136] He also made additional political connections. In New York City Spalding met with former ABCFM vice president William Dodge, who "assured [Spalding] of the warmest support in Washington."[137] Dodge sent out a circular among other "friends of Protestant religion" in the federal government, including William Blaine, Speaker of the House of Representatives; Schuyler Colfax, vice president of the United States; and Senator Samuel Clarke Pomeroy of Kansas.[138] In Philadelphia Spalding gained a patron in the railroad baron Jay Cooke, who donated money to Spalding's cause and entertained him at his "royal mansion."[139]

As 1870 neared its close Spalding arrived in Washington, DC. His visit could hardly have been better timed. In 1869, under President Ulysses S. Grant, the federal government had adopted the so-called Peace Policy toward Native Americans. The misleadingly named policy combined a push toward enticing Native peoples toward reservations with the same scorched-earth military tactics toward resisting tribes that Grant had implemented against the South as a Civil War general. But it also enlisted Christian denominations to take unprecedented authority on reservations, distributing supplies, teaching agriculture, establishing churches and schools, and teaching Native people to appreciate "the comforts and benefits of a Christian civilization."[140] In other words the government was now implementing on a national level the tactics Spalding and the other Oregon missionaries had unsuccessfully utilized in the 1840s, and they were doing so in partnership with Christian ministers. As the historian of US Indian policy Francis Paul Prucha has argued, this unprecedented cooperation of church and state in Indian affairs "might just as properly have been labeled the religious policy."[141] There was hardly a more opportune time for Spalding to present his case for the good that the Oregon missionaries had done among the Cayuse and Nez Perce Indians in service to the American nation.

On January 25 Spalding received the invitation he had long awaited: a chance to present his case before several influential senators, including Corbett and Pomeroy. No record of the results of this meeting exists, but one week later, on February 2, Pomeroy proposed a resolution calling for the secretary of the interior to deliver to the Senate any documents relating to the early missionary history of Oregon.[142] Meanwhile, Spalding had given Oregon's secretary of Indian affairs, A. M. Meacham, a copy of his history, which Meacham delivered to the secretary of the interior. Finally, on February 9, Vice President Colfax presented Spalding's document to the Senate, which unanimously ordered that it be printed.[143] And with that masterful bureaucratic maneuver Spalding's history was endorsed by the US Senate.

From the Senate chamber an amazed Spalding wrote to his wife, "Glory to God. Bless His Holy Name. Victory complete. . . . Every Senator seemed my friend." He had received a warmer welcome than he had imagined, and he had brought the attention of powerful people to his providential history of the United States. Moreover, President Grant had put the Nez Perce Reservation under the care of the Presbyterians, giving Spalding an opportunity to return to his old mission. "Tell my friends and enemies," he added, "that my visit to Washington to vindicate our faithful dead and Protestantism has been a complete success."[144]

Spalding's sense of triumph did not last long. Within a year after returning to the Northwest and his old mission at Lapwai he had another falling-out with his fellow missionary W. J. Monteith and was again ordered to leave Lapwai, this time by his own mission board.[145] Employing his usual persistence he again solicited testimonies in his support and was reinstated in 1873 as a missionary to the nearby Spokane people. By this date, however, his health had failed, and he was too feeble to move to the Spokane Reservation. He died at Lapwai on August 3, 1874, shortly after baptizing the Umatilla chief Umhawlawish and his wife. He christened the couple "Marcus and Narcissa Whitman."[146]

The Senate document that Spalding had for years labored to produce never circulated widely. Only two thousand copies of the document were printed in 1871, though Spalding did receive many letters from supporters requesting copies. Far more enduring were the legend of Marcus Whitman that Spalding invented and the providential view of American expansion that the legend instantiated. By virtue of his crusade to redeem the memory of his mission Spalding had created a narrative that would extend beyond the limits of his own writings to build the intellectual framework for regional and then national histories of American destiny.

Professionalizing Providence

In his first major article series on Oregon history the ex-missionary
William Gray described at length one of Oregon's earliest missionaries and pioneers: "A young man about twenty-five years of age,
medium height, black hair, wearing black whiskers.... dark blue
eyes, light complexion, round straight form, active and fearless in all his
motions... He was considered an ingenious man, persevering in anything
he undertook, often undertaking and accomplishing what others had
failed in. He had what was considered at that time a good practical education for a new country... his religious views were practical and progressive... in short he was, a kind of compound patriotic, philanthropic,
political, religious individual, philanthropy or generosity generally in the
ascendant."[1] This paragon of human perfection was Gray himself, a man
in the process of establishing himself as one of the preeminent founders
and caretakers of Oregon history. While Henry Spalding was in the midst
of his crusade to rectify the US government's unflattering history of the
Oregon missions, William Gray had begun his own historical quest. In
1870 he published his *History of Oregon,* which cemented him as one of
the leading authorities on Pacific Northwest history. The following year
Gray convened the inaugural meeting of Oregon's first state historical
association, the Pioneer and Historical Society (PHS). Intertwined with
both of these projects was Gray's desire to build a monument to his old

missionary companion Marcus Whitman—a movement that ultimately failed in its immediate goals but succeeded in making Whitman and the providential history of the West that he symbolized a central component of regional identity and professional historical inquiry.

Like Henry Spalding, William Gray believed that the ABCFM missionaries should be recognized as the true heroes of early Oregon settlement, and also like Spalding, Gray believed that the Oregon Country's Catholics were truly responsible for Whitman's death. But while Spalding disseminated this belief by means of local and national church networks and connections in the federal government, Gray used the emerging structure of the local historical society to grant his work legitimacy. In doing so, Gray and the historical society he founded both participated in and helped to shape two pivotal movements in American history writing: the professionalization of providential history and the growth of regional history in the American West.

The professionalization of providential history both prefigured and differed from the later professionalization that has been detailed by scholars of academic historiography, including Peter Novick and Robert Townsend. Novick's *That Noble Dream: The "Objectivity Question" and the American Historical Profession* traces the development of the discipline of American history from the 1880s to the 1970s, examining how academic historians helped create and then transform the historical profession through debates about the desirableness and attainability of objectivity in historical work.[2] Novick's analysis is centered on the practice of history in academic research universities; Novick sees the historical profession's origins and growth as contiguous with the development of research universities and the rise of the seminar method. However, as Townsend has demonstrated in *History's Babel: Scholarship, Professionalization, and the Historical Enterprise in the United States, 1880–1940,* universities were not the only centers of historical labor in the mid- to late nineteenth century. Other forms of historical authority coexisted and competed with the university, forming overlapping networks of authoritative practices that Townsend and others have described as "the historical enterprise."[3] However, Townsend focuses mainly on the AHA, a national organization founded in 1884, which he rightly identifies as representative of only a small sector of the historical enterprise.[4] Pioneer societies were founded decades before the establishment of the AHA or graduate programs in history. Like the AHA, these communities were settings for historical research, but unlike the AHA pioneer societies explicitly combined local pride and religious and racial exclusivity with historical pursuits. Hence they served as conduits for the transmission of a triumphal, Anglo-Protestant-centered narrative of the West that influenced American history writing into the twentieth century.

In the American West local historians, many of them with only a cursory education, circulated their narratives in newspapers, books, public lectures, pamphlets, and church sermons, and they dialogued with other histories drawn from these formats. These histories were embedded in the authors' personal experiences of the events described. In fact, personal experience was perhaps the primary marker of local historical authority. Gray was lauded as a "pioneer of pioneers, and historian of events in which he took so conspicuous a part."[5] Gray's fellow missionary Cushing Eells was described as one "whose opportunities in a residence of nearly fifty years, and associations with the men of early times, peculiarly fit him for an authentic narration of events preceding the settlement of the country."[6] Even Spalding's fanciful account of the Oregon missions was undergirded by his authority as a witness to the events he described.[7] In each case local historians' firsthand knowledge of events was not a liability but an advantage. Local experience, bolstered by personal reputation and affiliation with local power structures like the Pacific Northwest's Protestant establishment, was essential to historical authority in the West.

The importance of local experience was intertwined with the origins of the Oregon pioneer as a marker of white, Protestant identity. Oregon's pioneers—the region's earliest white American settlers—were not born, they were made. Or rather they made themselves, by asserting their authority as the region's founders, writing its first histories, forming organizations to commemorate their arrival in the Oregon Country, and, most crucial, delineating who were decidedly *not* pioneers: British and French Canadians loyal to the Hudson's Bay Company, Indians, Catholics and other religious minorities, and Americans who arrived too late to have undergone the defining experience of journeying to the Oregon Country via wagon train or dangerous sea voyage. Given these boundaries, Oregon's pioneers were overwhelmingly white, American-born Protestants, and they narrated the region's history in a distinctly providential key, one authenticated by their experiences of the events they witnessed and in which they took part.

The historian of British Columbia Chad Reimer has described history writing in the late nineteenth-century North American West as "pioneer history." According to Reimer, pioneer history served to establish moral examples for western settlers while granting western regions legitimacy by echoing eastern North American Great Men histories.[8] In the case of pioneer history, however, the Great Men were often men of ordinary backgrounds and means, distinguished not by their education, class, or family origins but by their rugged individualism and unique place in the broader history of westward expansion. Through pioneer history, writes Reimer, "ordinary people pursuing everyday tasks could . . . be players in the grand sweep of history for they lived in a privileged time and place: North America's far west had only recently come into the ambit of European civilization, and they were present when that happened."[9]

Though Reimer focuses on the Canadian West, his term "pioneer history" is useful because it explains how local figures who lacked traditional status markers were able to claim historical authority in the West. Reimer demonstrates that historical work served an essential purpose in Canadian western expansion by helping Anglo-European settlers develop a regional identity and by furthering the narrative that Anglo-European conquest of the West was both inevitable and laudable. However, pioneer history in the American West had a more explicitly providential framing than in the Canadian West. The belief that God had foreordained western lands to become part of the United States was essential to pioneer history's justification of white settlement and the displacement of Native peoples. Providentialism allowed pioneer historians to elide the violence of white settlement by attributing western conquest to a foreordained destiny rather than to forced removal and wars of extermination. It positioned Native peoples not as rightful possessors of the land but as obstacles to American progress.

In other words Gray and his historical allies were not only pioneer historians but also providential historians: historians who believed that the work and will of God were evident in historical events and who were shaped by Protestant notions of American identity and destiny. They thus characterized a new kind of providential history: pioneer providential history. Pioneer providential history combined Protestant triumphalism with an individualist, antiauthoritarian ethos. It prioritized the work of heroic individuals over purportedly stodgy institutions, including churches and missionary organizations. It also prioritized local expertise over formal education and credentials, including those of religious leaders. In these ways it extracted providential history from its obvious sectarian moorings. Yet, as Tracy Fessenden has observed of literary writing in this period, this apparent secularization belied a deeper embedding of Protestant ideals.[10] Pioneer providentialists may have critiqued individual Protestant religious leaders and church organizations, but on a more fundamental level they saw Protestantism as the foundation of western settlement and American identity as coterminous with Protestant allegiances. Catholics thus continued to appear in pioneer histories as they had in Spalding's more explicitly sectarian history of the Oregon missions. Pioneer historians simply shifted the emphasis away from doctrinal debates and toward Catholics' purported foreign allegiances, suspect whiteness, and antidemocratic principles. This was a fundamentally white, Protestant vision of the Pacific Northwest, one that both explained and figuratively erased the continued presence of Native peoples and religious minorities.

Though this vision of a white West endured past the nineteenth century, by the 1880s pioneer history began to fracture as western newcomers began to question both the special status given to the pioneers and the trustworthiness of local experience as a source of historical authority. In Oregon and Washington these struggles coalesced around the legacy of Marcus Whitman. Even as historians like Gray were using Whitman as a capstone for a providential history of the Pacific Northwest, other local historians sought to overturn the Whitman legend as a means of advancing their own vision for the Northwest's past and future, one still embedded in a vision of Anglo-American progress but unmoored from uncritical deference to the Northwest's earliest white settlers. I examine that struggle here and in so doing take a cue from recent work in the secularization of American public and academic life.

In *The Secular Revolution* Christian Smith argues that the secularization of American public life was not the natural result of the progress of modernity but rather was the product of overlapping and sometimes contradictory projects undertaken by "contending groups with conflicting interests seeking to control social knowledge and institutions."[11] These groups included some members of the Protestant establishment as well as religiously marginalized groups such as Catholics, Mormons, and freethinkers. Though not united in their views, Smith's secularizers tended to be concentrated in knowledge-producing professions like education and journalism, influenced by European intellectual currents, frustrated by the limiting nature of the Protestant hegemony, and committed to "quasi-religious visions of secular progress, prosperity, and higher civilization."[12]

The loci of professionalization that Smith describes, however, were not nearly as influential in the late nineteenth-century American West, where European influence was despised and the structures of intellectual and professional life were barely extant. Rather, in the West secularizing projects arose from local conditions that sometimes paralleled but often differed from those of the East: a climate marked by suspicion of religious authority, ongoing Protestant–Catholic conflict, a large percentage of loosely Protestant but ecclesiastically unaffiliated settlers, and a desire to make the Northwest a pinnacle of modern society. Out of these conditions a second class of pioneer historians sprang up: pioneer secularizers, who used their local authority to question the accounts of the pioneer providentialists and in so doing hoped to both modernize the Northwest's historical writing and undermine the power of the pioneer providentialists. Like Brouillet and other Catholic historians before him, pioneer secularizers prefigured some of the methodologies and claims that professional academic historians later used to dismantle the Whitman legend.

The legacy of Marcus Whitman became a battleground on which these two emerging schools of history collided: the pioneer providential historians like Gray, who sought to build a historical enterprise dedicated to loosely Protestant ideals and the valorization of Oregon's early pioneers; and the pioneer secularizers, who attacked pioneer providentialist history as inappropriately sectarian and insufficiently objective. In the process, they would once again remake the memory of Marcus Whitman and, by extension, the contours of historical understanding in the West.

Mr. Gray Becomes Dr. Gray, Esq.

Perhaps more than any of the other early interpreters of Marcus Whitman's life and death William Henry Gray demonstrates the extent to which nineteenth-century Anglo-Americans could remake their identities in the American West. Although Gray came from a humble background, had little professional training, and abandoned the mission that brought him to the Oregon Country, by the end of his life he had claimed a place as one of the Oregon Country's most respected pioneer citizens.

Gray was born on September 8, 1810, in Fairfield, New York, to Samuel and Rhoda (Barber) Gray.[13] Little is known about his family and early life. When he was a teenager his father died, and he became a cabinetmaker's apprentice in nearby Springfield, New York.[14] Gray also attempted to get an education, first at the Oneida Industrial Institute in Whittlesboro, New York, and then as a physician's apprentice in Utica. Both endeavors failed: his teachers at Oneida found him to be "an extremely dull scholar," and the Utica physician dismissed Gray for the same reason.[15] Just when it looked like Gray would be a cabinetmaker for life, he found an opportunity. A pastor with whom he was boarding had heard that the ABCFM was recruiting missionaries to work among the Indians of the Oregon Country. Gray applied to the board, stating that he'd be ready to leave immediately. He had few skills or endorsements to recommend him to the position. His own pastor warned the board that Gray had "by no means the qualifications that we think desirable for such a station."[16] But as the Oregon mission party was scheduled to leave shortly there was little time to vet Gray thoroughly, and so he was accepted to join Marcus and Narcissa Whitman and Henry and Eliza Spalding to establish a mission in the Oregon Country.[17]

Because Gray had neither the medical training of Marcus Whitman nor the ministerial education of Henry Spalding, the board assigned him to be the group's mechanic, or manual laborer.[18] Gray was supposed to assist with farming, construction, carpentry, and any other practical tasks that Whitman and Spalding needed to be carried out. The post was a poor fit. Gray resented being subject to Whitman's and Spalding's authority, shuttling back and forth between the two men's mission stations and having to spend his time doing manual labor rather than teaching and preaching. As he complained in a letter to a colleague, "For me to labor a little at this place pack up & go and labor a little at another & pack up & go to another & then pack up.... I do not feel that it is a pleasunt [sic] situation to occupy."[19] Gray longed to have a mission of his own, away from the orders of Whitman and Spalding.[20] The missionaries had been in the Oregon Country for scarcely a year when Gray convinced Spalding to allow him to return to the eastern United States to bring back a reinforcement of missionaries and supplies. Gray and his Nimiipuu and Flathead guides also drove a herd of horses to the East Coast, where they could sell some and trade the rest for cattle.[21] Gray did not notify Whitman of this decision until after he had left.[22] Though this incident was outlined in chapter 1, it is worth revisiting in greater detail here to fully explain Gray's role in what happened next.

The trip was an unmitigated disaster. Gray was supposed to travel the first leg of the journey with Francis Ermatinger, a Hudson's Bay Company trader. He would then join a party of American fur traders at the yearly trading rendezvous at Horse Creek in the Rocky Mountains.[23] But Gray grew impatient. He decided to go ahead without the fur company's protection, instead proceeding with only the small party of Native men to guard a large herd of horses. Gray wrote in his journal, "Our number is small, but God can protect us and carry us forward."[24] The experienced fur trader Jim Bridger disagreed, warning Gray, "The grace of God won't carry a man through these prairies! It takes powder and ball."[25] Bridger's warning proved correct: six weeks after leaving the Rendezvous Gray's party was ambushed by a band of Native men whom Gray identified as Sioux. The attackers killed all six of Gray's Native associates, sparing only Gray and two other whites.[26] All of the party's property was stolen in the skirmish, including the horses whose sale was meant to fund Gray's return trip. The incident infuriated members of the British and American fur trading community, who believed that Gray traded his life for those of his Native companions.[27]

Gray arrived in Fairfield, New York, in the fall of 1837, with only two bullet wounds and a hole in his hat to show for his trouble. He had lost all his supplies, the herd of horses, and his traveling companions on the journey. He did, however, manage to recruit eight additional missionaries for the Oregon Country, including Mary Augusta Dix.[28] Dix was the daughter of a pious Dutch Reformed family in Ithaca, New York. After a ten-day courtship Gray and Dix married.[29] Like the marriages of all the other Oregon missionaries, it was a marriage explicitly undertaken for the missionary cause. Gray's rather utilitarian proposal to Dix asked that, "Whatever connection may be formed let it only be that the gospel may be given to the ends of the Earth."[30] Gray also attended several months of public lectures at Fairfield Medical College, after which he saw fit to call himself a doctor, although upon his return to Waiilatpu, Marcus Whitman promptly ordered him to stop using that title.[31]

Even though Gray was nearly killed on the trip to the Northeast he planned the missionaries' return to Oregon with the same lack of caution that had resulted in the deaths of his Native companions. Under Gray's orders, the mission party did not bring sufficient supplies. The missionaries slept four to a tent, allowing no privacy for any of the newly married couples. The party ran out of food halfway through the journey and had to subsist solely on game meat.[32] At the Horse Creek rendezvous, a group of unidentified Indians arrived at the missionaries' camp seeking revenge for Gray's cowardice the previous summer and placing the whole company in danger.[33] The missionaries arrived at the Whitman Mission on August 29, 1838, with none of the promised supplies for the missions and six months of growing animosity toward Gray.[34] The Oregon missions never recovered. Quarrels forged in Gray's party combined with existing resentment between the Whitmans, the Spaldings, and Gray. Finally, in 1842, William and Mary Gray left the mission and moved to the fertile, more thickly settled Willamette Valley.[35]

But Gray was destined to be more than a failed missionary. His dismissal from the missions allowed him to pursue other causes. In the absence of a formal government, settlers in the Willamette Valley had been holding meetings since 1841 in order to address issues of probate and protection of property. Gray became involved in the meetings upon his arrival in the Willamette Valley.[36] From 1818 to 1846 the Oregon Country's national status was ambiguous since both the United States and Great Britain claimed the region. Unlike territories that were held solely by the United States, the Oregon Country's standing was vague, and settlers could not rely on the US government to appoint leaders or establish laws. While the Hudson's Bay Company acted as the de facto judicial and political authority for its workers, the American settlers had no clear authority to arbitrate disputes or prevent social disorder. Nor did they accept the leadership of the Hudson's Bay Company, which many Americans, including Gray, saw as a corrupt foreign monopoly.[37]

Given the need for an authoritative system outside of the Hudson's Bay Company, some of the Willamette Valley settlers, including Gray, began to argue that the Americans needed to form their own government. At a meeting held on May 2, 1843, at Champoeg, a Hudson's Bay Company trading post on the Willamette River, the American settler George LeBreton proposed that the settlers organize a provisional government. Gray seconded the motion, bringing it to a vote. Despite opposition from the Hudson's Bay–affiliated settlers who were present, the motion passed with fifty-two Americans voting for the government and fifty French Canadians and other Hudson's Bay–affiliated men voting against. Gray was subsequently appointed to serve on the new government's nine-person legislative committee and to the committees on military and land grants.[38]

From 1843 to 1849 Oregon's provisional government created its own structures: a set of Organic Laws, a legislature, courts, a post office, and a militia. Trappers and farmers with no qualifications other than good standing in their communities were appointed as legislators, army captains, and magistrates.[39] The legislature was so unfamiliar with legal and political theory that three of its members resisted opening their meetings to the public. According to Gray, this was because "they did not want to expose their ignorance of making laws."[40]

It was unlikely that other Oregonians would have protested, however. The ad hoc nature of the provisional government echoed the improvisational abilities of the Oregon Country's settlers as a whole. Emigrants to Oregon found few political, social, religious, or professional structures akin to those in the eastern United States. In their new homeland these settlers both replicated and subverted the structures they had left. A story one Oregon settler liked to tell captures this point: "[Settler] 2 and [settler] 3 were traveling together; 3 was from Cincinnati, Ohio. They had reached Independence, Missouri; says 3 to 2, 'Titles are very necessary in Missouri; what titles shall we take?' 'Well,' says 2, 'I will take *Major*.' 3 says, 'I will take *Doctor*.' They rode up to the best hotel in the place and called for lodgings."[41]

Gray too found himself able to adopt a number of professions, though not always successfully. From 1843 to the late 1860s, Gray drifted from one career to the next. He worked at the Oregon Institute, a school founded by Methodist missionaries, until the doctrinal disagreements became intolerable for both sides. He prospected (evidently without success) for gold in California in 1849 and along the Fraser River in British Columbia in the 1860s. He captained a steamboat, traveled with a US delegation to Alaska, served as a local judge and doctor.[42] During this time Gray also became a historian, in the same way he had entered into his other endeavors: by finding a niche and filling it.

Gray's *History of Oregon* and the Beginnings of Pioneer Providentialism

As Gray went about his various occupations, the Oregon Country was nearing the end of an epoch. Between 1840 and 1860 over fifty-three thousand people traversed the Overland Trail to settle in Oregon, along with more than two hundred thousand who went to California.[43] The emigrants believed themselves to be part of a unique historic event. Thousands of emigrants recorded their journeys in descriptions both cursory and richly detailed. The result was an outpouring of American folk writing—letters, diaries, memoirs, and trail guides—perhaps surpassed only by that of the Civil War.[44] However, by 1860, the overland movement was waning. Due to increasing conflict between emigrants and Indians, overland travel to Oregon had slowed from an all-time high of fourteen thousand emigrants in 1848 to only fifteen hundred in 1860.[45] With the advent of the transcontinental railroad in 1869 the overland trail became almost obsolete. Americans continued to emigrate to Oregon, but few took the slow, dangerous wagon route when trains and stagecoaches offered safer, easier, and faster transportation. The experience of traveling to Oregon had fundamentally changed.

Oregon's political situation had changed as well. Partly as a result of the killings of the Whitmans and their associates in 1847 the US government had extended territorial jurisdiction over Oregon in 1848. In

1859 Oregon became the thirty-third state in the Union. Washington and Idaho were carved off into territories in 1853 and 1863, respectively. For Oregon's earliest American settlers, territorial organization was both a blessing and a curse. On the one hand, the Hudson's Bay Company was no longer able to exercise de facto political power in the region. On the other hand, the federal government soon began to impinge on the power of Oregon's settlers, especially those who had been involved with the provisional government. It was within the purview of the US president to appoint territorial governors, state Supreme Court justices, Indian agents, and minor positions such as customs officials. Presidents from Polk to Lincoln chose to appoint eastern party loyalists who had never been to the Oregon Country. Northwesterners balked at these outside appointments, labeling the newcomers carpetbaggers and deriding their ignorance of local concerns.[46] Their complaints were not unfounded, as many of the early appointees abandoned their posts for other pursuits or became embroiled in scandal.[47] As early as 1850 established residents of Oregon Territory were lobbying their fellow citizens to demand that the federal government "appoint no man to office in Oregon, unless he be an Oregon man—one among us."[48]

Despite the fact that even the earliest American settlers had lived in the Oregon Country only since the 1830s, northwesterners who had arrived prior to 1848 began to see a clear separation between themselves and newcomers. They adopted the term "pioneer" to distinguish themselves from emigrants who came to the Oregon Country later and under less trying conditions as well as from the federally appointed carpetbaggers. In the late 1860s and early 1870s these early settlers began to form pioneer associations, publish accounts of Oregon's Pioneer Days, and advocate for clear distinctions between themselves and latecomers.[49] Through these and other activities the pioneers claimed authority over the Oregon Country's history. They were among the first architects of an Anglo-American history of the Pacific Northwest.

Oregonians had participated in history-making endeavors prior to 1860 (see chapter 2). However, as was the case with Henry Spalding and Jean-Baptiste Brouillet, most Oregonians entered into historical debate only in order to interpret specific events like the Cayuse War, to address specific perceived wrongs, such as the loss of Spalding's mission property, or to promote the settlement of the Pacific Northwest. Pioneer historians, by contrast, created a sustained, general history of the Oregon Country. Moreover, pioneer historians created a historical community, one composed of local historical associations, yearly reunions, and ongoing dialogue on historical questions pertinent to the region.

In the early 1860s this historical community existed only in an informal way, but pioneers were already expressing interest in their history, holding onto their Oregon Trail writings and other early documents and exchanging historical information with other pioneers. When the historian Frances Fuller Victor sought documents for her history of the Columbia River, she found that "all the old Oregonians had at one time or another cherished the idea of writing a book about Oregon," which made them unwilling to give up their old letters, diaries, and other written materials. "It proved to me that they all had a strong sense of the peculiar points in their history," Victor wrote.[50]

One of these pioneer historians was Elwood Evans, a lawyer and former Quaker originally from Philadelphia. In 1851 Evans moved from Philadelphia to the Oregon Territory to serve as deputy collector of customs for the territory. He quickly became involved in the region's politics, successfully lobbying to make Washington a separate territory from Oregon in 1852, serving intermittently in the territorial congress and as acting governor, and finally being appointed territorial secretary by Abraham Lincoln.[51] He also became one of the earliest and most prolific compilers of Pacific Northwest history. As early as 1861 Evans began writing to some of Oregon's earliest settlers and missionaries, asking for documents and information and making notes on his findings.[52] He felt a special sympathy for the early Oregon missionaries, "those early Christian Pioneers who were willing to leave home, society and friends, deny themselves all the pleasures and comforts of life and in many matters lay down life itself to impart glad tidings of salvation to the benighted Indian."[53] As Evans wrote to Gray and his missionary colleague Cushing Eells, "I frankly believe you will concur with me that there is much in our early history really valuable and instructive which ought to be preserved and that day after day it is becoming forgotten."[54]

On July 4, 1865, William Gray attended a historical lecture given by Evans.[55] The two men conversed, and Evans convinced Gray to produce his own history of the Oregon Country's early years.[56] The following year Gray published a series of articles on the Oregon missions in the Astoria, Oregon newspaper the *Marine Gazette*. The articles sparked interest beyond Gray's expectations. "Few articles had been given, however," Gray explained, "before there was a call for back numbers of the paper, which were not on hand."[57] Gray compiled a book from the articles, which would allow him to incorporate new information and critiques he had received from other interested readers, including Elwood Evans, the geologist and ethnologist George Gibbs, and Oregon State Representative J. H. D. Henderson.[58] The book also allowed Gray a chance to weigh in on a dispute between the Hudson's Bay Company and the US government. After the Ashburton Treaty set the US–Canada boundary line at the 49th parallel in 1846, the Hudson's Bay Company gradually abandoned its posts in the southern Oregon Country and moved most of its traders to British Columbia.[59] US settlers also began to encroach on the lands of the Puget Sound Agricultural Company, a Hudson's Bay Company subsidiary that had grown into a small enclave of former fur traders, many of whom were Catholic, and their Native and mixed-race families.[60] In 1869, after years of intermittent negotiations, the US government agreed to compensate the Hudson's Bay Company $450,000 for lost property and navigation rights to the Columbia River. Another $200,000 went to the Puget Sound Agricultural Company.[61] Gray saw the settlement as an insult to the true Oregonians, namely, Protestant missionaries and pioneers, who had fought tooth and nail to ensure that Oregon would become an American possession. "With an audacity only equaled by the arch-enemy of God and man," Gray said of the Hudson's Bay Company, "they come to our government and demand five millions of gold for facilitating the settlement of a country they had not the courage or power to prevent."[62] Like Spalding's before him, Gray's historical work was shaped by a sense of personal grievance and resentment at supposed interlopers in the West.

In 1870 Gray published his *A History of Oregon, 1792–1849: Drawn from Personal Observation and Authentic Information,* a 65-chapter, 624-page tome giving a detailed account of the Oregon Country's history from the American exploration of its coast in 1792 to 1849, when Oregon was formally organized as a US territory. Gray made no claims to "literary merit or attractive style" in his history; rather, he appealed to his "personal knowledge, observation, and participation in what is stated for one third of a century" and to the evidence—secondary sources, letters, and personal testimonies—he had meticulously collected.[63] The resulting project was an eccentric compilation of firsthand narrative, whole chapters of other author's books and letters, and liberally quoted letters and other primary documents, tied together by Gray's inimitable commentary.

Gray narrated events with the kind of cantankerous vividness that only an eyewitness could muster. His candid portraits of his fellow missionaries earned him much rancor from those who were still alive and would serve as a major source of negative information by later historians who wished to discredit Spalding, Whitman, and others. Gray described Henry Spalding as "below mediocrity" in his "professional character," and Asa Bowen Smith as "a man whose mind was so full of prejudices he could not reason with himself."[64] The missionary Elkanah Walker was "diffident, and unassuming, always afraid to say *amen* at the end of his prayers," while the missionary Cushing Eells was "made to move in a small circle, for his soul would be lost outside of it."[65] Indeed, as Elwood Evans wrote to Henry Spalding, "A stranger, picking . . . up [the lectures in the *Marine Gazette*], and not regarding them as a very egotistical autobiography, would be forced to conclude that in that period, there was in Oregon, one competent *man*, that the A.B.C.F.M. and Protestant denominations knew nothing of the proper *material* for missionaries, though there was 'one striking exception' to prove the rule, found in the wisdom of their *choice* of W. H. Gray."[66] Other early Oregonians fared no better in Gray's accounting. Oregon's first Indian agent, Elijah White, was a "puffball of folly and ignorance."[67] Robert Newell, an American who expressed doubts about organizing the provisional government, was "a hypocrite in action as well as profession."[68] Gray had nothing but contempt for the men of the Methodist mission, who he believed were more interested in maintaining their own sphere of influence than in ensuring the American possession of the Oregon Country.[69]

Nevertheless, Gray saved his choicest words for the Hudson's Bay Company. He argued that Great Britain's support of the "monster monopoly" was "one of the most gigantic frauds ever continued for a series of years by one professedly civilized and Christian nation upon another."[70] To Gray, the company was the ultimate example of the kinds of bureaucratic structures that had no place in the Oregon Country. Nearly every chapter of his book listed detailed accusations of the company's wrongs: overstepping their charter to trade in the Oregon Country, bringing Catholic missionaries to Oregon "for no other purpose than to facilitate their trade among the Indians, and to destroy the American influence in that country," and, most egregiously, fomenting the resentment that led to the murder of the Whitmans and twelve other Americans at the Waiilatpu mission.[71] In Gray's eyes the history of the Oregon Country could effectively be summed up as a battle between the Hudson's Bay Company's un-American, un-Christian stranglehold on the region and the tenacious, put-upon American Protestant missionaries, American settlers, and sympathetic allies who engaged in a David and Goliath struggle against the company's machinations. Gray and his fellow missionaries "formed the nucleus around which the American pioneer with his family gathered, and from which he drew his encouragement and protection."[72] In this framing Gray followed a common technique of western mythmakers that the historian Richard White has termed "inverted conquest."[73] Gray depicted Anglo-American Protestants as a beleaguered minority surrounded by hostile others, making the settlers' eventual triumph more spectacular and their opponents less sympathetic.[74]

But Gray was not content to depict Oregon missionaries as outnumbered victims; he also wanted to emphasize their heroism. The mythical Marcus Whitman served this goal perfectly. When Whitman was alive, he and Gray had had a tense relationship: Whitman had been frustrated with Gray's impulsiveness, while Gray was annoyed by Whitman's blunt demeanor.[75] Moreover, Gray had left the Whitman Mission by May 8, 1842, so he had no personal knowledge of Whitman's fateful winter ride of 1842–43.[76] Twenty-three years after Whitman's death, however, Whitman's actions as a missionary appeared prescient, paving the way for mass American migration to Oregon. And Gray now saw himself and Whitman as partners in ensuring American possession of Oregon, with Whitman going "to Washington to . . . defeat the Hudson's Bay Co. and Jesuits" while Gray left the mission to "combine the settlers then in Oregon in a self-sustaining and self-protecting Government."[77]

In his *History,* then, Gray elevated Whitman to the status of pioneer providential hero, foremost among the missionary pioneers. And as Gray reimagined Whitman as a pioneer hero, he also rewrote his own pioneer status: from a discontented manual laborer who abandoned Whitman's mission to a faithful and knowing partner in Whitman's efforts to save Oregon.

Though Gray dedicated only a dozen or so pages of the *History* to the story of Whitman's winter ride, he mentioned Whitman throughout the text as one of the primary heroes of early Oregon history and as a model pioneer. Gray described Whitman as a rough-hewn, stubborn, brave, dedicated figure, one who was not hemmed in by the stolid conventions of eastern gentility or shortsighted institutional fidelity. In Gray's portrait, Whitman was "a man of easy, *don't-care* habits" whose gruff manners, bluntness, and single-mindedness were both a liability and an asset.[78] While "a stranger would consider him fickle and stubborn" (an observation that perhaps betrayed some of Gray's past disagreements with Whitman), Gray asserted that Whitman was actually "sincere and kind, and generous to a fault," devoted wholly to the "objects of the mission," and "seldom manifesting fears of any danger that might surround him."[79] He was, in short, precisely Gray's ideal of a pioneer: a Protestant American who could both extend Anglo-Protestant power to the region and "*rough it*" in the West.[80]

While Gray's description of Whitman served to advance his notion of the model Protestant pioneer, it was Gray's narration of the Whitman Saved Oregon Story that most clearly situated Whitman within Gray's pioneer vision. Gray twice included the story of Whitman's winter ride in his *History;* the first time quoted verbatim from Spalding's lectures and the second time in his own words.[81] In this second retelling Gray depicted Whitman as a solitary hero bound to no authorities except God and country. Gray began with Whitman's arrival in Washington, DC, as Daniel Webster, the epitome of eastern formalism and complacency, stood ready to trade possession of the Oregon Country to Great Britain in exchange for "a small settlement in Maine and the fisheries on the banks of Newfoundland."[82] Gray wrote, "Just at this time, in the dead of winter, an awkward, tall, spare-visaged, vigorous, off-hand sort of a man, appeared at the [State] Department in his mountain traveling garb. . . .

Fig. 4. *Whitman Leaving Home on His Winter Ride to Save Oregon,* from
John Thompson Faris, *Winning the Oregon Country* (New York: Missionary
Education Movement of the United States and Canada, 1911). Marcus and
Narcissa Whitman Collection, Whitman College and Northwest
Archives, Walla Walla, Washington.

[O]n his way to Washington he had not stopped for a moment,
but pressed on with a vigor and energy peculiarly his own."[83] Rejected
by Webster, Whitman demanded an audience with President Tyler
himself.

Gray's account of Whitman's meeting with Tyler served as an ideal-
ization of pioneer authority, as the eyewitness testimony of an old Oregonian triumphed over the interests of powerful institutions. Though the
Hudson's Bay Company, the British government, and Webster himself had
all told Tyler that the Oregon Country was a worthless wasteland, Tyler
decided that Whitman's "personal representations" of the Oregon Country
were more valuable than those of the other parties, and he commissioned
Whitman to lead a wagon train of American settlers to Oregon. Gray concluded, "But that Dr. Whitman ... stood before the President of the United
States the only representative of Oregon and all her future interests and

greatness, a self-constituted, self-appointed, and without parallel self-periled representative ... that he should be able to successfully contend with the combined influences brought against him,—can only be attributed to that overruling power which had decreed that the nation, whose interests he represented, should be sustained."[84]

Here was the essence of Gray's view of providence. Providence was the force that propelled rugged, determined individuals to triumph over both foreign influences and complacent structures of authority for the good of the nation and Protestant Christianity. Providence worked against and in spite of all power structures except truly democratic organizations like the Oregon provisional government. In Gray's history providentialism joined with the lionization of the pioneer to create a pioneer providential history.

This pioneer providentialism was underscored by Gray's depiction of religious authorities. Whereas Spalding's providential history of Whitman had depicted both the ABCFM and Methodist missions as essential to Protestantism's stand against Catholicism in the Oregon Country, Gray's history portrayed all religious authorities, including the missions, as obstructions to providence and the pioneer spirit. Gray argued that Methodist leaders like Jason Lee were every bit as antagonistic to the provisional government as foreigners like the Catholic priests and the Hudson's Bay Company traders because the Methodists wanted to maintain sole authority in the Willamette Valley settlements.[85] More galling to Gray was the fact that the American board and Whitman's missionary companions apparently disapproved of Whitman's journey to Washington. After Whitman visited Washington, DC he visited the board's headquarters in Boston in order to request additional missionary reinforcements. There, Gray wrote, Whitman "met the cold, calculating rebuke for unreasonable expenses, and for dangers incurred without instructions or permission from the mission to come to the States."[86] The mission board refused to compensate Whitman for his journey, so Whitman had to sell "his own little private property" to fund his return trip to Oregon.[87] Worse still, the board had completely omitted Whitman and his associates from their half-century memorial retrospective, effectively erasing Whitman's heroism from the board's public history.[88] Gray regarded even Protestant religious organizations as roadblocks to independent-thinking, providentially ordained individuals. Individual pioneers like

Marcus Whitman, not church authorities or organizations, saved Oregon from becoming a British possession.

Though few critics were enamored of Gray's sprawling narrative and unconventional prose, the *History of Oregon* quickly elevated Gray to relative fame as one of Oregon's most well known historians and a pioneer authority on Oregon's early history.[89] The *History* received attention in local and national newspapers, including the *New York Evangelist,* the *San Francisco Bulletin,* the Portland *Oregonian,* and the *New York Tribune.*[90] Several reviewers expressed misgivings about Gray's accusations against the Hudson's Bay Company, the Catholic missionaries, and Gray's fellow Protestant missionaries. The reviewer for the *New York Tribune* worried that Gray "is too much a partisan to write history," while the reviewer for the Portland, Oregon, *New Northwest* commented, "Though the author's prejudices crop out very forcefully in some places, yet we think he clearly substantiates good reasons for them."[91] Despite these caveats, reviewers unanimously praised the book for its thoroughness and its wealth of primary source information.[92] Other historians quickly turned to the *History* for questions about Oregon's early years, referring to it for everything from the roots of the name Wallamet (now Willamette) to how many Anglo-American settlers there were in Oregon in 1834.[93] The influential historian Hubert Howe Bancroft even offered to delay the publication of his own history of the Pacific Northwest when he heard that Gray might publish a sequel to the *History.* (The sequel never came to fruition).[94]

Historians also turned to Gray as a reliable source for understanding Marcus Whitman's heroism. Over the next twenty years, books, newspaper articles, and other written works would cite Gray as they recounted the story of Whitman's ride to rescue the Pacific Northwest from Great Britain.[95] Spalding's crusade had brought the Whitman Saved Oregon Story into local consciousness and national governmental record, but Gray's *History* brought the story into academic and public historical discourse.

Thus Gray's *History* helped to inaugurate another strain of providential history—pioneer providentialism—while bringing the Whitman Saved Oregon Story to more readers than Spalding had ever reached. Yet the *History* was only one of the ways in which Gray established himself—and Marcus Whitman's legend—as a vital force in Pacific Northwest history. Even as he was writing his *History* Gray was forming Oregon's first state historical society and mobilizing it to build a monument to the newly minted savior of Oregon: Marcus Whitman.

Of Pioneers and Monuments

Gray not only engaged in the writing of pioneer history but also helped create a community of Pacific northwesterners who were devoted to the region's pioneer heritage and to the kind of independent institution building that had so profoundly shaped the Oregon Country's early years. He did so through founding, first, the Oregon Pioneer Society (OPS) and then, when that organization failed to sufficiently advance his vision of Oregon history, the PHS. Intertwined with these efforts was Gray's ongoing quest to build a monument to his former missionary companion Marcus Whitman. These two campaigns—the historical society and the monument—helped further define and establish the ideals of pioneer history while drawing a growing number of northwesterners into formal practices of history making.

Historical societies had been a part of local historical culture in the United States since the Massachusetts Historical Society was founded in 1791.[96] By the time Gray organized the OPS there were over one hundred historical societies in the US.[97] Combining historical research and writing, social gatherings, and local booster activities, historical societies helped to shape and solidify regional identities as well as the historical profession itself.[98]

As America's territorial reach expanded in the nineteenth century, local historical societies cropped up almost as quickly as settlements and governmental structures did. The first historical society in Indiana, for instance, was founded in 1808, eight years before Indiana became a state. The Wisconsin Territorial Legislature established the State Historical Society of Wisconsin in 1846, two years before Wisconsin statehood.[99] These societies helped boost the developing territories by touting their region's heroic founders, unparalleled natural resources, and unique importance to the nation.[100] Historical societies in new territories also aided in the expansion of US empire by elevating the territories' "true," Anglo-American

founders in the face of continuing resistance by Native peoples.[101] Califor-
nians organized the Society of California Pioneers in 1850 in the midst of
settlers' genocidal campaign against Native peoples, while the Historical
Society of Idaho Pioneers was founded in 1881, nine years before Idaho
statehood and only four years after the Nez Perce War of 1877.[102] Historical societies circumscribed the enduring presence of Native peoples in
the West by asserting that their states' true histories began with Anglo-
American settlement, while Indians belonged to a past, prehistoric era.

    In the territories and states of the American West the earliest histori-
cal societies were often pioneer societies. Pioneer societies were interested
in defining and protecting the memory and authority of a region's earliest
Anglo-American settlers.[103] They used membership requirements to separate early settlers from later settlers, men from women, and whites from
nonwhites. The California Society of Pioneers, for instance, originally restricted its First Class membership to men who had arrived in California
prior to 1849 and descendants of those men, while the Historical Society of
Idaho Pioneers restricted membership to men who had arrived in Idaho
Territory before July 4, 1864, and their male descendants.[104] Other exclusions were implied in the wording of pioneer society bylaws or imposed by
society members. Most bylaws included a provision whereby new members had to be voted into the association, ensuring a lasting homogeneity of
race and, often, religion.[105] Moreover, since pioneer society bylaws defined
pioneers as emigrants, Native peoples by definition could not be pioneers;
they could serve only as aids or obstacles to pioneer heroism, bit players in
their own stories.

    In other words when William H. Gray founded his pioneer his-
torical society in the 1870s he did not create its institutional structures
ex nihilo. Rather, he drew from existing patterns of pioneer society organization, adapting these structures to address regional and sectarian
issues. The result was the PHS, an association that helped to establish a
Pacific Northwestern regional identity and historical culture, both
through its own historical efforts and through the debates and fractures
that it sparked.

    The precursor to the PHS was an organization also founded, in
part or in whole, by Gray. On September 8 and 9, 1867, twenty-one white
male Oregon settlers convened in the state House of Representatives in

Salem, Oregon, in order to formally establish the OPS.[106] Few records exist of the OPS's early days, but, according to Hubert Howe Bancroft, William Gray was the "prime mover" in founding the group.[107] The OPS's constitution clearly defined pioneer identity in both membership requirements and directions for public events. Membership was restricted to those who had either been born to American settlers in Oregon or had arrived in Oregon before 1848 and remained in the region for seventeen years. Prospective members had to pay a three-dollar fee and be voted in by the society's existing members, ensuring that no early settler who had offended Oregon's pioneer establishment would be able to join the organization. Once a year the OPS was to have a procession in which members would march in order of the years they had arrived in the Oregon Country and wear badges with their emigration year "in a conspicuous place on his or her person."[108]

The men who founded the OPS had been part of an informal network of pioneers for years, characterized by their involvement in local government, business, and churches, their correspondence with one another, and their interest in regional history. In addition to Gray, they included Oregon's governor, George L. Woods; the businessman Alex P. Ankeny; and the former superintendent of Indian affairs J. W. Nesmith. Many of the founders had been connected with the Methodist missions in Oregon, and about half were active members of Protestant churches.[109]

But the society's membership is instructive for whom it excluded as well as included. There were no women among the founders. None of the members were Catholic, Native American, mixed-race, or connected to the Hudson's Bay Company.[110] While OPS did not expressly prohibit these populations from joining, the historical practices it advanced were designed to celebrate and valorize white, male, Anglo-American, broadly Protestant (or at least non-Catholic) settlers. In this way the society helped to promote the Oregon Country's Anglo-American Protestants as the true founders of the region and arbiters of its history.

Although the OPS's structure, rhetoric, and membership accorded with Gray's own ideals in many ways, by 1871 Gray had begun to feel that its approach was insufficient for his historical goals. As Bancroft has noted, the OPS was focused primarily on reunions and other social events, while Gray wanted an association that prioritized the collection and interpretation of historical documents.[111] While still serving as a member of the OPS Gray began to recruit Oregonians to a new society of his own invention: the PHS. A circular for the new society announced the PHS's documentary focus: "Its object shall be to collect, callate [*sic*], and publish, as soon as its funds will justify, sketches of the early discovery, settlement and settlers of the country. To prepare for, collect and preserve, all records of the past and present History of Oregon Territory and its several subdivisions. To establish a Public Library, and Reading Room. Securing, by voluntary subscription, the service, or by purchase, the aid of the press, in carrying forward its objects, and promoting social intercourse among its members."[112] Unlike the OPS, the PHS focused on producing authoritative histories of the Pacific Northwest.

Most of those whom Gray recruited to the PHS responded with great interest out of both a sense of duty to their adopted region and an eagerness to share their stories. J. C. Bell stated that the gathering of oral and written historical material was "an imperative duty we owe to those who sacrificed their lives to promote the interest of this Country," while Sam McKean wrote to Gray, "I felt truly gratified—I was pleased to my very *center*" that the PHS was interested in his personal reminiscences.[113] The reasons for Gray's successful recruitment are clear: he not only suggested that pioneers' experiences were worthy of preservation but also invited pioneers to serve as arbiters of Oregon history.

The PHS convened for its first full meeting on February 22, 1872.[114] The society was similar to the OPS in several ways: it was interested in defining pioneers as a select group of Oregonians, it excluded nonwhites and foreigners from full membership, and it included many members of Oregon's Protestant establishment.[115] On paper the PHS also maintained the same divisions between pioneers and nonpioneers that the OPS did. Those who had arrived in Oregon before 1848 could be elected corresponding members of the PHS, whereas those who had arrived after could be elected only as honorary members. While both corresponding and honorary members were allowed to vote in PHS matters, only the former could be addressed as pioneers, ensuring that "pioneer" remained an honorary title for a privileged few.[116]

Yet the PHS also differed from the OPS in significant ways. It held its meetings in Astoria, the site of the first Anglo-American settlement in the Oregon Country, rather than in Salem, the state capital. Astoria was closer to Gray's home than Salem, and Gray felt that its residents had been more supportive of his efforts than the authorities in Salem.[117] Salem was home to two power structures with which Gray had a testy relationship: the state government and the old Methodist mission. Astoria accorded better with Gray's vision of the Pacific Northwest as a place defined by the bravery of a few settlers working largely outside the structures of church and state.[118]

In addition to the difference in locations the PHS's mission was more explicitly historical than that of the OPS. It was clear from the PHS's inception that Gray intended it to rank among the top historical societies of the nation. The PHS collected biographical information from all of its members as well as primary and secondary source documents for its library.[119] Members of the PHS debated various historical questions at annual meetings. As the recording secretary of the PHS Gray corresponded with organizations like the State Historical Society of Wisconsin, the Southern Historical Society, the American Antiquarian Society, and the United States Centennial Commission, requesting and sending documents, soliciting and giving information, and advocating throughout the nation the importance of Oregon history.[120] In these ways the PHS defined and advanced the status of Oregon pioneers while moving beyond pioneer boosting to professionalization.

Yet for all his interest in professionalization, Gray nonetheless intended the PHS to advance a particular kind of history: one that, like Gray's writings, prioritized the Oregon Country's preterritorial years, criticized the Hudson's Bay Company and Catholics, and, most of all, lauded specific providential heroes like Marcus and Narcissa Whitman. The work of the PHS in collecting and debating historical materials gave this history the burnish of historical authority. If Gray's conclusions were supported by the work of an entire society of historians, then they could not be discounted as mere sectarian or nationalist propaganda. "Our Historical Society have carefully collected all the facts and documents ... that which enables them to speak from reliable testimony," Gray wrote to the secretaries of the ABCFM. He continued, "There can be no question as to the intent and designs of the British Government to hold Oregon by the influence and power of the Hudson's Bay Company ... and that Dr. Whitman

... was the cause of their defeat."[121] Addresses at the PHS's annual meetings echoed these claims. For instance, George Henry Atkinson's address of 1876 repeated the tale of Whitman saving Oregon from the British and praised the early Anglo-American settlers and missionaries for resisting the Hudson's Bay Company and "secret religious foes and plotters."[122] Atkinson concluded, in phrasing that combined Spalding's providentialism with Gray's pioneer boosting, "As the peaceful and successful founders of a Christian State, the American colonists in Oregon have been clearly led by the Prince of Peace. ... When the future historian shall write up the records of this State for the hundreds of thousands who will dwell where we do now, it will be his pleasant duty to inscribe the highest honors to the pioneer American colonists of Oregon, and place the name of the martyr, Whitman, above them all."[123]

The PHS thus both provided the structure for a practicing historical community and directed that historical practice toward projects that would reinforce Gray's opinions of the Pacific Northwest's past. But its most enduring legacy would be to bring the legacy of Marcus Whitman into public historical discourse through its campaign to "place the name of the martyr, Whitman, above them all." It reached this goal via a campaign to build a monument to Whitman, but while that effort brought public attention to the Whitman Saved Oregon Story it also unwittingly helped generate the seeds of that story's downfall.

Gray was not the first to suggest a monument to Marcus Whitman, but he was certainly the most vocal about it. In fact, in 1874, when Gray began his monument campaign, there had already been several attempts to memorialize Whitman. Cushing Eells had been working since 1859 to establish a school on the Whitman Mission grounds in honor of Whitman's work. This school, eventually restructured as Whitman College, served as a locus for the memorialization and popularization of Whitman in the 1890s.[124] Cushing's son Edwin Eells had attempted to introduce a bill in the Washington Territorial Legislature in 1869 to build a monument to Whitman, but the bill failed.[125] Two years later the Washington Territorial Legislator W. P. Winans successfully campaigned to name a county in Washington Territory after Whitman.[126] But Gray was not interested in a school or a county name: he wanted a statue. As he wrote to a member of the PHS, "Many men and warriors of much less merit . . . the Nation now delight to honor, in erecting over their remains a costly monument" while "Oregon's first volunteer and faithful Representative" Marcus Whitman had no such distinction.[127] Gray decided to mobilize the PHS to rectify that situation, initiating a campaign that would begin in 1874 but not come to fruition until after Gray's death.

Gray's desire for a physical monument was in keeping with trends in American public history in the 1870s. The Civil War had claimed the lives of at least 620,000 Americans. As the historian David Blight has argued, this unprecedented number of war casualties produced new interest in and practices of memorialization. Northern and southern women began decorating the graves of the dead with flowers in the earliest years of the Civil War, and by 1868 Memorial Day or Decoration Day had become an unofficial holiday in both the North and South.[128] The building of monuments was a more elaborate memorial undertaking that had the potential to unite still-grieving communities through the labor of fundraising and the ritual of monument unveiling. According to Blight, "By the 1890s hardly a city square, town green, or even some one-horse crossroads lacked a Civil War memorial of some kind."[129]

Monuments also served a civic purpose, helping to advance the notion of noble sacrifice that both the Union and the Confederacy embraced in their attempts to make sense of the war's losses.[130] Such language, like the story of Whitman, was shrouded in the language of providence. Mourning Americans on both sides described fallen soldiers as martyrs in a war ultimately brought on by God's mysterious will. The notion of providence both allowed for the possibility of sectional reconciliation by obscuring the war's concrete causes and politicized the war more deeply by embedding it in a broadly Protestant vision of national destiny.[131]

The Pacific Northwest had not experienced anywhere near the same kind of Civil War casualties as the eastern and southern parts of the nation. But northwesterners were aware of the memorialization projects being undertaken in other parts of the country. In 1875 the *Oregon City Enterprise* reported that "for soldiers killed in the civil war, eighty-five thousand headstones have already been completed in West Rutland, Vt."[132] Newspapers also covered the difficulties in completing the Washington Monument, a project that had taken on new importance as a symbol of national unity in the post–Civil War era.[133]

While Civil War casualties remained distant from many western-
ers' experiences, postbellum Pacific northwesterners were dealing with
losses of their own. The first generation of pioneers was dying. "The pioneers are fast departing. Father Walker & Mother Eells, Father Spaulding
[*sic*] & Mother Griffin, Mother Gray & Father Powers have all passed
over the river. How many more, I do not know," the PHS member W. A.
Tenney wrote to Gray in 1885.[134] Drawing attention to the Northwest's
pioneer heritage was an ideal way to demonstrate that though the Oregon Country had not suffered through the Civil War like the rest of the
nation had, it had its own tradition of noble sacrifice and patriotic martyrdom. The proposal to memorialize Whitman by means of a monument thus arrived at an opportune time. Monument building and
memorial ceremonies were on the upswing nationally, and northwesterners were looking for ways to promote their own history.

On February 21, 1874, Gray convinced the members of the PHS to
form the Whitman Monument Association. Gray, not surprisingly, was
appointed chairman, and prominent Astoria citizens rounded out the
committee: the PHS president T. P. Powers, John Hobson, W. D. Hare,
and A. Van Dusen. The committee determined to send canvassers to as
many counties as possible within the old Oregon Country in order to
solicit contributions.[135] It also prepared an address to be circulated
throughout the Northwest, one that utilized the language of martyrdom,
memorial, and sacrifice that was sweeping the nation. The address
opened, "It has ever been the custom of States and Nations, where Christianity and civilization prevails, to perpetuate the memories of great and
good men,—benefactors of mankind; and if we neglect longer to do justice to the memory of that noble and self-sacrificing martyr, we shall
prove ourselves unworthy of the enjoyment of the blessings and privi-
leges that now surround us, through his self-sacrificing efforts."[136]

After appealing to their readers' memorializing interests, the address then detailed the story of Whitman saving Oregon, told in Gray's
signature mode. Upon learning that Oregon was to be traded "for a tri-
fling consideration," Whitman, "without aid or counsel from any source,"
declared he would travel to Washington, DC, "brav[ing] mountain tem-
pests, and fac[ing] every danger" to save Oregon. "If any man, since the
days of Washington, deserves to be held in remembrance by his country-

men, and honored for his noble deeds, and sacrifices for patriotism and
truth—it is Dr. Marcus Whitman," the committee argued. The address
concluded, "In the name of the martyrd [sic] dead we make this appeal to
our generous people, hoping they will respond with willing hearts and
liberal hands."[137] The Pacific Northwest may not have played a central
part in the Civil War, but it now had its own patriotic heroes and martyred dead.

Despite the lofty language of the monument proposal and the willingness of a few volunteers to canvass assertively, the monument failed
to get enough contributions for the committee to proceed. The *Willamette Farmer* reported in 1877 that only $130.80 had been donated to
the fund, along with another $256.50 in unpaid pledges—nowhere near
enough to fund a major monument.[138] Gray lamented, "During the three
years we have been canvassing for funds we have procured but a small
amount in *cash* and *promises*."[139] Gray, always keen to suspect foreign
and Catholic intrigue, attributed the difficulties to Hudson's Bay Company and Catholic interference.[140] But there were other reasons for the
limited response. The monument Gray proposed would be expensive,
costing at least $5,000 for materials and transportation.[141] Furthermore,
the association had no land on which to put the monument. Gray insisted that the monument be built on the old mission grounds, where
Whitman and the other victims of the mission attack had been buried in
a mass grave.[142] However, that land was now owned by a farmer, Charles
Swegle, who was not interested in selling it.[143]

Yet Gray and the other PHS members did not give up so easily. In
1880, after a several-year hiatus, the Monument Association resumed its
campaign in earnest. The association convinced Swegle to donate the
two acres of land surrounding the Whitman Mission grave on the promise that the monument would be completed within five years.[144] It also
approved a design for the memorial. Gray had envisioned a statue of
Whitman holding a Bible in one hand and a flag in the other, but Reverend J. H. Hopkins, a prominent Episcopal clergyman from Williamsport,
Pennsylvania, recommended the winning design: a thirty-three- by
seven-foot Celtic cross made of Oregon granite. The Celtic cross would
be simpler and cheaper to carve than a statue, but the main motivation
for the design was its anti-Catholic symbolism. The cross, according to

Hopkins, dated from "the ancient ages, before Romanism was introduced" and would thus stand as a clear affront to Catholicism. An open Bible, a bald eagle, and the United States shield would be carved on panels at the bottom of the cross, underscoring the links between Protestantism and nationalism.[145] With the design and the land secured, Gray began soliciting quotes from lumber salesmen, stoneworkers, and granite suppliers. The Monument Association secured a donation of lumber for the fence and a promise of donation for the stone. The association also managed to harness some of the booster energy that was driving development in Walla Walla, the home of Whitman College and the closest town to the former Whitman Mission. While the Oregon Territorial Legislature rejected a bill to appropriate ten thousand dollars to the Whitman Monument, perhaps because of the monument's location in Washington Territory, the city of Walla Walla embraced the cause, offering to place the monument in front of the city courthouse.[146]

Gray was able to use local newspapers to keep the monument campaign in the public eye. The *Oregonian,* the *Walla Walla Statesman,* the *Astorian,* the *Willamette Farmer,* the *Dalles* [Ore.] *Times,* the *North Pacific Coast,* and the *Lewiston* [Ida.] *Teller* all published updates on the monument campaign.[147] Gray also cast a wider net for support, utilizing Protestant networks to recruit fundraising canvassers in the East and publishing letters from supportive easterners in northwestern papers. The *Astorian* for January 26, 1881, reported on letters received from two eastern supporters: William Augustus Mowry, a New England educator and eventual Whitman biographer, and John Henry Hopkins Jr., who had submitted the aforementioned Whitman Monument design. "With the hearty co-operation of such gentlemen as Hon. William A. Mowry and Rev. J. H. Hopkins," stated the paper "Mr. Gray can feel assured that the monument will be erected in due time."[148]

The newspaper coverage ensured that the tale of Whitman saving Oregon would be repeated frequently in print. Every announcement regarding the monument repeated the story, so that the very ubiquity of the reports gave the story the patina of factuality. Early reports on the Whitman Monument stated the matter more tentatively. A journalist for the *New Northwest* wrote, in 1874, shortly after the beginning of the monument campaign, "It is claimed—truthfully without a doubt—that mainly by the efforts of Dr. Whitman was the United States Government prevented from relinquishing her hold upon the region."[149] By 1880 regional newspapers were describing the same story as part of the "facts of history," supported by the testimonies of Whitman's fellow missionaries and the abundant documentary "proof" that "Great Britain made every effort to keep Oregon."[150]

But the very media attention the campaign received caused its downfall. As the Whitman Monument project increasingly brought Whitman into the public eye, it raised the hackles of several Pacific northwesterners who had doubted the Whitman Saved Oregon Story for years. As the monument became a very real possibility, these skeptics went public with their concerns. Their critiques sparked the Whitman controversy, a public debate that pitted the Whitman doubters against the Whitman boosters and, in the process, forge new understandings of history and secularism in the Oregon Country.

The First Whitman Controversy and the Makings of Pioneer Secularism

The Whitman Saved Oregon Story had its detractors ever since Spalding began to circulate the tale publicly in the 1860s. As I noted in chapter 2, the Oregon Country's Catholics denied the story from the beginning, but their objections did not reach beyond the Catholic press. Other Oregonians had also questioned the story. Some were pioneers who had been in the Oregon Country while Whitman was still alive and wondered why they had never heard him speak of such a notable act of heroism.[151] Others were researchers—journalists, writers, political figures, and historians—whose findings led them to question the key points of the story as well as Spalding's and Gray's veracity.

The first of these skeptics to publish her conclusions was Frances Fuller Victor, the Oregon writer, historian, and researcher for the famed historian Hubert Howe Bancroft. Victor was a relative latecomer to the Oregon Country, but like many Oregonians she knew the experiences of migration and self-reinvention. Born in 1826 in Rome, New York, Victor gradually moved West with her parents and sisters, from New York to Pennsylvania to Ohio. Her first marriage brought Victor to Nebraska

Territory, but she and her husband quickly separated. In 1862 Frances Fuller married Henry Victor, a naval engineer whose work brought the couple to San Francisco and then to Oregon.[152] Victor was already a writer when she came West, but the Pacific Northwest provided both a historical community and seemingly endless material for inspiration. She began corresponding with historians, including William Gray, Elwood Evans, and the influential Oregon judge Matthew Deady.[153] In 1870, the same year Gray published his *History*, Victor published *River of the West*, a depiction of the Oregon Country as told by the famous mountain man Joe Meek. Meek had no love for the Oregon missionaries, Methodist or ABCFM, and *River of the West* reflected those views. While Victor's book repeated the story of Whitman saving Oregon, it also, like Gray's *History*, accused the Methodist missions of being devoted to worldly gain. The Methodist missionaries, according to Victor, were "well-to-do, and continually increasing their worldly goods by sharp bargains and general acquisitiveness," so that they became "the aristocracy of American Oregon."[154] Victor's acerbic, witty critiques of the early Methodist missionaries would have been enough to cause controversy among Oregon's Protestant establishment, but more upsetting for the missionaries was Victor's comparatively positive portrayal of Oregon's early Catholic missionaries. "A little more of the same Jesuitical spirit would have softened and brightened the character of those [Protestant] missionaries to the future historian of Oregon," remarked Victor, scandalizing her Protestant readers.[155]

The depiction of missionaries in *River of the West* embroiled Victor in a public dispute with the former Methodist missionary Jesse Quinn Thornton. From 1870 to 1871 Victor and Thornton engaged in a scathing debate printed in the *Pacific Christian Advocate*, based in Portland, Oregon. Thornton argued that the book's irreverent treatment of the missions and of Christianity in general would compromise public morals. Thornton wrote, "Readers will seek in vain to find upon any of [*River of the West's*] pages a serious recognition of Christianity in any of its forms and aspects as the faith of the writer; or a sentence which embodies the idea of a Deity, who in her view of the subject, ever concerns himself in the affairs of men or even of nations."[156] In other words, Victor's text was not sufficiently providential; it made no mention of the hand of God in the events of the Pacific Northwest, nor did it privilege Protestant figures and viewpoints. Victor responded, "My course had been from the first, in gathering the material for my book, one of impartial hearing of all sides; that I had sought information far and wide, of all classes and denominations alike; that if there was a party who had not had a fair hearing, it was their own fault. I felt that I had shaken together and sifted the beliefs of all Oregon in writing my book."[157] It was this claim to impartiality—an impartiality based on the examination of primary sources without the framing of providential assumptions—that frustrated Victor's critics. The controversy faded within the year, neither side gaining a clear upper hand. It was not the last time Victor ran afoul of Oregon's old missionary community, however, nor the last time that two opposing views of history clashed in the Pacific Northwest.

Victor continued to write over the next few years, publishing the travelogue *All Over Oregon and Washington* in 1872 and beginning research for a volume on the Pacific Northwest's Indian wars.[158] But in 1875 her husband died in a shipwreck, forcing her to write for others in order to make ends meet.[159] In 1878 the San Francisco historian Hubert Howe Bancroft enlisted Victor to research and write for his multivolume US history series. Using Bancroft's massive historical library and his plan for the organization of the series, Victor and other contract writers drafted histories that Bancroft then published under his own name. While the extent of Victor's authorship is debated, it is likely she wrote the entirety of Bancroft's two-volume *History of Oregon,* all of the *History of Washington, Idaho and Montana,* and substantial portions of at least five other Bancroft works.[160] It was work for which Victor was underrecognized and underpaid. "Last year I wrote or worked fifty one weeks, every day except Sundays from 8 o clock in the morning until 6 in the evening," Victor lamented in 1879. Later in the letter, she added, "I often wish to do something for myself or to vary my theme, but have not the strength left."[161] Yet this work gave Victor the resources to explore more fully the Whitman Saved Oregon Story—an exploration that ultimately convinced her that the story was a fraud.

While writing *River of the West,* Victor had already discovered some inconsistencies in Gray's account of Whitman, but she still drew from portions of his *History* to give an abbreviated version of the Whitman

Saved Oregon Story.[162] The resources at Bancroft's library allowed Victor to find information on Whitman's 1842–43 ride that supported her initial doubts regarding the Whitman story. First, fishing rights along the eastern US–Canada border had been settled in the Treaty of 1818, so Spalding's tale of trading Oregon for a codfishery was utterly false.[163] Second, Spalding and Gray stated that the Oregon trade was proposed as part of the Ashburton Treaty of 1842, but negotiations on that treaty did not address the Oregon boundary. Even if Oregon had been discussed in the treaty proceedings, the negotiations had been concluded before Whitman's arrival in the East, so Whitman could not have influenced the treaty. Third, Whitman's available correspondence made no mention of treaty negotiations, only of mission business. In 1879 Victor wrote to her friend Elwood Evans, "I have entirely and completely unravelled [sic] the tangles that troubled you (and me) in 1870. The whole story is plain as A.B.C. You would enjoy the unfolding."[164]

Victor's information was enough to convince Evans, who had been harboring his own doubts about the Whitman story. Since 1864, when he had convinced Gray to start writing history, Evans had grown increasingly frustrated with Gray's "bitter, arrogant egotism" and relentless self-promotion.[165] He had also began to doubt the accounts of other Oregon missionaries like Henry Harmon Spalding, who he believed to be blinded by his "educated fanaticism," and Cushing Eells, who he saw as "an old man in his dotage" who had been duped by the other missionaries into believing the story of Whitman's heroic journey.[166] In the mid-1870s Evans was appointed territorial librarian of Washington Territory, and the position allowed him to access a wider array of documents on Pacific Northwest history.[167] He also began corresponding with former Hudson's Bay Company traders and early American settlers who knew Whitman personally. By 1880 Evans felt confident that he would be able to repudiate the " 'ridiculous twaddle' that Oregon was saved to the United States by a private citizen."[168]

As the Monument Association, with Gray at the helm, continued to raise the profile of the Whitman Saved Oregon Story, Victor and Evans worried that the Whitman Monument project would make Pacific northwesterners look ridiculous. Victor wrote to Evans, "The Historical Society of Astoria, of which Gray is the head and Grout will make fools of themselves by erecting a monument to Dr Whitman as the man who 'saved Oregon to the United States.' How Gray ever conceived the idea I do not know. Certain it is wrong whether intentionally or not. He will make Oregon a laughing stock for future generations if he persists in this thing. Dr Whitman and his wife should have a monument like any other good Christian folk; but the Daniel Webster story, and the Cod Fishery story and all the rest is bosh."[169] Victor's first plan to stop the Whitman Monument was to have Evans approach Gray quietly and inform him of his errors. "Cannot you present these facts to him privately, by letter, and stop the ridiculous nonsense," inquired Victor. "*Me* he would suspect of not holding a *missionary* in sufficient veneration."[170] But it soon became clear that Gray and other influential Oregonians were wholly devoted to making Marcus Whitman's alleged heroism as public as possible. Victor and Evans would have to make their objections public as well.

The opportunity arose following the publication of an article by Samuel Asahel Clarke, a journalist and Oregon pioneer of 1851, in the *Californian* of July 1880. The article, entitled "How Dr. Whitman Saved Oregon," told the Whitman story in enthusiastic fashion and made a plea for donations to the Whitman Monument Association.[171] Victor saw a possibility to print her findings, prepared as a rebuttal to Clarke, and the editors of the *Californian* obliged. In an article entitled "Did Dr. Whitman Save Oregon?" Victor presented her evidence about the treaty negotiations of 1842, arguing that "[Whitman] could say nothing [the government] did not already know; and as to the folly said to have been contemplated by Mr. Webster, of 'trading off Oregon for a cod-fishery,' it will be seen by the treaties quoted, that the fishery question had been settled ... 'forever,' by the convention of 1818." Perhaps to appease Whitman's many defenders, Victor concluded that the Whitman Saved Oregon Story was ultimately an injustice to Whitman, who "would have scorned to claim for himself honors which he had never won." Indeed, Victor asserted, "it is ... no kindness to his memory to place him in a false position, from which the reader of encyclopædias could easily rout him."[172]

"Did Dr. Whitman Save Oregon?" was the first published article to call into question the Whitman Saved Oregon Story. The article represented the beginning of the first Whitman controversy, the struggle between pro- and anti-Whitman partisans to control the legacy of Marcus

Whitman in public memory. The Whitman controversy raged for six years before fading and then being resurrected in 1900. It was a struggle to define not only Whitman's importance to the Pacific Northwest but also the parameters of history itself. Via the Whitman controversy, Victor, Evans, and their allies sought to champion a new kind of history: pioneer secularism.

Pioneer secular history was like pioneer providential history in several respects: it was concerned with creating a regional identity and a noble past for western settlers; it celebrated Anglo-American western expansion and upheld certain individuals as moral exemplars; and it appealed to local experience in order to bolster the historical authority of such models. But pioneer secular history diverged in basic ways from providential history. Its writers were, like Christian Smith's secularizers, largely outsiders to the Protestant establishment who sought to free Pacific Northwest history from Protestant dominance.[173] Victor was a Unitarian; Evans had been excommunicated from the Hicksite Quaker community of his youth for marrying a non-Quaker.[174] Other Whitman doubters, including Matthew Deady, Jesse Applegate, and Bancroft, were ambivalent about the Oregon Protestant mainline of Presbyterians, Methodists, and Congregationalists, and their research into early Oregon Protestants' letters and diaries did little to counter these sentiments. "Verily, crooked are the ways of the servants of the Lord in Oregon," Victor wrote to Evans after researching some of the maneuvers of Oregon's pioneer Protestant leaders.[175]

The pioneer secularists were outsiders in other ways as well. Compared to pioneer providentialists like Gray, most of the secularists were relative latecomers to the Oregon Country. Deady had arrived in the Northwest in 1849, Evans in 1852, and Victor in 1864. None of them held the coveted status of being pre-1848 pioneers. In addition, Victor's gender and family status precluded her from being a pioneer insider: she was a previously divorced, childless woman. In a tradition dating back to Spalding's lectures about Narcissa Whitman and Eliza Spalding, Pacific Northwest pioneer culture lionized Protestant women settlers as "pioneer mothers," women whose work of making homes and raising children in the West was crucial to the civilization of the frontier.[176] Though these women were honored in pioneer writings and ceremonies, they were neither expected nor encouraged to participate in recording and debating Northwest history. By contrast, Victor, who once described herself as "a bit of a blue[stocking]," actively encouraged women to seek fulfillment outside of the homemaking pursuits that defined the pioneer mother ideal. Victor's historical writing was an inextricable part of her quest to "establish the precedent of an intelligent, independent womanhood" not dependent on the opinions of men.[177] All of the secularizers were criticized for not being true pioneers, but the sharpest words were saved for Victor, whose very existence as a female pioneer historian called into question the boundaries of pioneer history and identity.

The pioneer secularizers resented the power of the Pacific Northwest's Protestant establishment and generally believed that any kind of religious bias was antithetical to a modernizing West. In their view freedom from religious bias was crucial to western identity. Secularizers believed—rightly—that many pioneers had come to the Oregon Country to be free of denominational constraints, and they identified these nonpious pioneers as the true founders of the Pacific Northwest. The secularist position became markedly clear in the late 1870s and early 1880s, when Pacific northwesterners, along with Americans across the nation, debated President Ulysses S. Grant's call for nonsectarian public schools. Elwood Evans, serving as speaker of the Washington Territorial Legislature, explained that in Washington Territory's public schools "books of a sectarian character are excluded as text-books, and no denominational doctrine is permitted to be taught."[178] The editors of the *West Shore,* a Portland literary magazine to which Frances Fuller Victor often contributed essays, wrote of the common school question in starker terms: "We believe we are giving expression to the honest expressions of every true Pacific coaster, when we say that our untrammeled, free-and-easy ways of living, doing business and enjoying life should never be exchanged for the strait-laced, sectarian methods that invariably obtain in the older States of our Union."[179] In the same way that pioneer secularizers sought an education system free of "sectarian methods," they also sought a nonsectarian history untainted by the bitter Protestant–Catholic conflict that had characterized early Oregon history.[180]

To advance their vision of a nonsectarian history pioneer secularizers appealed to local authority in terms that would lead to controversy with pioneer providentialists over the meaning of pioneer authority. While pioneer providentialists argued that historical authority was bound up in eyewitness testimony, pioneer secularists held that eyewitness testimony alone was unreliable and that historical authority rested on the meticulous interpretation of primary source documents to verify eyewitness accounts. As Evans wrote in his research notes, "I had too generously, too hastily believed Gray, Spalding, Atkinson.... I now, however, possess such *data* as leads me to a different, but I have no doubt, a *proper conclusion*." The acceptable data, Evans specified elsewhere in the document, were "facts, memoranda or documents," not the assurance of eyewitnesses.[181]

The secularists' prioritizing of primary source documents was not unique to the Pacific Northwest. Across the United States and Europe the nature of historical research was changing. Prior to the 1870s most American history writing was undertaken by nonprofessionals relying heavily on existing secondary source histories. This practice began to change in the late 1870s when German-trained historians such as Herbert Baxter Adams introduced European historical methods to the American academy. At the same time, university-based historians like Adams began to push for the professionalization of academic history, establishing clear standards of practice that separated university-based historical practice from the work of nonuniversity historians. Arguably the foremost of these standards was that historical writing must be based in original research in primary source documents.[182]

As primary sources became increasingly central to the practice of academic history, eyewitness testimony came under increasing scrutiny. In the post–Civil War era scientific magazines and journals explored the unreliability of memory.[183] Of special concern was the finding that eyewitnesses could recall events falsely even when they believed themselves to be reporting them accurately and honestly. As the neurologist George Miller Beard wrote in *Popular Science*, "The value of human testimony is impaired . . . through the emotions acting upon the reason, slowly, it may be, and unconsciously, so as to produce in due time sincere but utterly untrue convictions in regard to facts of observation."[184]

These changes had import for historians of the Oregon Country, where pioneer authority was largely constructed on eyewitness experience of and participation in the Oregon Country's early years of white American settlement. Historians of the Pacific Northwest had been collecting original documents and using them as evidence since the beginning of Oregon history writing. But earlier accounts, like those of Spalding, Brouillet, and Gray, had drawn equally heavily on eyewitness accounts, including and especially the memories of the writers. Reliance on memory and testimony was necessary in part because there was little or no documentation of many early events in the Oregon Country, as early settlers often lacked the time, supplies, or education to keep written records. Even those records that were made could be lost to fires, floods, frequent relocation, and other exigencies of western life. In the absence of eyewitness testimony some events would vanish from history altogether.[185] Eyewitness testimony was also necessary to the pioneers because it allowed them to smooth the rough edges of extant sources, adding context and mitigating unflattering information. Some pioneer documents, notably personal letters and diaries, had never been intended for public consumption. They included embarrassing details about petty arguments, grudges, discouragements, and failures.[186] The privileging of primary sources meant that eyewitnesses had less control over how narratives of early pioneer history were presented. The pioneer secularists' emphasis on source documents thus posed a triple threat to pioneer providentialists: it undermined the authority of pioneer experience, omitted information for which documentation could not be supplied, and risked exposing scandalous information about the Oregon Country's early Anglo-American settlers, especially the first Protestant missionaries.

The pioneer providentialists thus found themselves faced with a new class of historians who came from outside the pioneer Protestant establishment, rejected providential explanations of historical events, and insisted that primary source documents were more reliable than the memories of pioneers. If the Whitman Saved Oregon Story was proved to be false, the methods the providentialists used to create it would be considered suspect as well. The stakes of the debate became clearer in an article Victor published in the *Astorian* in 1881.[187] Gray's account of Marcus Whitman, Victor wrote, was "a tissue of fictions."[188] Victor's research had convinced her that it was impossible for Whitman to have influenced treaty negotiations in 1843, and furthermore, that Whitman had not

traveled east for patriotic reasons at all. Instead, Victor argued, Whitman
had gone directly to the ABCFM headquarters in Boston to protest the
ordered closure of the Cayuse mission so as not to lose his mission land
and the improvements he had made on it. In order to make this case Victor detailed the problems the board missionaries had faced—and
caused—in the Oregon Country: missionary infighting, "the bad conduct
of the Indians, and hopelessness of the mission among them, and the
expense, being situated far inland, and in no sense self-supporting."[189]
There was no secret Jesuit plot or codfishery trade, Victor asserted. The
real reasons for Whitman's ride were neither patriotic nor pious. On the
contrary, they revealed the fractures in a deeply dysfunctional missionary
community obsessed with petty slights and material gain.

The missionaries had documented many of these problems in their
writings, but pioneer providentialists had overlooked these details, pre-
ferring the eyewitness accounts that painted a more flattering picture of
the missions. The revelation undermined providentialists' claims that
Whitman had traveled across the continent to save Oregon from becoming a British possession. More broadly, it demonstrated that the
providentialists' reliance on eyewitness testimony and deference to missionary honor had resulted in misleading and inaccurate history. "I cannot pretend to say what the object of Mr. Gray in adopting the fiction
which he has imposed on the world as history," Victor wrote. "But this I
do say, and I can substantiate it; that until Mr. Gray, about 1866, set this
story afloat, nobody had ever heard of it." Victor acknowledged that
there were old pioneers who believed the story, but she attributed that to
their faulty memory of "events of more than twenty years before." She
concluded, "These circumstances remind me of what I once heard an
intelligent man say about evidences in court, that no two witnesses who
had seen the same thing, told the same story about it, and that people
often swore to lies."[190] Victor's exposé threatened missionaries' credibility as well as the established story of Whitman's heroism.

Gray responded to Victor's criticisms with a six-article series in the
Astorian.[191] The series reasserted Gray's claims about Whitman and the
terms of pioneer providential history—terms that Victor's historical
writing violated. Gray identified Victor as a writer "whom we believe to
be a woman possessed of a peculiar talent," a "quibbler" who "seeks no-

toriety."[192] He argued that just as Catholic missionaries had sought "not only to divide and destroy the American missions but the American settlements in Oregon," now Victor sought to "destroy the character and good name of the dead, and of the living."[193] By identifying Victor as a woman working outside and against the Northwest's Protestant settler community, Gray declared her to be an outsider to the pioneer historical establishment, a person who was by both gender and disposition unable to accurately represent Oregon's history. To counter Victor's critiques, Gray cited a number of pioneers—white, Anglo-American, male early settlers—who had testified to hearing Whitman discuss the political importance of his 1842–43 journey and his role in the Emigration of 1843.[194] In direct contradiction to Victor, Gray insisted that the testimonies of these "good witnesses" took precedent over written documents.[195]

Gray was the most prominent pioneer providentialist to take up the critiques of Victor and Evans, but he was not the only one. Other Pacific northwesterners, including the newspaper editor Edward Carpenter Ross and Myron Eells, the son of Whitman's compatriot and Whitman College founder Cushing Eells, rose to defend the Whitman story and its pioneer providential moorings. In 1884 Gray partnered with Ross and Myron Eells to collect their previously published defenses of Whitman into a pamphlet entitled *The Whitman Controversy*.[196] The *Whitman Controversy* articles demonstrated the extent to which the pioneer secularists had forced the pioneer providentialists to modify the terms of their arguments. Whereas Whitman's defenders had not felt the need to refer to primary source documents in their earlier work, they now contended with the pressures of advancing documentary evidence. The problem was that many of the aspects of Whitman's winter journey had little or no known documentation. The *Whitman Controversy* writers found themselves appealing to documentary evidence that no longer—or, in some cases, had never—existed. The records of the Oregon missions' meetings, including the meeting at which Whitman allegedly divulged his reasons for traveling to the east, allegedly disappeared during the attack on Whitman's mission.[197] A letter Whitman sent from Washington, DC was lost in "the great freshet in the Willamette about New Year's Day, 1853."[198] Many of Cushing Eells's historical documents were destroyed in a house fire in 1872.[199] In the absence of primary source evidence for Whitman's heroism, Whitman's defenders

relied on origin stories for once-extant documentary evidence that supported their case.

Even as the three authors capitulated in some ways to the pioneer
secularists' critiques, however, the articles firmly defended the assumptions of pioneer providential history: the trustworthiness of eyewitness
testimony, the centrality of pioneer authority, and the workings of providence in historical events. The authors argued that although memory
could sometimes be unreliable, documentary evidence could never sup-
plant the testimonies of those who had experienced Oregon's early days
for themselves. "The question is one of personal knowledge of events
that occurred in Oregon in 1842," Gray argued, not the "big Oregon historical rat's nest" of documents that Victor and Evans had collected.[200]
Gray and his cohistorians depicted what they saw as the absurdity of
Pacific Northwest latecomers like Evans and Victor determining what
still-living pioneers had seen or done. Ross wrote, "At the time [William
Gray and Cushing Eells] with their associates were discussing matters
. . . not likely to ever be forgotten by them, little Elwood Evans was struggling to master the 'combination' of his first pair of pants, or wondering
if the chestnuts on the hills of his native Pennsylvania were not ripe, and
never dreaming that the day would come when he would be able to tell
these old missionaries more of their doings out here than they had ever
known themselves."[201]

Intentionally using biblical phrasing, the authors of the tract appealed to the "great cloud of witnesses" who could reliably attest to Whitman's saving of Oregon.[202] Witnesses like the missionary Mary Walker,
who "left home, friends, early associations, and civilization behind her,
and came [to the Oregon Country] to teach and civilize," had long been
pillars of the Protestant community in the Oregon Country. If they
could not be believed, the authors asked, then "to whom can we look for
the truth?"[203] Victor's and Evans's critiques endangered not only the legacy of Marcus Whitman but also the special status of Oregon's pioneers,
who alone had the right to interpret early Oregon history.

Ultimately, *The Whitman Controversy* appealed to readers to have
faith in Whitman's deeds rather than in the research of Victor and Evans,
outsiders who could neither claim eyewitness status nor respect those who
could. Gray, Ross, and Eells firmly believed that providence would recon-

Fig. 5. Whitman Monument at Whitman National Historic
Site, 2010, Walla Walla, Washington. Despite Gray's campaigning,
the Whitman Monument would not be paid for or completed until
1897. Its final design was much different from the more elaborate
versions envisioned by Gray. Photographed by the author.

cile the discrepancies in the eyewitness accounts and documents. "As many
seeming difficulties in the Bible, where that book and secular history have
seemed to conflict, have been reconciled by the discoveries of the last fifty
years, so I am waiting for more light on the subject under discussion,"
wrote Myron Eells.[204] This would not be the last time that the Whitman
story's supporters likened the tale's authority to that of scripture.

The *Whitman Controversy* pamphlet was Gray's last major contribution to the Whitman debates. The Whitman controversy died down for a time, not to be resurrected until 1900. Gray died in 1889 after several years of failing health. The Whitman Monument efforts stalled, and the roughly eight hundred dollars the Monument Association had raised was deposited in Portland's Ladd and Tilton's Bank to draw interest.[205] The monument was not completed until 1897, and its pared-down design would resemble neither Gray's initial elaborate plan nor Hopkins's more subtle critique of Catholic Christianity.

Gray's legacy extended beyond the monument campaign, however. The PHS continued to operate until the turn of the twentieth century, ensuring that the mythology of the Oregon pioneers that Gray helped create would have expression in historical writings, reunions, and memorials.[206] The public historical culture Gray helped build and shape continued to flourish, though now it was split among providentialists and secularists contending for control of the region's history. And Gray had successfully made himself chief among these pioneers and historians; through his energetic self-reinvention he had risen from being a mediocre student with few prospects to become one of the region's vaunted pioneers. His life symbolized the kind of creative institution and identity building that characterized the Oregon Country in the four decades after statehood.

The pioneer secularists succeeded in redrawing some of the boundaries of historical debate in the Pacific Northwest, but for those outside of the territory debates over regional historical authority proved far less attractive than the story of Whitman itself. The 1890s would see the Whitman Saved Oregon Story become a national narrative, as eastern church historians took up Gray's *History* and rewrote the Whitman story for a national audience. Thanks to that national interest, the monument for which Gray campaigned finally became a reality in 1897. The Whitman story's day of reckoning would come but not before all Americans knew Marcus Whitman as the hero who "Added Three Stars to Our Flag."

Selling Providence

On December 5, 1897, Protestants in Washington, DC, crowded the city's First Congregational Church to commemorate the fiftieth anniversary of the death of Marcus Whitman, "who rode from Walla Walla to Washington [DC] to save the [N]orthwest to the United States."[1] The ceremony began with a choir service and continued with speeches by some of the city's prominent citizens, including the Civil War hero Oliver Otis Howard and the US Supreme Court justice David Josiah Brewer. The speakers lauded Whitman as "a man of God and a true patriot," one of the great heroes of American expansion. Justice Brewer declared, "His was a noble and heroic deed, and one that saved to his country a great State." Brewer continued, "If we eulogize the broad foresight of Secretary Seward, who purchased Alaska for $7,000,000, that country whose vast wealth we are now only beginning to realize, what honor should we give to Dr. Whitman, this missionary who saved to the United States the great northwest."[2]

Fifty years had passed since Whitman, his wife, Narcissa, and eleven other Americans died at the hands of members of the Cayuse Nation, and thirty years since Whitman's missionary companion Henry Harmon Spalding began to lecture on the fictional story of Whitman's 1842 ride to save Oregon from the British. Now, due to the concerted labor of a few wealthy, well-connected figures and the growing popularity of both western and expansionist tales, the story had captured the hearts of Christians across the nation. Churches in Chicago, Philadelphia, New York, and Boston hosted celebrations of Whitman's heroism. Whitman's story graced the meeting halls of the AHA and the pages of the *New York Times* and the *Ladies' Home Journal* alike. By 1895 the *Atlanta Constitution* could declare, "Every American is aware of the great ride of Marcus Whitman."[3]

Pacific northwesterners had raised questions about the Whitman Saved Oregon Story's accuracy in the 1880s, creating fractures within the region's community of pioneer historians. But even as northwesterners questioned the story of Whitman and the providential vision of history it embodied, easterners began to discover the story—many for the first time. A nationwide fundraising campaign for Whitman College enlisted Americans in the East and Midwest for Whitman's cause. The ABCFM, the organization that appointed and supervised Marcus Whitman, organized national days of remembrance in 1895 and 1897. A revitalized campaign for a Whitman Monument sprang up in Walla Walla, Washington, in 1890, sending calls for funds across the country. Alongside these projects the Whitman story proliferated in newspapers, magazines, books, sermons, and speeches. From 1885 to 1899 the Whitman story spread beyond its original, largely regional circle of dedicated promoters like Henry Spalding and William Gray to become widely accepted as national history and national myth. As the Whitman story spread, Americans remade Whitman again—this time, into a herald of American expansion and an ideal type of American masculinity. In an era of racial conflict, religious diversification, and imperial development, Whitman became a potent emblem of Anglo-American male ambition and a martyr for the white man's burden to civilize the world.

The story of Whitman was felicitously suited to the 1890s, an era in which white Americans were both enamored of the possibility of expanding US power beyond its North American borders and worried about the influx of foreign immigrants to the United States. The historian Matthew Jacobsen has argued that in the late nineteenth and early twentieth centuries foreign peoples, both at home and abroad, served as the foils against which native-born white Americans forged their identities. Native-born whites placed the world's peoples on an evolutionary spectrum that moved from savagery to civilization. Foreign and dark-skinned peoples were classified as savage: unfit for self-governance and requiring the tutelage of whites to train them in the virtues of capitalism and democracy. Print culture profoundly shaped Americans' understandings of race, nation, and imperial imperative. As Jacobsen states, "At once reflecting, circulating, and reinforcing such habits of seeing, writing of all sorts may be said to participate in a crucial manner in the political project of empire-building."[4]

Jacobsen brings together many fundamental themes in *Barbarian Virtues*—imperialism, global capitalism, emerging academic disciplines, immigration, and urban reform. Yet his analysis of foreignness and savagery does not examine the origins of "savagery" as a rhetorical term. As the scholars like Michael Gaudio and Roy Harvey Pearce have shown, concepts of savagery and civilization originated in Euro-American encounters with indigenous peoples, and narratives of these encounters cemented the terms upon which other concepts of race and civilization were constructed.[5] Nowhere were these concepts expressed more potently than in stories of missionary work among nonwhite peoples. Although missionary tales like the Whitman story originated prior to the 1890s, they took on a special meaning in the 1890s as expressions of Anglo-American racial destiny.[6] Missionary narratives like that of Marcus Whitman lionized white, native-born Americans who entered foreign lands to teach purportedly savage peoples the arts of civilization. These stories taught Americans to view American power as a benevolent extension of material and spiritual salvation. The equating of American governance and Christian salvation was especially true of stories about missionaries to Native America, as missionary incursion into Native lands often prefigured the formal expansion of American political jurisdiction. Missionary tales also taught their readers how to view foreign peoples: as uncivilized, unenlightened, barbaric groups who desperately needed American leadership. Such accounts conflated the rejection of American influence with rejection of Christ, thereby conferring divine sanction upon Euro-American supremacy. Americans in the 1890s saw an unbroken line from western expansion across the North American frontier to the extension of American power into farther-flung lands like Hawaii, Cuba, and the Philippines. As Americans looked beyond the borders of the continental United States to new potential sites of power and influence, the story of Marcus Whitman took on new meaning as a prequel to and herald of the global reach of American power.

Historians since Arthur Schlesinger have argued that imperialist ideals shaped American missionary work, but fewer scholars have examined how missionary narratives shaped domestic understandings of empire.[7] The late nineteenth-century modifications to the Whitman story grew out of and helped shape a new era in providential history: that of imperial providentialism. Imperial providentialism retained many of the teachings of earlier providentialism: that God acted in ways that could be objectively evaluated by historians, that God had specially chosen the United States to be a prosperous world power, and that Anglo-American expansion and the redemption of the world were coextensive. But it also exhibited a growing racial consciousness marked by the rise of scientific racism, the unprecedented growth of foreign immigration to the US, and increasing American intervention into the affairs of other nations. Whereas earlier understandings of divine providence had advanced a vision for the church, imperial providentialism advanced a vision for the Anglo-American "race." This reference to the Anglo-American race was no longer coded through appeals to Protestantism or pioneer identity, as it had been in the earlier nineteenth century. Instead, the survival and uplift of the white race were explicitly equated with the expansion of Christ's redemptive kingdom. John Henry Barrows, the president of Oberlin College, saw the rise of the white race as a harbinger of the coming unity of the Christian world. He declared, "The most hopeful feature of the outlook into the twentieth century is the certain predominance of Saxon nationalities. Within a hundred years the population, wealth and power of the United States will ... be such that other nations will sink into comparative insignificance before the colossal forces represented by American civilization."[8]

Missions were an integral part of this vision of the so-called Saxon race. White Americans turned to foreign and home missions both to ease anxieties about foreign immigration and to reinforce their self-understanding as the stewards of civilization. Home missions would serve as "antiseptic agencies" against the degradation of Anglo-American communities by foreign immigrants, while foreign missions would "introduce a new and higher type of manhood" to uncivilized nations.[9]

The story of Marcus Whitman aligned well with this vision of providence. Whitman had engaged in a civilizing mission that extended American power over a foreign region populated by supposedly savage people in need of Christianity and American institutions. His mission facilitated a major expansion of American territory. While historians like Gray and Spalding had emphasized the denominational and regional importance of Whitman's heroism, imperial providentialists highlighted the national and racial significance of the Whitman story. Whitman's ride was no longer simply a matter of rescuing Oregon Territory from British rule and Catholic influence. In the 1890s the narrative shifted: now Marcus Whitman rode "to Save an Empire."[10]

As missionary stories were shaping Anglo-American impressions of nonwhite, non-Protestant peoples at home and abroad, a second kind of civilization project was taking place in late nineteenth-century Protestant society. Even as American Protestants looked to civilize the nonwhite, non-Protestant world, they sought to promote a vision of civilized life in US cities, towns, and rural areas in an era of western expansion and urban growth. This project required large-scale capital investment, something that perpetually cash-strapped denominational and interdenominational organizations could rarely muster. The leaders of Christian colleges, missionary associations, and other Protestant endeavors thus turned to those who could fund the messages and projects of Protestant Christendom: wealthy capitalists who had benefited from the economic shifts of the Gilded Age and now sought to infuse their wealth with moral authority. Preachers and politicians continued to play a part in late nineteenth-century moral reform efforts, as they had in the past, but capitalists supplied the resources for such efforts and imbued those efforts with their political and financial sensibilities.

Late nineteenth-century capitalists have been popularly categorized as a monolithic group of robber barons, but more recent historians of the Gilded Age have emphasized the diversity of occupations, methods, and goals among capitalists of that era.[11] Wealthy industrialists and investors viewed their fortunes as both a confirmation of the rightness of their moral choices and as a mandate to use that wealth to shape a moral Protestant society.[12] These moral capitalists used their financial resources to fund educational and reform efforts—particularly emphasizing Christian colleges—as a means of advancing Christian civilization within the United States. The most prominent of these moral capitalists was the Scottish Presbyterian and steel magnate Andrew Carnegie, who funded 108 college libraries during his lifetime. Carnegie famously argued that wealth should be "regarded as a sacred trust, to be administrated by the possessor, into whose hands it flows, for the highest good of the people."[13] Carnegie thought the relentless pursuit of wealth could be sacralized by the commitment to giving philanthropically during one's lifetime. The businessman (and he was a business*man;* Carnegie and others rejected the possibility of women capitalists) could "prevent the ills of humanity" by giving to institutions that elevated the mind and rewarded industrious workers.[14]

In the 1890s the civilizing energies of imperial providentialism and the power of moral capitalism would align in the cause of Marcus Whitman. I trace this alliance here by focusing on the three figures whose partnership was indicative of the relationships between imperial providentialism and capital more generally. Stephen Penrose, the president of the financially destitute Whitman College fought to keep open the institution that served as a "living monument" to Whitman's legacy.[15] Like many colleges born of the Gilded Age, Whitman was born of the moral ambition of a particular capitalist, yet, unlike many others, it was explicitly founded in a bid to secure, for Christianity and civilization, the empire its namesake had inaugurated. Daniel Kimball Pearsons was a wealthy philanthropist who took up the cause of Whitman as part of his larger civilizing vision. Oliver Woodson Nixon was a journalist who would distill the story of Whitman for a wider audience. The efforts of these three men culminated in two major national celebrations that spoke to their success in making Whitman part of national consciousness: Marcus Whitman Day in 1895 and the fiftieth anniversary of Whitman's death in 1897.

"A School of High Moral Character"

Cushing Eells, a missionary colleague of Marcus Whitman and the founder of Whitman College, was born on February 16, 1810, in Blandford, Massachusetts, to Joseph and Elizabeth (Warner) Eells.[16] While many of Eells's future missionary companions—Henry Spalding, William Gray, and Marcus Whitman—had early lives marked by painful loss, unstable family lives, and failed career hopes, Eells appears to have enjoyed a happy childhood and a clear path to the ministry. He was the third of ten children, all of whom lived to adulthood. Though his father was not a minister, Eells came from a long line of reverends, graduates of the top Congregational and Presbyterian schools in the United States.[17] When Eells was seventeen his father, his minister, and a family friend encouraged him to go to college and study for the ministry. Though Eells initially refused, worrying that "he was not a bright enough scholar," he eventually acquiesced.[18] He studied at local academies before completing degrees at Williams College and East Windsor Seminary (now Hartford Seminary).[19]

During his studies Eells became involved with the Mills Society, one of many small associations that encouraged its members to consider missionary work. Through the society Eells learned about the exciting possibilities for doing missionary work in South Africa. In 1836 he applied to the ABCFM, and the following year he was ordained as a missionary to the Zulus.[20] During this time Eells had struck up a courtship with Myra Fairbanks, the eldest daughter of a pious Congregational family. The two married on March 5, 1838, and prepared to travel across the world to South Africa.[21]

Fate led them elsewhere however. In 1837 William H. Gray arrived at the board headquarters in Boston, making extravagant claims about the missionary prospects among the Native tribes in the Oregon Country. The board asked seven recently appointed foreign missionaries—Elkanah and Mary Walker, Asa and Sarah Smith, and the newly married Cushing and Myra Eells—to change their appointments, go to the Oregon Country with Gray and his new wife, and join the missionaries Marcus and Narcissa Whitman and Henry and Eliza Spalding in their labors among the Native peoples of the Oregon Country. The missionaries agreed and made the arduous cross-country journey with Gray in 1837–38.

They spent the winter of 1838 at the Whitman Mission, and then the Eellses and the Walkers established a new mission among the Spokane people at Tshimakain.[22] For the next nine years the Eellses labored among the Spokanes. Like the Whitman Mission, the Tshimakain Mission never succeeded in gaining converts, so the Eellses and Walkers placed their focus on civilizing projects like teaching English, literacy, and Anglo-American farming techniques and domestic skills.[23] Then, in 1847, the attack on the Whitman Mission plunged the eastern side of the Pacific Northwest into chaos. The Spokane Mission was nearly two hundred miles from where the Whitmans and their associates were killed, but none of the missionaries knew how far the violence would spread. The nearby Hudson's Bay Company post, Fort Colvile, prepared for an attack, while Cushing Eells and Elkanah Walker tried to head off rumors of an American attack on the Spokanes, rumors that threatened to incite the Spokanes to preemptory violence.[24]

Despite their difficulties the Eellses resisted abandoning their mission as long as they could in the wake of the Whitman Incident, though, as Eells wrote to Henry Spalding, "I am aware we may be exposed to great peril."[25] By June 1848, however, the retaliatory war against the Cayuses had made it unsafe for the Eells family to remain at Tshimakain. That month they moved to the Willamette Valley, escorted by sixty members of the Oregon militia.[26] As the Cayuse War raged, Colonel H. A. G. Lee of the Oregon militia banned American civilians from settling in the Columbia Plateau. The region would not be reopened to American settlement until 1858, after the Cayuses, Spokanes, and other peoples of the region had been relegated to reservations that encompassed but a small fraction of their original homelands.[27]

For ten years the Eells family supported themselves in various ways—teaching school, farming, and preaching.[28] But Cushing Eells never abandoned hope that he could return to the Columbia Plateau. "My eyes and ears have been open, & the enquiring thought has hundreds of times arisen has the Great Head of the Ch[urch] any further service for me to perform in the field formerly occupied by the O[regon] Mission?" Eells wrote to the ABCFM secretary in 1855.[29] In 1859, once civilians were allowed to reenter and settle in the Plateau, Eells visited the ruins of the Whitman Mission. The mission grounds had long since been abandoned, and the mass grave where the Whitmans lay had been neglected. At that moment, Eells later stated, "I believe that the power of the Highest came upon me."[30] Eells resolved to transform the old mission site into a proper memorial to the Whitmans. But unlike William

Gray, who campaigned to build a stone monument for Marcus Whitman, Eells did not intend to build a physical monument (see chapter 3). Rather, he sought to build a moral one: "a befitting monument to the memory of our martyred missionary colaborers in the form of a school of high moral character."[31]

The timing for this proposal was apt. In the wake of the removal of the Cayuse people and their neighbors to reservations, Anglo-Americans were flooding into the region surrounding the old Whitman Mission. As was often the case in the American West, institution building had not caught up with this energetic wave of settlement.[32] Eells convinced the Washington Territorial State Legislature to pass a charter establishing Whitman Seminary, a nondenominational, coeducational high school for the children of the settlers around the former Whitman Mission.[33] Though the charter did not mention a denominational affiliation, it was evident that Eells and those who partnered with him intended that the school would be de facto Congregationalist. The Oregon Congregational Association had been one of the first groups to express its support for the project; several of Eells's missionary companions, including Elkanah Walker and Henry Harmon Spalding, were part of the first board of directors; and all the members of the initial board of directors were associated with either Congregationalist or Presbyterian churches.[34] The school would thus serve as a beacon of Protestant authority in a rapidly growing and tumultuous region.

In 1862, much to his aging wife's dismay, Eells decided to sell his family's farm in Forest Grove, Oregon, and use the money to purchase the Whitman Mission site for the school.[35] In the Walla Walla Valley surrounding the mission the Eells family found a growing community of emigrants recently settled on the Cayuse people's ancestral homelands, including soldiers who had claimed Cayuse lands in the wake of the Cayuse War, speculators hoping to profit from the gold recently discovered in the area, and farmers and merchants hoping to outfit those speculators. These newcomers had recently established the town of Walla Walla about six miles from the Whitman Mission. As a supply center and wintering site for miners, Walla Walla had quickly earned a reputation for lawlessness. "Saloons, boarding houses, and gambling dens lined Main Street," writes the historian G. Thomas Edwards of Walla Walla's early days.[36] Cushing's wife, Myra, reported later that "if she could then have been permitted to return to Forest Grove, three hundred miles, she would have been tempted to make the journey on foot, yes, on her hands and knees."[37] Eells still lacked the funds to build his seminary or hire teachers. He hoped that by farming the Whitman Mission's land and seeking donations from churches and citizens of Walla Walla he could eventually save enough to construct a schoolhouse.[38]

For four years Eells failed to gain any sizable donations for the prospective seminary. Walla Walla's frenetic mining economy enticed few families or Congregational church members who might be interested in a Christian school. The trustees also disagreed on whether the seminary should be situated on the Whitman Mission site, six miles from Walla Walla, or in the center of town. Eells's original vision had been to found the seminary at the Whitman Mission site and encourage a "small, retired, but moral, educated, and religious town [to] grow up around it," away from the bustle and bad influence of Walla Walla.[39] But Walla Walla's wealthiest citizen had other ideas. It was the first time, but not the last, that wealthy donors shaped the moral vision of Whitman College.

Dorsey Syng Baker had made his fortune selling supplies to local miners and investing in one of the first steamboat operations in the region.[40] Baker was constantly looking for ways to boost Walla Walla, and a functioning school in downtown Walla Walla could bring in new customers for his various business endeavors.[41] In 1866 he offered to donate four acres of land so that Whitman Seminary could be established in the heart of Walla Walla.[42] Eells continued to worry about moving the school to the town, with its saloons, reputation for vigilante violence, and general disorder. Ultimately, however, he acquiesced, unable to refuse free property and hoping that a location in town might encourage more Walla Walla residents to support the school.[43]

Whitman Seminary opened its doors on October 13, 1866, with a faculty of three and a student body of twenty-one children and teenagers. The local Congregational minister, Peasley Badger Chamberlain, was appointed principal, underscoring the school's close ties with Protestant communities in the region. Walla Walla citizens turned out to observe the dedication of the seminary's two-story wooden building, one of the most impressive in town. But local curiosity would not be sufficient to sustain the school. When Whitman Seminary opened, it was already a thousand dollars in debt.[44] For the next thirty years the seminary's debt continued to increase, as the school fell prey to the unstable enrollment rates of a shifting population and competition from better-funded Episcopal and Catholic schools. After Chamberlain resigned in frustration over the school's lack of funds, several eastern-educated men took their turns as seminary principal. Although some succeeded better than others, each eventually resigned. In 1883, under the leadership of its first president, Alexander Anderson, the seminary was converted into the first college to be founded on the eastern side of the Pacific Northwest. But the expanded curriculum had little appeal for the mostly local students, children of farmers and small businessmen for whom bookkeeping and other vocational skills were more attractive than Greek and Latin.[45]

Cushing and Myra Eells worked tirelessly to help procure funds. Cushing gave money from his salary and other income, while Myra churned butter and raised chickens for the market, donating the proceeds to the seminary.[46] In 1883 and 1884 Eells undertook a cross-country fundraising trip to the eastern United States. On the advice of the American Congregational Education Society Eells lectured on Whitman's ride, hoping to raise eastern churches' interest in contributing to Whitman College. Despite a warm reception, however, Eells was unable to raise funds, as audiences were evidently more interested in tales of the pioneer missionary's exploits than in donating to his namesake college.[47] Nor did Eells have the social connections that might help him navigate the world of wealthy potential donors.[48] As Eells anxiously wrote in his diary in 1883, "Work and solicitude in behalf of Whitman College are painfully trying. ... Appearances are discouraging. My faith in God continues."[49] Cushing Eells died in 1893, not knowing whether the fledgling college would succeed or fail. According to his son Myron's records, Eells had given over ten thousand dollars of his own money to Whitman College during his lifetime as well as countless hours worrying, praying, and fundraising. But the fate of the college was still undecided.[50]

It may be surprising that Whitman College failed to win widespread local or national support, given its association with the missionary hero Marcus Whitman. But despite Whitman's growing fame in the 1860s, 1870s, and 1880s, promoters of the missionary had not yet found ways to mobilize his legend to generate widespread economic support. Henry Spalding's lectures and congressional document had reached some Protestant sympathizers but were never published widely. Gray's *History* was widely used by other historians, but, even so, Gray failed to raise sufficient popular support for a Whitman Monument. Although Marcus Whitman's fame had grown, in the early 1890s he remained a regional hero. Articles about his heroism indicated this fact. Eastern newspapers often introduced the story with prefaces like "It is not generally known . . .," highlighting the inconsistent spread of Whitman's fame.[51] It would take new kinds of advocates and a new set of historical exigencies to make Whitman's legend appeal to both the masses and to wealthy donors in ways that would convince them to open up their pocketbooks.

D. K. Pearsons and the Business of Moral Capitalism

In 1894 Stephen Beasley Linnard Penrose accepted an appointment as president of Whitman College. He was determined to find these advocates. Penrose had traveled west in 1890 as part of the Yale Band, a group of four Yale Divinity School graduates who had been commissioned by the American Home Missionary Society to fill ministerial positions in Washington State. From 1890 to 1894 Penrose had served as pastor of the First Congregational Church of Dayton, Washington, located about thirty miles from Whitman College. Dayton was at that time a small farming town of about eighteen hundred people, and its Congregational Church had been in a sorry condition. According to Penrose, it had no pastor and only six aged members, "three of them confirmed invalids and all of them over sixty years of age."[52] During his tenure as pastor Penrose worked energetically to bring eastern-style educational resources to Dayton and its surrounding communities, teaching Sunday school and day school, organizing two Chautauqua lecture societies, raising funds for the public library, and becoming a trustee of the struggling Whitman College.[53] Under his leadership the Dayton church went from a tiny, failing congregation to a self-supporting institution. Whitman College's trustees believed that Penrose might be able to work similar magic at Whitman. As one supporter of the college stated, "There is just one man who . . . can, I believe, save the institution from death and that is Rev. Mr. Penrose."[54]

Penrose assumed the presidency of Whitman College on October 2, 1894. He found an institution on the brink of financial ruin: the college's five faculty members had not been paid for a year, and the student body had shrunk from a high of almost two hundred students in 1889 to only thirty-four regular pupils.[55] Whitman had no endowment and carried a $13,500 debt. The citizens of Walla Walla were unable to contribute much assistance. The effects of the Panic of 1893 were still being felt in the Northwest, and railroad strikes, the decline of the mining industry, and low crop prices had undercut Walla Walla's prosperity.[56] "If wheat were not at twenty cents a bushel, our task would be easy," Penrose lamented.[57] Penrose needed to find a way to secure money quickly and to get most of it from outside Whitman College's immediate vicinity. In order to do this he needed assistance from those who were more experienced in the ways of Gilded Age fundraising and publicity. He resolved to travel east at his own expense to raise funds, much as Eells had done twenty years earlier. To demonstrate his faith that Whitman College could recover, he also cut his salary in half, using the rest of the money to help operate the school. "I believe in the College, and am willing to be poor if it may become rich," he wrote to Myron Eells.[58]

There was one person who might be able to help Whitman College: the wealthy Chicago philanthropist Daniel Kimball Pearsons, commonly called D. K., who was known for his generous donations to small Protestant-affiliated colleges such as Wisconsin's Beloit College.[59] Pearsons had offered Whitman College's previous president an attractive but seemingly unrealizable proposal: if Whitman College could raise $150,000 in donations, Pearsons gave another $50,000 for its endowment. Then-president Eaton had rejected the offer, knowing that if the school could not raise even $13,500 to cover its debt it could never reach the $150,000 goal.[60] But Pearsons extended the offer again when Penrose was appointed president, and Penrose was determined to find a way to appeal to Pearsons's generosity. The resulting fundraising campaign entwined Whitman College's fate with the world of Gilded Age moral capitalism and especially with the expanding power of moral capitalists in Chicago.

Like many of his wealthy peers, Pearsons had undergone a rags-to-riches transformation that undergirded his firm belief in the ability of hardworking people to achieve financial prosperity. He was born on

April 14, 1820, to a poor but pious farming family in the town of Brad-ford, in the Green Mountain region of Vermont.[61] From a young age, Pearsons was determined to get an education, but poverty forced him to leave Dartmouth College after only one year of study. After trying and failing to find work in Boston, Pearsons met a Baptist dairy farmer who hired him as a laborer and helped him attend the Baptist Manual Labor School in Worcester, Massachusetts. Eventually, he was able to attend medical school in Woodstock, Vermont.[62] In 1847 Pearsons, now a young doctor, married the twenty-eight-year-old Marietta Chapin, whose dedication to missionary and charitable causes would shape Pearsons's later philanthropic giving.[63]

By 1851 Pearsons had built a modestly successful medical practice in Massachusetts as well as a career lecturing on medical textbooks. A chance encounter with the former Oregon legislator Samuel Thurston, however, convinced the Pearsons that they would be more successful in the West, where land and resources abounded. At Marietta's urging, the Pearsons moved to rural Illinois in 1857 and then to Chicago in 1860.[64] Chicago's late nineteenth-century industrial boom had made it a key link between growing western communities and established eastern networks. The city's rise to primacy as a hub for lumber and agricultural products had created a wealthy class seemingly overnight, a develop-ment that paralleled the economic and industrial transformations hap-pening in other US cities.[65] Pearsons abandoned his medical practice for a career in the booming real estate market.[66] His first commission was to sell fourteen thousand acres in Champaign County, Illinois, to eastern-ers looking for farmland.[67] He quickly earned a reputation as an honest dealer and a scrupulously frugal man, and he put his earnings into new tracts of land, land loans, and railroad and bank shares. In twelve years he made a million dollars. When the Great Chicago Fire and the Panic of 1873 came along, Pearsons took advantage of the disasters and bought even more property at low prices.[68]

By 1887 Pearsons had amassed a fortune of $3.5 million.[69] He was nearly seventy years old by this time, mostly retired from active business endeavors, and he and his wife had no children.[70] "What am I going to do with this [money]?" he wondered. "I cannot carry it out of the world in my dead hands."[71] He decided to follow the example set by the banker and philanthropist George Peabody, who before his death had become famous for donating the vast majority of his fortune to charitable causes.[72] Pearsons spent the rest of his life giving away nearly all of his own fortune to the causes he saw fit. He and his wife donated to a variety of organizations, including Chicago Presbyterian Hospital, a Chicago school for indigent boys, and the 1893 World's Fair, but the bulk of their wealth they spent on colleges. Pearsons's poverty had kept him from receiving a liberal arts education; now he was determined to help "poor boys and girls . . . who have to hustle" to get the training he had been denied.[73] Pearsons's plan was simple: to support small, struggling Christian colleges, mostly ones located in the Midwest and West, by offering to supplement their fundraising efforts. Pearsons saw these "freshwater colleges"—named such by Pearsons because they were not part of the New England establishment of elite schools—as "direct products of the true American pioneer spirit," whose "sound, practical Christianity" would train up the western men and women "who make up the moral backbone of this nation."[74] From 1887 to 1893 Pearsons donated large sums of money to six colleges, all located in the Midwest and West.[75]

Pearsons's donations captured the attention of the press from Chicago to New York City. Professor Samuel Ives, writing for the Chicago Advance, dubbed Pearsons the "Friend of Christian Education" and lauded him for "inaugurating a new era of benevolence among the rich men of Chicago."[76] Pearsons himself, however, denied that his donations came from any particularly generous or pious spirit. As he told his nephew, Daniel Kimball Jr., "There never was a bigger mistake than calling me benevolent. I have not a spark of benevolence in me. I'm a hard-hearted, tight-fisted, penny-squeezing old curmudgeon[.] I haven't a trace of charity or kindness in my whole being." He explained further, "I give my money away because I want to be my own executor, and because coffins were not made to hold it. I want to know where my money goes and what good is accomplished with it. I haven't any children except my colleges. I have taken care of my kinsfolk. I haven't any poor or deserving relatives. You can see my giving is business."[77]

It was precisely this dedication to the "business" of giving, however, that marked Pearsons's philanthropy as the philanthropy of moral capitalism. To Pearsons, wealth was a means of exerting moral influence—and specifically the moral influence of mainline Protestantism—over society. Moral capitalists did not believe that great wealth necessarily implied great virtue; money could be earned by honest or dishonest means. Instead, such people believed that wealth could be sanctified through the practice of philanthropy. When John D. Rockefeller was criticized for making philanthropic donations with his oil money, which his detractors believed had been "tainted" by Rockefeller's ruthless business practices, Pearsons came to Rockefeller's defense. "This cry of 'tainted money' . . . is unfair. It is not American," Pearsons insisted. "It has become the rallying cry of the socialist, the drone and the discontented members of society, who hate those whose talents and fortune exceed their own."[78] Pearsons judged there was no such thing as "tainted money" if it was used for philanthropic causes. Philanthropy purified and sanctified all wealth, regardless of how the wealth had been amassed. As Pearsons argued, "Money invested that way [in Christian education] cannot be tainted. Devoted to the purpose of spreading the Word of Christ or the torch of knowledge any stain would be removed."[79] Moreover, Pearsons believed that his giving would act as a witness to other wealthy people. "You have got to put a lever under some rich people to make them charitable," he declared. This "lever" would convince wealthy people who were holding onto their money immorally—the "old rich cusses" as Pearsons described them—to become charitable as well.[80] Philanthropic giving, in other words, helped to civilize and Christianize the Gilded Age world of wealth, bringing the wealthy in line with the tenets of Protestant beneficence.

Pearsons did not intend simply to civilize the wealthy class through his giving. He also invested in projects that helped civilize the communities they reached: foreigners, foreign immigrants, and especially residents of rural and western communities within the United States. Pearsons believed that colleges were the most efficient way to accomplish this work. "If Christianity is fundamental to the elevation of the race," he wrote, "the Christian college is the instrument through which to advance Christian civilization."[81] Pearsons deemed that Christian colleges could help answer Anglo-Americans' growing anxiety about foreign immigrants as the nation struggled to accommodate the largest migratory wave it had ever experienced. Pearsons was convinced that "by education will America absorb and assimilate the large population which is now on her shores ... and thereby escape the danger which threatens from those who do not seem able to grasp the true spirit of civil and religious liberty—the cornerstone of our republic."[82] But it was not only the foreign-born that Pearsons sought to civilize. He saw the American West as another kind of foreign place, one where extractive economies, lack of religious and educational institutions, and roaming mobile populations in search of quick wealth had created a white, American-born society of people in need of civilizing. As Pearsons said of Colorado, "The bright young men perched upon the mountain peaks or nestling in deep basins walled in by peaks of gold, are not easily led into the practice of Christian virtues; the roughness of the miners and stockmen and the wildness of the frontier towns are against it."[83] Western colleges would help rein in the passions of young people—men above all—and train them in the Protestant habits of life and mind that Pearsons and other moral capitalists valued: industriousness, thriftiness, "wholesome restraint," and protection from "bad habits and bad associations."[84] These students, once trained in the moral habits of mind that marked civilized American Christianity, would help keep the nation "rooted and grounded in the old religious convictions" that Pearsons believed were necessary for continued US success and progress.[85]

Given his commitment to funding Christian colleges, it is not surprising that Pearsons took an interest in Whitman. In his renewed offer to Whitman College's president, Stephen Penrose, Pearsons agreed to donate $50,000 to Whitman College's endowment if the college could raise $150,000 by January 1, 1896. Penrose had been quietly raising donation pledges among the citizens of Walla Walla, but these pledges, like Pearsons's $50,000, were dependent on the success of the endowment campaign. None of the money could help the college meet its immediate debts, which included a year of back pay to its professors. Desperate, Penrose traveled to Chicago to ask for Pearsons's help. Whitman College could not raise the required $150,000 when it was still $13,500 in debt, Penrose explained.[86] Pearsons, according to Penrose, "delivered a lecture upon the heinousness of all debts in general and of this debt in particular," which nearly quashed Penrose's hopes for assistance.[87] But as it turned out, this lecture was merely the prelude to a donation: Pearsons wrote Penrose a check for the $13,500 on the spot, instructing him to "send that out and pay the teachers and clean it all up."[88] Moreover, Pearsons decided to take the young Penrose under his wing. Pearsons believed his own life was a model of fiscal success, down to the specifics of his daily routine, and he expected the recipients of his largesse to trust his prescriptions for healthy living, perseverance, and financial management. He directed Penrose to, like him, live frugally, take daily naps, and eat a bit of raw onion before every meal as a digestive tonic.[89] But interspersed with this mundane advice were instructions on how to mobilize the story of Marcus Whitman to gain the attention of donors. "Call together your Congressmen and Governor and your wise patriotic men from all parts of the state," Pearsons commanded Penrose, "and let them have a chance to honor the man who saved Washington and Oregon for our country."[90]

Like many Americans in the 1890s, Penrose had first discovered the tale of Whitman saving Oregon when he read William Barrows's 1884 popular history *Oregon: The Struggle for Possession.*[91] Penrose later recalled that he "realized at once the value of the story to the College as a basis of appeal to patriotic people and he resolved to make use of it in every legitimate way."[92] As a Pacific northwesterner and an academic Penrose was aware that there had been controversies over the Whitman story in the past, but he was thoroughly convinced of the story's truth and remained so throughout his life. He only needed a way to publicize the story more effectively to readers in the East.

"It Is Hard to Believe It Is Fact and Not Fiction"

Penrose had a capable ally in this endeavor: the prominent Chicago journalist Oliver Woodson Nixon, the literary editor of the *Chicago Inter Ocean.* Like Pearsons, Nixon had moved up in the late nineteenth-century world of moral capitalism, from early poverty to eventual fiscal success and widespread influence. But whereas Pearsons had gained his influence through wealth and philanthropy, Nixon had amassed wealth and power through that other vital organ of the Gilded Age world, the press. It was the last of the many occupations Nixon had undertaken. Like Pearsons, he had had to hustle in his earlier life. As a young man in Indiana Nixon had paid his way through school and begun a career in education. But boredom set in and called on him to go west. In 1850, at the age of twenty-five, Nixon traveled overland to the California Gold Rush, where he cut and sold cordwood to the miners, and then to Oregon, where he worked briefly as a schoolteacher. After a year of adventuring he went back East, dabbled in politics, earned his medical degree, and set up a practice in Cincinnati. The coming of the Civil War, however, forced another career change. Nixon served as medical director of the Union Army of the Mississippi, but a shell blast severely damaged his hearing, making further medical practice virtually impossible. During the war Nixon had discovered a talent for writing, penning letters about the war for publication in the *Cincinnati Commercial.* Upon his return from the war Nixon became involved in newspaper work. With the help of his wealthy brother, William, Nixon reorganized the *Cincinnati Chronicle* in 1868 and then bought out the *Cincinnati Times.* The brothers' success earned them the notice of the owner of the *Chicago Inter Ocean,* a newspaper that had been struggling in the wake of the Great Chicago Fire and the Panic of 1873.[93] In 1878 the Nixons moved to Chicago to take over the paper, Oliver Nixon serving as literary editor.[94] Nixon became associated with the moral capitalist world of Chicago and especially with D. K. Pearsons. Like Pearsons, Nixon was a churchgoing Protestant in the Reformed tradition as well as a firm believer in the power of businessmen to use their wealth to improve society. In 1889 Nixon delivered a paper for a meeting of the Chicago Congregational Club entitled "The Indirect Influence of Christianity Upon the General Business Community" for a meeting on the theme "The Christian Business Man."[95] It is unclear when Pearsons and Nixon first met, but by the 1890s they considered themselves fast friends. In fact, it had been Nixon who first convinced Pearsons to include Whitman College in his philanthropic efforts.[96]

According to Nixon, he had first heard the Whitman story during the 1850s, when he was a schoolteacher in Oregon.[97] This is possible though unlikely given the story's origin in 1848. In any case, it was not until the 1880s that Nixon became involved with the story's public dissemination. In 1884 Nixon's *Inter Ocean* published a sensational retelling of the Whitman story inspired by William Barrows's recently published *Oregon: The Struggle for Possession.* Based largely on Gray's *History of Oregon,* Barrows's *Oregon* received wide circulation and was written in an accessible style that would have appealed to a journalist like Nixon. No author was credited in the article, but as Nixon was the literary editor of the *Inter Ocean* he would have at least reviewed this content, if not written it himself.[98] From 1884 onward, every year on November 29, the anniversary of Whitman's death, Nixon published an editorial on Marcus Whitman and Whitman College, "calling upon the people of the United States to honor the memory of a neglected hero."[99]

But Nixon's most celebrated assistance to Whitman College and Marcus Whitman's legend came in book form. As he continued to publish articles and book reviews on Whitman, Nixon came to a realization that "no man can tell the story of Whitman in a newspaper article."[100] Newspaper articles were neither thorough enough to properly demonstrate Whitman's heroism nor widely distributed enough to reach his desired audience. In order to disseminate Whitman's legend more effectively and broadcast the story to a larger readership, Nixon wrote, "the people have got to be educated into the truth."[101]

In 1894 Nixon began collecting and expanding his editorials and sketches on Whitman into a book. He did not intend to write a scholarly biography. Instead, he sought to render the established story of Marcus Whitman saving Oregon in more vivid and sustained detail than had been previously attempted and to dedicate the book's proceeds to Whitman College. Nixon wrote to Penrose, "I base my main plea upon Whitman's patriotic work, & not upon his missionary success."[102] For a national fundraising campaign in the 1890s, when nationalism and overseas imperialism were at a peak, Whitman the patriotic hero would serve as a better subject for a biography than Whitman the martyred missionary. Whitman the missionary appealed to Presbyterians and Congregationalists, Whitman the pioneer appealed to Pacific northwesterners, but Whitman the patriotic hero had the potential to appeal to Protestant Americans in general. "The world loves a hero," observed Nixon.[103] This version of Whitman accorded with Nixon's vision of US power, in which the Far West stood as the "very gateway of the world's footsteps, and commerce and wealth"[104] Whitman the patriot was a hero for an imperial age.

On June 20, 1895, Nixon published his work, the 339-page *How Marcus Whitman Saved Oregon: A True Romance of Patriotic Heroism.* In his preface Nixon clarified that his biography was "not intended to be a history of the Oregon missions or even a complete biography of Dr. Whitman." Instead, Nixon would "bring out . . . in a series of sketches, the heroism and patriotism of the man who rendered great and distinguished service to his country, which has never been fully appreciated or recognized."[105] Nixon launched a concerted and savvy marketing campaign to promote the book, running weekly ads in the *Inter Ocean* and special deals on the book through the *Inter Ocean* and other Chicago papers.[106] He sent free copies to Congregationalist and Presbyterian ministers around the United States and, equally strategic, to other well-known moral capitalists like John D. Rockefeller, Andrew Carnegie, and John Wanamaker. While none of the famous philanthropists made large donations to Whitman College, apparently considering it Pearsons's project, they did form lasting relationships with Pearsons, corresponding privately and defending each other publicly.[107]

Handsomely illustrated and sprinkled with colorful anecdotes from Nixon's own days as a pioneer, the book was designed to appeal to both adults and younger readers. And appeal it did. The first edition sold out within five months, and the book had gone through five editions by April 1896.[108] While a few reviewers felt that Nixon claimed too much for Whitman, the vast majority agreed with the reviewer for the *Los Angeles Times,* who wrote, "The work is one of the most entertaining and instructive of its kind ever written."[109] The *Detroit Free Press* concurred: "No history was ever told more truthfully, and no story of patriotism ever more vigorously recited."[110] The reviewer for *Book News* stated with unknowing irony, "Dr. Nixon tells the story of Whitman's ride so dramatically that one can hardly believe it is fact and not fiction."[111] The book soon became a quasi-hagiography for pious Protestant readers, who often referred to it not by its title but simply as "The Life of Whitman."[112]

High production value and relentless promotion no doubt contributed to the book's success. But its popularity ultimately rested on the way it mobilized established tropes of providential history that were familiar to American Protestant readers. Like Spalding and other providential historians before him, Nixon believed that historical study could reveal God's divine plan for the United States and the world. "At this day it is easy to see from the light of history how God rules in the minds and hearts of men, as he rules nations," he observed.[113] Nixon regarded the

Whitman Saved Oregon Story as undeniable proof of God's providential plan for the United States and for Protestant Americans in particular. The engaging tale could be taught to children and used as evidence to counter the enemies of Protestant religion. Nixon wrote, "The best possible answer of the church and of the friends of missions to those who sneeringly ask, What good has resulted to the world for all the millions spent on missions? is to point to that neglected grave at Waiilatpui, and recite the story of heroism and patriotism of Dr. Marcus Whitman."[114]

Even as Nixon emphasized the hand of providence in Whitman's life he highlighted Whitman's independence from institutional structures and the importance of eyewitness testimony for arriving at an accurate record of Whitman's life. Nixon's work, in other words, conformed to the conventions of pioneer history. While Nixon dialogued with and sometimes relied on other historians in his account, his main source was his own experience in the West. Nixon appealed to his memory of crossing the plains to Oregon in 1850, experiencing life on the frontier, and hearing stories of Whitman from Oregon residents. As he stated, "I expect some of my critics will ask, as they have in the past: 'Who is your authority for this fact and that?' I only answer, I don't know unless I am [the] authority."[115] Like Spalding and Gray before him, Nixon relied on his own eyewitness experience and pioneer identity to legitimate his work.

For those interested in the mythology of the pioneers the book could not have come at a more opportune time. Only five years earlier the US Census had announced that the US frontier had officially closed—there was no longer any place in the continental United States that had a population of less than one person per square mile. The announcement furthered an already growing nostalgia for the mythical Wild West. Dime novels and traveling entertainment like Buffalo Bill's Wild West Show dramatized a West made up of savage Indians, vast landscapes, lawless frontier towns, and the constant thrill of adventure. For eastern audiences Nixon's claim to pioneer authority added a frontier mystique to his writing that lent his claims credibility. The *Chicago Interior* stated, "No writer could have produced a biography of Whitman of equal interest and merit, because this biographer himself followed Whitman's trail across the plains and through the great 'stony mountains' a few years after Whitman saved Oregon."[116] Others gravitated toward the book because of its vivid depictions of a West that readers believed was now lost forever. As the *St. Louis Post Dispatch* wrote of Nixon's book, "Those not interested in the object [of Whitman's ride] will nevertheless be intensely interested in the charming story, and its wild, free life which will never again be repeated. . . . They are the realities of American history which excel all romance."[117] But perhaps the clearest statement of frontier nostalgia came from a New York reader, George H. Hepworth, a reviewer for the *New York Herald*. "When I finished this volume I felt as though a sort of blizzard had blown through me, and I assure you, it was not an unpleasant sensation," he wrote. "The West is getting tame, but in the forties, oh, in the forties, it was worth visiting. And this volume carries you back to those old times, with many a racy incident and many a deed of prowess."[118] Frontier nostalgia and trust in pioneer authorities thus combined to attract readers to Nixon's book. Much like other sites of frontier mythmaking, Nixon's prose inspired readers to experience the conquest of the West through the eyes of those who had witnessed it.

Nixon did not simply invoke a pioneer vision of the past, however. He also shifted the terms of providential history to reflect American Protestants' growing imperial consciousness. Nixon's narrative emphasized, more than previous versions of the Whitman story, the nationalistic nature of missionary work, the divine right of the United States to acquire new territory and expand its influence, and the ways in which Whitman served as an ideal racial and religious type, combining bravery, grit, and the ideals of American civilization in equal measure. Nixon downplayed the denominational quarrels and Protestant–Catholic conflict that earlier versions of the Whitman story had emphasized. Instead, he depicted Whitman and his fellow missionaries as "intensely American" heroes who "thought it no abuse of their Christianity to carry the banner of the Cross in one hand and the banner of the country in the other."[119]

Whitman's ride was noteworthy not because it rescued the Oregon Country from Catholics or even from the British but because it awakened Americans to their imperial potential. Nixon made much of the apocryphal story that Whitman first laid claim to the far West in 1836,

Fig. 6. *Whitman Group on Fourth of July 1836*. Photograph from the painting.
Illustration from Myron Eells, *Marcus Whitman: Pathfinder and Patriot*
(Seattle: Alice Harriman, 1909). Marcus and Narcissa Whitman Collection,
Whitman College and Northwest Archives, Walla Walla, Washington.

stopping at the Continental Divide to plant the American flag and "take
possession of the western side of the American continent in [God's]
name."[120] Describing Whitman's ride, Nixon wrote, "Suddenly new blood
had been injected into American veins in and about Washington. They
saw a great fertile country, thirty times as large as Massachusetts, which
was rightfully theirs and yet claimed by a power many thousand miles
separated from it. The National blood was aroused."[121] This trope of the
"National blood" reverberated throughout Nixon's narrative. As he observed, "No other race of men . . . would undertake so great a journey" as
the Anglo-American pioneers who colonized the North American
West.[122] Whitman was first among this "race of men." The description
of the white race as a race of *men* was not incidental. Like his Anglo-
American Protestant contemporaries, Nixon viewed race through a gen-

MASSACRE OF REV. DR. WHITMAN OF THE PRESBYTERIAN MISSION.

Fig. 7. An artist's conception of the murder of Dr. Whitman. Illustration
from Clifford M. Drury, *Marcus Whitman, MD.* From Frances Fuller
Victor, *The River of the West: Life and Adventure in the Rocky Mountains and
Oregon.* Marcus and Narcissa Whitman Collection, Whitman College and
Northwest Archives, Walla Walla, Washington.

dered lens. Proper performance of masculinity and femininity was
crucial to the Anglo-American race's inherent superiority over other
cultures. To Nixon, white American pioneers including Marcus Whitman manifested white superiority through their manliness.

As the historian Gail Bederman has argued, late nineteenth-century
Anglo-American understandings of masculinity and race were shifting
toward a more rugged, rather than genteel, model of masculinity.[123] This
new emphasis bore out in *Marcus Whitman*'s textual and visual depictions of Whitman. Nixon described him as "the very best specimen of
American Christian manhood."[124] He had "muscles trained, and a brain
which never seemed to tire"; he was too busy to write much, but when he
did, "he was remarkably clear, precise, and forcible."[125] The images Nixon
commissioned for the text emphasized this manhood even more vividly.
At the time of *Marcus Whitman*'s publication the most widely circulated

Fig. 8. *Whitman Pleading for Oregon before President Tyler and Secretary Webster*. The Miriam and Ira D. Wallach Division of Art, Prints and Photographs: Picture Collection, New York Public Library, New York, NY.

image of Whitman was an 1870 engraving of his death at the hands of Cayuse attackers.[126] This image, created by Nathaniel Orr and Company for Frances Fuller Victor's *River of the West,* showed Whitman adorned in a suit, with cleanly groomed facial hair, unsuspectingly reading a book by the fire as a menacing looking Cayuse man, tomahawk in hand, approaches Whitman from behind. Orr's still, genteel depiction of Whitman contrasts sharply with his portrait of the Cayuse attacker, who is shown midstride, arm raised, with his cloak askew to reveal his bare arm and back. Narcissa Whitman stands behind the attacker, reaching out to try to stop the coming blow. Marcus Whitman is a passive presence in the image, unaware of his impending fate, as all the action happens around him.[127]

The images commissioned for Nixon's book are strikingly different. Whitman has traded his suit and close-cropped hair for head-to-toe buckskin and a fuller beard. He never appears seated; he is always acting. In the book's opening plate he is depicted at the start of his famous win-

ter ride, seated on a white horse and surrounded by Indians and mountain men and looking back at his wife in the distance.[128] In the illustration
of the book's pivotal scene at the White House, Whitman stands, illumi-
nated by a ray of sunlight, pointing out into the distance as he speaks to
President John Tyler and Secretary of State Daniel Webster. Tyler and
Webster are finely dressed and calmly seated as they listen to Whitman,
while Whitman towers above them, his chair behind him.[129] He is no
longer a passive martyr or an icon of genteel civilization; now he is a
strong, active frontiersman who brings the rugged West to the overcivi-
lized East.

When Penrose, Pearsons, and Nixon partnered to save Whitman
College they also refashioned the Whitman story into a tale that would
appeal to a national audience in an imperial age. But a promise and a
book were not sufficient to raise the needed $150,000. For that, the three
fundraisers needed to find ways to engage ordinary American Christians in the memorialization of Marcus Whitman and the future of
Whitman College.

"A New National Hero"

Even before Nixon published *Marcus Whitman* he, Penrose, and
Pearsons had realized that the fundraising campaign could succeed only
if it appealed to a wider audience and caught the attention of other
Christian leaders. Thus the three men engaged in a nationwide publicity
campaign, one that began in 1895 and culminated in 1897. Throughout
this campaign the men helped to enlist others in the cause of Whitman,
from church leaders and politicians to women's magazine publishers
and civic organizations. From Oregon to Washington, DC, Americans
would take up the cause of Whitman, retelling and reimagining his legacy through popular literature, sermons, memorial campaigns, and academic historical work.

Both the national campaign and the moral capitalist vision that
guided it would move in directions that Whitman College's supporters
did not anticipate. As more and more people took up the story of Whitman, competing efforts at memorialization sprang up, leading to conflict
between the many parties who wanted to claim Whitman for themselves.

Even Whitman's bones became a subject of dispute, as two parties sought to house them within their own reliquaries. Out of these struggles the memory of Marcus Whitman became both more widespread and more institutionalized, as organizations from across the nation took up Whitman's cause as their own.

As Nixon's *Marcus Whitman* attracted the attention of readers nationwide in 1895, the fundraisers engaged on two fronts. Penrose traveled throughout the Midwest and East, delivering lectures on Marcus Whitman's heroism, much as Henry Spalding had done three decades earlier. This Whitman, however, was more like Nixon's version of Whitman than Spalding's. Penrose presented Whitman as "a new national hero, who, though long since buried in a martyr's grave, is recognized today as worthy of a foremost place in the roll of our country's heroes."[130] Penrose presented Whitman College as a memorial to and an extension of Whitman's patriotic and civilizing work. As he wrote to the readers of the *New York Tribune,* "Education and religion are the foundations of the State. Could a more fitting memorial be erected to a great man?"[131]

Meanwhile, Nixon and Pearsons enlisted the Congregational ministers of Chicago to help in the fundraising campaign. Local ministers were taken with the story of Whitman, which seemed to align perfectly with Protestant religious and political interests. At a February meeting of the Congregational Club attended by some four hundred people, the Reverend Frank Gunsaulus lauded Whitman as the "Columbus of the Pacific" and placed him alongside George Washington and Abraham Lincoln in a "trinity of patriotism."[132] Gunsaulus, who wrote the foreword to Nixon's *Marcus Whitman,* contrasted Protestant America with Catholic France, arguing that while Napoleon would be forgotten figures like Washington, Lincoln, and Whitman will "go on forever, their names ever gaining fresh luster." To Gunsaulus, Whitman was evidence that "the Teutonic idea is gaining ascendancy over the Roman" and that the reason for this ascendancy was Protestant Christianity.[133] Congregational ministers like Gunsaulus created their own space within the Whitman story, adopting the imperial providentialism of Nixon but emphasizing even more strongly that Protestantism, and specifically Congregationalism, was the key to the white American race's special role in world affairs.

At the behest of Nixon and Pearsons, the Chicago Congregational Association agreed to designate June 29, the Sunday before Independence Day, as Whitman Sunday, in which all Congregational churches in the greater Chicago area would present sermons on Whitman and take up collections for Whitman College. Nixon, always the marketer, sent copies of his book to local ministers to aid them in their sermon preparation.[134] "If all these churches . . . do their duty, and attest their interest by making handsome bequests, as they should, there will remain no doubt about the success [of the Whitman College endowment campaign]," trumpeted the *Inter Ocean*. Forty-five area churches took up the call. The titles of the Sunday sermons echoed Nixon's and Gunsaulus's rhetoric: "Marcus Whitman, One of the Master Builders of the Nation," "Marcus Whitman, Patriot, Hero, Christian," and "Marcus Whitman: Model American," preached in German to Bethlehem Congregational Church's immigrant congregation.[135]

At the same time, Pearsons and Nixon worked on securing the support of the local and national press. Nixon continued to send out copies of his book and introduced Penrose to other newspaper editors. Under Nixon's leadership the *Inter Ocean* had consistently upheld Whitman's legend and Whitman College's needs, but neither cause had received much attention from Chicago's most prominent Congregationalist paper, the *Advance*. Since the *Advance* was the premier Congregationalist periodical in Chicago and one of the most prominent Congregationalist organs in the West, Pearsons decided to apply gentle pressure to the paper.[136] "I have given the *Advance* a little advice on matters, if they want the paper to be well received in Wash[ington State] they must show their hand in favour of Whitman College. I guess they will change their tune a little, they need a little business sense," he wrote to Penrose in October 1896.[137] From that point forward the *Advance* covered the tale of Marcus Whitman and the plight of Whitman College in earnest.

The success of the first Whitman Sunday prompted a second observation in June 1896. By this time over $100,000 of the required $150,000 had been raised for Whitman College's endowment. About two-thirds of those donations came from outside the Pacific Northwest, a testament to Whitman's growing fame and the energetic campaigns of Whitman College's supporters. As the college's boosters continued their work, audiences outside of Chicago began to take an interest. An article by George M. Baxter on Whitman's ride was published in the leading papers of Atlanta, Philadelphia, and Los Angeles as well as many smaller cities.[138] "To one man are the people of the United States indebted for the possession of the rich region which now comprises the states of Oregon, Idaho, and Washington and part of Wyoming," the article declared.[139] Journalists, pastors, and politicians invoked Whitman in civilizing causes at home and abroad. A writer for the *Interior* called on Protestant Christians to "Save [Utah] to Christ and the church as Marcus Whitman saved the great Northwest to the United States. Colonize [the Mormons]."[140] At a massive rally in New York City to help raise the Presbyterian Board of Home Missions out of debt, Rev. Charles Thompson invoked the crowd to give generously "in the name of Marcus Whitman, the Paul Revere of the West" and later on "in the name of our country, this darling of divine providence."[141] The Congregational minister William Elliot Griffis cited Whitman in the long history of providential US expansion that was now leading to the conquest of the Pacific. "If we read the past aright, the American people will not follow; they will lead," he asserted.[142]

While churches and the popular press incited much of the fervor surrounding Whitman, the memorialization efforts did not go unnoticed in academic circles. In the 1890s the American practice of history was being professionalized and standardized. Local historical societies like William Gray's PHS continued to influence and engage individual communities, but new institutions sprang up to centralize power within the discipline. The most prominent national historical body was the AHA, founded in 1884 to foster "the exchange of ideas and the widening of acquaintance, the discussion of methods and original papers."[143] By 1897 the association had grown to nearly one thousand members.[144] A year earlier the AHA had merged with the nation's largest church history organization, the American Society of Church History. While Henry Warner Bowden has claimed that this merger indicated a capitulation of church history to the rising methodology of scientific history, memorializations of Whitman demonstrate that this was not the case. Contrary to Bowden's assertion that by the 1890s "it had become virtually impossible to base church history on a confession of faith and still command respect in the scholarly world," many of the leading historians associated with the AHA continued to narrate history in expressly Christian, providential terms.[145]

In 1896 the AHA elected Richard Salter Storrs, a Congregationalist minister and longtime president of the ABCFM, to be its president.[146] Storrs's inaugural speech celebrated "the contributions made by plain, uncelebrated men to the development of these United States."[147] He focused on three such men: Eleazar Wheelock, the founder of Dartmouth College, Rev. Manassah Cutler, who helped facilitate the settling of the Northwest Territory after the Revolutionary War, and Marcus Whitman, whose contribution consisted "in saving Oregon to the United States and in pushing our western boundary to the Pacific Ocean."[148] Storrs's providential vision of history was not incidental but essential to his history writing. To him, providence was "not the dream of reverie; it is not the imagination of the devout; it is part of the solidest and grandest history of the world."[149] Moreover, this providential vision was a distinctly imperial vision. As Storrs declared in one of his sermons on foreign missionary work, "The bringing of India under British rule, the lifting of Australia toward the independent Christian life and power which it is soon fully to attain, the opening of China and Japan and Africa, and the building up of this nation for the purposes of God in the earth—a building-up only made possible by the discovery of this continent four hundred years ago—all these things illustrate to us God's intervention."[150] Storrs and other late nineteenth-century historians reasoned that the study of history was the study of the unfolding of God's plan for the world, which was now culminating in Anglo-American Christian world supremacy.

Moreover, historians like Storrs believed that the new methods of scientific history were not contrary to the assumptions of providentialism but rather were integral to God's providential plan. The new historical methods, they believed, would help historians locate God's providence in formerly hidden places. Herbert Baxter Adams praised Storrs's address on Whitman as a demonstration of "the real genius of history, as we are reminded in the new historical methods which consider institutions and manners and people rather than warriors and presidents."[151] Other historians associated with the AHA, including John Bach McMaster, William

Augustus Mowry, and Horace Scudder began to include the tale of Whitman Saving Oregon in their school textbooks.[152]

Nixon's and Penrose's activism helped to spread the story of Whitman across the eastern parts of the United States, where new interlocutors adopted the story—and its imperial providentialist framework—for their own patriotic and academic ends. Indeed, in certain respects the efforts of Nixon and Penrose proved to be too successful. The Congregational Educational Society, the primary fundraising organization for Congregational colleges in the East, felt that the fervor over Marcus Whitman was drawing too much money and attention away from other Congregational schools and from the Educational Society itself. In 1895 the society had offered to donate twenty-five thousand dollars to the college's endowment campaign if Penrose promised not to fundraise in New England, but the money never came. A tense feud erupted between Penrose and Frank Ferguson, the secretary of the Educational Society. Finally, Pearsons convinced the two men to make peace. They did, after all, both need Pearsons's money.[153] The quarrel made two things clear: first, that the Whitman story was gaining support for Whitman College outside of the usual Congregationalist networks; and second, although Congregationalist and Presbyterian communities continued to advance the Whitman story, moral capitalists were the arbiters between the various groups that claimed Whitman as their own.

The disagreement in the East was only one of the problems Penrose faced. If Whitman College was to meet its endowment, Pacific northwesterners had to make good on the fifty thousand dollars they had pledged. One of the stipulations of Pearsons's fund-matching proposal was that a substantial amount of the endowment money had to come from the Walla Walla area. As Nixon wrote to Penrose in October 1897, "To have the enthusiastic backing of the people of Washington is everything in the battle."[154] The Pearsons contingency meant that the campaign for Whitman College needed to extend to the Northwest, where the effects of the story had become a subject of controversy in some historical circles. Nixon, however, was not daunted. "Oh we will win, even if all the sects and the mugwumps combine against us," he assured Penrose.[155]

Some prominent citizens in the Pacific Northwest were already interested in memorializing Whitman. While pioneer secularist historians in the Northwest had raised questions about the Whitman story's accuracy in the 1880s, a large population of northwesterners still believed the tale. Whitman's champion William Gray had died in 1889, but his son, Judge John Henry Dix (J. H. D.) Gray, had taken over as president of Gray's PHS, and several of Gray's pioneer allies continued to make statements in support of Whitman in local newspapers and at pioneer reunions.[156] With William Gray's death, though, the effort to build a monument for Whitman had stalled. Penrose now turned his attention toward reigniting the monument campaign, hoping that it would bring the needed local support to nearby Whitman College.

The monument effort had lapsed for two reasons: low donations and the lack of title to the land upon which Whitman's grave was situated. Penrose began with the land. With the aid of the Reverend William Sylvester Holt, a Presbyterian minister, Orientalist, and former missionary to China, Penrose made one last plea to the land's owner, William Swegle, who had previously refused when the Whitman Monument Association took too long in their fundraising efforts. Their conversation is not recorded, but Penrose and Holt were evidently persuasive. In addition to asking for a donation of the five acres surrounding Whitman's grave, Penrose and Holt offered to purchase another two acres at the price of twenty dollars an acre, later changed to thirty dollars per acre.[157] Penrose had evidently learned from his association with Pearsons how to appeal to people's business sense.

On February 14, 1897, Swegle announced that he would donate the five acres of land surrounding Whitman's grave for a monument, on the condition that the monument be built within one year.[158] One week later a group of Oregonians, mostly members of Gray's PHS and the Oregon Pioneer Association (the renamed OPS) met in Portland's First Presbyterian Church to reestablish the Whitman Monument Association.[159] J. H. D. Gray took the lead in the meeting, reiterating his father's claims that Whitman had saved Oregon in 1842–43. Whereas easterners had claimed Whitman explicitly in the name of Anglo-American Protestant Christianity, and Congregationalism and Presbyterianism in particular, the reformed Whitman Monument Association hewed to a unifying vision of pioneer identity that obscured its various exclusions under the banner of Americanism. The association passed a motion that "whatever was to be done in the honor of Dr. Whitman would be regarded as coming from no denomination, district nor single people. It should be from Americans, without regard to geographical lines or religion."[160] Any adult who donated one dollar to the monument fund and any child who donated twenty-five cents could become a member of the association.[161] The advisory committee, however, would be comprised only of those who hailed from Oregon, Washington, and Idaho. Penrose was named to the Washington advisory board. Pearsons and Nixon were elected as honorary members of the board, an indication of how deeply entwined their names had been with that of Marcus Whitman.[162]

As the monument association was taking shape Penrose announced that Whitman College would observe a special memorial service on the fiftieth anniversary of Whitman's death. The association determined that the Whitman Monument should be dedicated on the same day and that the two events be combined. Penrose began visiting Portland, Tacoma, and other Pacific Northwest cities to raise interest in the fiftieth anniversary events.[163] Pearsons and Nixon also sent their best fundraiser, the young Virginia Dox, to deliver speeches in and around Walla Walla.[164] With the assistance of Pearsons and Nixon, Penrose was able to appeal to some of the leading wealthy citizens of Walla Walla, including previous Whitman College donor Dorsey Baker and the prominent banker Levi Ankeny.[165] The *Los Angeles Times* wrote approvingly, "The subscriptions being raised in the State of Washington for a monument to Rev. Marcus Whitman . . . are coming in rapidly. The monument should be a beautiful one, for if ever the title of soldier of the cross fitted one man more aptly than another, that man was Marcus Whitman."[166]

According to the new monument plans, the Whitman Mission's dead, including Marcus and Narcissa Whitman, would be reburied in a "mausoleum of brick" topped by "a slab of polished marble" incised with the names of the dead buried there and "a simple history of their heroic life and tragic death."[167] A twenty-six-foot, eleven-inch granite and marble shaft, inscribed simply with the word "Whitman" along the base, would be erected on a knoll overlooking the grave.[168] Unlike Gray's failed monument campaign in the 1870s and 1880s, the monument campaign now attracted attention outside the Northwest thanks to the fame that Nixon's book had brought Whitman in the Midwest and East.

Presbyterian and Congregationalist ministers in places ranging from Peoria, Illinois, to Rochester, New York, appealed to their congregations to donate to the Whitman Monument Association.[169] The Presbyterians in Philadelphia went still further: they began planning a memorial service in Philadelphia to be held concurrently with the service in Walla Walla, and they commissioned a statue of Whitman to be placed in the hall of statuary of the new million-dollar Witherspoon building, built to house the headquarters of the Presbyterian Board of Publications and Sabbath School Work. Whitman's statue was to be designed by the sculptor John Huston and placed in a line of Presbyterian providential heroes alongside Francis Makemie, the founder of Presbyterianism in the US, and biblical figures like Moses and John the Baptist.[170] The *San Francisco Chronicle* reported that the statue would be "heroic in size, representing the sturdy pioneer dressed in the rugged habiliments then in vogue on the frontier," underscoring the extent to which Whitman's status as providential hero had been linked with his reimagining as a paragon of Christian masculinity.[171]

The real momentum for the memorial came, however, when the ABCFM took up the cause. In a meeting held in New Haven, Connecticut, in mid-October the board voted to hold memorial services in Boston and Washington, DC, and to send representatives to the services in Walla Walla and Philadelphia. They also, at Nixon's suggestion, asked all Congregational churches to feature Whitman-themed sermons on the Sunday before November 29. Several hundred churches took up the call.[172] "While the [monument movement] is local, it proposes to give the movement a national character, for we are of those who believe that under God's guidance it is largely due to Whitman's foresight and prompt action that Oregon, Washington and Idaho are now United States soil," wrote Penrose's minister ally W. S. Holt for the *New York Observer and Chronicle*.[173]

Though Nixon and Pearsons publicly supported the monument events, privately it was clear they did so grudgingly. They both worried that the Whitman Monument campaign would take the public's attention (and finances) away from what they viewed as Whitman's true monument, Whitman College. A marble shaft was a visible goal and easy for donors to imagine, while an endowment for a college was a more abstract concept. To counter this disadvantage they proposed that seventy-five thousand

dollars in donations to Whitman College go to its own Whitman memorial: a stone building, the first of its kind at Whitman College.[174] Penrose
was in a bind. On the one hand, Pearsons and Nixon instructed Penrose
not to "let [the Whitman Monument] satisfy the people. Make them see
that the grand monument is to be Whitman College."[175] In order to do that,
Penrose must, they insisted, ensure that even if the other victims of the
Whitman Incident remained at the old gravesite, Marcus and Narcissa
Whitman's bones would be moved to the new building at Whitman College. "We want those sacred relics at the College," Nixon insisted.[176] But the
Monument Association balked at the suggestion, risking an unseemly
conflict over who should have the first claim to Whitman's remains. Worried about the potential for bad publicity, Pearsons and Nixon instructed
Penrose to relent to leaving the remains at the original grave. "We have already got such a hold upon the people that our work is bound to go forward," Nixon conceded.[177] Penrose worked out a compromise in which
Whitman's remains would be placed in a glass case in Walla Walla for a
temporary public viewing before being reinterred in the new mausoleum
at the original gravesite.[178] Bereft of Whitman's actual body, the college had
to find other ways to fashion itself as the premiere site of Whitman's memorialization.

Without the "sacred relics" of Marcus and Narcissa Whitman's bones,
Penrose turned his attention to making Whitman College the main interpreter of the fiftieth anniversary celebrations. He threw himself into the
memorial service preparations, recruiting speakers, members of the press,
and other high-profile attendees.[179] Penrose and the Monument Association agreed to split the responsibilities for the two-day celebration: Whitman College would preside over the events on November 29, and the
Monument Association would preside over November 30.[180] That way
Penrose would be able to set the interpretive tone for the entire two-day
gathering.

On November 29 three thousand people from around the Northwest and across the country gathered in Walla Walla for the festivities.
The day began at nine o'clock in the morning, when crowds flocked to the
Walla Walla Opera House to hear Rev. Moses Hallock speak. Hallock had
been a longtime trustee of Whitman College and had helped raise endowment funds in the East. He invoked Whitman in imperial providen-

tial terms, proclaiming, "Although it be a twice-told tale, familiar as household words to many who hear me tonight, you will listen yet once again while we put the emphasis where truth demands, and show the pivot on which, in the providence of God, this Northwest empire swung over into the lap of these United States."[181] Hallock then explained to the audience how "the sturdy plant which rooted on the rim of blue sea near Massachusetts" had carried "its fruits of free religion and free citizenship westward to the broad Pacific," overcoming "Spanish possessions and British ambitions" so triumphantly that "the blindest student of history cannot fail to discover the hand of a Father."[182] Whitman, of course, was the agent of this victory, secured by the hand of God. "Can we place too much emphasis on this man's deed? Impossible," Hallock concluded.[183] After recounting the story of Whitman's ride, Hallock turned to Whitman College, making it clear that it was the true monument to Whitman. "What Eells begun with his life-blood of loving economy, Dr. Pearsons is carrying forward with large generosity, and you will soon complete. No monument of granite can for one moment compare with that," Hallock asserted.[184] It was the civilizing mission of the Christian college, the institutions "that carve crude souls along fine lines of clean and Christlike character ... and send them out to bless the world," that would most properly speak to Whitman's legacy.[185] As American Protestants worried about how to maintain moral influence in the midst of rapid urban growth, economic corruption, and encounters with foreigners at home and abroad, Marcus Whitman offered Hallock and his listeners reassurance of the US's essentially Christian character and a moral vision for how to proceed amid Gilded Age social transformations.

The rest of the day continued with a showcase of Whitman College's resources. The sixty-voice Whitman Memorial Choir sang hymns, and Penrose gave the day's benediction. The college also managed something of a coup: Marcus Whitman Barnett, the great-great grandnephew of Marcus Whitman, presented Whitman College with a lock of Narcissa Whitman's hair, which Whitman's nephew, Perrin, had collected from Narcissa's body after her murder.[186] Whitman College would have its "sacred relic" after all.

The next morning the three thousand visitors processed to the local Oregon Railroad and Navigation Company depot, where two trains, whose services the railroad company had donated for the day, took them to the scene of the Whitmans' grave. There, the attendees discovered that bad weather had delayed the Whitman Monument's arrival, but the festivities continued back in Walla Walla, where more speeches and performances were to come. Again, the speakers' messages rang in an imperial providential key. "The future of America will be the greatest future which this world has ever beheld," stated William H. Scudder, a representative of the ABCFM. Marcus Whitman was "the pivotal point upon which the destiny of our country hung," and his bravery brought about the "upbuilding of this portion of the United States ... with liberty and fraternity at its corner stone."[187] The services closed with a communal singing of "America" and a final benediction by Penrose. The Washington State Congregational Association held its annual meeting immediately afterward, extending the meditations on Whitman for several more days.[188]

The memorial exercises at Walla Walla on November 29, 1897, were echoed in other places around the nation. Ministers from Boston to Fargo to New York City delivered Whitman-themed Sunday sermons on November 28, the day before the fiftieth anniversary.[189] The *Ladies' Home Journal* contributed the article "When Marcus Whitman Added Three Stars to Our Flag," complete with a map of the vast territory Whitman had won for the United States.[190] The celebration in Washington, DC, underscored the extent to which the Whitman story had captured the attention of religious and civic leaders alike. Held at the First Congregational Church of Washington, DC, it was part church service, part patriotic rally. Several of DC's political and religious leaders delivered speeches honoring the "hero and ... patriot," imagining Whitman as an exemplar of Christian and patriotic courage. As the retired US Army general Oliver Otis Howard proclaimed, "[Whitman] did not hesitate to face the labors and the perils the journey promised."[191] State Senator John I. Wilson of Washington offered a new addition to the Whitman Saved Oregon Story: after successfully leading the Emigration of 1843 back to Oregon at the close of his winter ride, Wilson stated, Whitman "unfurled the flag of the United States and with open Bible gave praise for the success of their enterprise."[192]

All in all, Penrose considered the services "a triumphant success" on account of the large attendance at Walla Walla, widespread celebrations throughout the country, and the way these commemorative efforts "contributed greatly to the fame of the College."[193] Shortly after the celebration, Whitman finally reached its $150,000 endowment goal, though with Pearsons's support it continued to raise funds for buildings and other additions.

More importantly, the college had solidified its position as the central site of interpretation of Marcus Whitman's legacy. Though the monument continued to attract tourists, Whitman College was to be the primary locus of the production and dissemination of material concerning Marcus Whitman. Through its published quarterlies, annual conferences, student work, and memorial events, Whitman College would shape both scholarly and popular depictions of Marcus Whitman into the present day. As Penrose stated in the college's first published quarterly in the spring of 1897, "Whitman College was founded in the interests of the Kingdom of God. The blood of the martyr was its seed."[194]

Moreover, through Penrose's writings and speeches the fundraising campaign itself would become part of the fabric of the Whitman myth. In his various tellings of Whitman College's history Penrose introduced three new characters into the narrative: "Cushing Eells, its founder, whose sainted memory is a benediction; Oliver W. Nixon, who has labored for it with word and pen; and Daniel K. Pearsons, whose great heart went out to the College in its time of need."[195] The "Saint, the Editor, and the Philanthropist" each helped to awaken Americans to the grand works of a national hero.[196] The Marcus Whitman they trumpeted in speeches, affirmed in memorial services, and supported with funds was not the Whitman of 1842 but a new creation, grown out of the traditions of providential history and reimagined for an era of academic professionalization, big capital, and imperial expansion.

But this Marcus Whitman was not to endure. Even as Whitman's fame reached its greatest height, doubters of the Whitman story were working quietly on research that promised to demolish the tale of Whitman's ride once and for all. In the process they would use the very same platforms that had helped to make Whitman a national figure in the 1890s: colleges, the press, and the AHA. As easily as these institutions had made Whitman, they could also undo him. Already the AHA and university history departments were fostering a new kind of historical research, one that focused on critical analysis of primary sources. It was only a matter of time before this research would lead others to the conclusions that regional historians like Frances Fuller Victor and Elwood Evans had discovered in the 1870s: the Whitman story was a fraud. And when this realization came, the press would find that reporting the debunking of the Whitman story was as lucrative as promoting it. The Whitman deniers would harness first the academy and then the popular media to publicize their message. Their work would shape not only the legacy of Marcus Whitman but also the contours of the American historical profession itself.

Debunking Providence

O n the afternoon of December 28, 1900, the Yale historian Edward Gaylord Bourne stood before the members of the AHA's sixteenth annual meeting in Ann Arbor, Michigan, and prepared to speak. The audience had come to hear what promised to be the sensational paper of the conference: a talk Bourne had provocatively titled, "The Legend of Marcus Whitman."[1] Bourne began by establishing how legends typically functioned in modern America: as ways of filling the gaps in documentary evidence or embellishing true histories "with the foliage of picturesque incident or winged words." The legend of Marcus Whitman, however, was different. In Bourne's words, it was a "complete legendary reconstruction of history" the likes of which had not been seen since the Middle Ages. Bourne's talk was not just critical, it was condemnatory. He explained that the tale of Marcus Whitman, celebrated by statues and sermons, printed in textbooks and encyclopedias, and extolled by the president of the AHA only four years earlier, was false. It was "not only without trustworthy contemporary evidence, but . . . irreconcilable with well established facts."[2] Bourne demonstrated through the use of primary sources that Whitman's ride of 1842–43 had nothing to do with saving Oregon and that the story of Whitman's ride was nothing more than "a figment of Spalding's invention."[3] "The results of this investigation will come to many as a shock,"

Bourne acknowledged.[4] But his intent was clear: the profession of history must have no loyalties to myth, nostalgia, or heroism. It had to be loyal only to the scientific production of narrative truth.

The assault on the Whitman Saved Oregon Story continued with a response from William Isaac Marshall, a Chicago principal who had been doggedly pursuing the unveiling of the Whitman story for over two decades. The real history of Marcus Whitman, Marshall argued, was marred by petty conflict, unheroic characters, and the wholesale failure of Whitman's mission. "It is without exception the most amazing story of small-souled and narrow-minded folly I have ever read," he asserted, and he quoted several unflattering passages from Whitman's, Spalding's, and the other missionaries' correspondence to prove his point.[5] Not only was the Whitman story untrue, it was invented to cover up the real and embarrassing flaws of Whitman and his missionary companions, flaws that would now come to light. The gild of the Gilded Age Whitman now flaked off; beneath, there was nothing but a failed minor missionary, promoted by capitalists and journalists seeking to sell an imperial story, not the historical truth.

Bourne and Marshall recognized that their words would come as a surprise to many of their listeners. And indeed they did. The revelation at the AHA sparked a nationwide controversy over Whitman's deeds. For the first time the Whitman Saved Oregon Story was questioned in the halls of power—not by a beleaguered Catholic minority or by Oregonians excluded from the local Protestant establishment, but by scholars who claimed and wielded authority through a newly created and rapidly transforming professional guild. This was the second Whitman controversy, and unlike its 1880s predecessor it entangled not only the Anglo-American communities of the Far West but also scholars, religious leaders, and political figures across the nation.

The Whitman Saved Oregon Story was only one of the tales that professional historians sought to undermine in this period. Popular myths like that of George Washington and the cherry tree, Paul Revere's midnight ride, and Columbus's alleged discovery of America also served as sites of conflict between old and new history, between the romantic and moralistic narratives of the nineteenth century and the emerging scientific history of the twentieth.[6] The Whitman story stands out among these, however, because it was so closely intertwined with the providential history that the new historians also sought to eliminate. Unlike Paul Revere's or George Washington's renown, Whitman's heroism was intrinsically linked to his status as a missionary. The Whitman story's appeal depended on listeners' assumption that the projects of Christianization and American expansion were coextensive, that missionary labor was necessarily patriotic labor. It also depended, to some extent, on the conviction that missionaries were trustworthy historians. Both of these assumptions were called into question in the early twentieth century.

The overturning of providential narratives and the questioning of well-loved legends were part of two larger changes happening in the American historical profession at the turn of the twentieth century. First, the ongoing professionalization of academic history was moving in new directions. The process of historical professionalization had begun in the mid-nineteenth century with the establishment of historical societies. By the late nineteenth century professionalization had produced new ways of teaching and researching history in the academy: a focus on original research using primary sources, the introduction of the seminar method in American academic historical classrooms, and a new emphasis on historical objectivity as the fundamental norm of historical writing.[7] In the twentieth century this process of professionalization increasingly created rifts in the historical community, as local historians, secondary school teachers, and other non-university-affiliated historians began to be excluded from positions of power within organizations like the AHA.[8]

The second, related process was that of the historical profession's secularization. Secularization is a contested and multivalent term: scholars have posited it as a project closely related to the politics of the nation-state, as a process by which the expansion of science marginalizes religion and as a further entrenching of (an albeit hidden) Protestantism.[9] The secularization of the American historical profession may be defined as (1) the removal of overtly sectarian language from academic historical narratives, (2) the abandonment of overt appeals to divine intervention in historical affairs, and (3) professional historians' self-conscious embracing of an attitude of objectivity and scientific realism over what they deemed to be myth, superstition, and bias. This three-part process was not always neatly sequential, but each component invariably occurred as historians sought to forge a coherent academic discipline out of a widespread, diffuse populist practice.

As the historian Peter Novick has famously shown, fin de siècle academic history was dependent on the notion of objectivity: a conviction that the past was an objective reality that could be revealed through specific methods of inquiry that, as in the natural sciences, revealed conclusions that were verifiable and unbiased. The so-called scientific historian was to act as "a neutral, or disinterested, judge," as Novick writes, and "must never degenerate into that of advocate or, even worse, propagandist."[10] According to this vision of the historian's craft, overt appeals to providence or celebrations of the triumph of Christianity were biased, polemical, or simply intellectually lazy. As a critic for the *American Historical Review* wrote of the providential historian and Whitman defender William Augustus Mowry's work, "Dr. Mowry regards our territorial acquisitions as a series of special providences and upon this theory contents himself with the externals of negotiation without making any attempt to present the underlying causes."[11] The reviewer saw Mowry's failure to properly examine historical causes as being directly related to his reliance on providentialism as an explanatory method.

Yet, as Novick also observes, while turn-of-the-century historians generally agreed that objectivity should be a standard of historical method, both "scientific history" and "objectivity" were contested terms. Moreover, as the historian Elizabeth Clark has demonstrated, even openly providentialist historians could and did view their work as being both scientific and objective; they simply defined these terms differently.[12] The church historian Philip Schaff, for instance, considered history to be a science insofar as it "traced a phenomenon back to its origins so as to locate its 'essence' or 'life force,' and then chronicled its subsequent development."[13] Schaff's view of historical science was thus shaped by both a Hegelian understanding of God in history and a belief in the evolution of civilizations.[14] The providential historians who defended Whitman likewise saw their work as being scientific and objective but in ways that differed from those of the new scientific historians. The providentialists defined objectivity and scientific history as a specific posture toward handling evidence and making arguments, not by the elimination of providential perspectives from historical writing. Their alternate definitions of scientific history and objectivity ultimately lost out to those of the new scientific historians, but only after vigorous debate.

The ideological convictions underlying these two processes—professionalization and secularization—owed much to earlier iterations of historical writing, especially the imperial providentialism of the late nineteenth century. Notions of civilization and progress continued to shape American historians' work in the twentieth century, but the terms of civilization were beginning to shift. Providential historians considered the civilizing process to be guided by the hand of God and marked by the primacy of Protestant Christianity. Their work emphasized God's providence as a factor in historical events and framed both US and world history as the spaces in which the salvation of the world would unfold. The new scientific historians, by contrast, did not view Christianity, civilization, and progress as being essentially linked, or, rather, they did not see them as being linked in the same ways. Scientific historians did not see the triumph of Protestant Christianity as the pinnacle of civilization's achievements; instead, they viewed progress as the gradual victory of science over superstition. As Herbert Baxter Adams wrote of the transition of scholarly authority from theological seminaries to history seminars, "Preachers became teachers, and the pro[p]aganda of religion prepared the way for the propaganda of science."[15]

The shifting nature of the relationship between religion and civilization was partly due to the interplay between history and other emerging academic disciplines, especially comparative religion and anthropology. These two disciplines were strongly influenced by social evolutionary models that depicted civilizations as progressing from belief in magic and superstition to enlightened religion and science. Myths coincided with the first and most primitive stage: magic. As the scholar of Judaism William Frederick Cobb stated, "Myth precedes religion, and dies when religion attains to self-consciousness."[16] Scholars explained the origins of myths in various ways—as faulty science, or attempts to understand the physical world; as accidents of language; as ways of explaining preexisting rituals—but they shared a conviction that myths were vestiges of primitivism.[17] Moreover, they argued that myths could be traced back to their primitive origins through rigorous source criticism combined with theories of

cultural evolution and anthropological study of modern day "primitives"—
the indigenous and in many cases colonized peoples of the Americas, Oce-
ania, and Africa. Thus definitions of myth took on a racial and religious
character: the darker-skinned, non-Christian peoples of the world were
depicted as having myths, while white Anglo-Americans, supposedly at the
top of the evolutionary schema, had abandoned myths in favor of scientific truth.

This view of myth created fractures within the Protestant historical
community. Nowhere were they more present than in the Whitman controversy. Some Protestant historians, like Marshall and Bourne, came to
believe that the future of Protestantism rested on its willingness to reject
sectarian bias and outdated legends and to embrace the mores of modern scientific inquiry. The Whitman critics regarded Protestants who
clung to their providential histories and their hero tales as no better than
the savages and medievals who represented the nadir of civilized life. It
is no coincidence that both of these terms had racial and religious connotations. They were the logical extension of the racialized understandings of progress that had come into vogue in histories of the 1890s—only
now, they were being applied not to darker-skinned, non-Protestant
peoples but to the Protestant historians who had helped create these
historical paradigms of progress.

Meanwhile, other Protestant historians fought against the emerging guild of scientific history by defending the Whitman story. Like the
historians who had been involved in the first Whitman controversy in
the 1880s, these Protestants worried that scientific historians' reliance
on original documents would lead them to ignore key oral history
sources. This was worrisome for pioneer historians who had staked their
claim to authority on their status as eyewitnesses to local history. But it
was not only local historians who feared the new scientific history. Some
Protestants saw clear parallels between the rise of biblical criticism and
the myth-busting work of the new historians. They worried that scientific history would undermine "much of well grounded history, including Biblical."[18] Moreover, they felt that the new historical methods would
rob historians of one of their most central social functions: creating a
usable past that appealed to its readers' moral and imaginative sensibilities. "[The new historians'] principal canon of criticism seems to be that

any striking story which appeals to the romantic in human nature ...
must be of 'such stuff as dreams are made on," wrote a critic for the *Chicago Advance*.[19] To these historians, scientific history's possible contributions to historical accuracy came at the cost of alternate knowledge
bases, biblical integrity, and a usable past.

Historians on both sides of the battle over Whitman's legacy understood that the stakes extended beyond the discrediting of a popular
tale. Bound up in the Whitman Saved Oregon Story were the providential assumptions, pioneer sensibilities, and racialized vision of religious
progress that had shaped the story and allowed it to permeate popular
and scholarly consciousness. Providential history had a symbiotic relationship with the Whitman story: as providential historians popularized
the story of Whitman's ride to save Oregon, the story validated providential historians' conviction that the hand of God was at work in earthly events. An attack on one was an attack on the other. For historians of
Whitman the choice was stark. They could defend the Whitman story
and the providential history that produced it and thus risk being associated with the sectarian and mythmaking tendencies that American historians had come to view as unseemly; or they could abandon Whitman
and providence in the hopes of saving not just the American historical
profession but American Protestantism itself.

"One of the Most Impudent Fabrications Ever Attempted"

William Isaac Marshall's response to Bourne's "The Legend of
Marcus Whitman" before the AHA marked the culmination of his life-
work. In many ways Marshall's biography and personality bear striking
parallels to the originator of the Whitman story, Henry Harmon Spalding. He was as dedicated to quashing the Whitman story as Spalding had
been to spreading it. His single-minded devotion to his cause and propensity for entering into conflict also caused many to dismiss him as a
monomaniac.[20] Yet, like Spalding's, Marshall's relentless pursuit of his
mission profoundly shifted the historical legacy of Marcus Whitman
and with it the shape of the American historical profession.

Marshall was similar to Spalding in another way: stymied by family
difficulties and lack of educational opportunities, he eventually reinvented

himself in the American West. Marshall was born in Fitchburg, Massachusetts, on June 25, 1840. When he was seventeen his father died, and Marshall
was forced to drop out of high school to support his family. He eventually
finished school under the tutelage of Pratt Rogers Spencer, the developer of
the Spencerian method of cursive writing and an early advocate of business
colleges.[21] Marshall embarked on a career as a schoolteacher, principal, and
superintendent, but at the age of twenty-six he decided to go west in search
of new opportunities. He went to the mining boomtown of Virginia City in
Montana Territory and remained there for nine years, working as a teacher
and earning his law license. Marshall never struck gold, but he found a way
to make a living via another western resource: Montana's stunning scenery.[22] He purchased stereopticon images of the recently designated Yellowstone National Park, returned to Fitchburg, and began a successful career as
a lecturer, introducing easterners to Yellowstone's natural wonders through
projected slides. He served as a literal as well as a figurative tour guide to
Yellowstone, organizing trips for parties of easterners and leading them personally through the park.[23] He gradually expanded his lecture series to encompass Utah and Mormon history, California's giant redwood forests, and
the history and scenery of the Rocky Mountains and the Pacific Coast.[24]

Through his work as a public lecturer on the West Marshall discovered the Whitman story. While on the lecture circuit he met William Augustus Mowry, a lecturer, educator, and prolific author of histories,
textbooks, and pedagogical treatises.[25] Originally from Uxburg, Massachusetts, Mowry had received a bachelor of arts degree from Brown University
and by 1877 was serving as the superintendent of schools in Salem, Massachusetts. Like most historians working in the 1870s, Mowry was neither
affiliated with a university nor had he received academic training in history.
But as a regular member of the New England Historical Society and, later,
the AHA, Mowry had gained a reputation as an authority on various historical subjects, including the Pacific Northwest.[26] He had been researching
the history of the acquisition of the Northwest by the United States when
he came in contact with William H. Gray, the pioneer historian and advocate of the Whitman Saved Oregon Story. Mowry learned from Gray's *History of Oregon* the story of Whitman's ride, and he became involved in both
western and eastern efforts to make Whitman's heroism more widely
known. He was elected an honorary member of Gray's PHS and also en-

couraged easterners to contribute to Gray's Whitman Monument Association.[27] At the same time, he began to lecture on Whitman's ride to educators
in New England. "It is a great surprise to me to find so few people here at
the East who know *anything* comparatively of the great work of Dr. Whitman," Mowry wrote to Gray in 1878. He continued, "I have had much satisfaction in presenting the facts of his work for Oregon, & how he saved it
to our country, before the teachers of New England, and one or two historical societies."[28] In the late nineteenth century the lecture circuit brought
public history to a wide audience, and the Whitman story was tailor-made
for this kind of spoken circulation.[29] Through his historical and educational connections Mowry helped the Whitman story gain acceptance in
the East.

When Marshall first heard the Whitman story from Mowry he was
suspicious: as he later wrote, the story "by no means agreed with my
previous notions of Oregon history."[30] Nevertheless, Marshall trusted
both Mowry and those upon whose testimonies Mowry's account was
based: namely, Whitman's fellow missionaries Henry Harmon Spalding,
William H. Gray, and Cushing Eells.[31] In the 1870s testimony from reputable eyewitnesses was still considered a primary source of historical
knowledge, and to a historian not familiar with local criticisms of Spalding's and Gray's honesty, few eyewitnesses would seem more trustworthy than Christian missionaries who had known Marcus Whitman
personally. There was another reason for Marshall to believe the story:
he "saw in it the material for a VERY POPULAR lecture on Oregon, especially for church lecture courses," one that he estimated could bring him
between ten thousand and twenty-five thousand dollars in revenue over
a period of years.[32] Over the next five years Marshall prepared for a new
two-lecture series on Whitman's ride while continuing to deliver lectures on other western topics. In 1882 Marshall embarked for the Pacific
Northwest to conduct his final research for the Whitman lectures. What
he found there permanently altered his view of Marcus Whitman and
launched him on a lifelong crusade to correct the historical record.[33]

In Oregon and Washington Marshall came in contact with several
local historians who doubted the Whitman story: Frances Fuller Victor,
Elwood Evans, and Matthew Deady.[34] As noted above, these scholars
were pioneer secularists, "secularists" insofar as they resisted the Protestant

culture of the Pacific Northwest's historical societies and argued that providentialist and sectarian biases made for inaccurate history, and "pioneer" historians insofar as they, like other historians in the Pacific Northwest, based their authority in part on their identity as pioneers, witnesses to the Pacific Northwest's early history. The pioneer secularists' critiques of the Whitman story had received little attention outside of the Pacific Northwest, but they were sufficient to reinforce Marshall's doubts about the Whitman story's accuracy.[35] Marshall resolved to conduct additional research before delivering his Whitman lectures rather than risk his historical reputation on what might be a falsehood.

Marshall spent the next five years visiting public libraries and archives in fifteen states, Canada, and the United Kingdom, at his own expense, offsetting the costs by continuing to lecture on other western topics.[36] Through this research he discovered that a major plot point in the Whitman story was false. Secretary of State Daniel Webster was neither ignorant of the Pacific Northwest's resources nor did he ever consider trading half of the then–Oregon Country for a codfishery. None of Webster's extensive records ever mentioned such a trade nor did any of Whitman's own correspondence.[37] This directly contradicted Whitman promoters' claims that Webster was convinced that the Oregon Country was "one unbroken waste of sand deserts and impassable mountains, fit only for the beaver, the gray bear, and the savage," and that Webster had "about traded [the Oregon Country] off ... for a codfishery in Newfoundland."[38] If Spalding and Gray had misrepresented the danger of the US losing Oregon, they had likely misrepresented other parts of the story as well. Marshall was incensed by this discovery. He was furious at the loss of a potentially profitable lecture series, at himself for being deceived, and especially at the missionaries and historians who had deceived him. "[The Whitman Saved Oregon Story] is one of the most impudent fabrications ever attempted to be palmed off on the credulity of mankind as history," he wrote to Myron Eells.[39]

In 1884, two years into his research, Marshall delivered his first lecture on Marcus Whitman at the Peabody Institute in Baltimore. It was not the celebratory hero story Marshall had planned in 1877, however; instead, it was Marshall's first public foray into the Whitman controversy. While conceding that Whitman's ride was heroic and daring, Marshall argued that the ride "was undertaken solely on missionary business, had no political purpose, accomplished no political result, and had no more to do with saving Oregon . . . to the United States, than it had with the election of Louis Napoleon to the presidency of the French Republic." With full confidence in his extensive primary source research, Marshall concluded, "No man who will read the evidence can doubt that if Marcus Whitman had never been born our [boundary] line would have been 49 degrees to the Pacific Coast, precisely as it is today."[40]

At this early point in Marshall's research he still believed that Whitman himself was a good, perhaps even a great, man, despite Spalding's and Gray's inflated tales of Whitman's heroism. This began to change when Marshall sought access to the records of Whitman's mission in the ABCFM archives. When the archives initially refused Marshall's request for access, the denial intensified his suspicions that not only was the Whitman story untrue but its falsity was being covered up by Whitman's supporters.[41] When Marshall did gain access to the records in 1887 he discovered hundreds of pages of correspondence between Whitman, his missionary colleagues, and their supervisors. This correspondence revealed what Marshall had suspected and others, like Frances Fuller Victor, had already known: the whole unflattering history of the ABCFM missions in Oregon, from the multiple petty conflicts between the missionaries to the board's order that the missions be closed in 1842. Marshall no longer believed that Whitman's ride had been a heroic, if ineffectual deed. He was now convinced that Whitman was "not in any sense of the term a great man, and that, though he was undoubtedly a very zealous man, he was far from being a wise, or a far-seeing, or a magnanimous, or a prudent, or a successful one."[42] He was also persuaded that Whitman's defenders must have been willfully ignorant, insane, or openly lying in their recounting of Whitman's heroism. As he wrote to Mowry, "When you read [my letter], you will not know at which to be the most amazed; your credulity in continuing to endorse the myth, or the audacious mendacity of Gray, Spalding and Eells in fabricating it."[43]

From that moment until his death in 1906 Marshall resolved to spend all available time and resources on disproving the Whitman story. "I most heartily wish I had never heard of it; but having been humbugged by it, I deem it my duty to put the real facts in the ca[s]e before the public," he explained to a colleague.[44] Why was Marshall's reply to this hoodwink so animated that he would devote so much time to its advertisement? Like Spalding before him, Marshall felt that he had been personally wronged by the creation and circulation of inaccurate history, and his future historical endeavors would be propelled by this sense of slight. Unlike Spalding, however, Marshall no longer believed that providential historical methods could determine the truth of history. Providential history had led Marshall to believe the stories of Spalding, Gray, and others. In order to expose the Whitman story he needed to rely on a different set of methods: the painstaking, document-based research of the new scientific history.

Marshall began work on what eventually became a two-volume exposé of the Whitman Saved Oregon Story. He reached out to other historians who had worked on the Whitman question. He earned the tepid support of a few scholars, including Hubert Howe Bancroft, who had never believed the Whitman story.[45] But most dismissed him for the same reason Spalding had been discounted twenty years earlier: they felt that Marshall's fiery writing style and seemingly obsessive quest to overturn the Whitman story proved he was a monomaniac.[46] Marshall did little to convince his colleagues otherwise. At one point he wrote William A. Mowry a 182-page copyrighted letter, painstakingly outlining every mistake he believed Mowry had made in his recent one-page *Congregationalist* article on Whitman. He followed up by promising Mowry that "I have a sincere respect for you, and so have given you this warning, that you may get to cover before the catastrophe comes. One half of the matter in my possession will not merely shatter the Whitman Saved Oregon Myth into fragments, but will grind it to impalpabel [sic] powder, whose existence will only be manifest by the strong sulphurous odor it will exhale from the amount of unscrupulous lying used to bolster it up."[47] Mowry, unpersuaded, proceeded with his planned biography of Whitman.

Marshall's abrasive tactics earned him little respect among his correspondents. "The opinion seems to be about unanimous that he is a crank of the first water. Such a man never exerts any very deep and abiding influence," wrote Mowry's friend, the Chicago Congregational minister Edward F. Williams.[48] Nor were the Whitman defenders' critiques limited to Marshall's obsessive tendencies; more broadly, they believed that Marshall lacked the qualities necessary to write objective history.

Mowry, Eells, and other Whitman boosters were established academics, trained in respected schools and published in reputable scholarly journals. Through these networks they had imbibed many of the principles of the new history, including its emphasis on objectivity. As Mowry wrote to Eells, "A successful historical student must have two qualities: (1) Unlimited patience and perseverance in studying the facts of the case. (2) Good judgment in interpreting these facts. I think Marshall has the first of these two qualities."[49] According to Mowry, Marshall was too "prejudiced against Whitman" to be taken seriously as a historian; his writing was "bombastic, egotistical, full of extreme statements and terribly in earnest."[50] Other historians agreed. "As a man I do not think Mr Marshall is respected very highly. His prejudices work against him," wrote Edward Williams. He concluded, "A partizan [sic] can never be trusted even if he tells the truth."[51] The habits of right history would, Williams suggested, be a bit more moderate in tone.

   It may seem surprising that providential historians were advocating objectivity in historical research and writing, as many scientific historians felt that appeals to divine providence necessarily violated the rules of objectivity. In fact, providential historians like Mowry and Eells saw no conflict between their providentialist convictions and the new history's emphasis on objectivity. To Eells, Mowry, and their fellow turn-of-the-century providential historians, "objectivity" entailed thorough and fair examination of all available evidence without imposing any preordained conclusions on said sources.[52] The providentialists believed that the objective examination of historical evidence—oral testimony and original source documents— did not preclude providential explanations of history but rather could bolster providential interpretations of history with the weight of objective evidence. In 1888, for instance, Eells gave a commencement address at Whitman College entitled, "The Hand of God in the History of the Pacific Coast," in which he used documentary evidence to illuminate "sixteen links in this chain of Providence which gave Oregon to the United States."[53] To the providentialists as well as to scientific historians, objectivity entailed a certain expectation of civility. Historians should not decide historical questions by, in Eells's words, "calling names, dealing in probabilities, or misstating an opponent's position" but simply by "weight of argument."[54] Objective historians, in other words, must recognize that documentary evidence could be fairly interpreted in more than one way and for this reason should treat their opponents with respect. As Mowry wrote to Marshall, "I claim the same right to my conclusions when I examine historical evidence that I would accord to you."[55] Providentialists viewed objectivity as a matter of public performance as well as of unbiased inquiry.

Being accepted into historical circles was also a matter of connections, another factor that Marshall lacked. Partly this was due to his tendency to lose friends because of his sharp language, but equally off-putting was Marshall's status as an outsider to established academic circles. Scholars like Eells and Mowry had received their graduate education in eastern universities and seminaries, where they had developed relationships with other researchers and learned a manner of academic etiquette that helped them with new introductions. Marshall, on the other hand, was nearly entirely self-taught in the ways of history. He read prolifically but had few interlocutors until he began his Whitman correspondence. Nor was Marshall's method of building academic community—contacting established academic historians out of the blue with scathing indictments of their work—very effective in gaining conversation partners or allies. Although Marshall had embraced the new methods of scientific history, above all the focus on original source documents, his writing style marked him as someone who had not yet learned the subdued language of academic historical writing, which regarded dispassionate and balanced prose as part and parcel of objectivity.

Despite Marshall's commitment to divulging the truth about the Whitman story he struggled for years to find a wider audience for his conclusions than a few lecture crowds and some grudging correspondents. He had finished the first draft of his Whitman exposé by the early 1890s, but the Panic of 1893 threw him into financial turmoil, forcing him to delay his search for a publisher.[56] He decided to turn his efforts toward a different strategy: If he could not afford to publish his work, he could at least keep the Whitman story from being "imposed upon the children of the nation through their school histories."[57] He began sending the authors of historical textbooks "typewritten criticisms of the amazing errors into which some of the ablest of our historians had fallen through accepting Gray, and Spalding, and C. Eells, and Barrows, and Nixon, and Mowry . . . and M. Eells as trustworthy authorities, instead of

going to original sources."[58] His letters reached such historical luminaries as John Fiske of Harvard, John Bach McMaster of the University of
Pennsylvania, and the social historian Edward Eggleston.[59] Instead of
simply exhorting them to stop publishing the Whitman story, as he had
Mowry and Eells, Marshall provided the historians with excerpts from
his evidence and offered to loan pieces from his large collection of documentary evidence.[60] Like Mowry, Eells, and other historians, these new
correspondents found Marshall's forceful manner of writing unprofes-
sional; Fiske, for instance, admonished Marshall, "I think the force of
your arguments would be enhanced if your style of expression were now
and then a little less vehement."[61] Nevertheless, most of the historians
found Marshall's overwhelming mass of evidence—government documents, material from the Hudson's Bay Company's archives, copies of
the missionaries' diaries and letters that had never before been presented
to the public—to be convincing. McMaster assured Marshall that "the
weight of evidence seems to be against the belief that Whitman rode to
Washington to save Oregon" and promised to edit the next edition of his
history textbook accordingly.[62] Fiske, despite his misgivings about Marshall's style, wrote to him, "You have entirely demolished the Whitman
delusion, and by so doing have made yourself a public benefactor."[63]

This positive reception notwithstanding, however, Marshall lacked
a public outlet for his research. Most of his correspondents agreed to
remove the Whitman story from subsequent editions of their textbooks,
but they preferred to do so quietly rather than stirring up public controversy.[64] Meanwhile, newspapers and pulpits continued to trumpet Whitman's heroism. It would take a more prominent and more widely
respected figure than Marshall to bring the Whitman story's inconsistencies into public light.

"Unceasing Critical Vigilance"

Edward Gaylord Bourne came late to the Whitman controversy,
but he brought with him a long career as a trained historian and respected academic. Bourne was as much an insider to the American historical profession as Marshall was an outsider. He was born in 1860 in
Strykersville, New York, to an educated family whose roots dated back to

Puritan times. His father, James Russell Bourne, was a Yale-educated Congregational minister. Bourne's early life, like Marshall's, had been marred by struggle. When he was ten years old he contracted the disease that eventually killed him: tuberculosis of the hip. He walked with a limp for the rest of his life.[65] The condition did not affect his love of learning, however, and Bourne quickly distinguished himself in his studies: first, in classical languages, then economics, and, finally, history. He earned bachelor of arts and doctoral degrees at Yale University, where he studied history under the tutelage of the sociologist and Herbert Spencer acolyte William Graham Sumner.[66] Bourne rose quickly through the historical ranks, his work on the Spanish empire in the Americas earning him wide recognition in the broader academic community. He served as a professor at Adelbert College (now Case Western University) before returning to a professorship at Yale in 1895.[67] Bourne immersed himself in shaping graduate historical work both at Yale and in academic institutions in general. He frequently corresponded with colleagues like Albert Bushnell Hart of Harvard, Frederick Jackson Turner of the University of Wisconsin, and the editor of the *American Historical Review*, J. Franklin Jameson, discussing the state of the historical profession and which books and methodologies should be taught.[68] He served as one of the editors of the *Yale Review* and as a member of several program committees for the AHA.[69] Unlike Marshall, Bourne was well connected, well trained, well known in academic circles, and deeply invested in the academic historical discipline's various professionalizing projects.

As a student and then as a faculty member at Yale Bourne had discovered a world of interrelated professionalizing humanities disciplines, including history, economics, sociology, literature, and anthropology/comparative religion. The boundaries between these disciplines were still somewhat fluid, and Bourne read widely. He was greatly interested in comparative religionists' theories of the development of myth, which he said was a fascinating study.[70] In an article for the *Yale Review* Bourne compared philological and anthropological theories of the evolution of primitive myths. Whereas philologists like Max Müller argued that myths and folktales developed out of an ancient, common Aryan culture, anthropologists like Andrew Lang believed that myths originated with "the most distant and wildest savages." As Bourne explained, "These stories in their essential features reflect the range of thought, fears, and beliefs of savage people, they even embalm in story form descriptions of their early customs." Moreover, while European cultures had "pruned off" the "crudities" of myths as they "advanced in culture," myths and folktales had endured "with little modification" among supposedly primitive groups like the San peoples of South Africa. This is the theory that Bourne found most convincing and most "likely to gain more and more assent" from scholars.[71] Myths, in other words, were holdovers from a more primitive state of civilization, albeit one that could still be found in contemporary so-called savage societies. Bourne's understanding of myths as constructs of primitive societies came to play an integral role in his analysis of the Whitman story.

Bourne was also deeply committed to the new scientific history, particularly its emphasis on investigation of original sources. "Historical critics tell us that tradition ceases to be trustworthy after it has passed through more than two hands," he wrote in the *Yale Review* in 1886. "How much better than traditions are the accounts of historical events which are handed on from one age to another without constant verification in the sources?"[72] This conviction too was shaped by advances in the study of religion, namely, the method of studying the Bible known as higher criticism. In an essay on Leopold von Ranke, whom both nineteenth-century historians and contemporary scholars commonly credited as the founder of scientific history, Bourne explained that one of Ranke's major innovations was "the systematic application of what is now familiarly known as the 'higher criticism' to works written since the invention of printing" and, later, to manuscript sources as well.[73] Bourne believed that higher criticism could solve the thorny issues of biblical interpretation that were then fracturing Protestant communities. "If Ranke had devoted himself to Hebrew history," he asserted, "the Biblical discussions of our own day would have taken place in the time of our fathers and grandfathers."[74] If higher criticism could modernize understandings of the Bible, perhaps it could usher in a modern understanding of history as well.

Bourne made his name as a historian by applying higher criticism to earlier historical studies in order to locate errors or identify hidden contexts. In 1891 he published a study arguing from textual evidence that the historian George Bancroft had begun his *Martin Van Buren to the End of His Public Career* as a campaign document to support Van Buren's presidential bid.[75] Bourne's work was highly praised by others in the historical community who hoped his studies would help to prove the worth of the new historical methods to skeptics. Andrew Cunningham McLaughlin of the University of Michigan, for instance, wrote to Bourne, "Your application of Higher Criticism to Bancroft's Van Buren is very interesting & clever. I hope it will teach ecclesiastical obstructionists a lesson."[76]

In his embrace of higher criticism as well as anthropological theories of myth Bourne was influenced by trends in the study of religion even as he labored to rid histories of their sectarian preferences. His familiarity with these trends positioned him to recast the Whitman story as a myth, with full cognizance that such a categorization would alter its historical reception.

Despite Bourne's interests in the study of myth and the use of original sources to correct erroneous history, it was not he but one of his students who first became aware of questions about the Whitman story. One of Bourne's master of arts advisees, Arthur Howard Hutchinson, began researching the Whitman story in the late 1890s. Hutchinson had become aware of the story when he attended the University of Washington in Seattle. Not only did Marcus Whitman appear relatively frequently in the Seattle newspapers but Edmund Stephen Meany, one of the University of Washington's most prominent history professors, was a firm believer in the Whitman story.[77] Knowing something about the regional debates over Whitman's legacy, Hutchinson was interested in using the new higher criticism methods to examine the documentary evidence on Whitman's ride. After poring through much of the same documentary base as Marshall, Hutchinson became convinced that the Whitman Saved Oregon Story was false. He brought his conclusions to Bourne, hoping to publish them.[78] Unfortunately, Hutchinson was a better researcher than he was a writer. He submitted his essay to the *American Historical Review,* but its editor, John Franklin Jameson, rejected it. "I should like to see the Marcus Whitman legend neatly exploded in the pages of Review," James wrote to Bourne. "But I think, to speak frankly between you and me, that the article is too ill written and treats problems of criticism too much in the spirit of a tyro."[79] Like Marshall,

Hutchinson failed to perform the work of a historian in a way that appeared sufficiently polished for a professionalizing discipline.

Bourne was not willing to let the Whitman question go unremarked, however. He wrote back to Jameson inquiring whether the *American Historical Review* would be interested in an article on the Whitman story written by him. Jameson answered in the affirmative, and Bourne, using Hutchinson's notes, began preparing the paper that became "The Legend of Marcus Whitman."[80]

In addition to borrowing from Hutchinson's work, Bourne drew on the research of Frances Fuller Victor, the Oregonian pioneer secularist who had been involved in the first Whitman controversy of 1880–85. In the 1880s Victor had been dismissed as an outsider by many of her peers in the Pacific Northwest's historical community, and her attacks on the Whitman story were disregarded as the story gained national momentum. After spending two decades working as an uncredited ghostwriter for Hubert Howe Bancroft, Victor seemed doomed to fade into obscurity along with her criticisms of the Whitman story. This changed when Jameson contacted Victor to ask about her research. Like Hutchinson, Victor sent a manuscript she had written on the Whitman question to be considered for publication in the *Review,* but Jameson rejected it, as he had already asked Bourne to write on the Whitman story and was unwilling to publish a second paper on the same subject.[81] As in the 1880s Victor's exclusion from the circles of historical influence prevented her work from reaching a wider audience. This time, however, it was not the pioneer establishment of the Pacific Northwest but the rising academic historical community that rejected her. Victor sent some of her sources to Bourne for review, hoping to at least receive credit for her research in Bourne's footnotes.[82] Bourne duly praised Victor for being the only historian who had the open-mindedness to change her view of the Whitman story's "legendary character" after having repeated the story in her earlier work.[83] Victor's influence was ammunition for Bourne's critics, who had already faced her once in the 1880s.

Thus Bourne's paper relied heavily on the labor of Hutchinson, Victor, and, later, Marshall.[84] His conclusions did not vary greatly from what Victor, Marshall, and others had been arguing since the 1880s: that Oregon was not in danger of being traded to Great Britain in 1842–43;

that Whitman did not influence US policy on the Oregon Country; and that Whitman traveled east to save his floundering mission, not to rescue Oregon. What Bourne did that others had not was to imbue the Whitman story with broader stakes by depicting it as a modern-day myth, with all of the connotations of primitiveness that such a designation entailed. As Bourne argued, the Whitman story was an aberration, a holdover from an earlier era; it "call[ed] to mind the Donation of Constantine or the story of William Tell."[85] The mention of the Donation of Constantine was not incidental. To Bourne and his fellow historians Catholicism continued to be a referent for superstition and primitiveness, as it had for earlier providential historians. Allusions to the Middle Ages were a similar kind of shorthand for unenlightened superstition. Even as scientific historians attempted to craft histories that were not shaped by sectarian commitments, "Catholicism" was a code word for distinguishing scientific history from naive or willfully ignorant superstition. It is telling that historians on both sides of the debate depicted the Whitman myth busting as iconoclasm, for the scientific historians saw their work as a kind of Protestant Reformation of history, a stripping away of layers of tradition in order to get back to the original and supreme text.[86] While their critics wondered, along with the Whitman supporter Samuel Clarke, if the scientific historians "are all infidels and hate the church and its missionaries," the scientific historians themselves saw their labor as strengthening Christianity by purifying its history according to the demands of the new scholarship.[87]

Bourne found the Whitman story troubling because it upended typical narratives of historical progress. It had emerged not in the Middle Ages but in "the latter half of the nineteenth century in the United States."[88] Bourne thus cast his critique of the Whitman story in moral terms. He asserted, "To trace the steps by which the imaginative reconstruction of this transaction, strangely distorting the relative significance of men and events, has slowly but steadily pushed aside the truth, until it has invaded not only the text-books but the works of historians whose reputation gives their utterances a certain authority, would give every one a new idea of the pervasive and subtle power of the legendary faculty of the human mind and of the need for unceasing critical vigilance."[89] The Whitman Saved Oregon Story served as a cautionary tale for historians and their readers: Americans could not take their advanced state of knowledge for granted but must constantly be on guard against primitive and medieval impulses toward mythologizing. The era of modern scholarship depended on the expulsion of myths.

Bourne placed the Whitman story within a new teleology of progress, one that owed much to earlier providential narratives even as it repudiated them for their reliance on unsound history. This teleology, for all its celebration of the triumph of science over superstition, was still broadly Protestant in its convictions.

"Sometimes Scientific History Is Not the Truth"

"American Historical Society Makes an Exposure" ran the title of the *Los Angeles Times* coverage the morning after Bourne delivered his AHA address. The article opened by stating, "It looks as though many pages printed in American histories concerning the exploits of Marcus Whitman . . . will have to be torn out."[90] Other media outlets concurred. "Everyone thinks he knows how Dr. Whitman undertook a perilous journey across the Rocky Mountains in 1842," noted the *Dial*. "A striking paper by Edward G. Bourne of Yale University . . . proved that this story is not only inaccurate in its details but unfounded in its main outlines."[91] More than simply accepting Bourne's conclusions, however, many journalists adopted his teleology. In their reporting, the implicit racial and religious categorizations of Bourne's paper became more explicit. "The hero worshiper of today must yield to the spirit of modern history, which with the other sciences has laid aside the careless bungling medieval methods, and builds its monuments of fame on the foundations of truth, not on legends," wrote the journalist Alice Carman.[92] The *Oregonian* contrasted the confuting of the Whitman story with the proliferation of myths in ancient times, explaining that "in our age written and printed records are preserved, and the mythopeic [sic] faculty of the human mind receives checks and corrections unknown in the composition of the Homeric poems or portions of the Biblical narratives." These articles demonstrated the extent to which the sensibilities that drove Bourne's and Marshall's critiques of the Whitman story had permeated the popular press.

Though many were persuaded by Bourne's arguments, not all Whitman devotees were ready to erase Whitman's ride from their histories. Supporters of the Whitman Saved Oregon Story recognized that the national attention Bourne's paper was receiving entailed a more serious challenge to the Whitman story than had ever been raised before. Shortly after the AHA annual meeting Mowry wrote to Myron Eells, entreating him to respond publicly to Bourne's and Marshall's accusations. "The friends of Dr. Whitman must surely rally and present the evidence that the truth gives for the great work which he did," Mowry wrote. "Unless this evidence is presented the public inevitably will be obliged to lean the other way."[93]

Some of Whitman's supporters attempted to refute the arguments of Bourne and Marshall by using the old logic of pioneer history: Bourne was an outsider who had no personal familiarity with the events of 1842–43, while those who supported the story of Whitman's ride had known Whitman personally or had lived in the Northwest during its early days of settlement. Oliver Nixon, the Chicago newspaper editor whose astute promotion of the Whitman story helped to bring the tale national fame, claimed that Bourne had made "a bad break" for himself by questioning the Whitman story. Echoing the language of apostolic succession, he asserted, "The chain of historic authority tracing the work of Whitman in saving Oregon and Washington to the United States is perfect and unbreakable."[94] A writer for the *Chicago Advance* argued that readers should trust Nixon over Bourne, for Nixon "lived in the days of the events about which he writes [and] could get much nearer the facts," while Bourne was "a Yale professor who discredits all the direct testimony of Whitman, and Spalding, and Eells, and Nixon . . . as 'legendary.'"[95] John Wilder Fairbank, who knew Cushing Eells personally, wrote, "Professor Bourne knows of his own knowledge nothing in the matter, and no man has a right in these days of history making, to talk . . . on a subject of which he is personally ignorant."[96] To defenders of the old pioneer historical methods Bourne's identity as an insider in eastern academic circles made him an outsider in the ways of pioneer history. He had neither the personal experience nor the regional familiarity to be considered a trustworthy authority.

Other critics, however, realized that the logic of pioneer history could not successfully refute Bourne and Marshall, for their work placed the very foundations of pioneer history in jeopardy. The two men's arguments did not simply reiterate the work of pioneer secularists like Frances Fuller Victor; they self-consciously asserted a new regime of historical authority that viewed the rejection of oral tradition as essential to the process of academic modernization. As Marshall wrote, history must be based on "the contemporaneous records written by the actors themselves instead of on the shifting quicksands of ingenious theories, resting in the doubtful recollections of men."[97] Their research into the original documents of Whitman's mission, moreover, had undercut the trustworthiness of the eyewitnesses to whom the Whitman defenders appealed. After obtaining access to the ABCFM archives and Henry Spalding's journal, Marshall, Hutchinson, and, by extension, Bourne had found material that discredited the story's main advocates. Spalding's journals showed that he was "evidently a monomaniac, utterly irresponsible for his utterances."[98] Gray, Marshall asserted, cast so much vitriol toward the Hudson's Bay Company and Catholics that he could "no more write a fair history of Oregon than a donkey can sing opera music."[99] Cushing Eells, who had been well-liked during his lifetime and measured in his writings, had not left such compromising materials, but the Whitman skeptics still determined that "Spalding's inventions ... displaced his own recollections," so that he became an unwitting supporter of the legend.[100] These were claims that the pioneer secularists had made in the 1880s, but since Marshall and Hutchinson were able to access more of the missionaries' private materials they had a clearer view of the grudges and feuds, the worries about Spalding's mental health, and the frustrations with Gray's partisanship and propensity for exaggeration that had characterized the troubled history of the Oregon missions.

The defenders of the Whitman story deemed that the scientific historians' criticisms of Spalding, Gray, and Cushing Eells transgressed the boundaries of interpretive etiquette. The older generation of historians believed there were certain moral imperatives that should guide the study of history. Historical inquiry, rather than being simply deconstructive, should have a morally constructive purpose. "I must confess to very little sympathy with this tendency [toward disproving legends] among historic writers unless some ethical or at least high scientific benefit to the world is to result," wrote the Civil War veteran Charles

Henry Howard.[101] Whitman's loyalists also believed that historians should respect the privacy of the dead by not revealing unseemly and arguably irrelevant details of their inner lives. In their view the exposés of Marshall and Bourne were tawdry as well as disrespectful. "The missionaries were human. They had their quarrels. They afterwords [*sic*] saw their sins; they sought forgiveness of each other and of God," Myron Eells wrote. Since the missionaries' affairs were "thus settled, they ought to stay settled," he argued, "and the public has no right to drag them out and parade them before the world now."[102] The true believers of the Whitman story acknowledged that certain elements of the tale—the codfishery deal, the priest who allegedly taunted Whitman, alerting him to the British plot—were probably exaggerated, yet they felt that most of the disseminators of the Whitman story were honest, principled people. Henry Parker, writing for the *Homiletic Review,* avowed that the witnesses to the Whitman story were "persons of unquestionable intelligence, character, and veracity."[103] He inquired, "What is any testimony worth, if their testimony is to be sniffed at and kicked aside?"[104]

According to the supporters of the Whitman story, not only did the Whitman critics exercise poor moral judgment in attacking the character of Whitman, Spalding, and other pioneers, but they did so for no better reason than to chase after fame and fleeting historical trends. Longtime Whitman booster Charles Howard opined, "The smashing of popular idols and the clearing away of the fogs of poetry and romance that are found to hang like a drapery around the heroes of the past, seems, just now, to be a fad." Howard believed that Bourne's tearing down of the Whitman story was nothing more than an attempt to prove that "he belongs to the true historian's cult."[105] Those who championed Whitman understood that the new methods of disproving the tale were influenced by scholarly work on myth. As one author wrote for the *Chicago Advance,* "Some of our younger historians are nothing if not critical. They hate legends. . . . [T]hey have no rest in their critical souls until they have traced such stories back to that fire mist of imagination from which legends are evolved."[106]

To supporters of the Whitman story the new history posed a serious threat not just to the old historical regime but also, and more troublingly, to Christianity itself. They recognized that the biblical texts had originated as oral tradition. The editors of the 1901 *Homiletic* expressed the stakes starkly, warning that "Professor Bourne's demand for original documents of contemporary data would demolish much of well grounded history, including Biblical."[107] Whatever the shortcomings of the Whitman advocates, they rightly perceived that attacking cherished American legends helped the new historians and their methods gain recognition and legitimacy. They also realized that the new history both drew upon and had implications for the study of religion in the academy.

The Whitman defenders utilized a variety of arguments to combat Bourne and Marshall. The most sustained defense, however, came from Myron Eells, a missionary to the Twana people of Skokomish in Washington State's Puget Sound region. Eells was uniquely well positioned for this work. First, he commanded respect among the Pacific Northwest's aging pioneer historians. Eells was one of the first white Americans born in the Pacific Northwest, he had met Marcus Whitman as a young child, and he was well connected to the Northwest's earlier generation of pioneer historians, including William H. Gray.[108] Second, he was highly educated in the ways of providential history. Like his father, Eells earned his master of divinity degree from Hartford Theological Seminary, where he attended lectures by providentialist scholars such as Philip Schaff, the founder of the American Society of Church History.[109] While Eells became more reserved in his use of providential language over time, he liberally sprinkled his writing with providentialist quotes from other historians and religious leaders, such as Rev. James Whitford Bashford's proclamation that "the Divine Providence is the key to our national history."[110] Third, Eells was established in both regional and national academic networks. He was a trustee of Pacific University in Oregon as well as of Whitman College, was recognized as an authority on early Oregon, and had published his linguistic and anthropological writings on indigenous peoples of the Pacific Northwest in peer-reviewed journals like *Science* and the *American Anthropologist*.[111] Eells thus had ties to each of the scholarly worlds that were coming into conflict in the early twentieth century. As he would come to discover, however, the transformations of American history's professionalization made it impossible for him to hold these increasingly divergent historical communities together.

Eells responded first with an article in the *Whitman College Quarterly,* which was republished as a stand-alone pamphlet, and then with multiple newspaper articles in the *Oregonian* and other periodicals. Eells also drafted a biography of Whitman entitled *Marcus Whitman: Pathfinder and Patriot,* a work that was not published until after his death.[112] In these works Eells attempted to synthesize the requirements of the new scientific history with the older pioneer providential methods. He argued that while it was true that oral testimony was sometimes inaccurate, historians had methods of assessing whether such testimony was reliable or not. Testimony that agreed with documentary evidence or that was affirmed by multiple witnesses could be considered more accurate and used in historical writing.[113] To omit valid testimony, Eells argued, was a disservice to the historical profession. Scientific historians' emphasis on original documents would be particularly unfair to the history of the early Anglo-American West because the first settlers tended to be mobile, poorly educated, and subject to adverse conditions for the preservation of documents. This matter was especially personal for Eells. The Eells family had lost two homes, along with most of their family records, to fires. "Although [Cushing Eells] refreshed his memory all he could from the writings of others, yet he had to rely on his memory for much," wrote Myron Eells. "It was either this or to lose much of the truth."[114] Eells concluded that scientific historians were too stringent in their requirements that documentary evidence alone be used to ground historical arguments. "Generally scientific history and the truth agree, but sometimes in order to obtain the truth it is necessary to go outside of scientific history, and sometimes scientific history is not the truth," Eells wrote.[115]

Eells pointed out that Bourne and Marshall did not consistently adhere to the methods they espoused. When it served their arguments, they did use oral testimonies as evidence. For instance, in 1899 Bourne interviewed Elizabeth McGary Lovejoy, the wife of Asa Lawrence Lovejoy, the Oregon lawyer who accompanied Whitman on his 1842–43 ride, and asked her what she remembered Asa telling her about Whitman's reasons for going east. Bourne then used Elizabeth Lovejoy's testimony as evidence that Whitman's journey had no political motive. "Can any other conclusion be reached than that Professor Bourne has decided that memory, even if it be a memory of a memory, fifty-seven years old, is of weight if on his side, but if it is on the other side and a single memory, not half as old, it is of no weight?" Eells inquired. "Does this not break down his whole argument?"[116] He pointed out as well that Bourne and Marshall had neglected crucial documentary evidence, namely an 1843 letter that Whitman had written to James Porter, President John Tyler's secretary of war. In the letter Whitman referenced a meeting he had with Porter and reiterated his ideas for offering protection to American settlers in Oregon. The letter proved that Whitman had met with high government officials in Washington, DC, for the purpose of encouraging Oregon settlement.[117] Bourne and Marshall must have known of this letter's existence because both Eells and Mowry pointed to it as evidence, but they ignored it entirely in their analyses. Eells thereby emphasized not only that scientific history was a methodology with serious limits but also that neither Bourne's nor Marshall's examinations were as consistently scientific as they claimed.

Eells was seen as a savior by many who believed in the Whitman story: those who wanted the story to be true because of their relationship to the frontier and those who wanted it to be true because of their relationship to the Christian heroism Whitman allegedly modeled. Because of Eells's status as a respected scholar and pioneer historian with personal knowledge of early Oregon history adherents of the Whitman story hoped his work might quell the criticisms of the Whitman tale. Samuel Clarke believed that Eells had established the truth of the Whitman story "beyond all question."[118] A journalist for the *Independent* stated that Eells's *Reply to Professor Bourne's "The Whitman Legend"* "riddles the assumption of an infallible 'scientific method' on the part of the anti-Whitmanites" and "casts a deserved reproach on the super-strenuosity, not to say ferocity, of their arguments."[119] Yet the very fact that Eells needed to critique Bourne and Marshall on the basis of scientific history revealed how effectively scientific history had supplanted older ways of historical thinking in the academy. This change in scholarly authority, more than any of the discoveries in the Whitman controversy, was what signaled the downfall of the Whitman Saved Oregon Story. By depicting the story as a pernicious legend incompatible with modernity, Bourne and Marshall had made it a public and scholarly symbol of the folly of the old ways of doing history.

The shift in scholarly consensus was evident in the fact that by 1902 the Whitman story had begun to appear in lists of tales that scientific history had disproven. Bourne's close friend the church historian Albert Bushnell Hart mentioned the Whitman story alongside the naive veneration of the Pilgrims, the myth of the Southern Cavalier, and Mason Weems's tale of George Washington and the cherry tree. He stated that the Whitman story was "the most interesting of the American myths," one that had been "resolved into its elementary gases" by Bourne.[120] The political scientist Frederic Austin Ogg of the University of Wisconsin also likened the Whitman story to that of Washington and the cherry tree, placing it in a genealogy that began with the myth that Rome was founded by Romulus and Remus.[121] "The Whitman legend is fatally damaged, so far as any use of it by trained historians is concerned," asserted J. Franklin Jameson in his *American Historical Review* assessment of Bourne's expanded Whitman essay.[122] Jameson conceded, however, that "the passionate revilings to which we have seen the accomplished critic subjected in many newspapers make it plain that the legend will die hard."[123]

Through a strange coincidence Eells, Marshall, and Bourne all died within a few years of each other: Eells and Marshall of old age, Bourne during a surgery to correct his tubercular hip.[124] Their deaths deprived the Whitman controversy of its most prominent partisans, and after their loss the academic portion of the Whitman controversy largely subsided. The posthumous publication of Eells's *Marcus Whitman: Pathfinder and Patriot* (1909) and Marshall's *Acquisition of Oregon, and the Long-Suppressed Evidence about Marcus Whitman* (1911) brought one more round of popular and scholarly debate about Whitman, but by 1910 it was clear that scholarly sentiment had shifted toward Bourne and Marshall. The popular press enthusiastically praised Eells's *Marcus Whitman,* hoping that it would stem the tide of growing skepticism toward the Whitman story. "A careful reading of the overwhelming mass of evidence in this book ought to put the matter of Whitman's purpose forever outside the realms of controversy," wrote a reviewer for the *Independent.*[125] A review in the *Magazine of History* noted, in a statement that would prove prescient, "If this volume fails to convince the doubters that Marcus Whitman, the missionary-explorer, was the person to whom posterity is indebted for Oregon . . . no evidence will be produced which may reasonably be expected to convince."[126] Marshall's work received favorable notice in the *American Historical Review* whereas Eells's *Marcus Whitman* was paid virtually no attention in the scholarly presses, indicating the extent to which the Whitman story and its proponents were no longer considered part of academic history.[127]

The divide between the recognition of Eells's and Marshall's work paralleled the growing divide between popular and scholarly conceptions of history. From 1901 onward more professional and regional historical associations abandoned the Whitman story every year. In 1907 the director of the Oregon Historical Society honored not Marcus Whitman but Hudson's Bay Company trader John McLoughlin as the "father of Oregon."[128] Within a few years most major encyclopedias and histories had removed the Whitman story or added a disclaimer.[129] By 1918 the *New Catholic Review* observed that the Whitman legend had been all but stricken from school textbooks. "The fascinating story of Marcus Whitman's saving Oregon to the United States has passed into the region of fable where it belongs," it stated.[130]

Yet the story continued to hold sway outside of the historical community, especially among the populations where it had first circulated: Pacific northwesterners and Protestants. In Washington State in 1905 a congressman sponsored an essay contest offering a one-hundred-dollar watch to the student who wrote the best essay on Marcus Whitman and provided as a template an essay that defended the Whitman story.[131] In 1907 citizens of Washington celebrated the sixtieth anniversary of Whitman's death and listened to Cushing Eells's grandson recount the story of Whitman's ride.[132] In 1909 the Walla Walla Commercial Club ordered two statues of Marcus Whitman to be cast, one to be placed in front of the state capitol and the other at Whitman College.[133] Ministers continued to lecture on "Marcus Whitman, the Nation Builder," and children continued to read about Whitman's brave deeds in books like *Why Our Flag Floats over Oregon* and *Heroes of the Cross in America*.[134] Though stricken from the avenues of formal history, the Whitman Saved Oregon Story continued to suffuse the folkways of American culture.

In the end Bourne's labeling of the Whitman story as a myth proved prophetic, for after its discrediting the story took on a kind of mythic character. On the one hand, scientific historians situated the disproving of the Whitman story within a broader vision of the triumph of human reason over sectarian superstition. On the other hand, supporters of the Whitman story began to see it as a symbol of the rejection of scientific history and the values for which it stood. "There is more truth and beauty and possibly more practical benefit . . . in the thrilling story of William Tell than in the remnants of history that some would-be historians have spared to us from which to reconstruct our idol if we can," C. H. Howard proclaimed in an article defending Whitman.[135] The use of the term "idol" was not incidental: as academic elites increasingly dismissed the Whitman story as ahistorical, those who continued to defend Whitman described him in more, not less, sacralized terms.

No piece of writing demonstrates such veneration more patently than an editorial written for the *Journal of Education* on the Whitman controversy in 1905. The journal's editor, Albert Edward Winship, opened by stating that the "spirit that discounts the part that Columbus had in the discovery of America, that tones down the halo on Washington's historic brow . . . and dulled the sound of the hoofs of Paul Revere's charger" had now attacked Marcus Whitman; but "as none of these modern hostile critics have dethroned Columbus, Washington . . . or Paul Revere, so they have not and will not make less sacred the name of Marcus Whitman."[136] After considering some of the arguments on both sides of the Whitman question Winship closed not with an academic argument but with an appeal to spiritual experience. He described a visit to the Whitman Monument, one of America's most interesting "sacred sites." At the monument Winship was overcome: "Without the least concern for the relative effect of the pleas of the historical attorneys I stood uncovered at the foot of the monument; with dimmed eyes I read in marble the names of the martyrs, and with unfeigned emotion stood on the sites of the mission houses in which precious blood was shed by sacrilegious hands."[137] Whitman no longer appeared in history books as the savior of Oregon, but here, at his grave, he could still be discovered by the faithful.

Under the banner of providential history Whitman was a martyr of flag and cross. In the world of pioneer history he was an independent trailblazer. The providentialists of the 1890s made him an emissary of American empire, and the scientific historians claimed that Whitman was just a man—well intentioned, perhaps even brave, but not a hero.

Now, exposed and dismissed by the scientific historians, Whitman became more sacred to those who still believed. Marcus Whitman was not just a martyr to the nation and to Christianity. He was also a martyr to the new critical spirit among academic historians, a spirit that the Whitman supporters believed would strike history of all its heroes and Christianity of its scriptures. He had been infused with Christlike splendor, his deeds doubted and his "precious blood ... shed by sacrilegious hands." Whitman's debunking was also his apotheosis.

After Providence

Providence did not disappear overnight. Despite the decisive victory scientific history secured by debunking the Whitman Saved Oregon story, both providential history and the Whitman story continued to haunt the halls of the academy, the pages of popular history, and spaces of public remembrance in the twentieth and twenty-first centuries.

Scholarly defenses of the Whitman story largely ceased after the death of Myron Eells in 1907, and scholars who did mention it included it only as a historical curiosity or a cautionary tale.[1] But the Whitman story had a longer life in popular history. Politicians and regional boosters found that like other spurious but patriotic tales like George Washington's cherry tree, the Whitman story was a useful legend. It contained the requisite themes of God and country (as well as a healthy dose of excitement) for stump speeches, tourism campaigns, and expressions of regional pride. Between the 1920s and the 1950s several constituencies attempted to revive the heroic Whitman, first in a massive pageant, then through the centennial celebration of the Whitmans' arrival in the Oregon Country, and finally with a likeness placed in the National Statuary Hall. But each of these memorialization campaigns highlighted the increasing fractures not only between scholarly and popular history but also between providential and nonprovidential interpretations of Whitman's legacy.

In 1923 the Whitman College president and tireless Whitman story promoter Stephen Penrose convinced the leaders of Walla Walla to
put on a massive pageant of regional history.[2] The resulting extravagan-
za, "The Pioneer Pageant, How the West Was Won," involved a six-and-a-
half-acre stage, an artificial river, fifteen thousand square feet of painted
scenery, and a volunteer cast of two thousand actors, dancers, and sing-
ers who came from Oregon and Idaho as well as Washington. Penrose
wrote the pageant's script, including a narrator who explained Walla
Walla's "sacred past" to three boys (and by extension, the audience). That
sacred past begins with the arrival of Marcus and Narcissa Whitman,
who brought with them "the home, the school, *the flag!*" and progresses
to the Whitman Saved Oregon Story, "the stuff / Of Heroes!" The narrator then declares, "Was there ever ride so great / To save an empire being
thrown away?"[3] The pageant continues with a representation of the attack on the Whitman Mission, the subsequent settler–Native wars, and,
finally, a "millennial vision" of the region's future, in which dancers symbolize the flourishing of farming, education, art, religion, labor, and law.[4]
The pageant dramatized the providential arc of Pacific Northwest history, from the civilizing efforts of missionaries to the removal of the
land's Native inhabitants and finally to a flourishing white civilization.

Over thirty thousand people attended the "Pioneer Pageant" during each of the two years of its performance, and for a moment it seemed
as if the play might signal a Whitman renaissance.[5] Despite the success
of the pageant, however, it was clear that Marcus Whitman's fame was
slipping, even in the region where his legend was strongest. Penrose had
wanted the entire pageant to focus on Whitman but was unable to convince other Walla Wallans on the pageant board to do so, both because
of the controversy over the Whitman story and because some board
members felt that other aspects of Walla Walla history were more significant.[6] In order to assuage Walla Walla business leaders' anxieties over
the potentially controversial Whitman material, Penrose insisted, "The
first three movements of the Pageant [excluding the final "millennial vision" section] are strictly historical, following with severe carefulness the
known incidents of early history."[7] The interests of providentialism and
capital were not aligning as seamlessly as they had thirty years earlier,
when Penrose used the Whitman story to help save Whitman College

from bankruptcy. More worrying to Penrose and other supporters of the Whitman story was the fact that outside of the Pioneer Pageant (and Warren G. Harding's much-maligned Independence Day speech of 1923), the tale of Whitman's ride was receiving almost no national attention. In a period when patriotic pageants were all the rage, the Pioneer Pageant and its retelling of the Whitman tale failed to garner lasting interest or support among the wider public. In 1928 the *Boston Globe* published a rendition of Whitman's ride in its series "Forgotten Episodes in American History," showing just how far Whitman's star had fallen outside of Walla Walla.[8]

Subsequent attempts to renationalize Whitman's memory served instead to demonstrate the extent to which even popular historians had embraced the methods of academic history. In 1936, the centennial anniversary of the arrival of the Whitmans in Oregon, President Franklin Delano Roosevelt signed an order declaring the Whitman Monument a national park. The wording of the order, however, illustrated the degree to which the debunking of the Whitman tale had permeated national discourse. The order said nothing about Whitman's ride, focusing instead on the Whitmans' service and subsequent deaths as missionaries.[9] The park's educational materials rejected the Whitman story as well. A 1947 guidebook to the site stated, "The myth that he 'saved Oregon' has been exploded, and historians generally agree that his labors did not alter the eventual political destiny of Oregon."[10] The Whitman Monument, originally envisioned by Whitman's companion William H. Gray as a physical testament to Whitman's heroic deeds, now became a site of academic historical interpretation mediated through the state. Whereas in the nineteenth century governmental structures had supported depictions of Whitman as a providential figure by reprinting Spalding's history of Whitman's mission and involving state officials in various Whitman commemorations, by the early twentieth century state and federal governments had largely adopted the findings of scientific historians.

State and local efforts to memorialize Whitman took place after the Second World War as well when the Washington State Legislature selected Marcus Whitman as the first of the state's two figures to be placed in the US Capitol Building Statuary Hall. The advocates of the statue, led by the Walla Walla Business and Professional Women's Club,

Fig. 9. *Marcus Whitman*, bronze by Avard Fairbanks, given in 1953.
Located in the National Statuary Hall, United States Capitol Building.
Image courtesy of Jeremy Sabella.

saw Whitman as an ideal champion for the postwar era. As both a patriotic and providential hero, Whitman could serve as an antidote to the
godless Communism of the country's Cold War foes. Goldie Rehberg of
the women's club concluded by saying, "It is great to know that the Bible
was the inspiration which led to the opening up of this beautiful State of
ours and where the Bible preceded, the American flag followed and established its purpose."[11] Vice President Richard Nixon proclaimed at the
unveiling ceremony, "I hope the spirit of Marcus Whitman . . . would be
one which will pervade this Capitol somehow so that those of us in the
Senate and House might reflect that same spirit in our handling of the
grave problems that confront America today."[12]

The statue, designed by Avard Fairbanks and installed in the Capitol
in 1955, itself evoked the Whitman story. It depicted Whitman in the midst
of his midwinter journey, dressed in buckskin and holding a Bible and
saddlebags, the caption below reading, "My Plans Require Time and Distance."[13] Nevertheless, the story was strikingly absent in the biographical
material that contextualized the statue's unveiling. The biography's authors,
the academic historians Ronald V. Sires and Robert Comegys, followed
scholarly consensus that the Whitman story was false, stating, "As far as
can be determined from written evidence, Whitman's remarks had no influence on actual government policy."[14] Instead, Sires and Comegys argued, Whitman should be remembered for "the zeal, tenacity, and
whole-hearted devotion with which he did his work and followed the call
of duty as he heard it."[15] The oral testimony that providentialist historians
had once used to support the Whitman story went entirely unmentioned
in Sires's and Comegys's biography, demonstrating the extent to which
written primary sources had supplanted oral testimony in academic history. The inclusion of the biography also illustrates the changing boundaries of historical work and the state. By the mid-twentieth century
governmental agencies were more reticent in their appeals to providentialism. Providential appeals intensified in other arenas of politics during the
Cold War, as seen in President Dwight D. Eisenhower's explicit reference
to divine providence in his 1953 Inaugural Address, but at the bureaucratic level academic history ruled the day.[16]

Nuanced academic histories of Whitman, however, failed to incite
the same excitement that the mythical tale of Whitman's ride had. Even as

Whitman's likeness was placed in the US Capitol, suggesting a possible resurgence of his fame, it became clear that other western archetypes had eclipsed him in popularity. By midcentury the providentially ordained West had been fully supplanted by another mythical West: that of the lawless Wild West, in which religious figures and perhaps even God were absent or impotent. A few authors tried to refigure Whitman to fit into this western universe, depicting him as a roughriding "Doctor in Buckskin," but it was an awkward fit for a missionary who was famous for establishing, not flouting, Anglo-American civilization in the West.[17] The degree to which this new western vision had overtaken the older providential model was captured in a 1955 newspaper article about the recently erected Whitman statue. A group of schoolchildren touring the Capitol stopped before the statue of Whitman. "I know him," exclaimed one of the children, "that's Davy Crockett!" The bemused reporter wrote, "Explanations proved futile after that, and now, the guards say, most adult visitors don't bother with them."[18] The more Whitman was stripped of his providential trappings, the less Americans seemed to be interested in him.

In the second half of the twentieth century transformations in historiography shifted Whitman's reputation again. The American Indian Movement of the 1960s and 1970s and the new western history of the 1980s and 1990s highlighted what Native communities had been saying for decades if not centuries: the Anglo-American conquest of the West was not a triumphant tale of civilization over savagery but a story of colonial violence, ethnic cleansing, and even genocide. If the providential Whitman was a hero, the revisionist Whitman was a villain, a representative of the arrogance of Anglo-American colonialism and religious intolerance. The new western historian Patricia Nelson Limerick noted that by the mid-1840s, "the [Whitman] mission began to look like an agency for the service of white people."[19] Other scholars have highlighted Whitman's theological and cultural rigidity, his anti-Catholicism, and his support for the displacement of the Cayuse people.[20] Popular remembrance has followed this shift in scholarly tone. In 2016 Whitman College officially discarded its mascot title, the Fighting Missionaries (represented in earlier decades by "Marc," a scowling, buckskin-wearing cartoon Whitman holding a Bible and a rifle). A survey of students, faculty, staff, and alumni determined that many believed the Missionaries moniker "celebrates the systematic oppression of Native Americans."[21] A vandal spray-painted "Genicide" [*sic*] on the college's statue of Whitman in October 2019.[22] Also in 2019 Washington legislators proposed a bill (still in committee when this book went to press) to replace Whitman's statues in both the US and Washington State capitol buildings with figures less implicated in American colonialism and Native dispossession.[23]

As Whitman's fame has shifted toward infamy in popular and academic historical circles, Whitman has become a useful figure for yet another constituency: conservative evangelical Christians frustrated by the marginalization of providential narratives in scholarly history and public school curricula. These new providentialists, including the lay historians Catherine Millard and William Federer, sought to recover the history of God's divine plan for the United States.[24] In *The Rewriting of America's History* Millard claimed that "America's true history" was being destroyed or covered up "through the rewriting and/or reinterpretation of American historical records: in our national parks, monuments, memorials, landmarks, shrines, and churches" and "through removal of key historic pieces that do not support the current ungodly bias."[25] In response to this threat, Millard offered a new providential history "dedicated to the glorious truth that this nation was established upon biblical principles . . . and God's faithful blessings are upon a people who confidently placed themselves under the protective banner of His care."[26]

Millard then offered a sort of revision of revisionist history: resurrecting the providential tales, including the Whitman Saved Oregon Story, that modern academic historians had disparaged and omitted. Millard's retelling of the Whitman story drew upon work by central promoters of the legend, including Henry Harmon Spalding and Warren G. Harding.[27] Harding, Millard argued, "left the most accurate legacy of the missionary zeal with which these Western states . . . were brought into the Union." But "in spite of this U.S. president's personal testimony to Whitman's valiant journey to prevent Oregon's annexation by England, Whitman's efforts are denigrated by modern historians who discredit the purposes for the trip, and even make out his cross-country ride to be legendary."[28] To Millard, as to the providential historians of the early twentieth century, the discrediting of the Whitman story represented a broader pattern of secular skepticism that had denuded history of its providential truths. Few evangelical authors have gone as far as Millard in repeating the Whitman Saved Oregon Story verbatim from Spalding or Harding, but many more embrace Whitman as a symbol of providentialism more generally.[29]

The tensions that arose in the early twentieth century between providentialism and science, archival evidence and oral testimony, and the scholarly and the popular continue to play out in the marginal historical communities of the new providentialists. It is in these spaces—these narrow communities of intense historical interest—where the Whitman story can still be heard and where it is, in its mythic form, still believed. This new providentialism can be seen not only in the affirming recollection of Whitman's heroism but also in conservative Christian communities' fascination with original historical documents and artifacts. Millard emphasizes that she has spent twenty-two years researching at the Library of Congress, "utilizing the original writings, documents, papers and works of the founding fathers as documentation for her books."[30] The providential historian David Barton is often lauded by his conservative supporters as having collected "thousands of original documents"; the conservative pundit Glenn Beck, for instance, praises Barton as "the Library of Congress in shoes."[31] One of the legacies of early twentieth-century battles over the nature of history, in other words, is that even providential historians now equate historical authority with possession of or research in original documents.

New providentialists' highly selective and often ahistorical use of original sources bears little similarity to the archival research of academic historians, yet contemporary conservative Christian lay historians like Barton and Millard use rhetoric that bears a striking resemblance to the language of the earlier historical battles. New providentialists argue that the dominant narrative of US history is a myth imposed by partisan historians. Their return to original documents will reveal the true history hidden by leftist scholars unable to see past their secular humanist and Marxist biases. Conservative Christian lay historians have weaponized the language of myth that scientific historians used to delegitimize providential historians in the early twentieth century. Now, they claim, academic historians are the mythmakers and lay providentialists the truth tellers.[32]

If Whitman's critics have not succeeded entirely at removing him from public historical celebration (after all, Whitman College still bears his name), neither have new providentialists succeeded in rehabilitating Whitman for a larger audience. The stalemate over Whitman's legacy evokes broader questions about the American historical profession's past and future. Peter Novick argued that by the 1980s "history no longer constituted a coherent discipline; not just that the whole was less than the sum of its parts, but that there was no whole—only parts."[33] The objectivity of scientific history was supposed to be an antidote to providence, but it had proven too amorphous to hold together a community of scholars with increasingly diverse interests and methodologies. And yet even as historians have struggled to find new teleologies to anchor their narratives, vestiges of older progress narratives continue to surface in historical writing. American historians have been "leaving providence behind" ever since the debunking of the Whitman Saved Oregon Story in 1900, but providence seems to keep catching up with them.[34]

Unsurprisingly, overt providential assumptions remained in the field of church history the longest. Facing the rise of fascism in Europe and increased pessimism in the US, William Warren Sweet closed the second volume of his seminal *Story of Religion in America* with the following injunction: "The student of church history has learned that God is in no hurry and so in patience he 'possesses his soul.' Church history is an excellent tonic when men are disturbed and fainting because of new and confusing voices. History says the ship has weathered many another storm, so do not throw up your hands because unaccustomed waters are rushing about your ears."[35] Yet Sweet tempered his providential encouragements with rigorous investigations into primary sources and a professed commitment to objectivity.[36] He sought, in other words, to be a scientific providentialist.

But even this effort would not ensure the endurance of an explicit providentialism. As Henry Warner Bowden observes, after 1906 "the weight of a naturalistic, nonprovidential perspective slowly crushed the old form of church history."[37] The atrocities of the Second World War, the increasing possibility of nuclear holocaust, and the slide into seemingly endless proxy wars convinced many historians that "the disasters and crimes of our century provide cases more difficult than the Book of

Job for anyone readily able to see God's hand in the design of major historical events."[38] Even theologians increasingly neglected or abandoned the doctrine of divine providence. The theologian Langdon Gilkey observed in 1963 that providence "[had] been left a rootless, disembodied ghost, flitting from footnote to footnote, but rarely finding secure lodgment in sustained theological discourse."[39] By 1973 the historian Matthew Anthony Fitzsimons could declare, "Serious historical inquiry is inevitably at odds with the idea of providence in history."[40]

Within church history specifically and religious history more broadly American historians have struggled to create broad syntheses that do not map onto the providential focus on Protestants. Long after church historians ceased to echo providential historians' optimism regarding God's guidance in earthly events, they maintained providential historians' focus on Protestants, especially Reformed Protestants, as the implicit or explicit producers and preservers of American culture.[41] The historian of American religion Catherine Brekus observed in 2016 that the canon of Protestant-centered history "has not been completely dismantled"; instead, scholars have constructed a "countercanon" emphasizing the "pluralistic, fractious, and transatlantic."[42] In this way the progress narrative of American religion has remained largely unchanged, even as religious diversity has replaced the Protestant center.

In the American West the long shadow of Frederick Jackson Turner's frontier thesis has created a different but equally influential progress narrative, one that locates the American character in the meeting of savagery and civilization. But as Kerwin Klein aptly notes, the Turnerian thesis mapped onto older categories of savagery and civilization that equated savagery with wilderness, prehistory or ahistory, and heathenism, and civilization with white settlement, history, and Christianity.[43] Though Turner gave credit to the savage side of the frontier for influencing this development, the end result of the frontier process was not a new wilderness but a new civilization, the United States. In other words, though Turner himself never mentioned divine providence, his thesis followed the contours of providential teleology from savagery to civilization. New western historians critiqued the Anglocentrism of the frontier model, but as Klein has observed, this myth busting easily replicates the progress narratives of the older frontier model.[44] In her classic work of new western history, Limerick described Turner's frontier thesis as a "creation myth" that is destined, like Christian creationism and indigenous American origin stories, to come into conflict with modern scholarship.[45] Donald Worster envisioned western historians of the 1960s "gathered around the banquet table, heads still bowed dutifully at the name of Frederick Jackson Turner, and a few still crossed themselves in reverence."[46] The myths changed, but the definition of myth—unscientific, primitive, pious, and destined to be displaced by enlightened truth—remained much the same.

In recent years Native American, First Nations, and other Indigenous scholars have called on non-Native historians to reconsider their assessments of myth and oral tradition. Historians' focus on written documents, they observe, has often relegated indigenous peoples to the realm of ahistory or prehistory, excluding Native voices from historical interpretation.[47] They have pointed out that oral traditions are far more durable and far less contradictory to written sources than non-Native academics have allowed.[48] And they have questioned the hegemony of Euro-American scholars' concept of historical time as linear and progressive.[49] In doing so, they have offered potential alternatives to the progress narratives that providence helped to embed in American history. Ironically, the very intellectual traditions that both providentialists and scientific historians excluded may present the best possibilities for moving beyond the historical battles of the nineteenth and twentieth centuries.

Continuing conflicts over myth in history attest to the challenges of imagining an American history without providence or the myth-busting progress narratives it generated. And yet, as the story of Marcus Whitman shows, history is constantly being reimagined. The boundaries between myth and history, primitiveness and progress, superstition and science are not fixed but instead are instantiated, questioned, and modified by specific people's debates about specific stories. The invention and reinvention of Whitman's heroism is a reminder that American history itself is an invention, born out of struggle and contention but also out of idealism, intellectual curiosity, and the desire for a usable past. And what is invented can be reinvented. After all, what's more American than reinvention?

Notes

Introduction

1. "History of Famed Oregon Trail Retold by President at Meacham," *Los Angeles Times,* July 4, 1923, 12.

2. Ibid.

3. "Refers to Doubt of Whitman Story," *New York Times,* July 4, 1923, 3.

4. This line was first attributed to Whitman by Whitman's associate, Cushing Eells, in 1883. Eells recalled the words from memory in a testimony whose accuracy has been questioned by historians. While Whitman did make statements reminiscent of this in subsequent letters, I have not been able to verify Eells's account of Whitman's statement. Sworn statement of Cushing Eells, August 23, 1883, reprinted in Myron Eells, *Marcus Whitman, M.D.: Proofs of His Work in Saving Oregon to the United States, and in Promoting the Immigration of 1843* (Portland: G. H. Himes, 1883), 9–10. The closest recorded statement of Whitman, written shortly after his journey east, is, "I cannot feel that we can look on and see foreign and papal influence making its greatest efforts and we hold ourselves as expatriated and neutral." Marcus Whitman to David Greene, Nov. 1, 1843, box A, Marcus and Narcissa Whitman Collection 1834–1936 (Whitman College and Northwest Archives, Whitman College, Walla Walla).

5. "Address of Rev. Charles L. Thompson, D.D.," delivered at a home missions rally at Carnegie Hall, New York, March 3, 1896, *The Church at Home and Abroad* 19, no. 112 (April 1896), 304.

6. "Marcus Whitman's Ride: Crossing the Continent in Midwinter to Save an Empire," *Detroit Free Press,* Oct. 11, 1891, 12.

7. Edward Gaylord Bourne, "The Legend of Marcus Whitman," *American Historical Review* 6, no. 2 (Jan. 1901): 276–300; 276.

8. Ibid., 277–78.

9. Peter Novick, *That Noble Dream: The "Objectivity Question" and the American Historical Profession* (New York: Cambridge University Press, 1988), 1.

10. Ibid., 4–6. See also Mircea Eliade, *The Sacred and the Profane: The Nature of Religion,* trans. Willard R. Trask (New York: Harcourt, Brace, & World, 1959), 95; Broni-slaw Malinowski, "Myth in Primitive Psychology," in *Magic, Science, and Religion and Other Essays* (Boston: Beacon, 1948), 78–79; Émile Durkheim, *Elementary Forms of the Religious Life,* trans. Joseph Ward Swain (New York: Macmillan, 1915), 101.

11. Nicholas Guyatt, *Providence and the Invention of the United States, 1607–1865* (Cambridge: Cambridge University Press, 2007). Guyatt coins the term "providential history" to describe "the idea that America had a special destiny in the divine plan for the world's redemption" (51). Guyatt is less interested in providentialism as a historical method or philosophy than in the ways in which the idea of American destiny has been deployed politically in different historical moments, for example, to promote a national identity distinct from that of Great Britain, to promote American expansion, or to main-tain a sense of national unity in the face of sectional and racial conflict (106, 224, 291). Other works that address providentialism are similarly interested in providentialism's political uses. See, for instance, Mark Noll, *The Civil War as Theological Crisis* (Chapel Hill: University of North Carolina Press, 2006); Matthew McCullough, *The Cross of War: Christian Nationalism and U.S. Expansion in the Spanish–American War* (Madison: Uni-versity of Wisconsin Press, 2014); Stephen H. Webb, "American Providence, American Violence," in *From Jeremiad to Jihad: Religion, Violence, and America,* ed. John D. Carlson and Jonathan H. Ebel (Berkeley: University of California Press, 2012), 91–110. While my book is also interested in the political mobilizations of providentialism, it is primarily focused on how providential convictions produced particular methods and institutions of historical writing that went on to shape the development of the American historical profession.

12. While acknowledging the fuzzy, contested nature of the definition of objectiv-ity held by historians, Novick summarizes the assumptions undergirding objectivity as "a commitment to the reality of the past, and to truth as a correspondence to that reality; a sharp separation between knower and known, between fact and value, and, above all, between history and fiction." Novick, *That Noble Dream,* 1–2. This book's definition of objectivity differs from Novick's for two reasons. First, the providential historians as well as the objective historians discussed here saw their work as illuminating the objective reality of the past. The difference was that providential historians believed that the di-vine acted in history and thus that the work of God in history was part of the objective reality that historical methods could discover. Second, both providential and objective historians took the posture of the disinterested observer at times in order to undergird their interpretations while at other times appealing to the authority of their direct expe-rience of historical events or to the moral rightness of their positions. The difference between their historical modes, then, was not whether historians appealed to an objec-tive reality or took the posture of neutral observers but rather whether their historical work accepted the notion of the divine acting in history to ensure the prosperity of American Protestantism.

13. Bourne, "The Legend of Marcus Whitman," 276–300; William I. Marshall, *Acquisition of Oregon, and the Long Suppressed Evidence about Marcus Whitman*, 2 vols. (Seattle: Lowman & Hanford, 1911); William A. Mowry, *Marcus Whitman and the Early Days of Oregon* (New York: Silver, Burdett, 1901); and Myron Eells, *Marcus Whitman, M. D.: Pathfinder and Patriot* (Seattle: Alice Harriman, 1909).

14. Clifford Merrill Drury, *Marcus and Narcissa Whitman, and the Opening of Old Oregon*, 2 vols. (Glendale, CA: A. H. Clark, 1973), 2:382–85, 387. See also Drury, *Marcus Whitman, M.D.: Pioneer and Martyr* (Caldwell, ID: Caxton Printers, 1937); Drury, *The Mountains We Have Crossed: Diaries and Letters of the Oregon Mission, 1838*, introduction to the Bison Books edition by Bonnie Sue Lewis (Lincoln: University of Nebraska Press, 1999); Drury, *Elkanah and Mary Walker: Pioneers among the Spokanes* (Caldwell, ID: Caxton Printers, 1940); Drury, *First White Women over the Rockies: Diaries, Letters, and Biographical Sketches of the Six Women of the Oregon Mission Who Made the Overland Journey in 1836 and 1838*, 3 vols. (Glendale, CA: A. H. Clark, 1963–66); Drury, *Henry Harmon Spalding* (Caldwell, ID: Caxton Printers, 1936); Drury, *Nine Years with the Spokanes: The Diary, 1838–1848, of Elkanah Walker* (Glendale, CA: A. H. Clark, 1976); Drury, *More about the Whitmans: Four Hitherto Unpublished Letters of Marcus and Narcissa Whitman* (Tacoma: Washington State Historical Society, 1979).

15. Julie Roy Jeffrey, *Converting the West: A Biography of Narcissa Whitman* (Norman: University of Oklahoma Press, 1991). Other scholarship of the last thirty years focuses primarily on the Whitman Mission as an incident in the history of Anglo-American conquest and cultural misunderstanding of Native peoples. Genevieve McCoy and Albert Furtwangler demonstrate the difficulties that Whitman and other missionaries had in translating the intricacies of Presbyterian doctrine into the Nez Perce language and American Protestant reading practices into a predominantly oral culture. Genevieve McCoy, "The Women of the ABCFM and the Conflicted Language of Calvinism," *Church History* 64, no. 1 (March 1995): 62–82; Albert Furtwangler, *Bringing Indians to the Book* (Seattle: University of Washington Press, 2000). The Whitman Mission also appears in some of the classic works of the New Western History of the 1980s and 1990s. Patricia Limerick discusses how the Whitmans, after their deaths, were cast as innocent victims rather than intruders on Cayuse land; Richard White discusses the Whitmans' mission as one of several factors that were impinging on Plateau Native lifeways in the nineteenth century. Patricia Nelson Limerick, *Legacy of Conquest: The Unbroken Past of the American West* (New York: Norton, 1987), 37–41; Richard White, "*It's Your Misfortune and None of My Own*": *A History of the American West* (Norman: University of Oklahoma Press, 1991), 72–73. More recent western histories also discuss the Whitman Mission as an instance of cultural misunderstanding and as a tool of Anglo-American expansion. Robert V. Hine and John Mack Faragher, *The American West: A New Interpretive History* (New Haven: Yale University Press, 2000).

16. Cameron Addis, "The Whitman Massacre: Religion and Manifest Destiny on the Columbia Plateau, 1809–1858," *Journal of the Early Republic* 25, no. 2 (Summer 2005): 257. I contest Addis's interpretation. By the twentieth century the main division over the Whitman story was not between Protestants and Catholics but between those

who accepted the findings of scientific historians like Edward Bourne and William Marshall and those who did not. The conflict was predicated not on "Old World religious scores" but on the new patterns of professionalization and secularization taking place in the academy and in American society as a whole. Robert Ross McCoy, *Chief Joseph, Yellow Wolf, and the Creation of Nez Perce History in the Pacific Northwest* (New York: Routledge, 2004), 70–83. McCoy follows the early twentieth-century historian Cornelius Brosnan in giving an erroneous date for the origin of the Whitman Story: the 1864 publication of the story in the *Sacramento Union,* McCoy, 80; S. A. Clarke, "Letter from Oregon," *Sacramento Daily Union,* Nov. 16, 1864, 2. William I. Marshall's 1911 *Acquisition of Oregon* shows that the Whitman Story appeared in two letters from the Oregon home missionary George Atkinson to the ABCFM in 1858 and 1859. Given that both Brosnan and McCoy discuss Marshall's work, this is a surprising oversight. I have discovered an even earlier iteration of the story, in an obituary in the *Boston Recorder* published in 1848, shortly after Whitman's death, and likely written or influenced by Henry Harmon Spalding, "Death of Dr. Marcus Whitman," *Boston Recorder,* June 16, 1848, 93.

17. For an overview of this shift, see Dana L. Robert, "From Missions to Mission to beyond Missions: The Historiography of American Foreign since World War II," in *New Directions in American Religious History,* ed. Harry Stout and D. G. Hart (New York: Oxford University Press, 1997), 362–93; Dana L. Robert, "Introduction," in *Converting Colonialisms: Visions and Realities in Mission History, 1706–1914,* ed. Dana Robert (Grand Rapids: Eerdmans, 2008), 1–20. For recent works emphasizing the influence of foreign missionaries on American culture, see Dana L. Robert, "The Influence of American Missionary Women on the World Back Home," *Religion and American Culture: A Journal of Interpretation* 12, no. 1 (Winter 2002): 59–89; Grant Wacker and Daniel Bays, eds., *The Foreign Missionary Enterprise at Home: Explorations in North American Cultural History* (Tuscaloosa: University of Alabama Press, 2003).

18. Henry Harmon Spalding, Lecture Series: "Early Oregon Missions: Their Importance in Securing the Country to Americans," *Walla Walla Statesman,* March 16–April 6, 1866; Myron Eells, *History of Indian Missions on the Pacific Coast: Oregon, Washington and Idaho* (Philadelphia: American Sunday-School Union, 1882); James Geddes Craighead, *Story of Marcus Whitman: Early Protestant Missions in the Northwest* (Philadelphia: Presbyterian Board of Publication and Sabbath-School Work, 1895); Joseph B. Clark, *Leavening the Nation: The Story of American Home Missions* (New York: Baker & Taylor, 1903); Mary Gay Humphreys, *Missionary Explorers among the American Indians* (New York: Scribner's, 1913).

19. Arthur Schlesinger pioneered the understanding of western missions as a form of cultural imperialism. See Schlesinger, "The Missionary Enterprise and Theories of Imperialism," in *The Missionary Enterprise in China and America,* ed. John K. Fairbank (Cambridge: Harvard University Press, 1974), 336–73. Building on Schlesinger, William Hutchinson has described foreign missions as providing the "moral equivalent for imperialism" in the late nineteenth and early twentieth centuries. See Hutchinson, "A Moral Equivalent for Imperialism: Americans and the Promotion of 'Christian Civilization,' 1880–1920," in *Missionary Ideologies in the Imperialist Era,* ed. William Hutchinson

and Torben Christensen (Aarhus, Denmark: Christensens Bogtrykkeri, 1982), 168. Andrew Porter contests this theory, arguing that "highly effective as missions were in promoting cultural change, they were amongst the weakest agents of 'cultural imperialism.'" Porter's study, however, is primarily concerned with European missions. I argue that the situation was different with American missionaries, particularly missionaries to Native nations, because American missionary entry into Native territory tended to be coextensive with the extension of US political and military control over those territories. Andrew Porter, "'Cultural Imperialism' and Protestant Missionary Enterprise," *Journal of Imperial and Commonwealth History* 25, no. 3 (September 1997): 388.

20. Robert, "The Influence of American Missionary Women," 59–89.

21. John H. Mitchell, "Oregon: Its History, Geography and Natural Resources," *National Geographic Magazine* 6 (Jan. 1894–March 1895): 256.

22. Henry Warner Bowden, *Church History in the Age of Science: Historiographical Patterns in the United States, 1876–1918* (Chapel Hill: University of North Carolina Press, 1971).

23. Ibid., 15–16, 25.

24. Elizabeth Clark, *Founding the Fathers: Early Church History and Protestant Professors in Nineteenth-Century America* (Philadelphia: University of Pennsylvania Press, 2011).

25. Ibid., 1.

26. Bowden, *Church History in the Age of Science,* 137; Clark, *Founding the Fathers,* 158–59.

27. For instance, Sir George Frazer, *The Golden Bough: A Study in Magic and Religion,* 2nd ed. (New York: Macmillan, 1922); Edward Burnett Tylor, *Primitive Culture: Researches into the Development of Mythology, Philosophy, Religion, Art, and Custom,* 2 vols. (London: John Murray, 1871), 1:431; Max Müller, *Lectures on the Science of Language: Delivered at the Royal Institution of Great Britain in April, May, and June 1861* (London: Longman, Green, and Roberts, 1861), 11–12; William Robertson Smith, *Lectures on the Religion of the Semites: First Series: The Fundamental Institutions* (New York: D. Appleton, 19–20).

28. Amanda Laugesen, *The Making of Public Historical Culture in the American West, 1880–1910: The Role of Historical Societies* (Lewiston, NY: Edwin Mellen Press, 2006). See also George A. Frykman, *Seattle's Historian and Promoter: The Life of Edmond Stephen Meany* (Pullman: Washington State University Press, 1998); Susan Schulten, "How to See Colorado: The Federal Writers' Project, American Regionalism, and the 'Old New Western History,'" *Western Historical Quarterly* 35, no. 1 (2005): 49–70; Jay Price, "The Small Town We Never Were: Old Cowtown Faces an Urban Past," in *Defining Memory: Local Museums and the Construction of History in America's Changing Communities,* ed. Amy K. Levin (Lanham, MD: Rowman & Littlefield, 2007), 97–108; Jessie L. Embry and Mauri Liljenquist Nelson, "Such Is Our Heritage: Daughters of Utah Pioneers Museums," in *Defining Memory,* 161–76.

29. Kerwin Klein, *Frontiers of Historical Imagination: Narrating the European Conquest of Native America, 1890–1990* (Berkeley: University of California Press, 1997).

30. Henry Nash Smith, *Virgin Land: The American West as Symbol and Myth* (Cambridge: Harvard University Press, 1950); also Jared Farmer, *On Zion's Mount: Mormons, Indians, and the American Landscape* (Cambridge: Harvard University Press, 2008); Joy Kasson, *Buffalo Bill's Wild West: Celebrity, Memory, and Popular History* (New York: Hill and Wang, 2000); David M. Wrobel, *Promised Lands: Promotion, Memory, and the Creation of the American West* (Lawrence: University Press of Kansas, 2002); Ari Kelman, *A Misplaced Massacre: Struggling over the Memory of Sand Creek* (Cambridge: Harvard University Press, 2013); Boyd Cothran, *Remembering the Modoc War: Redemptive Violence and the Making of American Innocence* (First Peoples: New Directions in Indigenous Studies, Chapel Hill: University of North Carolina Press, 2014).

31. Klein, *Frontiers of Historical Imagination*, 64–76.

32. Tracy Fessenden, *Culture and Redemption: Religion, the Secular, and American Literature* (Princeton: Princeton University Press, 2007), 6–9. See also Christian Smith, *The Secular Revolution: Power, Interests, and Conflict in the Secularization of American Life,* ed. Christian Smith (Berkeley: University of California Press, 2003); John Lardas Modern, *Secularism in Antebellum America* (Chicago: University of Chicago Press, 2011); Janet R. Jakobsen, "Ethics after Pluralism," in *After Pluralism: Reimagining Religious Engagement,* ed. Courtney Bender and Pamela E. Klassen (New York: Columbia University Press, 2010), 31–58.

ONE Providence and the Scandal of Missionary Failure

1. Marcus Whitman to David Greene, Oct. 29, 1840, typed transcript, box A, Marcus and Narcissa Whitman Collection, 1834–1936 (Whitman College and Northwest Archives, Whitman College, Walla Walla) (hereafter Whitman Collection.)

2. Ibid.

3. The classic work on the Whitman Mission, Clifford Merrill Drury's two-volume *Marcus and Narcissa Whitman, and the Opening of Old Oregon,* takes this approach, though Drury is less critical of the Whitmans than subsequent historians would be. Drury was himself a Presbyterian minister and was sympathetic to the Whitmans' evangelistic and civilizing goals, if not to the ways in which the Whitmans executed those goals. Drury, *Marcus and Narcissa Whitman, and the Opening of Old Oregon,* 2 vols. (Glendale, CA: A. H. Clark, 1973). More recent treatments of the Whitman Mission that focus on cultural misunderstanding (or the missionaries' all-out refusal to understand Indian cultures) include Julie Roy Jeffrey, *Converting the West: A Biography of Narcissa Whitman* (Norman: University of Oklahoma Press, 1991); Genevieve McCoy, "The Women of the ABCFM and the Conflicted Language of Calvinism," *Church History* 64, no. 1 (March 1995): 62–82; Albert Furtwangler, *Bringing Indians to the Book* (Seattle: University of Washington Press, 2000), and Patricia Nelson Limerick, *Legacy of Conquest: The Unbroken Past of the American West* (New York: Norton, 1987), 35–41.

4. Roberta Conner and William L. Lang, "Early Contact and Incursion, 1700–1850," in *Wiyáx̱ayx̱t/As Days Go By/Wiyáakaa'awn: Our History, Our Land, and Our People—the Cayuse, Umatilla, and Walla Walla,* ed. Jennifer Karson (Pendleton, OR: Tamástslikt Cultural Institute; Portland: Oregon Historical Society; Seattle: distributed by

University of Washington Press, 2006), 23–60; Larry Cebula, *Plateau Indians and the Quest for Spiritual Power, 1750–1850* (Lincoln: University of Nebraska Press, 2003); Theodore Stern, *Chiefs and Change in the Oregon Country: Indian Relations at Fort Nez Percés, 1818–1855,* vol. 2 (Corvallis: Oregon State University Press, 1993); Christopher Miller, *Prophetic Worlds: Indians and Whites on the Columbia Plateau* (New Brunswick: Rutgers University Press, 1985); Deward E. Walker Jr., *Conflict and Schism in Nez Percé Acculturation: A Study in Religion and Politics* (Pullman: Washington State University Press, 1968).

5. Barbara Alice Mann goes furthest in depicting the Whitman Mission in the context of Anglo-American colonialism, claiming that the Whitmans and their fellow missionaries used their mandate to evangelize as a ruse to take Indian land and accusing the missionaries of intentionally committing genocide against the Indians by poisoning them. While Mann's account deserves merit for its attention to Cayuse oral history, it fails to address the complex relations between missionaries and American nationalism in nineteenth-century America as well as the poor state of medical knowledge among American doctors, including Whitman, in the early nineteenth century. Cameron Addis depicts the Whitman Mission as an instance of Manifest Destiny but slights the Cayuse view of events when he blames the Whitman Massacre in part on the Cayuses' "overreliance on a supernatural framework." See Barbara Alice Mann, *The Tainted Gift: The Disease Method of Frontier Expansion* (Santa Barbara, CA: Praeger, 2009), 83–112; Addis, "The Whitman Massacre: Religion and Manifest Destiny on the Columbia Plateau, 1809–1858," *Journal of the Early Republic* 25, no. 2 (Summer 2005): 221–58; 256–57.

6. Samuel Worcester, *Eleventh Annual Report of the American Board of Commissioners for Foreign Missions* (Boston: Crocker & Brewster, 1820), 77.

7. Absalom Peters, *The Ninth Report of the American Home Missionary Society* (New York: James Van Norden, 1835), 9.

8. Jeffrey, *Converting the West,* 48.

9. Marcus Whitman to B. B. Wisner, June 27, 1835, typed transcript, box A, Whitman Collection.

10. Myron Eells, *Marcus Whitman: Pathfinder and Patriot* (Seattle: Alice Harriman, 1909), 23. Eells continues, "Many a time were tears seen on his face, as he thought of the disappointment in this object of life." Medical school was much less intensive than theological study in the early nineteenth century: Whitman completed his medical training in sixteen weeks, whereas ministry in a Presbyterian or Congregationalist church demanded four years of college and three of seminary. Drury, *Marcus and Narcissa Whitman,* 71.

11. Marcus Whitman to David Greene, June 27, 1834, typed transcript, box A, Whitman Collection.

12. This was William Clark of the Lewis and Clark Expedition of 1804–6. The Nez Perce tribe remembered Clark from his visit to Nez Perce country during that expedition, during which he successfully treated several sick Nez Perces, demonstrated US technological prowess, and made promises of future trade. See James Ronda, *Lewis and Clark among the Indians* (Lincoln: University of Nebraska Press, 1984), 220–35; Elliott West, *The Last Indian War: The Nez Perce Story* (Oxford: Oxford University Press, 2009), 20–23.

13. Gabriel P. Disoway, "The Flat-Head Indians," *Christian Advocate and Journal and Zion's Herald,* March 1, 1833, 105.

14. Ibid.

15. Ibid.

16. Later Protestant authors added a long speech to the story, in which one chief states that he has come "from the land of the setting sun" in search of "the white man's Book of Heaven." Catholics, on the other hand, claimed that the natives came seeking "Black Robes," or Catholic priests. The earliest appearance of the common version of this story, which describes the "Flatheads" as searching for the "white man's Book of Heaven" is in William Barrows's *Oregon: The Struggle for Possession* (Boston: Houghton Mifflin, 1884), 111. However, Barrows's poetic phrasing is clearly drawn from Henry Harmon Spalding's version of the story, in which the "Flatheads" are in search of the "Book of God" or "Book of Heaven." See Spalding, "Lectures by Rev. H. H. Spalding. Early Oregon Missions: Their Importance in Securing the Country to Americans," Lecture 2, *Walla Walla Statesman,* Feb. 16, 1866, 2; Henry Harmon. US Congress, Senate. Spalding, "Letter from the Secretary of the Interior, Communicating, in Compliance with the Resolution of the Senate of the 2d Instant, Information in Relation to the Early Labors of the Missionaries of the American Board of Commissioners of Foreign Missions in Oregon, Commencing in 1836. February 9, 1871.—Referred to the Committee on Indian Affairs and Ordered to Be Printed," 41st Congress, 3rd Session, 1871, 5. Also Ferenc Szasz and Margaret Szasz, "Religion and Spirituality," in *Oxford History of the American West,* ed. Clyde Milner II, Carol A. O'Conner, and Martha A. Sandweiss (New York: Oxford University Press, 1994), 359–92, 364; Furtwangler, *Bringing Indians to the Book,* 13–57.

17. Samuel Parker, *Journal of an Exploring Tour beyond the Rocky Mountains, under the Direction of the A.B.C.F.M. in the Years 1835, '36, and '37,* 3rd ed. (Ithaca: Mack, Andrus, & Woodruff, 1842), 80; Narcissa Whitman to Clarissa Whitman, August 30, 1836, in *First White Women Over the Rockies: Diaries, Letters, and Biographical Sketches of the Six Women of the Oregon Mission who Made the Overland Journey in 1836 and 1838,* vol. 1, *Where Wagons Could Go: Narcissa Whitman and Eliza Spalding* (Glendale, CA: A. H. Clark, 1936), 92.

18. Bishop Rosati recorded the incident in an 1831 letter to the editor of the *Society for the Propagation of the Faith:* Joseph Rosati to the Editor of the *Annales de la propagation de la foi,* 5 (1832): 599–600. His account, while still tailored to encourage missionary support, appears to be most accurate. Furtwangler analyzes the various written accounts in *Bringing Indians to the Book,* 13–57.

19. Cebula, *Plateau Indians,* 93–94. The *Christian Advocate* was the most widely circulated periodical of its time, reaching over thirty thousand households. Furtwangler, *Bringing Indians to the Book,* 121.

20. Acts 16:9, King James Version.

21. Margaret Szasz, *Indian Education in the American Colonies, 1607–1783* (Albuquerque: University of New Mexico Press, 1998), 101.

22. Richard W. Cogley, *John Eliot's Mission to the Indians before King Philip's War* (Cambridge: Harvard University Press, 1999), 1–10, 45–47; Paul William Harris, *Nothing*

But Christ: Rufus Anderson and the Ideology of Protestant Foreign Missions (New York: Oxford University Press, 1999), 21–23.

23. John M. Coward, *Newspaper Indian: Native American Identity in the Press, 1820–1890* (Urbana: University of Illinois Press, 1999), 68–72; Tim Garrison, *Legal Ideology of Removal: The Southern Judiciary and the Sovereignty of Native American Nations* (Athens: University of Georgia Press, 2002), 24–31.

24. Harris, *Nothing But Christ,* 12–14, 23.

25. Disoway, "The Flat-Head Indians," 108.

26. This station was not among the "Flatheads" (really Nez Perces) who had sent emissaries to St. Louis in 1831 but among the Kalapuya people of Oregon's fertile Willamette Valley. Lee believed this mission field would be more promising because, as he argued, the Native people of the Willamette Valley were more numerous and the Willamette Valley could support a mission colony better. Gray Whaley, *Oregon and the Collapse of Illahee: U.S. Empire and the Transformation of an Indigenous World, 1792–1859* (Chapel Hill: University of North Carolina Press, 2010), 105–10. For the Methodist Mission's history, see Robert J. Loewenberg, *Equality on the Oregon Frontier: Jason Lee and the Methodist Mission, 1834–43* (Seattle: University of Washington Press, 1976).

27. At this time missions to the indigenous peoples of North America were classified as foreign missions. See Mark T. Baker, *Presbyterian Missions and Cultural Interaction in the Far Southwest, 1850–1950* (Chicago: University of Illinois Press, 2005), p. 69, note 34.

28. "Convention of 1818," Junius P. Rodriguez, *The Louisiana Purchase: A Historical and Geographical Encyclopedia* (Santa Barbara, CA: ABC-CLIO, 2002), 85–86.

29. Drury, *Marcus and Narcissa Whitman,* 1:54–55; Whitney Cross, *Burned-Over District: The Social and Intellectual History of Enthusiastic Religion in Western New York, 1800–1850* (Ithaca: Cornell University Press, 1950), 3.

30. Marcus Whitman to B. B. Wisner, June 27, 1835, typed transcript, box A, Whitman Collection; B. B. Wisner to Marcus Whitman, June 14, 1834, typed transcript, folder 1, Marcus and Narcissa Whitman Papers, 1834–97, Oregon Historical Society Research Library, Portland, Oregon (hereafter Marcus and Narcissa Whitman Papers, OHS); B. B. Wisner to Marcus Whitman, July 17, 1834, typed transcript, Marcus and Narcissa Whitman Papers, OHS.

31. H. P. Strong to B. B. Wisner, Dec. 1, 1834, typed transcript, Marcus and Narcissa Whitman Papers, OHS; David Greene to Marcus Whitman, Jan. 1, 1835, typed transcript, Whitman Collection.

32. Whitman to Greene, June 21, 1835, typescript copy, Whitman Collection; Drury, *Marcus and Narcissa Whitman,* 119–20, 122. The traders became much more friendly toward Whitman after he successfully treated many of the company for a cholera outbreak (Whitman to Greene, June 21, 1835; Drury, *Marcus and Narcissa Whitman,* 1:124). Also see Fred R. Gowans, *Rocky Mountain Rendezvous: A History of the Fur Trade Rendezvous, 1825–1840* (Provo: Brigham Young University Press, 1976), 121–35.

33. Whitman to Greene, Nov. 7, 1835, Whitman Mission National Historic Site Web Site, Accessed March 6, 2015, http://www.nps.gov/whmi/learn/historyculture/marcus-letter-november-7-1835.htm.

34. Parker, *Exploring Tour,* 77.

35. Ibid.

36. Whitman to Greene, Nov. 7, 1835, transcript, on Whitman Mission National Historic Site Web Site; Parker, *Exploring Tour,* 78. The personal disagreements between the two missionaries also likely contributed to their separating early. See Whitman to Greene, May 10, 1839, typed transcript, box A, Whitman Collection.

37. Drury, *Marcus and Narcissa Whitman,* 1:111.

38. Harris, *Nothing But Christ,* 31–32; Jeffrey, *Converting the West,* 36–37.

39. For changes in notions of women's virtue and spiritual aptitude more generally, see Catherine Brekus, *Strangers and Pilgrims: Female Preaching in America, 1740–1845* (Chapel Hill: University of North Carolina Press, 1998), 149–54. For these shifts in missions specifically, see Dana L. Robert, "The Christian Home," in *Converting Colonialism: Visions and Realities in Mission History,* ed. Dana L. Robert (Grand Rapids: William B. Eerdman's, 2008), 136–38.

40. Robert, "The Christian Home," 140–41; Mary Kupiec Cayton, "The Canonization of Harriet Newell: Women, the Evangelical Press, and the Foreign Mission Movement in New England, 1800–1840," in *Competing Kingdoms: Women, Mission, Nation, and the American Protestant Empire, 1812–1960,* ed. Barbara Reeves-Ellington, Kathryn Kish Sklar, and Connie A. Shemo (Durham: Duke University Press, 2010), 85–88; Leonard Woods, *Memoir of Mrs. Harriet Newell, Wife of the Rev. Samuel Newell, Missionary to India* (New York: American Tract Society, 1827). Narcissa Whitman recalled reading about Harriet Newell when she was young; Jeffrey, *Converting the West,* 45.

41. Jeffrey, *Converting the West,* 37.

42. Drury, *Marcus and Narcissa Whitman,* 1:163–65.

43. David Greene to the Whitmans and Spaldings, March 4, 1836, typed transcript, Marcus and Narcissa Whitman Papers, OHS.

44. There is no indication that Whitman or his mission board understood the significance of this gesture by the Nez Perces; in fact, ABCFM secretary David Greene scolded Whitman for bringing the boys east, suggesting they would be spoiled by the attention. Whitman to Greene, Jan. 6, 1836, typed transcript, box A, Whitman Collection.

45. Parker, *Exploring Tour,* 119.

46. Edwin Vincent O'Hara, *Pioneer Catholic History of Oregon* (Portland: Glass & Prudhomme, 1911), 72.

47. Robert H. Ruby and John A. Brown, *Indians of the Pacific Northwest: A History* (Norman: University of Oklahoma Press), 74.

48. Cebula, *Plateau Indians,* 11–20; West, *Last Indian War,* 36–37.

49. Marcus Whitman to David Greene, Sept. 5, 1836, typed transcript, box A, Whitman Collection.

50. Narcissa Whitman to Edward and Harriet Prentiss, June 3, 1836, in *Where Wagons Could Go,* 51.

51. Ibid.

52. Marcus Whitman to David Greene, July 16, 1836, typed transcript, box A, Whitman Collection.

53. Narcissa Whitman to Brother Oren and Sister Nancy [Loomis], Oct. 24, 1836, *Where Wagons Could Go,* 331.

54. Narcissa Whitman to Jane Prentiss, March 31, 1836, in *Where Wagons Could Go,* 47.

55. This is not the Fort Walla Walla that is now a museum in Walla Walla. The old Fort Walla Walla, originally known as Fort Nez Perce, was about twenty-five miles west of the mission and was abandoned in 1855. Drury, editor's note, *Where Wagons Could Go,* 93.

56. Narcissa Whitman to Rev. Leverett and Mrs. Hull, Nov. 25, 1836, box A, Whitman Collection.

57. Narcissa Whitman to Parents, Brothers & Sisters, Nov. 1, 1836, box A, Whitman Collection.

58. Conner and Lang, "Early Contact and Incursion," in *Wiyáxayxt/As Days Go By/Wiyáakaa'awn,* 34.

59. Robert H. Ruby and John A. Brown, *Cayuse Indians: Imperial Tribesmen of Old Oregon* (Norman: University of Oklahoma Press, 1972), 3–12.

60. Asa Bowen Smith to his parents, Sept. 15, 1838, *The Mountains We Have Crossed: Diaries and Letters of the Oregon Mission, 1838,* ed. Clifford M. Drury (Lincoln: University of Nebraska Press, 1999), 157.

61. Ruby and Brown, *Cayuse Indians,* 3.

62. West, *Last Indian War,* 5–6.

63. Marcus Whitman recorded in 1837 that the younger Cayuses no longer understood the Cayuse language and spoke only Nimiipuutímt. Marcus Whitman to David Greene, May 5, 1837, typed transcript, box A, Whitman Collection. See also Ruby and Brown, *Cayuse Indians,* 12.

64. West, *Last Indian War,* 8–10.

65. Lillian Alice Ackerman, *A Necessary Balance: Gender and Power among the Indians of the Columbia Plateau,* The Civilization of the American Indian Series, vol. 246 (Norman: University of Oklahoma Press, 2003), 49–53; Cebula, *Plateau Indians,* 15; McCoy, *Chief Yellow Wolf,* 21–26

66. Alvin M. Josephy, *The Nez Perce Indians and the Opening of the Northwest* (New Haven: Yale University Press, 1971), 84–90.

67. Henry Spalding, "Letter from the Rocky Mountains," dated July 11, 1836, published in the *New York Evangelist,* Oct. 22, 1836, 171.

68. Clifford M. Drury, *Henry Harmon Spalding* (Caldwell, ID: Caxton Printers, 1936), 115.

69. Jeffrey, *Converting the West,* 84.

70. Drury, *Marcus and Narcissa Whitman,* 1:226.

71. The Spaldings spent their first winter in a teepee, while Whitman built a sod-roofed lean-to. Drury, *Marcus and Narcissa Whitman,* 231–33.

72. Marcus Whitman to David Greene, May 18, 1837, typed transcript, box A, Whitman Collection; Whitman to Greene, May 27, 1840, box A, Whitman Collection; Marcus Whitman to his brother, copy, handwritten, May 24, 1841, box A, Whitman Collection.

73. Marcus Whitman to David Greene, May 5, 1838, typed transcript, box A, Whitman Collection.

74. Marcus Whitman to David Greene, copied by Narcissa Whitman, Oregon Country, Oct. 25, 1836, typed transcript, box A, Whitman Collection.

75. Henry Harmon Spalding to David Greene, Oct. 2, 1839, typed transcript, box A, Whitman Collection. See also Cornelius Rogers to Elkanah Walker, July 8, 1839, box 1, folder 18, Oregon Mission Papers, 1837-72, Beinecke Rare Book and Manuscript Library, Yale University, New Haven (hereafter Oregon Mission Papers); Marcus Whitman to Elkanah Walker, Nov. 5, 1841, box 1, folder 1, Whitman Family Papers, 1838-47 (hereafter Whitman Family Papers), Beinecke Library, Yale University.

76. Asa Bowen Smith to Elkanah Walker, April 27, 1840, box 1, folder 13, Oregon Mission Papers.

77. Ibid.; Marcus Whitman to Elkanah Walker, Dec. 27, 1839, box 1, folder 1, Whitman Family Papers; Henry Harmon Spalding to Elkanah Walker, Clear Water, Dec. 11, 1839, box 2, folder 14, Oregon Mission Papers. As Genevieve McCoy demonstrates, the missionaries themselves struggled to make sense of many of the doctrines they sought to teach the natives, since nineteenth-century Calvinism was a contested and often contradictory body of beliefs that encompassed elements of Arminianism. McCoy, "The Women of the ABCFM Oregon Mission and the Conflicted Language of Calvinism," 65-69. The missionaries among the Nez Perce were more successful at learning the language. Eliza Spalding and Asa Bowen Smith both became fluent, and Henry Spalding printed the first books in the Nez Perce language in 1839. Drury, *Marcus and Narcissa Whitman*, 171-72, 225.

78. Marcus Whitman to David Greene, May 18, 1837, typed transcript, box A, Whitman Collection; Marcus Whitman to David Greene, May 27, 1840, typed transcript, box A, Whitman Collection; Marcus Whitman to brother, May 24, 1841, typed transcript, box A, Whitman Collection; Henry Harmon Spalding to Elijah White, in White, *Concise View of Oregon Territory, Its Colonial and Indian Relations* (Washington, DC: T. Barnard, 1846), 19-24.

79. Marcus Whitman to David Greene, Oregon Territory, March 12, 1838, typed transcript, box A, Whitman Collection.

80. Elizabeth Vibert, *Traders' Tales: Narratives of Cultural Encounters in the Columbia Plateau, 1807-1846* (Norman: University of Oklahoma Press, 1997), 145-47; Robert T. Boyd, *People of the Dalles: The Indians of Wascopam Mission* (Lincoln: University of Nebraska Press, 2005), 66; Eugene S. Hunn and James Selam, *Nch'i-wána, "The Big River": Mid-Columbia Indians and Their Land* (Seattle: University of Washington Press, 1990), 219-25.

81. Marcus Whitman to David Greene, May 18, 1837, typed transcript, box A, Whitman Collection; Marcus Whitman to David Greene, May 27, 1840, typed transcript, box A, Whitman Collection; Marcus Whitman to brother, May 24, 1841, copy, handwritten, box A, Whitman Collection.

82. Henry Perkins to Mr. and Mrs. Walker, Wascopam House, March 7, 1839, box 1, folder 11, Oregon Mission Papers.

83. Jeffrey, *Converting the West*, 151.

84. Ibid.; US House, "Letter from the Secretary of the Interior, transmitting, in compliance with the resolution of the House of the 15th instant, the report of J. Ross Browne, on the subject of the Indian war in Oregon and Washington Territories, report prepared for the Committee on Military Affairs," 35th Congress, 1st session, 1858, 31.

85. Narcissa Whitman to Clarissa Prentiss, Waiilatpoo, Oregon Country, May 2, 1840, Marcus and Narcissa Whitman Papers, box 1, folder 20, Washington State University Library Manuscripts and Archives, Pullman, WA; Narcissa Whitman to Clarissa Whitman, Waiilatpu, Oregon Country, May 2, 1840, in Drury, *Where Wagons Could Go*, 137.

86. Ruby and Brown, *Cayuse Indians*, 76.

87. Gray's later writings especially indicated the level of bitter discord among the missionaries; see, for instance, his description of Spalding as "inclined in the early part of his missionary labors to accumulate property for the especial benefit of his family." William H. Gray, *History of Oregon, 1792–1849, Drawn from Personal Observation and Authentic Information* (Portland: American News Company, 1870), 110; also William H. Gray to Elkanah Walker, May 7, 1841, box 1, folder 3, Oregon Mission Papers; Mary Augusta Dix Gray to Sisters in Christ (Mary Walker and Myra Eells), Oct. 23, 1839, box 1, folder 3, Oregon Mission Papers; Marcus Whitman to David Greene, Waiilatpu, Oct. 22, 1839, typed transcript, box A, Whitman Collection.

88. Gray, *History of Oregon*, 110; see also William H. Gray to Elkanah Walker, March 28, 1842, box 1, folder 3, Oregon Mission Papers; Gray to Walker, May 7, 1841, box 1, folder 3, Oregon Mission Papers.

89. Narcissa Whitman to her father, Stephen Prentiss, Oct. 10, 1840, transcribed in "Mrs. Whitman's Letters," in *Transactions of the Twenty-First Annual Reunion of the Oregon Pioneer Association for 1893* (Portland: G. H. Himes, 1894), 129.

90. Marcus Whitman to David Greene, March 12, 1838, typed transcript, box A, Whitman Collection; Henry Spalding and Marcus Whitman to David Greene, April 21, 1838, box A, Whitman Collection.

91. Marcus Whitman to David Greene, Oregon Country, Oct. 30, 1838, typed transcript, box A, Whitman Collection.

92. Drury, "At Waiilatpu: The Whitman Home," *Where Wagons Could Go*, 134.

93. Mary Walker, Diary, Oct. 21, 1838, in *Diary of Mary Richardson Walker, 1838*, in Drury, *Elkanah and Mary Walker, Pioneers among the Spokanes* (Caldwell, ID: Caxton Press, 1940), 81; Mary Walker, Diary, Feb. 1839, *Elkanah and Mary Walker*, 117; Asa Bowen Smith to Elkanah Walker, April 20, 1839, box 1, folder 13, Oregon Mission Papers; Asa Bowen Smith to Elkanah Walker, Feb. 22, 1840, box 1, folder 13, Oregon Mission Papers; Marcus Whitman to Elkanah Walker, June 30, 1839, box 1, folder 1, Whitman Family Papers; Jeffrey, *Converting the West*, 140–42.

94. Mary Walker, Diary, Oct. 27, 1838, *Diary of Mary Richardson Walker*, 80.

95. Marcus Whitman to David Greene, Oct. 22, 1839, transcript, box A, Whitman Collection; Asa Bowen Smith to Elkanah Walker, Oct. 12, 1840, box 1, folder 13, Oregon Mission Papers; Francis Norbert Blanchet, *Historical Sketches of the Catholic Church in Oregon during the Past Forty Years* (Portland: 1878), 10, 27–50.

96. For practical reasons some Catholic missionaries did want the Indians to settle, but they never put as much effort into farming or teaching farming as the Protestants did. James R. Gibson, *Farming the Frontier: The Agricultural Opening of the Oregon Country, 1786–1846* (Seattle: University of Washington Press, 1985), 159–60, 168.

97. Henry Harmon Spalding to Elkanah Walker, Clearwater, Dec. 11, 1839, box 2, folder 14, Oregon Mission Papers; Marcus Whitman to David Greene, May 18, 1837, typed transcript, box A, Whitman Collection; Marcus Whitman to David Greene, May 27, 1840, typed transcript, box A, Whitman Collection; Marcus Whitman to brother, May 24, 1841, typed transcript, box A, Whitman Collection; Henry Harmon Spalding to Elijah White, in White, *Concise View of Oregon Territory,* 19–24.

98. Mark Thiel, "Catholic Ladders and Native American Evangelization," *U.S. Catholic Historian* 27, no. 1 (Winter 2009): 49–59; Philip M. Hanley, *History of the Catholic Ladder* (Fairfield, WA: Ye Galleon Press, 1993); Boyd, *People of the Dalles,* 187–88.

99. This ladder is now owned by the Oregon Historical Society and can be viewed at "Protestant Ladder," *Oregon History Project,* accessed March 6, 2015, http://www.ohs.org/education/oregonhistory/historical_records/dspDocument.cfm?doc_ID=1BD1D5D9-CBEA-5E8B-C0609C63D5C881B1. Also see the companion article, Kris A. White and Janice St. Laurent, "Collections: Mysterious Journey: The Catholic Ladder of 1840," *Oregon Historical Quarterly* 97, no. 1, special issue, *Catholic Missionizing in the West* (Spring 1996): 70–88.

100. Andrew Fisher, *Shadow Tribe: The Making of a Columbia River Indian Identity* (Seattle: University of Washington Press, 2010), 32; *Annual Report of the Commissioner of Indian Affairs to the Secretary of the Interior for the Year 1873* (Washington: Government Printing Office, 1874), 159. The quote is part of Joseph's explanation of why the Nimiipuu did not want churches on their reservation.

101. Narcissa Whitman to Elvira Perkins, March 23, 1839, *Mrs. Whitman's Letters, 1839–1847* (Salem: Oregon Pioneer Association, 1894), 167.

102. Narcissa Whitman to Jane Prentiss, Sept. 18, 1838, box 1, folder 3, Whitman Family Papers.

103. Joyce Badgley, *Seeing the Elephant: The Many Faces of the Oregon Trail* (Lubbock: Texas Tech University Press, 2003), 37; Laurie M. Carlson, *On Sidesaddles to Heaven: The Women of the Rocky Mountain Mission* (Caldwell, ID: Caxton Press, 1998), 103–4.

104. Marcus Whitman to David Greene, Waiilatpu, Oct. 22, 1839, typed transcript, box A, Whitman Collection.

105. Marcus Whitman to Elkanah Walker, Nov. 18, 1840, box 1, folder 1, Whitman Family Papers; Marcus Whitman to David Greene, March 28, 1841, July 13, 1841, Oct. 22, 1841, typed transcripts, box A, Whitman Collection; Furtwangler, *Bringing Indians to the Book,* 127.

106. William H. Gray to David Greene, April 15, 1840, Papers of the American Board of Commissioners for Foreign Missions, microfilm, reel 783, unit 6, Yale Divinity School Library Special Collections (hereafter ABCFM Papers).

107. Asa Bowen Smith to David Greene, Oct. 21, 1840, reel 783, unit 6, ABCFM Papers.

108. David Greene to the Oregon Missions, Feb. 25, 1842, reel 783, unit 6, AB-CFM Papers.

109. Neither Whitman nor Lovejoy kept a journal of their travels, but Lovejoy later wrote his recollections in a letter to George Atkinson in 1876. See Atkinson, "Centennial Paper: The American Colonist in Oregon: An Address Delivered before the Pioneer Historical Society of Oregon, at Astoria, Feb. 22, 1876" (Astoria, OR, 1876).

110. This plan is detailed in Marcus Whitman to James W. Porter, Secretary of War, June 22, 1844, typed transcript, box B, Whitman Collection. Whitman's plan never came to fruition: ironically, it would take Whitman's death for the US government to provide military protection to emigrants.

111. Marcus Whitman to David Greene, May 30, 1843, typed transcript, box B, Whitman Collection.

112. Whitman to Greene, Nov. 1, 1843, typed transcript, Whitman Collection.

113. Ibid.

114. Marcus Whitman to Stephen Prentiss, May 16, 1844, box 1, folder 1, Whitman Family Papers.

115. Ibid.

116. Ibid. Also see Whitman to Henry Brewer, May 25, 1844, box B, Whitman Collection; Marcus Whitman to H. F. Wisewell, June 29, 1845, box B, Whitman Collection; Whitman to Greene, May 18, 1847, typed transcript, box B, Whitman Collection; Whitman to Elkanah Walker, Waiilatpu, July 15, 1845, and Oct. 27, 1845, box 1, folder 1, Whitman Family Papers.

117. The emigration of 1842 was made up of only 125 people. West, *Last Indian War,* 46.

118. Ibid., 46–47.

119. Marcus Whitman to David Greene, April 8, 1844, typed transcript, box B, Whitman Family Papers.

120. Marcus Whitman to David Greene, Nov. 11, 1841, and enclosed letter from Archibald McKinlay, Oct. 4, 1841, typed transcript, Whitman Collection. Also see McKinlay's later recollection of the incident in Archibald McKinlay to Elwood Evans, Lac La Hache, British Columbia, Oct. 3, 1880, box 1, folder 33, Elwood Evans Papers, Beinecke Library.

121. Marcus Whitman to David Greene, April 8, 1845, transcript at "Dr. Whitman Selected Letters," Whitman Mission National Historic Site, accessed Sept. 25, 2012, http://www.nps.gov/whmi/historyculture/marcus-letter-april-8-1845.htm.

122. Marcus Whitman to David Greene, April 8 1844, box B, Whitman Collection.

123. Marcus Whitman to David Greene, Oct. 25, 1845, box B, Whitman Collection; Whitman to Elkanah Walker and Cushing Eells, Waiilatpu, Feb. 3, 1846, box 1, folder 2, Whitman Family Papers.

124. Antone Minthorn, "Wars, Treaties, and the Beginning of Reservation Life," in *Wiyáx̣ayx̣t/As Days Go By/Wiyáakaaʾawn, Our History, Our Land, Our People,* ed. Jennifer Karson, foreword by Alvin P. Josephy (Pendleton, OR: Tamástlikt Cultural Institute, 2006), 64; Addis, "Whitman Massacre," 222–23; Ruby and Brown, *Cayuse Indians,* 73–75; Drury, *Marcus and Narcissa Whitman,* 2:59–60, 132.

125. Washington Irving, *Astoria; or Enterprise beyond the Rocky Mountains* (Paris: Baudry's European Library, 1836), 71; Robert Boyd, *The Coming of the Spirit of Pestilence: Introduced Infectious Diseases and Population Decline among Northwest Coast Indians, 1774–1874* (Vancouver: University of British Columbia Press, 1999), 46.

126. Marcus Whitman to David Greene, Waiilatpu, Oregon Country, April 8, 1845, transcript at Whitman National Historic Site: Dr. Whitman Selected Letters, accessed Sept. 25, 2012, http://www.nps.gov/whmi/historyculture/marcus-letter-april-8-1845.htm.

127. Marcus Whitman to Elkanah Walker and Cushing Eells, Waiilatpu, Nov. 25, 1845, box 1, folder 2, Whitman Family Papers.

128. Marcus Whitman to David Greene, April 1, 1847, typed transcript, box B, Whitman Collection.

129. Marcus Whitman to Elkanah Walker and Cushing Eells, Waiilatpu, Nov. 25 1845, box 1, folder 2, Whitman Family Papers.

130. Statement of John Young and Augustus Raymond, Jean-Baptiste Brouillet, "Letter from the Secretary of the Interior, transmitting, in compliance with the resolution of the House of the 15th instant, the report of J. Ross Browne, on the subject of the Indian war in Oregon and Washington Territories, report prepared for the Committee on Military Affairs," 35th Congress, 1st session, 1858, 22–23; Stern, *Chiefs and Change,* 170. Gray himself denied this, citing a statement from Joel Palmer as evidence, in Gray, *History of Oregon,* 367.

131. Addis, "Whitman Massacre," 242.

132. David S. Jones, *Rationalizing Epidemics: Meanings and Uses of American Indian Mortality since 1600* (Cambridge: Harvard University Press, 2004), 2.

133. Narcissa Whitman to Abigail R. Smith, Feb. 8, 1847, box B, Whitman Collection.

134. Whaley, *Oregon and the Collapse of Illahee,* 62, 92–95; Boyd, *Coming of the Spirit of Pestilence,* 238–42. The diseases did not begin with the missions (there had been several serious epidemics before Jason Lee's arrival), but the missions did serve as a breeding ground for disease.

135. As Robert Boyd has shown, the measles epidemic most likely did not originate at the Whitman Mission, but given that measles arrived contemporaneously with the American emigration of 1847 it was natural that the Cayuse would blame the mission for the epidemic. Boyd, "The Pacific Northwest Measles Epidemic of 1847–1848," *Oregon Historical Quarterly* 95 no. 1, *Early Contacts between Native Americans and Euro-Americans* (Spring 1994): 6–47, 6–7.

136. John L. Lewes to Elkanah Walker, Fort Colvile, Jan. 2, 1848, Oregon Mission Papers.

137. Jean-Baptiste Brouillet, "Letter from the Secretary of the Interior, transmitting, in compliance with the resolution of the House of the 15th instant, the report of J. Ross Browne, on the subject of the Indian war in Oregon and Washington Territories, report prepared for the Committee on Military Affairs," 35th Congress, 1st session, 1858, 22–23.

138. Cebula, *Plateau Indians*, 118; Furtwangler, *Bringing Indians to the Book*, 100. Robert Boyd theorizes that Cayuse sweat baths, useful for ailments such as arthritis, may have also contributed to high death rates. *Coming of the Spirit of Pestilence*, 108.

139. William Craig, Statement, Exec. Doc. 58, 25–27; Josephy, *Nez Perce Indians*, 250.

140. Ruby and Brown, *Cayuse Indians*, 104.

141. Drury, *Marcus and Narcissa Whitman*, 2:241.

142. Ibid., 246–47.

143. For Cayuse accounts, see Minthorn, "Wars, Treaties, and the Beginning of Reservation Life," 63–64; editorial, "Whitman Yesterday and Today," *Confederated Umatilla Journal* 25, no. 6 (June 2017): 6A; editorial, "The Whitman Incident and the Cayuse Five," *Confederated Umatilla Journal* 26, no. 12 (December 2019): 6A. Mary Ann Bridger, the child of the trapper Jim Bridger and Cora Insala, a Flathead woman, was the only non-Cayuse witness to this first interaction and died of measles while in captivity. Matilda Sager Delaney, a survivor, described Bridger's account in *A Survivor's Recollections of the Whitman Massacre* (Spokane: Esther Reed Chapter, Daughters of the American Revolution, 1920), 15–16.

144. Accounts of the attack are numerous; Ruby and Brown, *Cayuse Indians*, 109–112, provides the most complete synthesis of the varying accounts. See also Drury, *Marcus and Narcissa Whitman*, 2:229–95; Jeffrey, *Converting the West*, 217–20. Primary source accounts include Mary Saunders, *Whitman Massacre: A True Story by a Survivor of This Terrible Tragedy Which Took Place in Oregon in 1847* (1916; repr. Fairfield, WA: Galleon Press, 1977); Eliza Spalding Warren, *Memoirs of the West: The Spaldings* (Portland: Marsh Printing, c. 1916), 23–32.

145. West, *Last Indian War*, 50.

146. Delaney, *A Survivor's Recollections*, 22–23.

147. Henry Harmon Spalding to Elkanah Walker and Cushing Eells, Fort Walla Walla, Jan. 1, 1848, Oregon Mission Papers; Peter Skene Ogden to Elkanah Walker, Fort Nez Perces, Dec. 31, 1847, Oregon Mission Papers.

148. Ruby and Brown, *Cayuse Indians*, 128–43.

TWO Providential History

1. Robert H. Ruby and John Arthur Brown, *The Cayuse Indians; Imperial Tribesmen of Old Oregon*, The Civilization of the American Indian Series, 189–204. (Norman: University of Oklahoma Press, 1972).

2. Henry Harmon Spalding, "Lectures by Rev. H. H. Spaulding, Early Oregon Missions—Their Importance in Securing the Country to Americans," *Walla Walla Statesman*, Lecture 1, Feb. 9, 1866, 1.

3. Henry Harmon Spalding, "Lectures by Rev. H. H. Spaulding, Early Oregon Missions—Their Importance in Securing the Country to Americans," *Walla Walla Statesman*, Lecture 4, March 2, 1866, 1.

4. See, in particular, John Fea's discussion of the work of George Bancroft in *Why Study History? Reflections on the Importance of the Past* (Grand Rapids: Baker Academic,

2013), 69–70. Scholars have used the term "providential history" in their work but rarely defined it; see, for instance, Catherine A. Brekus, "Writing Religious Experience: Women's Authorship in Early America," *Journal of Religion* 92, no. 4 (October 2012): 484; Francis J. Bremer, "John Winthrop and the Shaping of New England History," *Massachusetts Historical Review* 18, Massachusetts and the Origins of American Historical Thought (2016): 1–17; Mark A. Chancey, "Rewriting History for a Christian America: Religion and the Texas Social Studies Controversy of 2009–2010," *Journal of Religion* 94, no. 3 (July 2014): 329; Harry Clark Maddux, "God's Responsibility: Narrative Choice and Providential History in Mather's 'Biblia Americana' Commentary on Ezra," *Early American Literature* 42, no. 2 (2007): 305–21. This book differs from Arthur Schlesinger's definition of providential history insofar as it focuses on providential history as a method rather than as an interpretive focus on human fallibility and the temporary nature of human institutions; see Arthur Schlesinger, "America: Experiment or Destiny?" *American Historical Review* 82, no. 3 (June 1977): 506–7.

5. Hollis Read, *The Hand of God in History, or Divine Providence Historically Illustrated in the Extension and Establishment of Christianity* (Hartford: H. E. Robbins, 1855), iv.

6. Nicholas Guyatt, *Providence and the Invention of the United States, 1607–1865* (Cambridge: Cambridge University Press, 2007), 3. Scholarship on providentialism has tended to focus on Europe; see Alexandra Walsham, *Providence in Early Modern England* (New York: Oxford, 1999); Michael P. Winship, *Seers of God: Puritan Providentialism in the Restoration and Early Enlightenment* (Baltimore: Johns Hopkins University Press, 1996).

7. William Hutchison, *Errand to the World: American Protestant Thought and Foreign Missions* (Chicago: University of Chicago Press, 1987), 8.

8. Julie Roy Jeffrey, *Converting the West: A Biography of Narcissa Whitman,* The Oklahoma Western Biographies (Norman: University of Oklahoma Press, 1991), 42.

9. Electa VanValkenburg to Henry Harmon Spalding, June 23, 1868, box 5, Spalding Collection, 1832–1997, Whitman College and Northwest Archives, Whitman College, Walla Walla, Washington (hereafter Spalding Collection).

10. Huntington Lyman to Henry Harmon Spalding, Aug. 12, 1871, box 6, Spalding Collection.

11. William I. Marshall, *Acquisition of Oregon: And the Long Suppressed Evidence About Marcus Whitman,* 2 vols. (Seattle: Lowman & Hanford, 1911), 1:122. Other historians date the story's origins even later; see Cameron Addis, "The Whitman Massacre: Religion and Manifest Destiny on the Columbia Plateau, 1809–1858," *Journal of the Early Republic* 25, no. 2 (Summer 2005): 253.

12. Henry Harmon Spalding to Elkanah Walker, box 2, folder 17, Oregon Mission Papers, Beinecke Library, Yale University (hereafter Oregon Mission Papers); "Sandwich Islands: Annual Report of the Mission, 5th June, 1841," *Missionary Herald* 38, no. 3 (March 1842), 94.

13. Asa Bowen Smith to David Greene, Sept. 28, 1840, Papers of the American Board of Commissioners for Foreign Missions, 1811–1919, microfilm, Yale Divinity School Library Special Collections, Yale University, reel 783.

14. Hubert Howe Bancroft, *Works of Hubert Howe Bancroft*, 39 vols. *History of Oregon* (San Francisco: History Company, 1886), 29:665, note 46; Edward G. Bourne, "The Legend of Marcus Whitman," *American Historical Review* 6, no. 2 (1901): 281; James Braden Zischke, "Marcus Whitman: A Biographical Interpretation" (PhD diss., Stanford University, 1950), 248; Clifford M. Drury, *Henry Harmon Spalding* (Caldwell, ID: Caxton Press, 1936), 358.

15. Editorial note to Henry Harmon Spalding, "Early Oregon Missions: Their Importance in Securing This Country to Americans," Albany [OR.] States' Rights Democrat, 1866–1867, preserved in a scrapbook by Elwood Evans, Beinecke Library, Yale University, 65.

16. Drury, *Henry Harmon Spalding*, 18–19, 21–22. Spalding was "bound out" to the Broats, an arrangement in which the adoptive family was given a sum of money and bound by contract to raise the child until the age of twenty-one. Ibid., 23–24.

17. Ibid., 35–36.

18. Ibid., 33–34; Samuel Newell, *The Conversion of the World, or the Claims of Six Hundred Millions and the Ability and Duty of the Churches Respecting Them*, 2nd ed. (Andover, MA: Flagg & Gould, 1818), 18; Spalding, Diary, Nov. 26, 1836, typed transcript, box 2, Spalding Collection.

19. Caroll Cutler, *A History of Western Reserve College, 1826–1876* (Cleveland, Crocker's, 1876), 19; J. C. White, "Reminiscences of Lane Seminary," *Pamphlet Souvenir of the History of Lane Seminary: Papers Read Before the Lane Club* (Cincinnati, 1889), 7.

20. Henry Spalding, Diary, Nov. 26, 1836, typed transcript, box 2, Spalding Collection.

21. Robert H. Abzug, *Cosmos Crumbling: American Reform and the Religious Imagination* (New York: Oxford University Press, 1994), 116–24; White, "Reminiscences of Lane Seminary," 11.

22. Spalding to the Directors of the A.B.C.F.M., August 7, 1835, box 1, Spalding Collection.

23. Lyman Beecher, *A Plea for the West* (Cincinnati: Turman & Smith, 1835), 11–12.

24. Spalding, "Early Oregon Missions: Their Importance in Securing This Country to Americans," *Albany [OR] States' Rights Democrat*, 1866–67, preserved in a scrapbook by Elwood Evans, Beinecke Library, Yale University, 3.

25. Drury, *Henry Harmon Spalding*, 55–56. For similar controversies at Western Reserve, see ibid., 47–48.

26. For example, John L. Lewes to Elkanah Walker, Jan. 2, 1848, box 1, folder 4, Oregon Mission Papers; James Douglas to George Abernethy, Dec. 7, 1847, in *Oregon Spectator*, Dec. 10, 1847, 1; Peter Skene Ogden to Elkanah Walker, Vancouver, March 18, 1848, box 1, folder 8, Oregon Mission Papers.

27. George L. Curry, "The Massacre at Waiilatpu," *Oregon Spectator*, Jan. 20, 1848, 1.

28. Ogden to Walker, Vancouver, March 18, 1848, box 1, folder 8, Oregon Mission Papers; Jean-Baptiste Brouillet, "Letter from the Secretary of the Interior, transmitting, in compliance with the resolution of the House of the 15th instant, the report of J. Ross

Browne, on the subject of the Indian war in Oregon and Washington Territories," report prepared for the Committee on Military Affairs, 35th Congress, 1st session, 1858, 19.

29. Henry Spalding to David Greene, Oregon City, Oregon Country, Jan. 24, 1848, transcript, box 2, Spalding Collection; Henry Spalding, Letter to the Editor, *Oregon American and Evangelical Unionist* 1, no. 1, Feb. 8, 1848, 12–15; Jean-Baptiste Brouillet, *Authentic Account of the Murder of Dr. Whitman and other Missionaries, by the Cayuse Indians of Oregon, in 1847, and the Causes which Led to that Horrible Catastrophe* (Portland: S. J. McCormick 1869), 84–85. One of these was Brouillet's interpreter, probably Jean Toupin of Fort Walla Walla, and the other was the son of Tilokaikt, who, as noted in chapter 1, had a volatile relationship with Whitman and, according to trial records, allegedly participated in the Whitman killings. Drury, *Henry Harmon Spalding,* 337.

30. Henry Spalding to David Greene, Jan. 24, 1848, transcript, box 2, Spalding Collection; Drury, *Henry Harmon Spalding,* 341.

31. Ruby and Brown, *Cayuse Indians,* 160.

32. Alvin M. Josephy, *The Nez Perce Indians and the Opening of the Northwest,* Yale Western Americana Series (New Haven: Yale University Press, 1965), 260–62.

33. Henry Harmon Spalding to the Bishop of Walla Walla, or Either of the Catholic Priests, *Oregon Spectator,* Jan. 20, 1848, 1. "Below" was a common term for the settlements south of the Columbia River.

34. "A Bill to Authorize the Governor to Raise a Regiment of Volunteers, Etc.," *Oregon Spectator,* Jan. 6, 1848, 1.

35. Spalding to David Greene, Jan. 24, 1848, typed transcript, box 2, Spalding Collection.

36. Spalding, letter to the editor, *Oregon American and Evangelical Unionist* 1, no. 1, Feb. 8, 1848, 13–15.

37. For general anti-Catholicism at this time, see Elizabeth Fenton, *Religious Liberties: Anti-Catholicism and Liberal Democracy in Nineteenth-Century America* (Oxford: Oxford University Press, 2011), 53; Dana L. Robert, *Occupy until I Come: A. T. Pierson and the Evangelization of the World* (Grand Rapids: W. B. Eerdman's, 2003), 78–79; for anti-Catholicism in Oregon, see Malcolm C. Clark, "The Bigot Disclosed: 90 Years of Nativism," *Oregon Historical Quarterly* 75, no. 2 (June 1974): 112, 115–18.

38. Spalding to Walker, Oct. 22, 1839, box 2, folder 14, Oregon Mission Papers.

39. Henry Spalding to Elkanah Walker, Oct. 26, 1846, box 2, folder 17, Oregon Mission Papers.

40. Henry Harmon Spalding, letter to the editor, *Oregon American, and Evangelical Unionist,* 1, no. 1, Feb. 8, 1848, 12–15.

41. Ibid, 15.

42. Henry Spalding to Dudley Allen, Sept., 1848 [no day listed], typed transcript, box 2, Spalding Collection.

43. Henry Spalding, letter to the editor, *Oregon American and Evangelical Unionist,* 1, no. 2, June 21, 1848, 24.

44. Henry Spalding, letter to the editor, *Oregon Spectator,* Feb. 8, 1848, 13–14.

45. Henry Spalding, "The Actors in the Tragedy," *Oregon American, and Evangelical Unionist* 1, no. 8 (May 23, 1849), 118–19.

46. Ibid., 125–28.

47. J. B. A. Brouillet, "Journal of the Principal Events that Occurred in the Walla Walla Country from the Arrival of the Bishop and His Clergy Until the Moment They Left That Country for the Willamette Settlement," in J. Ross Browne, U.S. Congress, House, *Indian War in Oregon and Washington Territories. Letter from the Secretary of the Interior, Transmitting, in Compliance with the Resolution of the House of the 15th Instant, the Report of J. Ross Browne, on the Subject of the Indian War in Oregon and Washington Territories. January 25, 1858.—Referred to the Committee on Military Affairs, and Ordered to Be* Printed, 35th Cong., 1st Sess., 1858, 33–41., "Addison," letter to the editor, *Oregon American, and Evangelical Unionist,* 1, no. 7, March 1, 1849, 108.

48. Henry Spalding, letter to the editor, *Oregon American and Evangelical Unionist,* 1, no. 2, June 21, 1848, 24. For the *Spectator*'s policy, see W. G. T'Vault, "To the Public," *Oregon Spectator,* Feb. 5, 1846, 2.

49. Newspaper heading, *Oregon American, and Evangelical Unionist,* 1, no. 1, Feb. 8, 1848, 1; Drury, *Henry Harmon Spalding,* 356; Herbert Lang, "The Pioneer Printing Press of the Pacific Coast," *Transactions of the Fifteenth Annual Reunion of the Oregon Pioneer Association for 1887* (Portland: George H. Himes, 1887), 96–97.

50. [J. S. Griffin], "Note from the Editor," *Oregon American, and Evangelical Unionist,* 1, no. 8, May 23, 1849, 113.

51. "Information Received," *Oregon American, and Evangelical Unionist,* 1, no. 8, May 23, 1849, 115.

52. Brouillet, *Authentic Account,* 86.

53. Henry Spalding, letter to the editor, *Oregon American, and Evangelical Unionist,* 1, no. 2, June 21, 1848, 24.

54. Henry Spalding, letter to the editor, *Oregon American, and Evangelical Unionist,* 1, no. 8, May 23, 1849, 118.

55. "Death of Dr. Marcus Whitman," *Boston Recorder,* June 16, 1848, 93. The obituary states that it was taken from the Chicago Herald, probably the Presbyterian-funded *Western Herald/Herald of the Prairies.* The original *Herald* article appears to be lost.

56. For instance, referring to the Catholic missionaries indiscriminately as Jesuits, the emphasis on Whitman being "clothed in skins" and "traversing icy streams," and the reference to the "grasp of Great Britain" and the Jesuits' schemes. See Henry Harmon Spalding to Elwood Evans, Aug. 13, 1867, box 3, folder 44, Elwood Evans Papers, Beinecke Library, Yale University; Spalding, Henry Spalding, "History of Indian Affairs Among the Nez Perces," *Oregon Pacific,* November 9, 1865, typescript copy in William I. Marshall Papers, Beinecke Library, Yale University; Henry Spalding, "Early Missions in Old Oregon: Their Importance in Securing the Country to Americans," *Albany States Rights Democrat,* Nov. 17, 1866—Sept. 1867, collected in scrapbook by Elwood Evans, Beinecke Library, Yale University, 22–25.

57. "Eighth Annual Report of the Western Reserve Seminary," *Minutes of the General Assembly of the Presbyterian Church in the United States of America; with an*

Appendix (Philadelphia: William F. Geddes, 1832), 42; James B. Walker, *Experiences of Pioneer Life in the Early Settlements and Cities in the West* (Chicago: Sumner, 1832), 114, 244-46.

58. The *Ohio Observer* published a run of Spalding's letters to Dudley Allen in articles entitled "Letter from Rev. H. H. Spaulding, Missionary to Oregon," on Nov. 17, 1847, Dec. 1, 1847, Dec. 15, 1847, Dec. 29, 1847, and Jan. 5, 1848. The letters, written prior to Whitman's death, dealt with everyday life at the Nez Perce Mission.

59. Jeffrey, *Converting the West*, 17.

60. Harriet Newell and Leonard Woods, *Memoirs of Mrs. Harriet Newell Wife of the Rev. S. Newell, American Missionary to India, Who Died at the Isle of France, Nov. 30, 1812, Aged 19: Also a Sermon on Occasion of Her Death, Preached at Haverhill, Massachusetts* (London: Booth, 1816), 211.

61. Ibid.; Maria Monk et al., *Awful Disclosures of Maria Monk: As Exhibited in a Narrative of Her Sufferings During a Residence of Five Years as a Novice, and Two Years as a Black Nun, in the Hotel Dieu Nunnery at Montreal* (New York: Howe & Bates 1836).

62. Society for the Propagation of the Faith, "Notice Sur Les Missions Du Diocèse De Québec" (Québec City: Society for the Propagation of the Faith, 1839), 76.

63. John Claudius Pitrat, *Americans Warned of Jesuitism: Or, the Jesuits Unveiled* (Louisville: Hulls & Shannon, 1851). Also Herman Norton, *Startling Facts for American Protestants! Progress of Romanism since the Revolutionary War; Its Present Position and Future Prospects* (New York: American Protestant Society, 1844); Samuel Finley Breese Morse, *Foreign Conspiracy against the Liberties of the United States: The Numbers of Brutus, Originally Published in the New-York Observer* (New York: Leavitt, Lord, 1835).

64. Jon Gjerde and S. Deborah Kang, *Catholicism and the Shaping of Nineteenth-Century America* (Cambridge: Cambridge University Press, 2012), 46, 127, 86-90.

65. O. B., letter to the editor, *Oregon American, and Evangelical Unionist*, 1, no. 4, July 19, 1848, 63. See also R. W. Ford, letter to the editor, *Oregon American, and Evangelical Unionist*, 1, no. 4, July 19, 1848, 63; G. W. C., letter to the editor, *Oregon American, and Evangelical Unionist*, 1, no. 5, Aug. 2, 1848, 74-75.

66. Herbert Lang, "The Pioneer Printing Press of the Pacific Coast," *Transactions of the Seventeenth Annual Reunion of the Oregon Pioneer Association for 1889* (Portland: Himes, 1890), 94-97.

67. George H. Himes, "The Beginnings of Christianity in Oregon," *Oregon Historical Quarterly* 20 (March-Dec. 1919), 171.

68. Patricia O'Connell Killen and Mark Silk, *Religion and Public Life in the Pacific Northwest: The None Zone*, Religion by Region Series (Walnut Creek, CA: Altamira Press, 2004), 9-23.

69. Addis, "The Whitman Massacre," 246-47.

70. Ruby and Brown, *Cayuse Indians*, 94-98. In this way the pre-1848 political situation in the Oregon Country was somewhat akin to what Richard White describes in the Great Lakes region: an "area between the historical foreground of European invasion and occupation and the background of Indian defeat and retreat," in which the balance

of power was such that whites could "neither dictate to Indians nor ignore them." White, *The Middle Ground: Indians, Empires, and Republics in the Great Lakes Region, 1650–1815* (Cambridge: Cambridge University Press, 2011), x.

71. John David Unruh, *The Plains Across: The Overland Emigrants and the Trans-Mississippi West, 1840–60* (Urbana: University of Illinois Press, 1979), 186–87.

72. "Interesting from Oregon," *Weekly Alta Californian*, Dec. 15, 1849; Ruby and Brown, *Cayuse Indians*, 154.

73. Ibid., 159. Marcus Whitman to Elkanah Walker, Dec. 27, 1839, box 1, folder 1, Whitman Family Papers; Josephy, *Nez Perce Indians*, 88.

74. "Tribes Join History Center to Track Graves of Indians," *Eugene (OR) Register-Guard*, Sept. 29, 1996, 3C.

75. Antone Minthorn, "Wars, Treaties, and the Beginning of Reservation Life," in *Wiyáx̣ayx̣t/As Days Go By/Wiyáakaa'awn*, ed. Jennifer Karson Engum, foreword by Alvin P. Josephy (Pendleton, OR: Tamástlikt Cultural Institute, 2006), 64; Ronald B. Lansing, *Juggernaut: The Whitman Massacre Trial, 1850* (Pasadena: Ninth Judicial Circuit Historical Society, 1993), 46.

76. Ruby and Brown, *Cayuse Indians*, 168.

77. Will Bagley, *So Rugged and Mountainous: Blazing the Trails to Oregon and California, 1812–1848* (Norman: University of Oklahoma Press, 2010), 398.

78. Frances Fuller Victor, *The River of the West: Life and Adventure in the Rocky Mountains and Oregon; Embracing Events in the Life-Time of a Mountain-Man and Pioneer: With the Early History of the North-Western Slope, Including an Account of the Fur Traders, the Indian Tribes, the Overland Immigration, the Oregon Missions, and the Tragic Fate of Rev. Dr. Whitman and Family: Also, a Description of the Country, Its Condition, Prospects, and Resources, Its Soil, Climate, and Scenery, Its Mountains, Rivers, Valleys, Deserts, and Plains, Its Inland Waters, and Natural Wonders: With Numerous Engravings* (Hartford: Columbian Book Company, 1870), 496–97.

79. Lansing, *Juggernaut*, 92–93; Hubert Howe Bancroft and Frances Fuller Victor, *History of Oregon*, The Works of Hubert Howe Bancroft (San Francisco: History Company, 1886), 2:95.

80. "Later from Oregon," *New York Daily Tribune*, Aug. 22, 1850, 3.

81. Francis Norbert Blanchet, *Historical Sketches of the Catholic Church in Oregon, During the Past Forty Years* (Portland, 1878), 181–82.

82. Melinda Marie Jetté, *At the Hearth of the Crossed Races: A French-Indian Community in Nineteenth-Century Oregon, 1812–1859* (First Peoples: New Directions in Indigenous Studies, Corvallis, OR: 2015).

83. Brouillet, *Authentic Account*, 18; Jean-Baptiste Brouillet, J. Ross Browne, *Letter from the Secretary of the Interior, transmitting, in compliance with the resolution of the House of the 15th instant, the report of J. Ross Browne, on the subject of the Indian war in Oregon and Washington Territories*, prepared for the Committee on Military Affairs, 35th Congress, 1st session, 1858, 15. According to Brouillet, after Blanchet gave Gilliam the Catholic side of the story, Gilliam exclaimed, "Mr. Spalding could not have spoken so without being crazy" (Brouillet, *Authentic Account*, 18).

84. See, for instance, "By Last Night's Mail the California News," *Boston Daily Atlas,* July 9, 1850, 2; *Washington Daily Globe,* Dec. 28, 1850, 2.

85. "Proceedings of a Special Meeting of the Citizens of Linn County, O.T.," *Oregon Spectator,* Dec. 12, 1850, 1.

86. Susan M. Griffin, *Anti-Catholicism and Nineteenth-Century Fiction,* Cambridge Studies in American Literature and Culture (Cambridge: Cambridge University Press, 2004), 15.

87. Brouillet, *Authentic Account,* 20, see also 36.

88. Ibid., 23.

89. Ibid., 5–6.

90. Ibid., 4, 9.

91. Ibid., 5.

92. For instance, Bourne, "Legend of Marcus Whitman," 281–84; Marshall to William Augustus Mowry, Nov. 10, 1898, box E, Whitman Collection; T. C. Elliott to Edwin Eells, Dec. 24, 1907, Thompson Coit Elliott Papers, OHS, and earlier antecedents in Hubert Howe Bancroft, *History of Oregon,* 1:699; Harvey Kimball Hines to Elwood Evans, April 14, 1884, box 3, folder 25, Elwood Evans Papers.

93. H. A. G. Lee, letter to the editor, *Oregon Spectator,* July 13, 1848, 1.

94. *An Act to create the Office of Surveyor-General of the Public Lands in Oregon, and to provide for the Survey, and to make Donations to Settlers of the said Public Lands,* U.S. Statutes at Large 31 (1850): 496–500.

95. U.S. Congress, Senate, C. M. Walker, *Memorial of the Legislature of Oregon, praying for the extinguishment of the Indian title and the removal of the Indians from certain portions of that Territory, January 6, 1851.* Referred to the Committee on Territories. January 10, 1851, 31st Congress, 2nd Session.

96. Ruby and Brown, *Cayuse Indians,* 175–77.

97. Ibid., 196–97, 202–3.

98. Ibid., 218–20; Terence O'Donnell, *An Arrow in the Earth: General Joel Palmer and the Indians of Oregon* (Portland: Oregon Historical Society Press, 1991), 249–50; Donald L. Cutler, *Hang Them All: George Wright and the Plateau Indian War, 1858* (Norman: University of Oklahoma Press, 2016), 78–80.

99. Cutler, *Hang Them All,* 123–28.

100. Boyd Cothran, *Remembering the Modoc War: Redemptive Violence and the Making of American Innocence* (First Peoples: New Directions in Indigenous Studies, Chapel Hill: University of North Carolina Press, 2014), 18.

101. Ruby and Brown, *Cayuse Indians,* 191–92, 252–53.

102. US Congress, House, Congressional resolution, "Indian Hostilities in Oregon," *Congressional Globe,* Jan. 20, 1858, 35th Congress, 1st Session, 339.

103. US Congress, House, *Documentary History of the Revolution. Letter from the Secretary of State, on the subject of the contract entered into by Edward Livingston, late Secretary of State, with Matthew St. Clair Clarke and Peter Force, for the collection and publication of the Documentary History of the American Revolution,* 23rd Congress, 2nd Session, Dec. 24, 1834.

104. US Congress, Senate. *Memoir, historical and political, on the northwest coast of North America, and the adjacent territories; illustrated by a map and geographical view of those countries. By Robert Greenhow, translator and librarian to the Department of State.* 26th Congress, 1st Session, Feb. 10, 1840.

105. US Congress, Senate. *Mr. Jarnagin, from the Committee on Indian Affairs, reported the following resolution: Resolved, that the Secretary of War prepare, or cause to be prepared under his direction, a statement exhibiting a true history of the relations between the United States and the several Indian tribes,* 29th Congress, 1st Session Jan. 15, 1846.

106. US Congress, House. Browne, "Indian War in Oregon and Washington Territories. Letter from the Secretary of the Interior, Transmitting, in Compliance with the Resolution of the House of the 15th Instant, the Report of J. Ross Browne, on the Subject of the Indian War in Oregon and Washington Territories. January 25, 1858.—Referred to the Committee on Military Affairs, and Ordered to Be Printed," 2.

107. Ibid., 3.

108. Ibid.

109. Drury, *Henry Harmon Spalding,* 358.

110. US Congress, House, Department of the Interior, William P. Dole, *Annual Report of the Commissioner of Indian Affairs, 1862,* 37th Cong., 3rd sess., Nov. 26, 1862, 426; Drury, *Henry Harmon Spalding,* 368.

111. Spalding to Elwood Evans, Feb. 12, 1867, box 3, folder 44, Elwood Evans Papers, Beinecke Library, Yale University.

112. Henry Spalding to Elwood Evans, Feb. 12, 1867, box 3, folder 44, Elwood Evans Papers; "Early Oregon Missions: Their Importance in Securing This Country to Americans," Lecture Eight, *Albany [OR] States Rights Democrat,* collected in a scrapbook by Elwood Evans, p. 28, Beinecke Library.

113. Henry Spalding to S. B. Treat, Walla Walla, Washington Territory, April 21, 1866, transcript, Henry Harmon Spalding Papers, 1829–74, Oregon Historical Society Research Library, Portland (hereafter Spalding Papers).

114. Henry Spalding to G. H. Atkinson, Dec. 1, 1866, box 2, Spalding Papers.

115. Henry Harmon Spalding to Elwood Evans, March 8, 1867, box 3, folder 44, Elwood Evans Papers.

116. Ibid. Spalding is apparently referring to Presidents Abraham Lincoln and Andrew Johnson.

117. Henry Spalding to P. F. Marshall, Aug. 4, 1870, Spalding Papers; Spalding to Elwood Evans, Brownsville, Ore., Feb. 12, 1867, box 3, folder 44, Elwood Evans Papers; "Early Oregon Missions: Their Importance in Securing This Country to Americans," Lecture Eight, *Albany [OR] States Rights Democrat,* collected in a scrapbook by Elwood Evans, p. 28.

118. Henry Spalding to Esther Lorinda Bewley Chapman, Walla Walla, Washington Territory, March 26, 1866, box 4, Whitman Collection.

119. Henry Spalding, "Lecture by Rev. H. H. Spaulding," *Walla Walla Statesman,* Jan. 19, 1866, 2.

120. Henry Spalding to Esther Lorinda Bewley Chapman, Walla Walla, Washington Territory, March 26, 1866, box 4, Whitman Collection.

121. Henry Spalding to Elwood Evans, Feb. 12, 1867, box 3, folder 44, Elwood Evans Papers; "Early Oregon Missions: Their Importance in Securing This Country to Americans," Lecture One, *Albany [OR] States Rights Democrat,* Nov. 17, 1866, collected in a scrapbook by Elwood Evans, 3.

122. "Early Oregon Missions: Their Importance in Securing This Country to Americans," Lecture One, *Albany [OR] States Rights Democrat,* Nov. 17, 1866, collected in a scrapbook by Elwood Evans, 3.

123. For Whitman's own claims, see Marcus Whitman to Stephen Prentiss, May 16, 1844, Whitman Family Papers. Also see Whitman to Henry Brewer, May 25, 1844, Whitman Collection; Marcus Whitman to H. F. Wisewell, June 29, 1845, Whitman Collection; Whitman to Greene, May 18, 1847, Whitman Collection; Whitman to Elkanah Walker, Waiilatpu, July 15, 1845 and Oct. 27, 1845, Whitman Family Papers. For the evolution of Spalding's story, see especially G. H. Atkinson to the Secretary of the American Board, Nov. 20, 1858, and Sept. 7, 1859, Papers of the American Board of Commissioners for Foreign Missions, microfilm, reel 783, unit 6, Yale Divinity School Library Special Collections.

124. Henry Spalding, "History of Indian Affairs among the Nez Perces," *Oregon Pacific,* Nov. 9, 1865, typescript copy in William I. Marshall Papers, Beinecke Library, Yale University; Henry Spalding, "Early Missions in Old Oregon: Their Importance in Securing the Country to Americans," *Albany States Rights Democrat,* Nov. 17, 1866— Sept. 1867, collected in scrapbook by Elwood Evans, Beinecke Library, 22–25.

125. For example: "Do you believe, from your long acquaintance with the Nez Perces and Cayuse Indians, that the Protestant missions established among them in 1836 were productive of good both in elevating the natives from the wretched condition of want and ignorance of letters, of cultivation, and of God, in which the missionaries found them, to a comparatively high state of civilization and Christian attainments; as also in securing the constant friendship and firm alliance of the Nez Perces nation to the Americans and American government?" U.S. Congress, Senate, Committee on Indian Affairs, *Letter from the Secretary of the Interior, communicating, in compliance with the resolution of the Senate of the 2d instant, information in relation to the early labors of the missionaries of the American Board of Commissioners of Foreign Missions in Oregon, commencing in 1836,* 41st Congress, 3rd Session, Doc. No. 37, February 9, 1871, 49.

126. Ibid., 49.

127. Electa VanValkenburg to Henry Spalding, Oct. 6, 1869, box 5, Whitman Collection; "The Former Oregon Mission: A Great Wrong," *Missionary Herald,* Oct. 1869, 314; "The Veteran Missionary," *New York Evangelist,* March 2, 1871, 1.

128. Henry Spalding to P. F. Marshall, August 4, 1870, Spalding Papers; Henry Spalding to Rachel Griffin Spalding, Jan. 6, 1871, Spalding Papers; Henry Spalding to Rachel Griffin Spalding, Jan. 9, 1871, Spalding Papers; Henry Spalding to Rachel Griffin Spalding, May 6, 1871, Spalding Papers; "The Oregon Mission and the U.S. Government," *New York Evangelist,* Dec. 22, 1870, A6; "The Veteran Missionary," *New York Evangelist,* March 2, 1871, 1.

129. U.S. Congress, Senate, Committee on Indian Affairs, *Letter from the Secretary of the Interior, communicating, in compliance with the resolution of the Senate of the 2d instant, information in relation to the early labors of the missionaries of the American Board of Commissioners of Foreign Missions in Oregon, commencing in 1836*, 41st Congress, 3rd Session, Doc. No. 37, February 9, 1871, 49. 45.

130. Ibid., 49.

131. Henry Harmon Spalding to C. H. Hale and Elwood Evans, March 4, 1869, box 3, folder 44, Elwood Evans Papers, Beinecke Library, Yale University.

132. Obituary, H. W. Corbett, *New York Times*, April 1, 1903; "Corbett, Henry Winslow," *Biographical Dictionary of the United States Congress, 1774–2005* (Washington: Government Printing Office, 2005), 874; Josephy, *The Nez Perce Indians and the Opening of the Northwest*, 473.

133. "Smith, Joseph Showalter," *Biographical Dictionary of the United States Congress, 1934–35*.

134. J. S. Smith to Henry Spalding, Jan. 8, 1870, box 5, Spalding Collection.

135. Ibid.; Drury, *Henry Harmon Spalding*, 391–92.

136. "An Evening with an Old Missionary," *Chicago Advance*, Dec. 1, 1870, 9; "The Veteran Missionary," *New York Evangelist*, March 2, 1871, 1; Drury, *Henry Harmon Spalding*, 387–91.

137. Drury, *Henry Harmon Spalding*, 389.

138. U.S. Congress, Senate, Committee on Indian Affairs, *Letter from the Secretary of the Interior, communicating, in compliance with the resolution of the Senate of the 2d instant, information in relation to the early labors of the missionaries of the American Board of Commissioners of Foreign Missions in Oregon, commencing in 1836*, 41st Congress, 3rd Session, Doc. No. 37, Feb. 9, 1871, 44.

139. Drury, *Henry Harmon Spalding*, 391; Henry Spalding to R. J. Spalding, Jan. 9, 1871, Spalding Papers.

140. Francis Paul Prucha, *The Great Father: The United States Government and the American Indians* (Lincoln: University of Nebraska Press, 1984), 481–82. See also Jennifer Graber, "'If a War It May Be Called': The Peace Policy with American Indians," *Religion and American Culture: A Journal of Interpretation* 24, no. 1 (2014): 36–69.

141. Prucha, *The Great Father*, 482.

142. *Journal of the Senate of the United States of America, 1789–1893*, Feb. 2, 1871, 205.

143. U.S. Congress, Senate, Committee on Indian Affairs, *Letter from the Secretary of the Interior, communicating, in compliance with the resolution of the Senate of the 2d instant, information in relation to the early labors of the missionaries of the American Board of Commissioners of Foreign Missions in Oregon, commencing in 1836*, 41st Congress, 3rd Session, Doc. No. 37, February 9, 1871, 3.

144. Henry Spalding to R. J. Spalding, Feb. 9, 1871, Spalding Papers.

145. Drury, *Henry Harmon Spalding*, 406–7.

146. Ibid., 414–15.

THREE Professionalizing Providence

1. William Henry Gray, "History of Oregon," Article No. 4, *Astoria (OR) Marine Gazette,* Sept. 12, 1865, collected in a scrapbook by Elwood Evans, Elwood Evans Papers, Beinecke Library, Yale University (hereafter Evans Papers).

2. Peter Novick, *That Noble Dream: The "Objectivity Question" and the American Historical Profession* (New York: Cambridge University Press, 1988). See also Ellen Fitzpatrick, *History's Memory: Writing America's Past, 1880–1980* (Cambridge: Harvard University Press, 2002); Ian Tyrrell, *Historians in Public: The Practice of American History, 1890–1970* (Chicago: University of Chicago Press, 2005); Tyrrell, "Public at the Creation: Place, Memory, and Historical Practice in the Mississippi Valley Historical Association, 1907–1950," *Journal of American History* 94.1 (2007): April 24, 2010, http://www.historycooperative.org/journals/jah/94.1/tyrrell.html.

3. Robert Townsend, *History's Babel: Scholarship, Professionalization, and the Historical Enterprise in the United States, 1880–1940* (Chicago: University of Chicago Press, 2013), 3–4.

4. Townsend argues that the AHA is a suitable focus for his study because "the activities and membership of the American Historical Association (AHA) provide ample evidence about other emerging professions in the discipline" and "new professions emerged first within, and then through formal separations from, the AHA." (Townsend, *History's Babel,* 7). I argue that the position of the pioneer historian emerged outside of the purview of the AHA and was based in local connections rather than national historical communities.

5. "William H. Gray," *Oregon Native Son and Historical Magazine* 1, no. 1 (May 1899): 46–48.

6. Preface, Cushing Eells's lecture series on early Oregon history (title not included in clipping), *Walla Walla Union,* Feb. 2, 1885. Collected in scrapbook, "Oregon Missions," by Elwood Evans, Elwood Evans Papers.

7. "The Veteran Missionary," *New York Evangelist,* March 2, 1871, 1.

8. Chad Reimer, *Writing British Columbia History, 1784–1958* (Vancouver: University of British Columbia Press, 2009), 35.

9. Ibid.

10. Tracy Fessenden, *Culture and Redemption: Religion, the Secular, and American Literature* (Princeton: Princeton University Press, 2007), 9.

11. Christian Smith, "Preface," in *The Secular Revolution: Power, Interests, and Conflict in the Secularization of American Life,* ed. Christian Smith (Berkeley: University of California Press, 2003), vii.

12. Smith, "Introduction: Rethinking the Secularization of Public Life," *Secular Revolution,* 1–96, 2.

13. Lois Meeth, "Meeth Family Tree," Ancestry Library, accessed Aug. 8, 2014, http://trees.ancestrylibrary.com/tree/3999849/family?cfpid=6123360688.

14. Clifford M. Drury, introduction to journal of William Henry Gray, *The Mountains We Have Crossed: Diaries and Letters of the Oregon Mission, 1838,* introductions

and editorial notes by Clifford Merrill Drury, introduction to the Bison Books edition by Bonnie Sue Lewis (Lincoln: University of Nebraska Press, 1999), 233.

15. Clifford M. Drury, *Marcus Whitman, M.D.: Pioneer and Martyr* (Caldwell, ID: Caxton, 1937), 45–47.

16. Drury, *The Mountains We Have Crossed*, 234.

17. Ibid., 233.

18. "Indians West of the Rocky Mountains," *Missionary Herald*, 33, no. 1 (Jan. 1837), 24.

19. William H. Gray to Elkanah Walker, May 7, 1841, box 1, folder 3, Oregon Mission Papers, Beinecke Library, Yale University (hereafter Oregon Mission Papers).

20. Eliza Hart Spalding, "Diary of Eliza Hart Spalding, October, 1836," in *First White Women over the Rockies: Diaries, Letters, and Biographical Sketches of the Six Women of the Oregon Mission Who Made the Overland Journey in 1836 and 1838*, vol. 1: *Where Wagons Could Go: Narcissa Whitman and Eliza Spalding*, ed. Clifford Merrill Drury (Glendale, CA: Arthur H. Clark, 1963), 196–97; William H. Gray to Elkanah Walker, Oct. 4, 1839, box 3, folder 23, Oregon Mission Papers; William H. Gray to Elkanah Walker, Dec. 3, 1839, box 3, folder 23, Oregon Mission Papers.

21. Marcus Whitman to David Green, May 5, 1837, typed transcript, box A, Whitman Collection, Whitman College and Northwest Archives, Walla Walla, Washington (hereafter Whitman Collection). The meaning of "Flathead" is unclear here; while Flathead typically refers to the Bitterroot Salish people, Gray and other white settlers used the term indiscriminately for a number of northwestern tribes.

22. Marcus Whitman to David Greene, Waiilatpu, Oregon Country, Oct. 22, 1839, box A, Whitman Collection.

23. Horse Creek in what is now southeastern Wyoming, just north of present-day Laramie and Cheyenne. See Fred Gowans, *Rocky Mountain Rendezvous: A History of the Fur Trade Rendezvous, 1825–1840* (Provo: Brigham Young University Press, 1976), 82–83.

24. William H. Gray, "June 15, Thursday," in *William H. Gray, Journal of His Journey East, 1836–1837*, ed. Donald R. Johnson (Fairfield, WA: Ye Galleon Press, 1980), 49.

25. Robert M. Utley, *After Lewis and Clark: Mountain Men and the Paths to the Pacific*, maps by Peter H. Dana (Lincoln: University of Nebraska Press, 1997), 168.

26. Gray, *William H. Gray, Journal of His Journey East*, 67–70.

27. Utley, *After Lewis and Clark*, 168.

28. Robert L. Welch, *The Presbytery of Seattle 1858–2005: The "Dream" of A Presbyterian Colony in the West* (Philadelphia: Xlibris, 2006), 58.

29. Clifford M. Drury, "Mary Augusta Dix Gray," *The Mountains We Have Crossed*, 237–39.

30. Quoted ibid., 239.

31. Marcus Whitman to David Greene, Oct. 22, 1839, box A, Whitman Collection.

32. Drury, Introduction, "Myra Fairbanks Eells," in *First White Women over the Rockies: Diaries, Letters, and Biographical Sketches of the Six Women of the Oregon Mission Who Made the Overland Journey in 1836 and 1838*, vol. 2, *On to Oregon: The*

Diaries of Mary Walker and Myra Eells, ed. Clifford Merrill Drury (Glendale, CA: Arthur H. Clark, 1966), 58.

33. Myra Fairbanks Eells, Diary, July 5, 1838, in *On to Oregon,* 99–100.

34. Mary Walker described Gray as "exceedingly fractious" in her diary entry for June 10, 1838, in *On to Oregon,* 91; see also diary entries of Mary Walker and Myra Eells for August 29, 1838, in *On to Oregon,* 166; Utley, *After Lewis and Clark,* 169.

35. Henry Harmon Spalding, written confession of sin to Elkanah Walker, Feb. 23, 1842, box 2, folder 17, Oregon Mission Papers; Marcus Whitman to Elkanah Walker, June 30, 1840, box 1, folder 1, Whitman Family Papers; Narcissa Whitman to Mary Walker, March 8, 1841, typed transcript, box A, Whitman Collection; Marcus Whitman to Elkanah Walker, Nov. 18, 1840, box 1, folder 1, Whitman Family Papers; Marcus Whitman to David Greene, March 28, 1841, typed transcript, box A, Whitman Collection; Marcus Whitman to David Greene, July 13, 1841, typed transcript, box A, Whitman Collection; Marcus Whitman to David Greene, Oct. 22, 1841, typed transcript, box A, Whitman Collection; Albert Furtwangler, *Bringing Indians to the Book* (Seattle: University of Washington Press, 2000), 127.

36. William H. Gray, *A History of Oregon, 1792–1849, Drawn from Personal Observation and Authentic Information* (Portland: American News Company, 1870), 199–204, 260–61.

37. Carlos Schwantes, *The Pacific Northwest: An Interpretive History* (Lincoln: University of Nebraska Press, 1989), 112–13.

38. Gray, *History of Oregon,* 279–81.

39. Terrence O'Donnell, *An Arrow in the Earth: General Joe Palmer and the Indians of Oregon* (Portland: Oregon Historical Society Press, 1991), 80; Marie Merriman Bradley, "Political Beginnings in Oregon: The Period of the Provisional Government, 1839–1849," *Oregon Historical Quarterly* 9, no. 1 (March 1908): 51.

40. Gray, *History of Oregon,* 338.

41. Ibid., 125. Similarly, the trapper Robert Newell was nicknamed "Doctor" for his ability to make simple herbal remedies, and eventually the nickname became a formal title. T. C. Elliot, " 'Doctor' Robert Newell: Pioneer," *Oregon Historical Quarterly* 9, no. 2 (June 1908): 104. The institutional structures of the professions (i.e., medicine, law, divinity) were still in development during this time, but in the West the instability or outright absence of regulation in the professions was intensified because government and educational institutions were still developing, and it was difficult to verify claims of professional training back east. For the development of the professions in the US and Europe in the nineteenth century, see Magali Sarfatti Larson, *Rise of Professionalism: A Sociological Analysis* (Berkeley: University of California Press, 1977), 2–9.

42. "William H. Gray," *Oregon Native Son and Historical Magazine* 1, no. 1 (May 1899): 46–48.

43. John D. Unruh Jr., *The Plains Across: The Overland Emigrants and the Trans-Mississippi West, 1840–1860* (Urbana: University of Illinois Press, 1979), 120.

44. Ibid., 4.

45. Ibid., 119–20.

46. James B. Weatherby and Randy Stapilus, *Governing Idaho: Politics, People, and Power* (Caldwell, ID: Caxton Press, 2005), 82–83; Schwantes, *Pacific Northwest*, 134–35; Richard W. Etulain, "Abraham Lincoln and the Trans-Mississippi West: An Introductory Overview," in *Lincoln Looks West: From the Mississippi to the Pacific*, ed. Richard W. Etulain (Carbondale: Southern Illinois University Press, 2010), 40–41; Carleton W. Kenyon, "Legal Lore of the Wild West: A Bibliographical Essay," *California Law Review* (1968): 682–83.

47. Robert W. Johannsen, "Oregon Territory's Movement for Self-Government, 1848–1853," *Pacific Historical Review* 26, no. 1 (Feb. 1957): 18; Ronald H. Limbaugh, *Rocky Mountain Carpetbaggers: Idaho's Territorial Governors, 1863–1890* (Moscow: University of Idaho Press, 1982), 48.

48. Johannsen, "Oregon Territory's Movement for Self-Government, 1848–1853," 20.

49. Peter Boag, "Death and Oregon's Settler Generation: Connecting Parricide, Agricultural Decline, and Dying Pioneers at the Turn of the Twentieth Century," *Oregon Historical Quarterly* 115, no. 3 (Fall 2014): 350–53; Matthew Dennis, "Natives and Pioneers: Death and the Settling and Unsettling of Oregon," *Oregon Historical Quarterly* 115, no. 3 (Fall 2014): 287–88. Boag's genealogy of Oregon pioneer associations begins with the founding of the Oregon Pioneer Association in 1873, and Dennis follows this chronology. However, as I demonstrate in this chapter, there were efforts to institutionalize pioneer socialization, memorialization, and history prior to 1873, the most important being the Oregon Pioneer Society, founded in 1867.

50. Frances Fuller Victor to Elwood Evans, Feb. 5, 1866, box 3, folder 53, Elwood Evans Papers.

51. John Maceachern, "Elwood Evans, Lawyer-Historian," *Pacific Northwest Quarterly* 52, no. 1 (Jan. 1961): 15–16.

52. Ibid., 16.

53. Elwood Evans to Cushing Eells, Jan. 6, 1862, box 1, folder 15, Elwood Evans Papers.

54. Ibid.

55. W. H. Gray, "History of Oregon," Article No. 1, *Astoria [OR] Marine Gazette*, n.d., collected in a scrapbook by Elwood Evans, Elwood Evans Papers. The place of the lecture is not noted in Gray's or Evans's records.

56. Ibid.

57. Gray, *History of Oregon*, 3.

58. Elwood Evans to William H. Gray, Feb. 17, 1869, William H. Gray Collection, 1836–72, Whitman College and Northwest Archives (hereafter Gray Collection); George Gibbs to William H. Gray, Oct. 24, 1866, Gray Collection; J. H. D. Henderson to William H. Gray, March 17, 1866, Gray Collection.

59. Richard Somerset Mackie, *Trading Beyond the Mountains: The British Fur Trade on the Pacific, 1793–1843* (Vancouver: University of British Columbia Press, 1997), 121.

60. Emma Milliken, "Choosing between Corsets and Freedom: Native, Mixed-Blood, and White Wives of Laborers at Fort Nisqually, 1833–1860," *Pacific Northwest Quarterly* 96, no. 2 (2005): 96.

61. *Memorials Presented to the Commissioners, under the Treaty of July 1, 1863, between Great Britain and the United States, for the Final Settlement of the Claims of the Hudson's Bay and Puget Sound Agricultural Companies, Presented April 17, 1865* (Washington: Government Printing Office, 1865); George S. Boutwell, "Letter from the Secretary of the Treasury Inclosing [*sic*] a Letter from the Secretary of State asking an Appropriation to Pay the Awards under the Hudson's Bay and Puget Sound Agricultural Company's Treaties with Her Britannic Majesty," Executive Document No. 220, House, 41st Congress, 2nd Session, March 29, 1870, 2.

62. Gray, *History of Oregon*, 78.

63. Ibid., 3, 4.

64. Ibid., 107, 110.

65. Ibid., 178.

66. Elwood Evans to Henry Harmon Spalding, Feb. 23, 1867, Spalding Collection.

67. Gray, *History of Oregon*, 282.

68. Ibid., 342.

69. Ibid., 263, 310.

70. Ibid., 3.

71. Ibid., 33, 602, 558.

72. Ibid., 66.

73. Richard White, "Frederick Jackson Turner and Buffalo Bill," in *The Frontier in American Culture*, ed. James Grossman (Berkeley: University of California Press, 1994), 27–30.

74. Ryan E. Burt, "'Sioux Yells' in the Dawes Era: Lakota 'Indian Play,' the Wild West, and the Literatures of Luther Standing Bear," *American Quarterly* 62, no. 3 (2010): 621.

75. William H. Gray to Elkanah Walker, July 18, 1839, box 1, folder 3, Oregon Mission Papers; William H. Gray to Elkanah Walker, March 28, 1842, box 1, folder 3, Oregon Mission Papers; Marcus Whitman to Elkanah Walker, Dec. 27, 1839, box 1, folder 1, Whitman Family Papers; Marcus Whitman to Elkanah Walker, Nov. 18, 1840, box 1, folder 1, Whitman Family Papers.

76. William H. Gray to Marcus Whitman, M.D., May 8, 1847, box 1, folder 3, Oregon Mission Papers. Gray would later argue that he was present at the meeting of the missionaries in September of 1842, in which Marcus Whitman notified his associates that he would travel to Washington, DC. It is possible that he returned to the mission for that meeting, but his letter of May 8, 1842, makes it clear that Gray was already settled in the Willamette Valley before Whitman began his ride. See William H. Gray, "The Whitman Controversy: Recollections of W. H. Gray," in *The Whitman Controversy, Articles by Ed. C. Ross, Rev. M. Eels and W. H. Gray in Reply to Mrs. F. F. Victor and Elwood Evans* (Portland: G. H. Himes, 1885), 36–37.

77. Gray to David Newsom, Feb. 6, 1876, Gray Collection; Gray, draft letter to Joseph Holman, March 23, 1876, Gray Collection.

78. Gray, *History of Oregon*, 107–8.

79. Ibid., 108.

80. Ibid.

81. Ibid., 289–91, 315–19.

82. Ibid., 291.

83. Ibid., 315.

84. Ibid., 316.

85. Ibid., 268, 349.

86. Ibid., 317. The ABCFM disputed this. "Bibliographical: Gray's *History of Oregon*," *Missionary Herald, Containing the Proceedings of the American Board of Commissioners for Foreign Missions* 66, no. 4 (April 1870), 131.

87. Gray, *History of Oregon,* 317.

88. Ibid., 318. The memorial volume also stated that Samuel Parker's exploring tour of the Oregon Country revealed "no field for a great and successful mission," an assessment that offended Gray. Rufus Anderson, *Memorial Volume of the First Fifty Years of the American Board of Commissioners for Foreign Missions.* 5th ed. (American Board of Commissioners for Foreign Missions, 1862), 380.

89. "William H. Gray," *Oregon Native Son and Historical Magazine* 1, no. 1 (May 1899): 46–48, 46.

90. "Bibliographical: Gray's History of Oregon," *Missionary Herald, Containing the Proceedings of the American Board of Commissioners for Foreign Missions,* 66, no. 4 (April 1870), 131; "New Publications," *New York Tribune,* March 1, 1870, 6; untitled review, *New York Evangelist,* March 31, 1870, 8; untitled review, *Independent* 22, no. 1109 (March 3, 1870), 8; "Criticisms of New Books," *New York Herald,* Feb. 21, 1870, 5; "New Publications," *San Francisco Daily Bulletin,* March 12, 1870, 1; "Mr. Gray's 'History of Oregon,'" *Oregonian,* April 1, 1870, 2.

91. "New Publications," *New York Tribune,* March 1, 1870, 6; "History of Oregon," *New Northwest* [Portland], Aug. 18, 1871, 2.

92. "Books and Authors," *Hearth and Home,* March 12, 1870, 187; "New Publications," *New York Tribune,* March 12, 1870, 6; "Editor's Book Table," *American Antiquarian,* July 1, 1879, 2, 1.

93. "Our River's Name: Wallamet, Wallamette or Willamette," *Oregonian,* Oct. 22, 1874, 2; S. A. [Samuel Asahel] Clarke, "Oregon Pioneer History: Sketches of Early Days—Men and Times in the Forties," *Willamette Farmer,* April 16, 1881, 1.

94. Hubert Howe Bancroft to William H. Gray, San Francisco, Calif., July 21, 1878, Gray Collection.

95. For instance, Myron Eells, *Marcus Whitman: Pathfinder and Patriot* (Seattle: Alice Harriman, 1909), 289; William A. Mowry, *Marcus Whitman and the Early Days of Oregon* (New York: Silver, Burdett, 1901), 229; William Barrows, *Oregon: The Struggle for Possession* (Boston: Houghton Mifflin, 1884), 241; Oliver W. Nixon, *How Marcus Whitman Saved Oregon: A True Romance of Patriotic Heroism, Christian Devotion and Final Martyrdom, with Sketches of Life on the Plains and Mountains in Pioneer Days,* introduction by Frank W. Gunsaulus, 2nd ed. (Chicago: Star Publishing, 1895), 134.

96. Eileen K. Cheng, *The Plain and Noble Garb of Truth: Nationalism and Impartiality in American Historical Writing, 1784–1860* (Athens: University of Georgia Press, 2008), 29.

97. Ibid.

98. Terry A. Barnhart, "'A Common Feeling': Regional Identity and Historical Consciousness in the Old Northwest, 1820–1860," *Michigan Historical Review* 29, no. 1 (Spring 2003): 51; Michael Kammen, *Mystic Chords of Memory: The Transformation of Tradition in American Culture* (New York: Vintage Books, 2013), 272.

99. Barnhart, "A Common Feeling," 60, 63.

100. Amanda Laugesen, *The Making of Public Historical Culture in the West: 1880–1910: The Role of Historical Societies* (Lewiston, NY: Edwin Mellen Press, 2006), 22, 98. Though Laugesen is primarily interested in the work of historical societies from 1880 to 1910, her descriptions aptly describe associations in the West that were founded between the 1850s and 1870s.

101. David M. Wrobel, *Promised Lands: Promotion, Memory, and the Creation of the American West* (Lawrence: University Press of Kansas, 2002), 121–23; Clyde Milner, "The View from Wisdom: Four Layers of History and Regional Identity," in *Under an Open Sky: Rethinking America's Western Past,* ed. William Cronon, George Miles, and Jay Gitlin (New York: W. W. Norton, 1992), 213–15.

102. "Constitution of the Society of California Pioneers, Organized August, 1850; Amended May 4th, 1863," *Transactions of the Society of California Pioneers, January 1st to May 7th, 1863,* part 1, vol. 2 (San Francisco: Alta California Book and Job Office, 1863), 11; Kammen, *Mystic Chords of Memory,* 274. Benjamin Madley has convincingly argued that California settler violence against the Yuki people in particular constituted genocide. Madley, "California's Yuki Indians: Defining Genocide in Native American History," *Western Historical Quarterly* 39, no. 3 (2008): 303–32. See also Boyd Cothran, *Remembering the Modoc War: Redemptive Violence and the Making of American Innocence* (First Peoples: New Directions in Indigenous Studies, Chapel Hill: University of North Carolina Press, 2014).

103. Glen Gendzel, "Pioneers and Padres: Competing Mythologies in Northern and Southern California, 1850–1930," *Western Historical Quarterly* 32, no. 1 (Spring 2001): 55–57.

104. *Constitution and By-Laws of the Society of California Pioneers: Organized August, 1850* (San Francisco: C. Bartlett, 1853), 1; *Constitution, By-Laws and Prospectus of the Historical Society of Idaho Pioneers* (Boise: Milton Kelly, 1881), 5.

105. For instance, *Constitution and By-Laws of the Society of California Pioneers,* 3; *Constitution, By-Laws and Prospectus of the Historical Society of Idaho Pioneers,* 6; *Constitution, By-Laws and List of Members of the Society of Arizona Pioneers, Organized February 9, 1884* (Tucson, 1890), 12–13; "Oregon Pioneer Society," *Oregon City Weekly Enterprise,* Dec. 5, 1868, 1.

106. "Oregon Pioneer Society," *Oregon City Weekly Enterprise,* Dec. 5, 1868, 1.

107. Bancroft, *History of Oregon,* 2:693.

108. "Oregon Pioneer Society," *Oregon City Weekly Enterprise,* Dec. 5, 1868, 1.

109. Ibid.

110. Ibid.

111. Bancroft, *History of Oregon,* 2:693.

112. "Circular of the Pioneer and Historical Society of Oregon: Extract from Constitution," circa 1871, Gray Collection.

113. J. C. Bell to Gray, July 14, 1874, Gray Collection; Sam McKean to Gray, Oct. 2, 1871, Gray Collection. Also E. N. Condit to Gray, Jan. 9, 1878, Gray Collection; H. W. Corbett to Gray, Jan. 22, 1872, Gray Collection; B. F. Dowell to Gray, Nov. 11, 1871, Gray Collection; O. S. Phelps to Gray, Feb. 8, 1872, Gray Collection.

114. "Proceedings of the Pioneer and Historical Society of Oregon," *Oregonian*, Feb. 29, 1872, 1.

115. Prominent Protestants included the home missionary and Pacific University trustee G. H. Atkinson, US Senator H. W. Corbett, and the Indian agent Edwin Eells. G. H. Atkinson to Gray, Dec. 23, 1875, Gray Collection; H. W. Corbett to Gray, Jan. 22, 1872, Gray Collection; Edwin Eells to Gray, Jan. 10, 1872, Gray Collection.

116. W. A. Tenney to Gray, July 20, 1874, Gray Collection. However, Gray did extend corresponding membership to a few non-Oregonians, including members of his extended family and prominent easterners who Gray felt might raise the PHS's profile. The New York newspaper editor Horace Greeley, the Massachusetts educator William A. Mowry, and Gray's uncle, U. H. Dunning of Adams, New York, were all offered corresponding membership. Horace Greeley to Gray, Oct. 4, 1871, Gray Collection; William A. Mowry to Gray, Feb. 7, 1878, Gray Collection; U. H. Dunning to Gray, Nov. 20, 1871, Gray Collection.

117. Gray to editor of the *Willamette Farmer*, draft, May 22, 1875, Gray Collection.

118. Ibid.

119. O. S. Phelps to Gray, Feb. 8, 1872, Gray Collection; S. E. Barr to Gray, July 30, 1874, Gray Collection; David T. Genose, undated letter, received by PHS on May 22, 1872, Gray Collection; Silas B. Smith to Gray, May 27, 1872, Gray Collection.

120. H. C. Mays, Southern Historical Society, to Gray, Sept. 28, 1878; Lyman C. Draper, State Historical Society of Wisconsin, to Gray, Oct. 21, 1875; Stephen D. Peet, Editorial Office of the *American Antiquarian*, Jan. 6, 1880; James A. Smith, Centennial Executive Committee, to Gray, March 25, 1876.

121. Gray to secretaries of the A.B.C.F.M., June 10, 1880, Gray Collection.

122. George H. Atkinson, "The 'American Colonist' in Oregon: An Address Delivered before the Pioneer Historical Society of Oregon, at Astoria, Feb. 22, 1876, by the Rev. George H. Atkinson, D.D.," reprinted in Myron Eells, *Biography of Rev. G. H. Atkinson* (Portland: F. W. Baltes, 1893), 268. Also see address by Rev. William Roberts, "The Days of the Pioneer," *Oregonian*, May 19, 1884, 6; "Annual Meeting: Proceedings of the Oregon Pioneer and Historical Society, of Oregon, May 11, 1882," *Astorian*, 1.

123. Atkinson, "The 'American Colonist' in Oregon," 272.

124. Tom Edwards, *Triumph of Tradition: The Emergence of Whitman College, 1859–1924* (Walla Walla: Whitman College, 1992), 3–22.

125. Myron Eells, *Marcus Whitman, Pathfinder and Patriot*, 294.

126. "An Act to Organize the County of Whitman," *Statues of the Territory of Washington, Made and Passed at a Session of the Legislative Assembly Begun and Held at Olympia on the Second Day of October, 1871 and Ended on the Thirtieth Day of November, 1871* (Olympia: Prosch & McElroy, 1871), 134–36.

127. Gray to David Newsome, draft, Feb. 6, 1876, Gray Collection.

128. David W. Blight, "Decoration Days: The Origins of Memorial Day in North and South," in *The Memory of the Civil War in American Culture,* ed. Alice Fahs and Joan Waugh (Chapel Hill: University of North Carolina Press, 2004), 94–95.

129. Ibid., 105.

130. Ibid., 105–8; Blight, *Race and Reunion: The Civil War in American Memory* (Cambridge: Belknap, 2001), 97; Anne E. Marshall, *Creating a Confederate Kentucky: The Lost Cause and Civil War Memory in a Border State* (Chapel Hill: University of North Carolina Press, 2010), 87–88.

131. Harry S. Stout, *Upon the Altar of the Nation: A Moral History of the Civil War* (New York: Viking, 2006), 249–51; Guyatt, *Providence and the Invention of the United States,* 302.

132. "News Column," *Oregon City Enterprise,* Dec. 10, 1875, 4. See also "Decoration Day," *Willamette Farmer,* June 13, 1874, 1.

133. "The National Washington Monument," *Oregon City Enterprise,* July 28, 1876, 2; *New Northwest,* January 16, 1879, 1.

134. W. A. Tenney to Gray, Nov. 26, 1885. Also see "A Veritable Pioneer," *Willamette Farmer,* November 30, 1877, 4; Boag, "Death and Oregon's Settler Generation," 349–50.

135. "Dr. Marcus Whitman," *Willamette Farmer,* July 18, 1874, 11.

136. W. H. Gray et al., "Address to the People on the Subject of the Erection of a Monument to the Memory of the Late Dr. Marcus Whitman," approved at a meeting of the Pioneer and Historical Society's committee on the Whitman Monument, Astoria, Feb. 21, 1876, Beinecke Library, Yale University.

137. Ibid.

138. "Oregon Pioneer Historical Society," *Willamette Farmer,* March 19, 1875, 5.

139. Gray to Charles Swegle, draft, Nov. 29, 1877, Gray Collection.

140. Gray to David Newsom, Feb. 6, 1876, Gray Collection.

141. For comparison, a monument being commissioned in California at the same time cost only one thousand dollars. "The Whitman Monument," *New Northwest,* Nov. 6, 1874, 2.

142. Gray, untitled note dated July 4, 1876, Gray Collection.

143. Gray to Charles Swegle, draft, Nov. 29, 1877, Gray Collection.

144. "Committee Meeting," *Marshfield Coast Mail,* July 31, 1880, 4; Charles Swegle to Gray, July 25, 1881, Gray Collection.

145. "The Whitman Monument: The Design Prepared by Rev. Dr. Hopkins Accepted," *Oregonian,* Feb. 11, 1883, 3.

146. "Pioneer and Historical Society Meeting," *Astorian,* May 13, 1882, 3.

147. W. H. Gray, "Annual Meeting of the Pioneer and Historical Society of Oregon," *Daily Astorian,* Feb. 24, 1881, 1; "Oregon Pioneer Historical Society," *Willamette Farmer,* March 19, 1875, 5; "Pioneer Historical Society," *Eugene City Guard,* March 17, 1877, 1; "The Whitman Monument," *Idaho Tri-Weekly Statesman,* Aug. 21, 1880, 1.

148. "The Whitman Monument," *Daily Astorian,* Jan. 26, 1881, 2.

149. "The Whitman Monument," *New Northwest,* Nov. 6, 1874, 2.

150. "Dr. Marcus Whitman," *Willamette Farmer,* Sept. 24, 1880, 4.

151. Alexander Abernethy to Elwood Evans, Feb. 18, 1885, box 3, folder 4, Evans Papers; Jesse Applegate to Elwood Evans, Oct. 4, 1867, in scrapbook, "Oregon Missions: Whitman Massacre," compiled by Elwood Evans, Beinecke Library, Yale University.

152. Sheri Bartlett Browne, "A Lovely But Unpredictable River: Frances Fuller Victor's Early Life and Writing," *Oregon Historical Quarterly* 112, no. 1 (Spring 2011): 13, 26.

153. Frances Fuller Victor to Elwood Evans, Nov. 15, 1865, box 3, folder 53, Evans Papers; Victor to Gray, Nov. 30, 1866, Gray Collection; Hazel Emery Mills, "The Emergence of Frances Fuller Victor—Historian," *Oregon Historical Quarterly* 62, no. 4 (Dec. 1961): 314.

154. Frances Fuller Victor, *The River of the West: Life and Adventure in the Rocky Mountains and Oregon* (Hartford, CT: R. W. Bliss, 1870), 295.

155. Ibid., 294.

156. Newspaper clipping of J. Quinn Thornton's reply to Victor, *Pacific Christian Advocate,* circa 1870, in scrapbook, "Oregon Missions," compiled by Elwood Evans, Beinecke Library, Yale University.

157. Victor, "Mr. Thornton's Review of 'The River of the West,'" *Pacific Christian Advocate,* June 11, 1870.

158. Victor to Evans, Dec. 15, 1871, box 3, folder 53, Evans Papers.

159. Browne, "A Lovely But Unpredictable River," 26.

160. Mills, "The Emergence of Frances Fuller Victor—Historian," 324–25.

161. Victor to Evans, Jan. 7, 1880, box 3, folder 53, Evans Papers.

162. Victor, *River of the West,* 308–9; Victor to Evans, Jan. 7, 1880, box 3, folder 53, Evans Papers.

163. Victor to Evans, Dec. 9, 1879, box 3, folder 53, Evans Papers.

164. Evans to Hines, draft, April 12, 1881, box 3, folder 25, Evans Papers.

165. Ibid.

166. Ibid.

167. Sean Lanksbury et al., "Profiles of Washington Territorial Librarians—Elwood Evans, 1877–1879," *Between the Lines: Washington State Library Blog,* accessed 6 March 2015, http://blogs.sos.wa.gov/library/index.php/2013/10/profiles-of-washington-territorial-librarians-elwood-evans-1877-1879/.

168. Evans to Charles H. Phelps, editor of the *Californian,* draft, Nov. 19, 1880, box 3, folder 1, Evans Papers.

169. Victor to Evans, Dec. 9, 1879, box 3, folder 53, Evans Papers.

170. Ibid.

171. S. A. Clarke, "How Dr. Whitman Saved Oregon," *Californian* 2, no. 7 (July 1880): 19.

172. Victor, "Did Dr. Whitman Save Oregon?" *Californian* 2, no. 9 (Sept. 1880): 229.

173. Smith, *Secular Revolution,* 2.

174. Evans to J. S. Griffin, draft or copy, Feb. 2, 1862, box 3, folder 2, Evans Papers; Mills, "Emergence of Frances Fuller Victor—Historian," 336.

175. Victor to Evans, Jan. 7, 1880, box 3, folder 53, Evans Papers.

176. See, for instance, Spalding to Evans, May 30, 1868, box 3, folder, 44, Evans Papers; Gray, "Notes of History of Oregon—Contributed by W. H. Gray Esq—to Astoria Marine Gazette—commencing Aug. 22, 1865," Lecture 2, compiled in a scrapbook by Elwood Evans, Beinecke Library, Yale University. The ideal of the pioneer mother was found throughout the West, though it took different forms in different regions. See Brenda D. Frink, "San Francisco's Pioneer Mother Monument: Maternalism, Racial Order, and the Politics of Memorialization, 1907–1915," *American Quarterly* 64, no. 1 (March 2012): 85–113.

177. Rosemary Stremlau, "Frances Fuller Victor's Promotion of Strong, Independent Womanhood: Women and Marriage Reconstructed in 'The New Penelope,'" in *Portraits of Women in the American West,* ed. Dee Garceau-Hagen (New York: Routledge, 2005), 68.

178. Elwood Evans, *Washington Territory: Her Past, Her Present, and the Elements of Wealth which Ensure Her Future: Address Delivered at the Centennial Exposition, Philadelphia, Sept. 2, 1876 and in Joint Convention of the Legislature of Washington Territory, Oct. 13, 1877* (Olympia: Clarence Bagley, 1877), 50.

179. "Godless Schools," *New Northwest,* Aug. 25, 1881, 3; "Portland Public Schools," *West Shore* 6, no. 6 (June 1880): 163–64; "The New Educational Bill," *Astorian,* April 16, 1884, 2.

180. Elwood Evans, *History of the Pacific Northwest: Oregon and Washington,* 2 vols. (Portland: North Pacific History, 1889), 1:206.

181. Marginal notes by Evans, Myron Eells, "Myron Eells—Critique of Evans' Address," in scrapbook, "Marcus Whitman," compiled by Elwood Evans, Beinecke Library, Yale University; Victor to Evans, Feb. 17, 1884, box 3, folder 53, Evans Papers.

182. Townsend, *History's Babel,* 13, 18; Henry Warner Bowden, *Church History in the Age of Science: Historiographical Patterns in the United States, 1876–1918* (Chapel Hill: University of North Carolina Press, 1971), 15–16.

183. For instance, W. H. Burnham, "Memory, Historically and Experimentally Considered," *American Journal of Psychology* 2, no. 4 (Aug. 1889): 568–622; Wilbert W. White, "Talks on Memory: II," *Chautauquan* 9, no. 3 (Dec. 1888): 157; "Illusions of Memory," *Eclectic Magazine of Foreign Literature* 31, no. 6 (June 1880): 686.

184. George M. Beard, "The Scientific Study of Human Testimony," *Popular Science* 13 (June 1878): 180–81.

185. Ed. C. Ross, "The Whitman Controversy," in *Whitman Controversy,* 60–68; Ross, "Dr. Marcus Whitman," in *Whitman Controversy,* 21–24.

186. For instance, Henry Harmon Spalding had left his diary to Myron Eells via J. S. Griffin, with the instructions "that [Eells] should never let the enemies of Mr. Spalding use it to his injury." Eells recognized that Spalding's writings included his disagreements with other missionaries and other information that could reflect poorly on Spalding and was thus deeply conflicted about whether to make the whole diary or only excerpts available to the public. Eells, "As to the Value of Historical Testimony," *Oregonian,* March 22, 1903, 32.

187. Victor, "Did Dr. Whitman Save Oregon?" *Astorian,* March 6, 1881, 1.

188. Ibid.

189. Ibid.

190. Ibid.

191. Gray, "Did Dr. Whitman Save Oregon?" *Astorian,* March 15, 1881, 1; Gray, "Did Dr. Whitman Save Oregon?: Article Two," *Astorian,* April 5, 1881, 1; Gray, "Did Dr. Whitman Save Oregon?: Article Three," *Astorian,* May 8, 1881, 1; Gray, "Did Dr. Whitman Save Oregon?: Article Four," *Astorian,* May 19, 1881, 1; Gray, "Did Dr. Whitman Save Oregon?: Article Five," *Astorian,* June 4, 1881, 1; Gray, "Did Dr. Whitman Save Oregon?: Article Six," *Astorian,* June 9, 1881, 1.

192. Gray, "Did Dr. Whitman Save Oregon?: Article 3," *Astorian,* April 5, 1881, 1.

193. Ibid.

194. Ibid.

195. Ibid.

196. Ed. C. Ross et al., *The Whitman Controversy, Articles by Ed. C. Ross, Rev. M. Eels and W. H. Gray in Reply to Mrs. F. F. Victor and Elwood Evans* (Portland: G. H. Himes, 1885).

197. Myron Eells, "Dr. Whitman: Reply to Honorable Elwood Evans," in *Whitman Controversy,* 49.

198. W. C. McKay to Myron Eells, Feb. 21, 1885, *Whitman Controversy,* 69–70.

199. Myron Eells to Gray, July 20, 1882, Gray Collection.

200. Gray, "The Whitman Controversy: Recollections of W. H. Gray, Astoria, January 20, 1885," in *Whitman Controversy,* 25, 28.

201. Ross, "The Whitman Controversy," *Whitman Controversy,* 62.

202. Ibid., 67, from Hebrews 12:1, King James Version.

203. Ibid., 64.

204. Myron Eells, "Dr. Whitman: Reply to Honorable Elwood Evans," in *Whitman Controversy,* 23.

205. Clifford Merrill Drury, *Marcus and Narcissa Whitman and the Opening of Old Oregon,* 2 vols. (Glendale, CA: A. H. Clark, 1973), 2:384.

206. F. G. Young, "Functions of the Oregon Historical Society," *Oregon Historical Quarterly* 6, no. 4 (Dec. 1905): 405.

FOUR Selling Providence

1. "Laud Whitman's Deed: Services in Memory of the Pioneer Missionary," *Washington Post,* Nov. 29, 1897; 2.

2. Ibid.

3. "The Walla Walla Massacre," *Atlanta Constitution,* Nov. 10, 1895, 2.

4. Matthew Frye Jacobsen, *Barbarian Virtues: The United States Encounters Foreign Peoples at Home and Abroad, 1876–1917* (New York: Hill & Wang, 2000), 110.

5. Michael Gaudio, *Engraving the Savage: The New World and Techniques of Civilization* (Minneapolis: University of Minnesota Press, 2008); Roy Harvey Pearce, *Savagism and Civilization: A Study of the Indian and the American Mind* (Berkeley: University

of California Press, 1988); Lee D. Baker, *From Savage to Negro: Anthropology and the Construction of Race, 1896–1954* (Berkeley: University of California Press, 1998), 26–81.

6. For instance, Samuel W. Pond, *Two Volunteer Missionaries among the Dakotas, or, The Story of the Labors of Samuel W. and Gideon H. Pond* (Boston: Congregational Sunday-School and Publishing Society, 1893); J. E. Godbey and A. H. Godbey, *Light in Darkness, or, Missions and Missionary Heroes: An Illustrated History of the Missionary Work Now Carried on by All Protestant Denominations in Heathen Lands* (Des Moines: Burnett & Company, 1891); E. P. Tenney, *Triumph of the Cross, or, The Supremacy of Christianity as an Uplifting Force in the Home, the School, and the Nation* (Boston: Balch Brothers, 1895).

7. Arthur Schlesinger pioneered the understanding of American missions as a form of cultural imperialism. See Schlesinger, "The Missionary Enterprise and Theories of Imperialism," in *The Missionary Enterprise in China and America,* ed. John K. Fairbank (Cambridge: Harvard University Press, 1974), 336–73. Building on Schlesinger, William Hutchinson has described foreign missions as providing the "moral equivalent for imperialism" in the late nineteenth and early twentieth centuries. See Hutchinson, "A Moral Equivalent for Imperialism: Americans and the Promotion of 'Christian Civilization,' 1880–1920," in *Missionary Ideologies in the Imperialist Era,* ed. William Hutchinson and Torben Christensen (Aarhus, Denmark: Christensens Bogtrykkeri, 1982), 168–78. For a critique of this formulation, see Andrew Porter, " 'Cultural Imperialism' and Protestant Missionary Enterprise," *Journal of Imperial and Commonwealth History* 25, no. 3 (Sept. 1997): 367–91.

8. John Henry Barrows, "The Future of Christian Missions," *New York Evangelist,* Dec. 28, 1899, 16.

9. J. M. W., "70th Anniversary of the Congregational Home Missionary Society," *Outlook,* June 13, 1896, 1111; James S. Dennis, "Christian Missions and National Development," *New York Evangelist,* Feb. 16, 1899, 9.

10. "Marcus Whitman's Ride: Crossing the Continent in Midwinter to Save an Empire," *Detroit Free Press,* Oct. 11, 1891, 12.

11. Richard R. John, "Who Were the Gilders? And Other Seldom-Asked Questions about Business, Technology, and Political Economy in the United States, 1877–1900," *Journal of the Gilded Age and Progressive Era* 8, no. 4 (Oct. 2009): 474–80.

12. John H. Hamer, "Money and the Moral Order in Late Nineteenth- and Early Twentieth-Century American Capitalism," *Anthropological Quarterly* 71, no. 3 (July 1998): 138–39.

13. Andrew Carnegie, "Wealth and Its Uses," *Andrew Carnegie's College Lectures: "Wealth and Its Uses," in the (Butterfield) Practical Course, Union College, Schenectady, N.Y. "Business," Founder's Day, 1896, Cornell University, Ithaca, N.Y. With the Story of How He Served his Business Apprenticeship* (New York: F. T. Neely, 1896), 28.

14. Ibid., 29.

15. "Proceedings of the Pioneer and Historical Society of Oregon, May 11, 1882—Report of the Recording Secretary and of the Committee on Whitman Monument," *Daily Astorian,* May 13, 1882, 1.

16. Myron Eells, *Father Eells; or, The Results of Fifty-Five Years of Missionary Labors in Washington and Oregon; a Biography of Rev. Cushing Eells, D.D., with an Introduction by L. H. Hallock* (Boston: Congregational Sunday-School and Publishing Society, 1894), 15. This biography was written by Cushing Eells's son Myron in conjunction with Myron's brother, Edwin, from their interviews and reminiscences of their parents. Since Cushing Eells's property was twice destroyed by fire, once in 1841 and again in 1872, many of Cushing's own writings were lost. Though the biography occasionally takes a hagiographic tone, it remains the most accurate record of Cushing Eells's life up to 1872.

17. Ibid., 15–17.

18. Ibid., 25.

19. Ibid., 26–29.

20. Ibid., 29–30.

21. Ibid., 31–32.

22. Robert L. Welch, *The Presbytery of Seattle 1858–2005: The "Dream" of A Presbyterian Colony in the West* (Philadelphia: Xlibris, 2006), 58.

23. Diary of Mary Walker, January 1845, *First White Women over the Rockies: Diaries, Letters, and Biographical Sketches of the Six Women of the Oregon Mission Who Made the Overland Journey in 1836 and 1838*, vol. 2: *On to Oregon: The Diaries of Mary Walker and Myra Eells*, ed. Clifford M. Drury (Glendale, CA: Arthur H. Clark, 1966), 277; Paul Kane, *Wanderings of an Artist among the Indians of North America from Canada to Vancouver's Island and Oregon through the Hudson's Bay Company's Territory and Back Again* (London: Longman, Brown, Green, Longman's, and Roberts, 1859), 307–8.

24. Letters of John L. Lewes to Elkanah Walker, Dec. 13, 1847, Jan. 2, 1848, Jan. 14, 1848, Feb. 10, 1848, Feb. 12, 1848, box 1, folder 4, Oregon Mission Papers.

25. Cushing Eells to Henry Harmon Spalding, Jan. 28, 1848, Eells Collection, Whitman College and Northwest Archive, Whitman College, Walla Walla (hereafter Eells Collection).

26. Myron Eells, *Father Eells*, 140–41.

27. Robert Ross McCoy, *Chief Joseph, Yellow Wolf, and the Creation of Nez Perce History in the Pacific Northwest* (New York: Routledge, 2004), 102.

28. Myron Eells, *Father Eells*, 129–51.

29. Cushing Eells to S. B. Treat, draft, Jan. 6, 1855, box 1, Eells Collection.

30. Myron Eells, *Father Eells*, 173.

31. Cushing Eells to S. B. Treat, August 25, 1859, draft, box 1, Eells Collection.

32. G. Thomas Edwards, *Triumph of Tradition: The Emergence of Whitman College, 1859–1924* (Walla Walla: Whitman College, 1992), 8–9.

33. "An Act to Establish an Institution of Learning in Walla Walla County," in *Acts of the Legislative Assembly of the Territory of Washington; Containing, also, the Memorials and Resolutions Passed at the Seventh Regular Session, Begun and Held at Olympia, December 5, 1859* (Olympia: Edward Furste, 1860), 422–23.

34. Edwards, *Triumph of Tradition*, 6.

35. Myron Eells, *Father Eells*, 180.

36. Edwards, *Triumph of Tradition*, 9.

37. Myron Eells, *Father Eells,* 182.

38. Edwards, *Triumph of Tradition,* 8–9.

39. Myron Eells, *Father Eells,* 182.

40. Miles C. Moore, "A Pioneer Railroad Builder," *Oregon Historical Quarterly* 4, no. 3 (Sept. 1903): 195.

41. Ibid., 196.

42. P. B. Chamberlain, "Whitman Seminary," *Walla Walla Statesman,* June 8, 1866, 2.

43. Edwards, *Triumph of Tradition,* 9–10.

44. Ibid., 11–13.

45. Ibid., 15–20, 22, 37–42.

46. Ibid., 16.

47. Ibid., 56–58.

48. Ibid., 58.

49. Myron Eells, *Father Eells,* 203, 209, 206–7.

50. Ibid., 318.

51. "The Rev. Dr. Marcus Whitman's Patriotism, from the *Cincinnati Times-Star,*" *Presbyterian Home Missionary,* Jan. 1, 1884, 13. For similar statements, see S. A. Clarke, "How Dr. Whitman Saved Oregon," *Californian* 2, no. 7 (July 1880): 19; "The Missionary ahead of the Railroads," *Chicago Advance,* Sept. 13, 1883, 610.

52. Stephen Beasley Linnard Penrose, *Whitman: An Unfinished Story* (Walla Walla: Whitman, 1935), 143.

53. As Brenda K. Jackson argues, the re-creation of eastern middle-class institutions in the American West was a widespread phenomenon in the 1890s. Jackson, *Domesticating the West: The Re-creation of the Nineteenth-Century American Middle Class* (Lincoln: University of Nebraska Press, 2002), 6–8.

54. Leoti L. West, *The Wide Northwest: Historic Narrative of America's Wonder Land as Seen by a Pioneer Teacher* (Spokane: Shaw & Borden, 1927), 184.

55. Penrose, *Whitman,* 107, 144.

56. Ibid., 144.

57. Penrose to Myron Eells, Oct. 27, 1894, Stephen B. L. Penrose Papers, 1894–1947, Whitman College and Northwest Archives, Walla Walla.

58. Ibid.

59. "Beloit's Best Friend: Dr. D. K. Pearsons of Chicago Proves Its Benefactor," *Chicago Tribune,* June 25, 1891, 2

60. Edwards, *Triumph of Tradition,* 114–15.

61. Edward Franklin Williams, *Life of Dr. D. K. Pearsons, Friend of the Small College and of Missions* (New York: Pilgrim Press, 1911), 3–4.

62. Ibid., 6–8.

63. Daniel K. Pearsons Jr., *Daniel K. Pearsons: His Life and Works* (Elgin, IL: Brethren Publishing House, 1912), 33–34. The author of this biography was D. K. Pearsons's nephew. Pearsons Sr. had no children, so his nephew was named after him instead.

64. Williams, *Life of Dr. D. K. Pearsons,* 10, 16–20.

65. William Cronon, *Nature's Metropolis: Chicago and the Great West* (New York: W. W. Norton, 1992), 81–97; Robert Lewis, *Chicago Made: Factory Networks in the Industrial Metropolis* (Chicago: University of Chicago Press, 2008), 21–44; Elaine Lewinnek, *Chicago's Early Suburbs and the Roots of American Sprawl* (New York: Oxford University Press, 2014), 3–33; Glenda E. Gilmore, "An Overview of the Progressive Era," in *Who Were the Progressives?*, ed. Glenda E. Gilmore (Boston: Bedford/St. Martin's, 2002), 3–18.

66. Williams, *Life of Dr. D. K. Pearsons,* 20; Pearsons Jr., *Daniel K. Pearsons,* 96.

67. Williams, *Life of Dr. D. K. Pearsons,* 40–41.

68. Pearsons Jr., *Daniel K. Pearsons,* 142.

69. "Dr. D. K. Pearsons Expects to Live a Century," *Phrenological Journal and Science of Health* 110 (Oct. 1900): 134.

70. Pearsons Jr., *Daniel K. Pearsons,* 198–99.

71. D. K. Pearsons Sr., *A Lesson in Practical Philanthropy: Dr. D. K. Pearsons's Method of Helping Poor Colleges. An Address Delivered before the Civic–Philanthropic Conference at Battle Creek, Mich., October 18–23, 1898* (Battle Creek, MI, 1898), 6.

72. Pearsons Jr., *Daniel K. Pearsons,* 111–12.

73. Ibid., 66; Pearsons Sr., *Lesson in Practical Philanthropy,* 6.

74. Pearsons Sr., "Lecture on the 'Freshwater' College," in Pearsons Jr., *Daniel K. Pearsons,* 47–48.

75. Samuel Ives Curtiss, "Dr. D. K. Pearsons: The Friend of Christian Education," *Chicago Advance,* Jan. 26, 1893, 65.

76. Ibid.

77. Pearsons Jr., *Daniel K. Pearsons,* 255.

78. Ibid., 114.

79. Ibid., 115.

80. Ibid., 183.

81. Ibid., 276.

82. Ibid., 353–54.

83. Ibid., 275–76.

84. Ibid., 53.

85. Pearsons Sr., "Lecture on the 'Freshwater' College," in Pearsons, Jr., *Daniel K. Pearsons,* 44.

86. Penrose, *Whitman: An Unfinished Story,* 145.

87. Ibid., 148.

88. Pearsons Jr., *Daniel K. Pearsons,* 257.

89. Pearsons Sr. to Penrose, Oct. 20, 1897, Penrose Papers; also Pearsons Sr., to Penrose, Oct. 23, 1894, Penrose Papers; Pearsons Sr., to Penrose, Oct. 16, 1896, Penrose Papers; Pearsons Sr., to Penrose, Nov. 26, 1896, Penrose Papers.

90. Edwards, *Triumph of Tradition,* 143.

91. Penrose, *Whitman: An Unfinished Story,* 145. Evidence of the text's popularity is shown by the fact that by 1888 it was already in its fifth edition. Barrows, *Oregon: The Struggle for Possession.* American Commonwealth Series. 5th ed. (New York: Houghton Mifflin, 1883, 1888), front matter.

92. Penrose, *Whitman: An Unfinished Story*, 145.

93. "Oliver W. Nixon," in *History of the Republican Party and Biographies of Its Supporters, Illinois Volume*, ed. David Ward Wood (Chicago: Lincoln Engraving and Publishing, 1895), 188–90.

94. "A Prominent Journalist: Interview with Dr. O. W. Nixon, the Maker of the *Chicago Inter Ocean*," *Los Angeles Times*, Feb. 15, 1885, 1.

95. "Church Affairs. Among the Ministers," *Chicago Inter Ocean*, Nov. 19, 1889, 6.

96. Penrose, *Whitman: An Unfinished Story*, 147; Williams, *Life of Dr. D. K. Pearsons*, 199.

97. Oliver W. Nixon, *How Marcus Whitman Saved Oregon: A True Romance of Patriotic Heroism, Christian Devotion and Final Martyrdom, with Sketches of Life on the Plains and Mountains in Pioneer Days*, introduction by Frank W. Gunsaulus, 2nd ed. (Chicago: Star Publishing, 1895), 5–6.

98. "Dr Whitman's Ride: How Oregon Was Snatched from the Hudson's Bay Company," *Cleveland Plain Dealer* (from the *Chicago Inter Ocean*), July 28, 1884, 3.

99. "Honor to Whom Honor Is Due," *Whitman College Quarterly* 1, no. 1 (Jan. 1897): 20.

100. Nixon to Penrose, Dec. 21, 1894, Penrose Papers.

101. Ibid.

102. Ibid.

103. Nixon, *How Marcus Whitman Saved Oregon* 99.

104. Ibid., 275–76.

105. Ibid., 5.

106. For instance, advertisements for *How Marcus Whitman Saved Oregon*, *Chicago Inter Ocean*, Dec. 7, 1895, 10; Dec. 19, 1895, 10; Dec. 21, 1895, 4; Dec. 24, 1895, 12.

107. Nixon to Penrose, May 8, 1897, Penrose Papers; Williams, *Life of D. K. Pearsons*, 149, 249–51.

108. "Notes," *Congregationalist*, Oct. 3, 1895, 40; "Literary Notes," *Los Angeles Times*, April 19, 1896, 20. According to Nixon none of these editions were very large—the biggest edition was thirty-eight hundred books. Nixon to S. W. Pratt, Chicago, March 8, 1898, Pratt Collection.

109. "Fresh Literature," *Los Angeles Times*, July 8, 1895, 6; "Claiming Too Much," *San Francisco Chronicle*, Aug. 30, 1896, 22; "Fact and Fiction for the Holidays: Dr. Nixon Tells Once More How Marcus Whitman Saved Oregon and Made Himself Famous," *New York Herald*, July 13, 1895, 11; "Literary Field," *Cleveland Plain Dealer*, Aug. 25, 1895, 7; "How Marcus Whitman Saved Oregon," *Springfield (Mass.) Republican*, Oct. 20, 1895, 6.

110. "Books of the Week: How Marcus Whitman Saved Oregon," *Detroit Free Press*, Aug. 24, 1896, 7.

111. "How Marcus Whitman Saved Oregon," *Book News: A Monthly Survey of General Literature* 7 (Sept. 1894–August 1895), 509.

112. For instance, "Chicago Ministers' Meeting," *Chicago Advance*, June 11, 1896, 857; Williams, *Life of Dr. D. K. Pearsons*, 199.

113. Nixon, *How Marcus Whitman Saved Oregon*, 175.

114. Ibid., 98.

115. Ibid., 5.

116. Advertisement for *How Marcus Whitman Saved Oregon, Chicago Inter Ocean,* Aug. 2, 1896, 5.

117. "New Books," *St. Louis Post-Dispatch,* Aug. 16, 1896, 28.

118. "Fact and Fiction for the Holidays: Dr. Nixon Tells Once More How Marcus Whitman Saved Oregon and Made Himself Famous," *New York Herald,* July 13, 1895, 11.

119. Nixon, *How Marcus Whitman Saved Oregon,* 100.

120. Jonathan Edwards, *Marcus Whitman, M.D., the Pathfinder of the Pacific Coast and Martyred Missionary of Oregon* (Spokane: Union Printing, 1892), 13–14, quoted in Nixon, *How Marcus Whitman Saved Oregon,* 76–77.

121. Nixon, *How Marcus Whitman Saved Oregon,* 167

122. Ibid., 154.

123. Gail Bederman, *Manliness and Civilization: A Cultural History of Gender and Race in the United States, 1880–1917* (Chicago: University of Chicago Press, 1996), 18.

124. Nixon, *How Marcus Whitman Saved Oregon,* 125.

125. Ibid., 121.

126. The uncredited image was first produced for and published in Frances Fuller Victor's *River of the West* (Hartford, CT: R. W. Bliss, 1870), 410.

127. Ibid., 411.

128. Nixon, *How Marcus Whitman Saved Oregon,* n.p. I have not been able to find the name of the illustrator of these images; he or she is not mentioned in the book's credits, advertisements, or Nixon's correspondence.

129. Ibid., 128.

130. "An Unknown Hero. A Movement to Give Recognition to Dr. Marcus Whitman. His Lively Trip," *Cleveland Plain Dealer,* May 6, 1895, 8.

131. Stephen B. L. Penrose, "A Tribute to a Great Hero," *New York Tribune,* April 29, 1895, 5.

132. "Dr. Gunsaulus on Marcus Whitman," *Chicago Inter Ocean,* Feb. 19, 1895, 6.

133. "Honors to Whitman: Story of the Man Who Saved Oregon Told Last Night," *Chicago Inter Ocean,* Feb. 19, 1895, 3.

134. "Dr. Marcus Whitman," *Chicago Inter Ocean,* June 29, 1895, 12.

135. "Congregational (Whitman Sunday)," *Chicago Inter Ocean,* June 29, 1895, 13.

136. "The Advance," in Alfred Theodore Andreas, *History of Chicago from the Earliest Period to the Present Time,* 3 vols. (Chicago: A. T. Andreas, 1886), 3:709.

137. Pearsons to Penrose, Oct. 17, 1896, Penrose Papers.

138. George M. Baxter, "Marcus Whitman's Ride," in *Philadelphia Inquirer,* Aug. 23, 1896, 30; *Wheeling (WV) Sunday Register,* Aug. 23, 1896, 6; *Los Angeles Times,* Aug. 23, 1896, 16; *Atlanta Constitution,* Aug. 23, 1896, A4.

139. George M. Baxter, "Marcus Whitman's Ride: The Hero Who Saved the Great Northwest," *Atlanta Constitution,* Aug. 23, 1896, A4.

140. "Piths and Points: Budding and Grafting Christian Colonization," *Interior*, Nov. 12, 1896, 1471.

141. "Address of Rev. Charles L. Thompson, D.D.," *New York Evangelist*, March 5, 1896, 29.

142. William Elliot Griffis, "America in the Far East: V.—The Pacific Ocean and Our Future There," *Outlook*, Jan. 14, 1899, 110.

143. Herbert Baxter Adams, "Secretary's Report of the Organization and Proceedings, Saratoga, September 9–10, 1884," in *Papers of the American Historical Association* (New York: G. P. Putnam's Sons, 1886), 1:5.

144. James Schouler, "A New Federal Convention: From the Annual Report of the American Historical Association for 1897, pages 19–34" (Washington: Government Printing Office, 1898), 21.

145. Henry Warner Bowden, *Church History in the Age of Science: Historiographical Patterns in the United States, 1876–1918* (Chapel Hill: University of North Carolina Press, 1971), 67.

146. "Its First Session Here: Meeting of the American Historical Association," *New York Times*, Dec. 30, 1896, 2.

147. Herbert Baxter Adams, *Annual Report of the American Historical Association for the Year 1897* (Washington: Government Printing Office, 1897), 13.

148. Ibid., 14.

149. "The Permanent Motive in Missionary Work: The Address by Richard S. Storrs," *Congregationalist*, Oct. 5, 1899, 481.

150. Richard S. Storrs, "Our Country's Tribute," *Addresses on Foreign Missions Delivered before the American Board of Commissioners for Foreign Missions* (Boston: Congregational House, 1900), 90.

151. Untitled Article, *Independent*, Jan. 7, 1897, 19.

152. Horace Scudder, *A Short History of the United States of America for the Use of Beginners* (New York: Sheldon, 1890), 200–201; Scudder, *A History of the United States of America with an Introduction Narrating the Discovery and Settlement of North America* (New York: Butler, Sheldon, 1897), 310–12; John Bach McMaster, *A School History of the United States* (New York: American Book Company, 1897), 332; Wilbur Fisk Gordy, *A History of the United States for Schools* (New York, 1898), 285–86; William A. Mowry and Arthur May Mowry, *A History of the United States for Schools* (New York, 1896), 418.

153. Edwards, *Triumph of Tradition*, 160; Pearsons to Penrose, Sept. 21, 1897, Penrose Papers; Pearsons to Penrose, Oct. 8, 1897, Penrose Papers; Pearsons to Penrose, Oct. 28, 1897, Penrose Papers; Pearsons to Penrose, Nov. 22, 1897, Penrose Papers.

154. Nixon to Penrose, Oct. 17, 1896, Penrose Papers.

155. Nixon to Penrose, June 8, 1897, Penrose Papers.

156. "Oregon Pioneers: Annual Meeting of an Interesting Nature," *Astorian*, May 20, 1896, 4.

157. "Whitman Monument Proposed," *Tacoma Daily News*, Feb. 15, 1897, 1; "Whitman Monument. Dr. Penrose, of Walla Walla, an Ardent Supporter of the Dead Hero," *Oregonian*, March 4, 1897, 10.

158. "Whitman Monument Proposed," *Tacoma Daily News,* Feb. 15, 1897, 1.

159. "For a Monument to Marcus Whitman," *Oregonian,* Feb. 15, 1897, 8; "Whitman's Grave: Pioneers Will Tonight Discuss Question of a Monument," *Oregonian,* Feb. 16, 1897, 10; "Dr. Marcus Whitman His Neglected Grave to Be Marked with a Monument," *Oregonian,* Feb. 17, 1897, 10.

160. "Dr. Marcus Whitman His Neglected Grave to Be Marked with a Monument," *Oregonian,* Feb. 17, 1897, 10.

161. "The Whitman Monument. How Long Shall the Neglected Grave Utter Its Mute Reproach," *Oregonian,* April 24, 1897, 4; J. E. Walker, "The Whitman Christian Endeavor Society," *Golden Rule* 11, no. 39 (1897): 794.

162. "Now for a Monument Victims of the Cayuse War to Be Remembered," *Oregonian,* Feb. 24, 1897, 10.

163. "Lecture Tonight," *Dalles Daily Chronicle,* Feb. 2, 1897, 3; "Oregon Notes," *Oregonian,* June 28, 1897, 2.

164. Nixon to Pearsons, May 8, 1897, Penrose Papers.

165. Penrose, *Whitman,* 152.

166. Untitled article, *Los Angeles Times,* March 8, 1897, 6.

167. "The Whitman Monument: Contract for Its Construction Awarded," *Tacoma Daily News,* Aug. 3, 1897, 4.

168. Ibid.

169. "Presbyterial," *Interior,* April 29, 1897, 544; "News from Our Churches: The Interior," *Chicago Advance,* Feb. 25, 1897, 258; "Amoung [*sic*] the Philadelphia Churches," *New York Evangelist,* April 15, 1897, 13.

170. James M. Walton, "Ministers and Churches," *New York Evangelist,* Sept. 8, 1898, 29.

171. "The Savior of Oregon," *San Francisco Chronicle,* Dec. 20, 1897, 4.

172. "Board of Foreign Missions: It Is Decided to Observe the Anniversary of the Massacre of Marcus Whitman," *Chicago Tribune,* Oct. 15, 1897, 5; "Minutes of the Annual Meeting," *Missionary Herald, Containing the Proceedings of the American Board of Commissioners for Foreign Missions* 93, no. 11 (Nov. 1897): 477; "Whitman Memorial Service: Life of the Great Missionary to Be the Theme in Congregational Pulpits," *New Haven Register,* Nov. 17, 1897, 5; untitled article, *Grand Forks Daily Herald,* November 24, 1897, 4; untitled article, *New Haven Register,* Nov. 20, 1897, 20; "Church Notes," *Philadelphia Inquirer,* March 20, 1897.

173. W. S. Holt, "The Whitman Monument," *New York Observer and Chronicle,* Nov. 11, 1897, 627.

174. Pearsons to Penrose, May 20, 1897, Penrose Papers.

175. Nixon to Penrose, May 8, 1897, Penrose Papers.

176. Ibid.

177. Ibid., Oct. 29, 1897, Penrose Papers.

178. "At Whitman's Grave Preparing the Ground for the Mausoleum. The Bones and Other Relics Collected," *Oregonian,* Oct. 25, 1897, 3.

179. "Monument to Dr. Marcus Whitman" *New York Evangelist,* Nov. 25, 1897, 11.

180. "The Whitman Anniversary," *Whitman College Quarterly* 1, no. 4 (Dec. 1897): 3.

181. "Dr. Hallock's Address," *Whitman College Quarterly* 1, no. 4 (Dec. 1897): 7.

182. Ibid.

183. Ibid., 26–27.

184. Ibid., 25–26

185. Ibid, 26

186. Ibid., 29. There are multiple locks in various repositories that are claimed to be Whitman's hair, since giving and taking locks of hair was a common token of affection and remembrance in the mid-nineteenth century. Narcissa sent locks of her hair to family and friends back home. More gruesomely, when soldiers in the Cayuse War came across Whitman's grave and found her body dug up by animals, they cut locks of her hair as mementos before reburying her and the other victims' bodies. Trevor Bond, "Hair and History," *Washington State University Magazine,* online, accessed Jan. 14, 2015, http://wsm.wsu.edu/s/index.php?id=1153.

187. "Mr. Scudder's Address (imperfectly reported)," *Whitman College Quarterly* 1, no. 4 (Dec. 1897): 50.

188. Ibid.

189. "Church Notes," *Philadelphia Inquirer,* March 20, 1897, 5.

190. George Ludington Weed, "When Dr. Whitman Added Three Stars to Our Flag: How Oregon Was Saved for the Union," *Ladies' Home Journal* 14, no. 12 (Nov. 1897): 9.

191. "Laud Whitman's Deed: Services in Memory of the Pioneer Missionary," *Washington Post,* Nov. 29, 1897, 2.

192. Ibid.; "In Memory of Dr. Whitman," *Washington Times,* Nov. 29, 1897, 2.

193. Penrose to T. C. Elliot, Dec. 4, 1897, Penrose Papers.

194. "The Aim of Whitman College," *Whitman College Quarterly* 1, no. 1 (Jan. 1897): 22.

195. "Honor to Whom Honor Is Due," *Whitman College Quarterly* 1, no. 1 (Jan. 1897): 21.

196. Ibid.

FIVE Debunking Providence

1. F. H. Hodder, "The Marcus Whitman Legend," *Dial* 32 (Jan. 1, 1902): 40; "The Meeting of the American Historical Association at Detroit and Ann Arbor," *American Historical Review* 6, no. 3 (1901): 419–20.

2. Edward Gaylord Bourne, "The Legend of Marcus Whitman," *American Historical Review* 6, no. 2 (Jan. 1901): 276–300, 277.

3. Ibid., 296.

4. Ibid.

5. William Isaac Marshall, "Marcus Whitman: A Discussion of Professor Bourne's Paper," in *Annual Report of the American Historical Association for the Year 1900* (Washington: Government Printing Office, 1901), 221–36, 231.

6. "The Midnight Ride Paul Revere Didn't Take," *Detroit Free Press,* Dec. 2, 1908, 4; Joseph Rodman, "The Hatchet and the Cherry-Tree: The First Printed Version," *Critic* 44, no. 2 (Feb. 1904): 116.

7. Peter Novick, *That Noble Dream: The "Objectivity Question" and the American Historical Profession* (New York: Cambridge University Press, 1988), 32–34; Robert Townsend, *History's Babel: Scholarship, Professionalization, and the Historical Enterprise in the United States, 1880–1940* (Chicago: University of Chicago Press, 2013), 13–18.

8. Townsend argues that the exclusion of non-university-affiliated historians from AHA leadership and other positions of power occurred primarily in the period from 1926 to 1940 (*History's Babel,* 8). However, my research suggests that this pattern of exclusion was present at the beginning of the American historical profession's development and that the debunking of myths and the removal of overt providentialism were essential tools by which the new historians distinguished themselves from the old. Townsend himself hints at earlier fractures in the historical profession when he cites an 1895 review by the historian Maurice Bloomfield, who writes, "The professional scholar alone is capable of measuring and presenting the measurements of the difficulties and uncertainties that attach to any line of facts" (*History's Babel,* 17).

9. For instance, Talal Asad, *Formations of the Secular: Christianity, Islam, Modernity* (Stanford: Stanford University Press, 2003); Christian Smith, *The Secular Revolution: Power, Interests, and Conflict in the Secularization of American Public Life* (Berkeley: University of California Press, 2003); Tracy Fessenden, *Culture and Redemption: Religion, the Secular, and American Literature* (Princeton: Princeton University Press, 2007).

10. Novick, *That Noble Dream,* 2.

11. F. H. H., Review, *The Territorial Growth of the United States,* by William A. Mowry, *American Historical Review* 8, no. 3 (April 1903): 562.

12. Elizabeth Clark, *Founding the Fathers: Early Church History and Protestant Professors in Nineteenth-Century America* (Philadelphia: University of Pennsylvania Press, 2011), 141–42, 155.

13. Ibid., 158–59.

14. Ibid., 159–61.

15. Herbert Baxter Adams, "New Methods of Study in History," *Journal of Social Science* 18 (May 1884): 225.

16. William Frederick Cobb, *Origines Judaicae: An Inquiry into the Heathen Faiths as Affecting the Birth and Growth of Judaism* (London: A. D. Innes, 1895), 41.

17. See, for example, Edward Burnett Tylor, *Primitive Culture: Researches into the Development of Mythology, Philosophy, Religion, Art, and Custom,* 2 vols. (London: John Murray, 1871), 1:431; Max Müller, *Lectures on the Science of Language: Delivered at the Royal Institution of Great Britain in April, May, and June 1861* (London: Longman, Green, and Roberts, 1861), 11–12; William Robertson Smith, *Lectures on the Religion of the Semites: First Series: The Fundamental Institutions* (New York: D. Appleton, 1889), 19–20.

18. I. K. Funk and D. S. Gregory, Editor's Introduction, "How Oregon Was Saved to the United States, *Homiletic* 17 (July–Dec. 1901): 21.

19. "The Legend of Marcus Whitman," *Chicago Advance,* Jan. 17, 1901, 41.

20. William Augustus Mowry to Myron Eells, Boston, Mass., April 24, 1888, box E, Whitman Collection, Whitman College and Northwest Archives, Walla Walla, Wash.

21. Ellen Foster Marshall, "William Isaac Marshall: A Biographical Sketch," in William I. Marshall, *Acquisition of Oregon, and the Long Suppressed Evidence about Marcus Whitman,* vol. 1 (Seattle: Lowman & Hanford, 1911), 23.

22. Ibid., 23–24.

23. As Lee Whittlesey notes, although Marshall purchased the photographs of Joshua Crissman to use in his lectures, the photographs were often mistakenly credited to him. Lee H. Whittlesey, *Storytelling in Yellowstone: Horse and Buggy Tour Guides* (Albuquerque: University of New Mexico Press, 2007), 44–46.

24. Untitled article, *Zion's Herald,* June 29, 1876, 53, 26; "Detailed Daily Program, July 2–August 28," *Chautauquan* 7 (Oct. 1886–July 1887): 637.

25. William A. Mowry to Edward F. Williams, Feb. 14, 1899, box E, Whitman Collection.

26. "William A. Mowry Dies at His Home in Hyde Park," *Boston Herald,* May 23, 1917, 12.

27. Mowry to William H. Gray, Feb. 7, 1878, Gray Collection; "The Whitman Monument," *Astorian,* Jan. 26, 1881, 2.

28. Mowry to William H. Gray, Feb. 7, 1878, William H. Gray Papers.

29. For the role of public lectures as a forum for public history, see Andrew Chamberlain Rieser, *Chautauqua Moment: Protestants, Progressives, and the Culture of Modern Liberalism* (New York: Columbia University Press, 2003), 207–15.

30. Marshall to George Henry [G. H.] Himes, Aug. 24, 1888, box 1, folder 2, George H. Himes Papers, Oregon Historical Society Research Library, Portland, Oregon (hereafter Himes Papers).

31. Ibid.

32. Ibid.

33. Marshall, *Acquisition of Oregon,* 10.

34. Marshall to Myron Eells, Aug. 8, 1882, box E, Whitman Collection.

35. Ibid.

36. Ibid., July 23, 1887, box E, Whitman Collection.

37. Ibid.

38. This claim originated in Spalding's history of the Oregon Missions, published by the US Senate in 1871. See US Congress, Senate, Henry Harmon Spalding, *Letter from the Secretary of the Interior, Communicating, in Compliance with the Resolution of the Senate of the 2d Instant, Information in Relation to the Early Labors of the Missionaries of the American Board of Commissioners of Foreign Missions in Oregon, Commencing in 1836. February 9, 1871.—Referred to the Committee on Indian Affairs and Ordered to Be Printed,"* 41st Congress, 3rd Session, 1871, 22; and was repeated by Gray and Barrows. See also William Henry Gray, *A History of Oregon, 1792–1849, Drawn from Personal Observation and Authentic Information* (Portland: American News Company, 1870), 289–90; William Barrows, *Oregon: The Struggle for Possession.* American Commonwealth Series, ed. Horace Scudder. 5th ed. (Boston: Houghton Mifflin, 1884, 1888), 229.

39. Marshall to Myron Eells, July 23, 1887, box E, Whitman Papers.

40. Marshall, *Acquisition of Oregon*, 1:11.

41. Ibid., 12.

42. Ibid., 17

43. Marshall to William A. Mowry, Nov. 10, 1898, box E, Whitman Collection.

44. Marshall to Himes, Aug. 24, 1888, Himes Papers.

45. Mowry to Myron Eells, April 24, 1888, box E, Whitman Collection.

46. Marshall to Mowry, Nov. 10, 1898, box E, Whitman Collection.

47. Ibid., July 20, 1887, box E, Whitman Collection.

48. Edward F. Williams to Mowry, Jan. 14, 1899, box E, Whitman Collection.

49. Mowry to Eells, Feb. 1, 1899, box E, Whitman Collection.

50. Ibid.

51. Williams to Mowry, Jan. 14, 1899, box E, Whitman Collection.

52. Eells, *A Reply to Professor Bourne's "The Whitman Legend"* (Walla Walla: Statesman Publishing, 1902, reprinted from the *Whitman College Quarterly* 4, no. 3): 28.

53. Eells, "Hand of God in the History of the Pacific Coast: Annual Address Delivered Before the Trustees, Faculty, Students and Friends of Whitman College at the Sixth Commencement, June 1, 1888" (Walla Walla, 1888), 13.

54. Eells, *Reply to Professor Bourne's "The Whitman Legend,"* 28.

55. Mowry to Marshall, Dec. 9, 1898, box E, Whitman Collection.

56. Marshall, "Why His Search (?) for the Truth of History was a Failure: Being a Review of Rev. Myron Eells's 'Reply to Professor Bourne,'" *History vs. the Whitman Saved Oregon Story: Three Essays towards a True History of the Acquisition of the Old Oregon Territory (Being Nearly One-Twelfth of All our Domain on this Continent), which was the Longest, the Most Remarkable–and When Truthfully Told–the Most Interesting Struggle We Have Ever Made for Territory* (Chicago: Blakely Printing, 1904), 48.

57. Ibid., 49.

58. Ibid.

59. Ibid.; Leslie M. Scott, "John Fiske's Change of Attitude on the Whitman Legend," *Oregon Historical Quarterly* 13, no. 2 (June 1912): 160–74.

60. Bourne, "The Legend of Marcus Whitman," in *Essays in Historical Criticism* (New York: Charles Scribner's Sons, 1901), 51.

61. Marshall, *Reply to Professor Bourne's "The Whitman Legend,"* 230.

62. Quoted in Marshall, "Marcus Whitman: A Discussion of Professor Bourne's Paper," *Annual Report of the American Historical Association for the Year 1900*, 230; also Marshall to Mowry, Jan. 12, 1900, box E, Whitman Collection; Marshal to Mowry, May 15, 1899, box E, Whitman Collection.

63. John Fiske to Marshall, July 28, 1900, box E, Whitman Collection.

64. Fiske to Marshall, July 28, 1900, box E, Whitman Collection; Marshall to Mowry, Jan. 12, 1900, box E, Whitman Collection.

65. James Ford Rhodes, "Tribute to Edward Gaylord Bourne," *Proceedings of the Massachusetts Historical Society*, 3d series, vol. 1 (1907, 1908): 399–400.

66. Ibid., 405.

67. Ironically, Adelbert College (previously known as Western Reserve College) was where Henry Harmon Spalding had studied. However, I have not found any evidence that Bourne knew of Spalding during his time teaching at Adelbert. In his "Legend of Marcus Whitman," Bourne states, "My eyes were first opened to the intricacies and curious origin of the legend by a very careful investigation conducted under supervision by one of my students, Mr. Arthur Howard Hutchinson." Bourne, "Legend of Marcus Whitman," p. 277, note 1.

68. George B. Adams to Bourne, Feb. 21, 1895, box 1, folder 1, Edward Gaylord Bourne Papers, 1874–1970 (hereafter Bourne Papers), Yale University Manuscripts and Archives, New Haven; Nicholas Butter to Bourne, Sept. 24, 1894, box 1, folder 2, Bourne Papers; Edward T. Devine to Bourne, March 14, 1894, box 1, folder 4, Bourne Papers; Ephraim Emerton to Bourne, Jan. 24, 1897, box 1, folder 4, Bourne Papers; Albert Bushnell Hart to Bourne, Oct. 25, 1897, box 1, folder 6, Bourne Papers.

69. A. Howard Clark to Bourne, Jan. 13, 1900, box 1, folder 11, Bourne Papers; Clark to Bourne, Jan. 29. 1900, box 1, folder 11, Bourne Papers; Brian J. Clinch to Bourne, Sept. 30, 1899, box 1, folder 11, Bourne Papers; A. C. McLaughlin to Bourne, Feb. 21, 1900, box 2, folder 14, Bourne Papers; Albert Bushnell Hart to Bourne, Dec. 12, 1899, box 1, folder 13, Bourne Papers.

70. Bourne, "Some Recent Books on Folk Lore," *New Englander and Yale Review* 11 (Sept. 1887): 165.

71. Ibid. For Lang's theory of myth, see Lang, *Custom and Myth* (London: Longmans, Green, 1884), especially pages 53–57.

72. Bourne, "Method of Historical Study," *New Englander and Yale Review* 9 (Nov. 1886): 925.

73. Bourne, "Leopold von Ranke," *Annual Report of the American Historical Association for the Year 1896*, 2 vols. (Washington: Government Printing Office, 1897): 1:65–82, 76.

74. Bourne, "Leopold Von Ranke," *Essays in Historical Criticism*, 245–76, 256.

75. Bourne, "Bancroft's Life of Van Buren," *Christian Register*, Dec. 17, 1891.

76. A. C. McLaughlin to Bourne, Ann Arbor, Mich., Jan. 11, 1892, box 1, folder 7, Bourne Papers.

77. *Catalogue of Yale University, 1902–1903* (New Haven: Tuttle, Morehouse & Taylor, 1902), 540; for Meany's advocacy of the Whitman Story, see Robert Ross McCoy, *Chief Joseph, Yellow Wolf, and the Creation of Nez Perce History in the Pacific Northwest* (New York: Routledge, 2004), 70–71, 77–80.

78. Arthur Hutchinson to Bourne, n.d., c. 1900, box 1, folder 13, Bourne Papers; Hutchinson to Bourne, Oct. 11, 1900, box 1, folder 13, Bourne Papers; Hutchinson to Bourne, n.d., c. 1901, box 1, folder 13, Bourne Papers.

79. J. Franklin Jameson to Bourne, Oct. 28, 1899, box 1, folder 13, Bourne Papers.

80. Ibid., Nov. 2, 1899, box 1, folder 13, Bourne Papers.

81. Ibid., Nov. 15, 1900, box 1, folder 13, Bourne Papers.

82. Ibid., Aug. 18, 1899, box 1, folder 13, Bourne Papers; Ibid., Nov. 15, 1900, box 1, folder 13, Bourne Papers.

83. Bourne, "Legend of Marcus Whitman," note 1, p. 288.

84. For Marshall's influence on Bourne, see Marshall, *Acquisition of Oregon,* 1:8–9; Bourne, "Essays in Historical Criticism," 50–52.

85. Bourne, "Legend of Marcus Whitman," 276.

86. For instance, "History's Iconoclasts," *Seattle Mail and Herald,* Dec. 14, 1901, n.p. newspaper clipping in box I, Whitman Collection; H. J. Haskell, "Myths of American History," *Independent,* July 5, 1906, 31; "Marcus Whitman," *Independent,* Nov. 29, 1909, 1206; "The Whitman Controversy," *Independent,* Feb. 3, 1910, 275; C. H. Howard, "Not a Legend," *Interior,* Feb. 14, 1901, 201.

87. S. A. Clark to William A. Mowry, Nov. 8, 1902, box E, Whitman Collection; T. C. Elliott to Edwin Eells, Dec. 24, 1907, box 5, folder 1, Thompson Coit Elliott Papers, 1903–1937, Oregon Historical Society Research Library, Portland (hereafter Elliott Papers).

88. Bourne, "Legend of Marcus Whitman," 276.

89. Ibid.

90. "American Historical Society Makes an Exposure," *Los Angeles Times,* Dec. 29, 1900, 14. See also "Now Deny That Marcus Whitman Saved Oregon," *San Francisco Chronicle,* Dec. 29, 1900, 2; "Ride of Dr. Whitman; Story of How He Saved Oregon Called a Mere Legend . . . Proofs that There Is No Truth in It," *Washington Post,* March 17, 1901, 27.

91. "The Marcus Whitman Legend," *Dial* 32 (Jan. 1–June 16, 1902): 40.

92. Alice Carman, "The Whitman Myth," clipping from unknown newspaper, box E, Whitman Collection; "A Scathing Review," *Oregonian,* Sept. 3, 1902, 8.

93. William A. Mowry to Myron Eells, Feb. 11, 1901, box E, Whitman Collection.

94. "Whitman of Oregon," *Interior,* Jan. 17, 1901, 68.

95. "Religious World: The Legend of Marcus Whitman," *Chicago Advance,* Jan. 17, 1901, 75.

96. "Did Marcus Whitman Save Oregon," *Fitchburg Sentinel,* Feb. 12, 1901, 1.

97. Marshall to Elliot, July 10, 1888, box 5, folder 1, Elliott Papers.

98. William I. Marshall to unknown recipient, draft, July 10, 1888, box E, Whitman Collection.

99. Marshall to Myron Eells, April 2, 1887, box E, Whitman Collection.

100. Bourne, "Legend of Marcus Whitman," 285.

101. Howard, "Not a Legend," *Interior,* Feb. 14, 1901, 201.

102. Myron Eells, "As to the Value of Historical Testimony," *Oregonian,* March 22, 1903, 32; see also Eells to T. C. Elliott, Jan. 27, 1903, box 5, folder 1, Elliott Papers.

103. Henry Parker, "How Oregon Was Saved to the United States, or, Facts about Marcus Whitman, M. D.," *Homiletic* 14 (July–Dec. 1901), 25.

104. Ibid.

105. Howard, "Not a Legend," *Interior,* Feb. 14, 1901, 201.

106. "Religious World: The Legend of Marcus Whitman," *Chicago Advance,* Jan. 17, 1901, 75.

107. I. K. Funk and D. S. Gregory, Editor's Introduction, "How Oregon Was Saved to the United States," *Homiletic* 14 (July–Dec. 1901): 21.

108. Eells and Gray had previously collaborated on the *Whitman Controversy* pamphlet of 1885. *The Whitman Controversy, Articles by Ed. C. Ross, Rev. M. Eels and W. H. Gray in Reply to Mrs. F. F. Victor and Elwood Evans* (Portland: G. H. Himes, 1885). See also Michael J. Paulus Jr., "Cultural Record Keepers: The Myron Eells Northwest History Collection, Whitman College," *Libraries and the Cultural Record* 43, no. 2 (2008): 215.

109. *Minutes of the General Association of Connecticut, at the One Hundred and Sixty-First Annual Meeting, Held in Meriden, June 21–22, 1870, with Reports* (Hartford: Case, Lockwood & Brainard, 1870), 101. For Schaff's historical providentialism, see Stephen R. Graham, "'Cosmos in the Chaos': Philip Schaff's Vision of America," *American Presbyterians* 67, no. 4 (Winter 1989): 260–61.

110. Myron Eells, *Marcus Whitman: Pathfinder and Patriot* (Seattle: Alice Harriman, 1909), 307.

111. Eells, "The Thunder Bird," *American Anthropologist* 2, no. 4 (Oct. 1889): 329–36; Eells, "The Chinook Jargon," *American Anthropologist* 7, no. 3 (July 1894): 300–312; Eells, "Twins among the Indians on Puget Sound," *Science* 20, no. 504 (Sept. 30, 1892): 192–93; Eells, "Aboriginal Geographic Names in the State of Washington," *American Anthropologist* 5, no. 1 (Jan. 1892): 27–36; C. L. Higham, "Saviors and Scientists: North American Protestant Missionaries and the Development of Anthropology," *Pacific Historical Review* 72, no. 4 (Nov. 2003): 549–51.

112. Eells, *A Reply to Professor Bourne's 'The Whitman Legend'"* (Walla Walla: Statesman Publishing, 1902, reprinted from the *Whitman College Quarterly* 4, vol. 3); Eells, "As to the Value of Historical Testimony," *Oregonian*, March 22, 1903, 32; "Public Opinion on Whitman Question: Rev. Eells Reviews Professor Bourne's Article from the Whitman Side," *Oregonian*, May 31, 1903, 15; Eells, "Professor William I. Marshall's Seven Mistakes," *Oregonian*, Dec. 17, 1905, 45; Eells, *Marcus Whitman: Pathfinder and Patriot.*

113. *Reply to Professor Bourne's 'The Whitman Legend,'"* 29, 36.

114. Ibid., 38.

115. Ibid., 37.

116. Ibid., 44.

117. Ibid., 89.

118. For instance, S. A. Clark to William A. Mowry, Nov. 8, 1902, box E, Whitman Collection. See also Mowry to Eells, Feb. 1, 1899, box E, Whitman Collection; William A. Mowry to Myron Eells, Feb. 11, 1901, box E, Whitman Collection; "What Marcus Whitman Did Do," *Congregationalist and Christian World*, Aug. 16, 1902, 239.

119. "The Whitman Controversy," *Independent*, Nov. 13, 1902, 2712.

120. Albert Bushnell Hart, "Imagination in History," *American Historical Review* 15, no. 2 (Jan. 1910): 227–51, 242.

121. Frederic Austin Ogg, "Paolo Toscanelli and the Discovery of America," *New England Magazine* 30, no. 6 (Aug. 1904): 664–73, 666.

122. J. Franklin Jameson, untitled review of Bourne, *Essays in Historical Criticism*, *American Historical Review* 7, no. 4 (July 1902): 745–47, 746–47.

123. Ibid., 747.

124. "Death of Professor Marshall," *Oregonian*, Nov. 16, 1906, 5; "Pays Tribute to Memory of Late Myron Eells," *Oregonian*, Feb. 21, 1907, 2; "Obituary: Prof. Edward Gaylord Bourne," *New York Tribune*, Feb. 25, 1908, 5.

125. "Marcus Whitman," *Independent*, Nov. 23, 1909, 1206; also "On the Book Table," *Chicago Advance*, Sept. 9, 1909, 340; "With Authors and Books," *Idaho Statesman*, Oct. 27, 1909, 4; "Marcus Whitman as Missionary," *Springfield (Mass.) Republican*, Oct. 31, 1909, 27.

126. Review of *Marcus Whitman, Pathfinder and Patriot*, *Magazine of History with Notes and Queries* 11 (1909): 180.

127. Reviews of Marshall included Leslie M. Scott, untitled review, *Oregon Historical Quarterly* 12, no. 4 (Dec. 1911): 375–84; Charles W. Smith, untitled review, *American Historical Review* 17, no. 2 (Jan. 1912): 385–86. The only two scholarly reviews of Eells were a short, positive review in the *Bulletin of the American Geographical Society* and a review essay in the *Washington Historical Quarterly*. Charles Smith, the reviewer for the *Washington Historical Quarterly*, stated that Marshall's *Acquisition of Oregon* "closes the case for the negative." See untitled review, *Bulletin of the American Geographical Society* 42, no. 4 (1910): 299; Charles W. Smith, untitled review essay, *Washington Historical Quarterly* 3, no. 2 (April, 1912): 154.

128. Frederick V. Holman, *Dr. John McLoughlin: The Father of Oregon* (Cleveland: Arthur H. Clark, 1907).

129. See, for example, "Whitman, Marcus," in *Encyclopædia Britannica*, ed. Hugh Chisholm, 11th ed. (New York: Encyclopædia Britannica, 1911), 610; "Whitman, Marcus," *New International Encyclopædia*, vol. 28 (New York: Dodd, Mead, 1916), 611; David Saville Muzzey, *An American History* (New York: Ginn, 1920), 267; J. N. Larned, *A History of the United States for Secondary Schools* (Boston: Houghton Mifflin, 1903), 436–37; "Whitman, Marcus," *Americana: A Universal Reference Library*, ed. Frederick Converse Beach, vol. 22 (New York: Scientific American Compiling Department, 1911), n.p. One exception was William A. Mowry, who continued to print the Whitman story in his school textbooks until at least 1914. Mowry and Arthur May Mowry, *First Steps in the History of Our Country* (New York: Silver, Burdett, 1914), 233–35, 315.

130. Martina Johnston, "The Growth of a Modern Myth," *New Catholic World: A Monthly Magazine of General Literature and Science* 107 (1918): 637.

131. The congressman was Francis W. Cushman. "Cushman Offers Prize," *Olympian*, Oct. 30, 1905, 3; "Cushman Prize for Essay," *Olympia Daily Recorder*, Nov. 10, 1905, 2; "Marcus Whitman by E. A. Winship," *Walla Walla Statesman*, Nov. 16, 1905, 3.

132. "Address by Governor Recites Story of Terrible Tragedy of First Pioneer's Death," *Olympian*, Nov. 30, 1907; "Northwest Territory Honors Memory of Marcus Whitman," *Idaho Statesman*, Dec. 3, 1907, 8.

133. "Governor Hays Speaks at Unveiling of Statue," *Olympian*, Sept. 24, 1909, 4.

134. "Summer Church Work Planned," *Philadelphia Inquirer*, June 25, 1910, 9; "A Nation Builder Worthy of Honor," *Montana Anaconda Standard*, July 4, 1910, 7; "Red-Blooded American Heroes: Marcus Whitman the Saviour of Oregon," *Wilkes-Barre Times Leader*, March 10, 1911, 10; Don O. Shelton, *Heroes of the Cross in America* (New

York: Literature Dept., Presbyterian Home Missions, 1904); Leavitt Homan Hallock, *Why Our Flag Floats Over Oregon, or, The Conquest of Our Great Northwest* (Portland, ME: Smith & Sale, 1911).

135. Howard, "Not a Legend," *Interior,* Feb. 14, 1901, 201.

136. "Marcus Whitman," *Journal of Eduation* 61, no. 18 (May 4, 1905): 490.

137. Ibid., 492.

SIX After Providence

1. Leslie M. Scott, "John Fiske's Change of Attitude on the Whitman Legend," *Oregon Historical Quarterly* 13, no. 2 (June 1912): 161–62; Joseph Schafer, "What We Remember," *Wisconsin Magazine of History* 6, no. 2 (Dec. 1922): 235–36; George A. Frykman, "Edmond S. Meany, Historian," *Pacific Northwest Quarterly* 51, no. 4 (Oct. 1960): 163; Thomas A. Bailey, "The Mythmakers of American History," *Journal of American History* 55, no. 1 (June, 1968): 10, note 19; Robert J. Loewenberg, "Saving Oregon Again: A Western Perennial?" *Oregon Historical Quarterly* 78, no. 4 (Dec. 1977): 332.

2. Stephen B. L. Penrose, in collaboration with Percy Jewett Burrell, "Historical Introduction," *The Pioneer Pageant, How the West Was Won* (1923), n.p., Haas Arts Library Special Collections, Yale University.

3. Ibid., act 1, scene 2, n.p.

4. Ibid., act 2, scene 4, n.p.

5. "Northwest Pageant to Be Reproduced," *Washington Post,* May 18, 1924, ES9.

6. Penrose, Introduction, *Pioneer Pageant,* n.p.

7. Penrose to F. S. Hoyt, Houghton Mifflin Company, New York, Feb. 28, 1926, Penrose Papers.

8. "Forgotten Episodes," *Boston Daily Globe,* Oct. 27, 1926, 18.

9. US Congress, House, Committee on Public Lands, Knute Hill, "Establishment of Whitman National Monument," 74th cong., 2nd sess., June 17, 1935.

10. "Whitman National Monument, Washington" (Washington: US Department of the Interior, National Park Service, 1941, 1947), 13.

11. "Remarks by Mrs. Goldie Rehberg," in US Congress, Senate, *Acceptance of the Statue of Marcus Whitman presented by the State of Washington. Proceedings in the Capitol and the Rotunda, United States Capitol,* 83rd Cong., 3rd sess., Jan. 1, 1955, 43–45. See also "Address of William O. Douglas," 53–59.

12. "Remarks of Vice President Nixon of the United States," US Congress, Senate, *Acceptance of the Statue of Marcus Whitman presented by the State of Washington. Proceedings in the Capitol and the Rotunda, United States Capitol,* 83rd Cong., 3rd sess., Jan. 1, 1955, 70.

13. "Task Given to Sculptor," *Oregonian,* Nov. 22, 1949, 28; "Marcus Whitman Statue Unveiled in U.S. Capitol," *Oregonian,* May 23, 1953, 6.

14. Ibid., 11–12.

15. Ibid., 15.

16. Dwight David Eisenhower, "Inaugural Address," Delivered Jan. 20, 1953, in *Public Papers of the Presidents of the United States: Dwight D. Eisenhower, Containing the*

Public Messages, Speeches, and Statements of the President, Jan. 20, 1953 to Dec. 31, 1953, 2nd. ed. (Washington: Government Printing Office, 1960), 3.

17. For instance, T. D. Allen, *Doctor in Buckskin* (New York: Harper, 1951); William O. Steele, *We Were There on the Oregon Trail* (New York: Grosset and Dunlap, 1955); Herbert E. Arnston, *Caravan to Oregon: A Boy's Wagon-Train Adventure* (New York: Binfords and Mort, 1957); Wyatt Blassingame and Richard Glendinning, *The Frontier Doctors* (New York: Franklin Watts, 1963). Whitman also achieved temporary fame in the western comic book and trading card industries. See Bowman Wild West trading card, Famous Characters, "Marcus Whitman," #C-14; "Marcus Whitman, Blazer of the Oregon Trail," *Real Life Comics* 25 (Sept. 1941); "Oregon Trailblazer," *True Comics* 38 (Aug. 1944); "Marcus Whitman," Western Comics 6 (1948); Lee Ames, "Trappers' Rendezvous," *Kit Carson Tales* 21 (Feb. 1953).

18. "Random Notes from Washington: Hero Stands in for Davy Crockett," *New York Times,* June 20, 1955, 12; Robert C. Albright, "More Fame for Davy," *Washington Post and Times Herald,* July 3, 1955, E1.

19. Patricia Nelson Limerick, *Legacy of Conquest: The Unbroken Past of the American West* (New York: Norton, 1987), 40.

20. For instance, Thomas E. Jessett, "Christian Missions to the Indians of Oregon," *Church History* 28, no. 2 (June, 1959): 147–56; Jessett, Communication, *Church History* 29, no. 1 (March 1960): 89–90; Robert H. Ruby and John A. Brown, *Indians of the Pacific Northwest: A History* (Norman: University of Oklahoma Press, 1981), 75–78, 101–6; Richard White, "*It's Your Misfortune and None of My Own*": *A History of the American West* (Norman: University of Oklahoma Press, 1991), 72–73; Barbara Alice Mann, *The Tainted Gift: The Disease Method of Frontier Expansion* (Native America: Yesterday and Today, Santa Barbara, Calif.: ABC-CLIO, 1996), 83–110; Robert V. Hine and John Mack Faragher, *The American West: A New Interpretive History* (New Haven: Yale University Press, 2000), 184–85.

21. Neal Christopherson, Whitman College Mascot Survey Results: Executive Summary, March 2016, available at Marra Clay and Ellen Ivens-Duran, "College to Choose New Mascot," *Whitman Wire,* April 6, 2016, https://whitmanwire.com/news/2016/04/06/college-to-choose-new-mascot/. An image of Marc can be found at Whitman College Arminda Collections, Other Whitman Collections, Whitman College and Northwest Archives, accessed Jan. 10, 2019, https://arminda.whitman.edu/object/arminda29421.

22. Thomas Yawzinski, "Marcus Whitman Statue Vandalized on Whitman College Campus," KEPR, Oct. 14, 2019, https://keprtv.com/news/local/marcus-whitman-statue-vandalized-on-whitman-college-campus.

23. Tom Banse, "Proposal to Replace Marcus Whitman Statues Stokes Anger in Olympia," *NW News Network,* Jan. 30, 2019, https://www.nwnewsnetwork.org/post/proposal-replace-marcus-whitman-statues-stokes-anger-olympia; Washington State Senate Bill 5327, "An Act Relating to the creation of a work group to study and make 2 recommendations on a statue to replace Marcus Whitman; creating new sections; and providing expiration dates," 66th Legislature, 2019 sess., Jan. 16, 2019.

24. Catherine Millard, *The Rewriting of America's History* (Traverse City, MI: Horizon Books, 1991), iii.

25. Ibid.

26. Ibid., iv

27. Ibid., 207.

28. Ibid., 209. Also see Millard, "The Preacher Who Rode for an Empire," *Great American Statesmen and Heroes* (Camp Hill, PA: Horizon Books, 1995), 181–87.

29. For instance, Pat Robertson, *America's Dates with Destiny* (Nashville: Thomas Nelson, 1986), 126–27; Newt Gingrich, *Rediscovering God in America: Reflections on the Role of Faith in Our Nation's History and Future* (Nashville: Thomas Nelson, 2000), 60; Stephen K. McDowell, *Building Godly Nations: Lessons from the Bible and America's Christian History* (Charlottesville, VA: Providence Foundation, 2004), 7, 77, 154; Peter Marshall and David Manuel, *From Sea to Shining Sea for Young Readers: 1787–1837* (1986; repr. Grand Rapids: Revell, 2009), 359–62; Glover Shipp, *In God We Trust . . . Or Do We? Our Nation Built on a Christian Foundation* (Eugene: Resource Publications, 2011), 99. William Federer has reprinted the Harding speech in multiple texts purporting to furnish primary source evidence of America's Christian heritage; see William J. Federer, *America's God and Country: Encyclopedia of Quotations* (St. Louis: Amerisearch, 1994), 687–88; Federer, *Treasury of Presidential Quotations* (St. Louis: Amerisearch, 2004), 216–28; Federer, *Prayers and Presidents: Inspiring Faith from Leaders of the Past* (St. Louis: Amerisearch, 2010), 163–65. David Barton's WallBuilders organization has reprinted the Whitman Saved Oregon Story in lesson 5 of its Lessons for Christian Heritage Week, available at WallBuilders, "American Christian Heritage Week Lessons," https://wallbuilders.com/chw/lessons/lesson-5-american-republic/.

30. "Biography," Christian Heritage Ministries Web Site, accessed Feb. 26, 2015, http://www.christianheritagemins.org/biography.htm. Despite the wording of this biography, Millard appears to have never been employed at the Library of Congress; she simply conducted research there. Sid Roth, "Our Guest: Catherine Millard," It's Supernatural Web Site, accessed Feb. 27, 2015, http://www.itssupernatural.net/2015/01/15/our-guest-dr-catherine-millard.

31. "Blaze Magazine Interview with David Barton: 'Saving History,'" The Blaze Web Site, accessed Feb. 27, 2015, http://www.theblaze.com/stories/2012/07/06/blaze-magazine-interview-with-david-barton-saving-history.

32. Millard, *Rewriting of America's History*, 13, 2.

33. Peter Novick, *That Noble Dream: The "Objectivity Question" and the American Historical Profession* (New York: Cambridge University Press, 1988), 576.

34. Amanda Porterfield, "Leaving Providence Behind," *Church History* 80, no. 2 (June 2011): 366.

35. William Warren Sweet, *The Story of Religion in America*, 3rd ed. (New York: Harper, 1950), 451.

36. James L. Ash, "American Religion and the Academy in the Early Twentieth Century: The Chicago Years of William Warren Sweet," *Church History* 50, no. 4 (1981): 454–55.

37. Henry Warner Bowden, *Church History in an Age of Uncertainty: Historiographical Patterns in the United States, 1906–1990* (Carbondale: Southern Illinois University Press, 1991), 219.

38. M. A. Fitzsimons, "The Role of Providence in History," *Review of Politics* 35, no. 3 (July 1973): 396. See also Lewis O. Saum, "Providence in the Popular Mind of Pre–Civil War America," *Indiana Magazine of History* 72, no. 4 (Dec. 1976): 316; Martin Marty, *Righteous Empire: The Protestant Experience in America* (New York: Dial Press, 1970), 188–98.

39. Langdon B. Gilkey, "The Concept of Providence in Contemporary Theology," *Journal of Religion* 43, no. 3 (July 1963): 171.

40. Fitzsimons, "The Role of Providence in History," 386.

41. Peter W. Williams, "Does American Religious History Have a Center?" *Church History* 71, no. 2 (June 2002): 387.

42. Catherine A. Brekus, "Contested Words: History, America, Religion," *William and Mary Quarterly* 75, no. 1 (Jan. 2018): 5.

43. Kerwin Klein, *Frontiers of Historical Imagination: Narrating the European Conquest of Native America, 1890–1990* (Berkeley: University of California Press, 1997), 138.

44. Ibid., 2–3.

45. Limerick, *Legacy of Conquest,* 323.

46. Donald Worster, *Under Western Skies: Nature and History in the American West* (New York: Oxford University Press, 1994), 8.

47. For instance, the collection *Natives and Academics: Researching and Writing about American Indians,* ed. Devon A. Mihesuah (Lincoln: University of Nebraska Press, 1998); Donna L. Akers, "Removing the Heart of the Choctaw People: Indian Removal from a Native Perspective," *American Indian Culture and Research Journal* 23, no. 3 (Sept. 1999): 63; Linda Tuhiwai Smith, *Decolonizing Methodologies: Research and Indigenous Peoples* (New York: Zed Books, 1999), 28–35; Mary Jane Logan McCallum, "Indigenous Labor and Indigenous History," *American Indian Quarterly* 33, no. 4 (Fall 2009): 523–44; Nēpia Mahuika, *Rethinking Oral History and Tradition: An Indigenous Perspective* (New York: Oxford University Press, 2019).

48. Donald L. Fixico, "The Native American Researcher: Another View of Historical Documents," *Midwestern Researcher* 8, no. 2 (1983): 5–15; Lisa Brooks, *Our Beloved Kin: A New History of King Philip's War* (New Haven: Yale University Press, 2018), 12–14, 72–106.

49. Tuhiwai Smith, *Decolonizing Methodologies,* 55–56; Leslie Marmon Silko, *Yellow Woman and a Beauty of the Spirit: Essays on Native American Life Today* (New York: Simon & Schuster, 2013), 25–47.

Index